Jewish Ireland in the Age of Joyce

Jewish Ireland in the Age of Joyce

A SOCIOECONOMIC HISTORY

Cormac Ó Gráda

PRINCETON UNIVERSITY PRESS

PRINCETON AND OXFORD

Library of Congress Cataloging-in-Publication Data

Ó Gráda, Cormac.
Jewish Ireland in the age of Joyce : a socioeconomic history /
 Cormac Ó Gráda.
p.   cm.
Includes bibliographical references and index.
ISBN-13: 978-0-691-12719-4 (hardcover)
ISBN-10: 0-691-12719-0 (hardcover)
1. Jews—Ireland—History. 2. Jews—Ireland—Social conditions.
3. Ireland—Ethnic relations. I. Title.
DS135.17202 2006
941.5′004924—dc22   2006004943

British Library Cataloging-in-Publication Data is available

This book has been composed in Sabon

Printed on acid-free paper. ∞

pup.princeton.edu

Printed in the United States of America

3   5   7   9   10   8   6   4   2

For Asher Benson and Nick Harris

Ní bheidh a leithéidí ars ann

אזעלעבע מעבססיו קאבעו מעד בישסזייו

CONTENTS

List of Illustrations and Tables ix

Acknowledgments xi

INTRODUCTION 1

CHAPTER 1
Arrival and Context 9
  Leaving Home: History and Memory 12
  The Migration in Context 21

CHAPTER 2
"England-Ireland" and Dear Dirty Dublin 30
  Mortality 33
  Living Standards 40
  Interwar Dublin 41
  Water and Sanitation 42
  The Jewish Community in Context 43

CHAPTER 3
"They Knew No Trade But Peddling" 45
  The Weekly Men 47
  The Old and the New Peddling 56
  "The Jewman Moneylender" 61

CHAPTER 4
Self-Employment, Social Mobility 72
  Artisans 72
  Occupational Mobility 73
  Immigrants as Entrepreneurs and Workers 84
  Technical Appendix: More on Age and Occupational
    Choice in the United States 92

CHAPTER 5
Settling In 94
  Housing and Settlement 94
  Six Streets in Little Jerusalem 105
  Within-Street Clustering 108
  Cork and Belfast Jewries 115

CHAPTER 6
Schooling and Literacy 122

CHAPTER 7
The Demography of Irish Jewry   129
   The 1911 Population Census   131
   The Fertility Transition   134
   Jewish and Gentile Fertility   136
   Infant and Child Mortality   143
   Mortality in Jewish Ireland   147
   Culture Mattered   152
   Technical Appendix: Accounting for the Variation in
      Fertility and Infant/Child Mortality   154

CHAPTER 8
Culture, Family, Health   160
   Litvak Culture   164
   Food, Drink, and Health   171

CHAPTER 9
Newcomer to Neighbor   178
   In the Beginning   179
   Remembering Limerick   191
   Autobiographical Memory   194
   Social Learning across Communities?   200
   A Note on Litigation between Jews   202

CHAPTER 10
Ich Geh Fun "Ire"land   204
   Religion   205
   From Little Jerusalem to Rathgar and Beyond   206
   Decline   209

APPENDIX 1
Letters to One of the Last "Weekly Men"   217

APPENDIX 2
Mr. Parnell Remembers   221

APPENDIX 3
Louis Hyman, Jessie Bloom, and *The Jews of Ireland*   224

Notes   229

Bibliography   271

Index   295

LIST OF ILLUSTRATIONS AND TABLES

FIGURES

1.1.	The Pale and Its Provinces	15
1.2a.	Emigration of Jews and Others from Russia, 1880–1914	20
1.2b.	Emigration from Russia, Italy, and Central Europe to the United States, 1880–1914	20
1.3.	The Litvak Shtetls	24
2.1.	Age Distributions of Deaths (%) by Socioeconomic Group in Dublin Registration Area, 1883–87 and 1901–10	37
2.2.	Wages in Dublin and Great Britain, 1880–1914	40
4.1a–p.	Shifting Shares of Several Occupations or Occupational Groups	78–83
5.1.	Chancery Lane 1913	98
5.2a.	Dufferin Avenue	100
5.2b.	Greenville Terrace	100
5.2c.	Longwood Avenue	101
5.2d.	Oakfield Place	101
5.3a, b.	The Streets of Little Jerusalem	109–110
5.4a–f.	Density of Jewish Settlement on Six Streets	111–112
5.5a–f.	Within-Street Clustering	113–114
5.6.	The Suburbanization of Dublin Jewry	116
7.1.	Ages at Death of Dublin Jews born 1899–1903	152

TABLES

1.1.	Correlations between Migration Flows to the United States, 1880–1914 (First Differences)	21
1.2.	Shtetls of Origin	25
2.1.	The Jewish and Russian-Born Populations of Dublin, Belfast, Cork, Ireland, and Great Britain, 1871–1936/37	32
2.2.	Infant and Child Mortality in Dublin and Belfast	39
3.1.	Main Occupations of Ireland's Russian-Born Residents, 1891–1911	49
3.2.	Jewish Businessmen in Ireland, Liverpool, and Manchester in 1893	52
3.3.	Average Size of Loans Made by Jewish Moneylenders and Traders c. 1910–13	65
4.1.	Age and Occupation in the Dublin Jewish community, 1911	74

4.2a. The Occupational Profile of Jews and Others in Ireland, 1926   75

4.2b. The Occupational Profile of Jews and Others in Ireland, 1946   76

4.3. Occupations of Russian- and Russian-Polish-Born Males in England and Wales, 1881–1911   86

4.4. Percent of the Jewish Male Labor Force in Selected Occupations in London, Lancashire, Yorkshire, and the Rest of England and Wales   89

4A.1. Impact of Age, Marital Status, and Years in United States on Occupation: Marginal Effects   92

4A.2. Impact of Age, Marital Status, and Years in United States on Occupational Status: Marginal Effects   93

5.1. Median Year of Enrollment by Grid Area   120

6.1. Literacy and Age Heaping in Dublin in 1911   123

7.1. Housing and Occupations: 1911 Dublin Database   133

7.2. Births, Deaths, and Natural Increase in Vilna and Kiev Provinces, 1858–69   137

7.3. Average Age at Marriage in Little Jerusalem   139

7.4. Duration and Average Number of Children   140

7.5. Percentage Childless by Duration   141

7.6. Marital Fertility in Belfast and Cork   142

7.7. Marital Fertility by Confessional Group in 1946   143

7.8. Mortality Rate per Thousand Births of Children under Five Years by Mother's Nationality, Manhattan, 1915   145

7.9. Marriage Duration, Fertility, and Mortality in Ireland and Dublin before 1911   148

7.10. Child Survival Prospects in Belfast and Cork   149

7A.1. Accounting for the Variation in Fertility: Marginal Effects   155

7A.2. Mean Values of Variables   156

7A.3. Accounting for the Variation in Mortality: Marginal Effects   158

8.1. Working-class Diets in Glasgow in 1911–12   175

ACKNOWLEDGMENTS

THIS BOOK has its origins in researches into urban historical demography. A curiosity about whether some well-known features of Jewish demography elsewhere a century ago were replicated in Ireland, and the reasons for them, prompted my broader interest in the history of Irish Jewry. In attempting to come to grips with what was a completely new research field for me, I incurred many intellectual debts.

Without the awards of Social Science and Humanities Research Council of Ireland (SSHRCI) Senior Research Fellowship in 2002–3 and a Visiting Fellowship at Princeton University's Shelby Cullom Davis Center in 2003–4, I could not have produced this book. The SSHRCI award allowed me to build up some databases, to read widely, to produce some preliminary quantitative results, and to talk to lots of people. The stimulating and supportive environment at Princeton gave me the opportunity to write a first draft, try out some of the material in seminars, and avail of Princeton's almost unrivaled library facilities. I am particularly grateful to Gyan Prakash, then director of the center, and to Jennifer Houle, its administrator. In addition, a grant from the University College Dublin Faculty of Commerce permitted me to avail of the excellent research assistance of Rebecca Stuart and Brian Carr.

I am immensely grateful to all those who helped along the way. Many thanks in particular to Maurice Abrahamson, Guy Beiner, Asher Benson, the late Mark Berger, Andy Bielenberg, Mickey Brennan, Joe Briscoe, Barry and Carmel Chiswick, Louis Cullen, David Dickson, Maria Diemling, Michael and Mady Edelstein, Chris Friedrichs, Thelma Frye, Tom Garvin, Katrina Goldstone, Tim Guinnane, Michael Haines, Brian Hanley, Nick Harris, Wim Jongman, Bill Jordan, Liam Kennedy, Carla King, Joe Lee, Olga Litvak, Martin Maguire, Louis Marcus, Joel Mokyr, Graham Mooney, Fergus Mulligan, Joel Perlmann, Éamon Ó Ciosáin, Niall Ó Ciosáin, Fionn Ó Gráda, Tim O'Neill, Manus O'Riordan, Ray Refaussé, Stuart Rosenblatt, Jim Smith, Arthur Sugerman, Brendan Walsh, Harold Waterman, and Stephen Wheatcroft for comments and guidance on various points. I am particularly grateful to Guy Beiner, Asher Benson, Michael Brennan, Máire Ní Chiosáin, and Fionn Ó Gráda for reading and commenting on most of an earlier draft at a crucial stage.

Princeton Firestone Library achieved feats impossible in Dublin: it produced roll after roll of the *Jewish Chronicle* on microfilm, and even photocopied relevant excerpts from Harley's rare *Commercial Directory of the*

Jews (1893). Archivists at the University of Tulsa, the American Jewish Archives in Cincinnati, the University of Washington, Hebrew University Department of Oral History, and the YIVO Institute of Historical Research were all extremely helpful. I am especially thankful to Gerry Lyne at the National Library for directing me to some very useful source material. Raphael Siev, ever obliging, gave me the run of the archives of the Irish Jewish Museum. I am grateful to Professor Séamus Ó Catháin for permission to cite material belonging to the Irish Folklore Commission. Stephen Hannon drew the maps of Dublin and Lithuania and Seán Ó Domhnaill helped with the jacket design.

My interest in Ireland's Jewish past introduced me to some of Ireland's Jewish present. Making contact with and getting to know several members of the community described in this book has been an exciting and rewarding experience. Letting go of the book is not letting go of these friendships. I hope the dedication speaks for itself.

This work is based in part on interviews with people familiar with the Jewish community. A mail drop to houses on half a dozen streets in Dublin's former Jewish neighborhood elicited many anecdotes, impressions, and cups of tea. I am grateful to the many inhabitants of Saint Kevin's Parade, Dufferin Avenue, Martin Street, Greenville Terrace, Saint Kevin's Road, and Longwood Avenue, who replied to my initial inquiry, and to those whom I subsequently met or talked to by phone. I am also grateful to the members of Saint Kevin's Community Centre who fielded my questions and shared their reminiscences with gusto and humor in March 2003.

At Princeton University Press, Peter Dougherty was both enthusiastic and demanding. At the Press, I am also grateful to Sophia Efthimiatou, Brigitta van Rheinberg, Sara Lerner, and Jenn Backer.

Finally, I am thankful to my immediate and extended families for all kinds of help. *Tuigeann siad.*

Jewish Ireland in the Age of Joyce

Introduction

Arbutus Place: Pleasant Street: pleasant old times . . .
M. Shulomowitz, Joseph Goldwater, Moses
Herzog, Harris Rosenberg, M. Moisel, J. Citron. . . .
With swaying arms they wail in pneuma over
the recreant Bloom.
—*James Joyce,* Ulysses

Ninety-five percent of the population of Ireland is
Catholic, five percent is Protestant; I am Chief
Rabbi of the rest.
—*I. Jakobovitz, chief rabbi of Ireland, 1948–59*

THE ADVENTURES of Leopold Bloom in Dublin on 16 June 1904 (Blooms-day) are familiar to lovers of literature everywhere. James Joyce's decision to give such a prominent role to a Dublin Jew (or half-Jew) in *Ulysses* has ensured Ireland's capital city an enduring role in Jewish studies.[1] Yet although a *Ulysses* without its Bloom is inconceivable, Joyce's central character sprang from a community rarely mentioned in social and economic histories of the city or, indeed, in discussions of Jewish migration generally. There is a good reason for this: the small size of that community. In 1866, the year of the apocryphal Leopold Bloom's birth, the Jewish population of Dublin numbered about two hundred souls and that of Belfast at most a few dozen. Dublin's Jewish quarter, where Leopold Bloom would spend so many "pleasant times," did not yet exist.

In the following decades Dublin and Ireland were very much marginal destinations for the more than two million Jewish men, women, and children who left eastern and central Europe in search of a better life. On the eve of World War I the Jewish population of greater Dublin numbered barely three thousand, one-tenth that of Manchester or Montreal, and a much smaller fraction of that of London or New York. Other Irish destinations were of even less import. Yet the immigration, miniscule though it was in relative terms, spawned a vibrant Jewish community that would sustain itself for several decades. The small size of the community shaped its occupational profile and influenced its acculturation; it also compromised its viability in the long run. The unimportance of immigration in modern Irish history, at least before the era of the Celtic Tiger in the 1990s, lends the case of Ireland's Jews a particular interest.[2]

Over the years, Ireland's Jewish immigrants and their families have been the subjects of a small number of scholarly works and evocative and increasingly elegaic memoirs and television documentaries. Bernard Shillman's *Short History of the Jews in Ireland* (1945), Louis Hyman's *Jews of Ireland to the Year 1910* (1972),[3] and Dermot Keogh's *Jews in Twentieth-century Ireland: Refugees, Anti-Semitism, and the Holocaust* (1998) are foremost among the former, while Nick Harris's *Dublin's Little Jerusalem* (2002), Stanley Price's *Somewhere to Hang My Hat: An Irish-Jewish Journey* (2002), and Valerie Lapin's documentary *Shalom Ireland* (2003) are the most recent examples of the latter. Somewhere in between, part social history, part personal or communal memoir, are Ray Rivlin's *Shalom Ireland* (2003) and David Marcus's *Buried Memories* (2004). Somewhat less accessible, though no less useful, are the unpublished dissertations of Gerry E. Moore (1981, 1984) and Mark Duffy (1985), and Micheál Ó Meachair's Irish-language introduction to Judaism (2004), which includes a brief account of Irish Jewry. Shillman and Hyman deal mostly with the pre-1900 era, while the main focus of Keogh's study is indicated by its title. Moore is also concerned with communal relations, while Duffy concentrates on the economic condition of the pre-1914 Jewish community and its first steps toward middle-class respectability. The immigrants are also commemorated in a small Irish Jewish Museum, located in a former synagogue at 3/4 Walworth Road, a little street by Dublin's Grand Canal that was once, albeit fleetingly, completely Jewish.[4] The museum's collection of artifacts and documents also represents, sadly, an Irish Jewish community in decline, both in terms of numbers and vibrancy. More memoirs are in progress, and the expatriate community maintains a vicarious existence on the Internet.

What prompted the immigrants to forsake their (mainly) Lithuanian towns and villages? Why did they opt for Dublin and a few other places in an Irish economy not then noted for its economic dynamism? How did they fare relative to their coreligionists who chose other destinations? Did they differ from them in terms of skills, wealth, and origins? How did they and their children adapt or assimilate? Why did an apparently vibrant community begin to decline in the 1940s? Such questions, still largely unanswered, are the focus of this study. They relate to the economic and social histories of both Jewry and Ireland.

Leopold Bloom's creator lived between 1882 and 1941. The main analytic focus of this study is the economic history and demography of Dublin's and Ireland's Jewish community between the 1870s and the 1940s—hence "the age of Joyce." The history of Irish Jewry in this period—or, to be more precise, of the numerically dominant newcomers from eastern

Europe—is one of resilience and successful adjustment to the challenges and limited opportunities it faced. This is reflected in the growing size of this always close-knit and sometimes fractious community, in its wealth of communal institutions, and in its shifting occupational profile and geographical location. Ireland's relative economic backwardness shaped both the number and the occupational profile of its immigrants. They started out as a classic proto-capitalist "middleman minority," carving out trading niches previously unimagined or shunned by the native majority. Like the other ethnic "Mercurians" (devotees of Mercury, the Greek god of merchants), merchants, and other service providers described by historian Yuri Slezkine, they peddled dry goods and household furnishings on credit to the Irish poor, and engaged in petty moneylending—socially useful but low-prestige callings reliant on a poor clientele.[5] The small size of the Irish Jewish community meant proportionately more self-employment, fewer masters, and fewer servants than in larger urban communities such as New York's Lower East Side and London's East End. Even before World War I the number of rambling peddlers in Ireland was declining, although the credit draper (who sold dry goods on the system of installment credit known colloquially as the "never-never") survived into the 1950s and 1960s. For the immigrants acculturation entailed shifting to more "respectable" and more rewarding ways of making a living, mainly in manufacturing and the professions. The shift was also associated with movement from the initial areas of settlement to more middle-class neighborhoods.

In Dublin the very first immigrants settled in tenement housing, but they soon moved on to modest streets off the South Circular Road and Lower Clanbrassil Street on the southern edge of the city, engaging in petty trading and skilled craftwork for a living. Within a decade or two, the more successful switched to middle-class housing in the same area. On the eve of World War II many of these (or their children) had already shifted across the Grand Canal, leapfrogging the area immediately to its south as far as the middle-class suburbs of Rathgar and Terenure. They left the traveling, the moneylending, and the tailoring behind them, opting instead for careers in dentistry, medicine, and the law, or became merchants and factory owners. In Belfast's Jewish community, these patterns were replicated.

The economic trajectory of post-1870s Irish Jewry has left its mark on a wide variety of sources. Manuscript census enumeration forms provide snapshots of first-generation immigrants and their children. School enrollment records capture the community's eagerness to educate its children, and reveal the community's shifting occupational structure and its gentrification in suburbia. Naturalization records from the 1910s offer complementary insights into how the immigrants made a living in the early decades. Commercial directories chronicle the community's settlement patterns. Autobiographical memoirs and taped conversations and interviews offer insights into the immigrants' acculturation and adaptation. Communal records, newspapers, and numerous public and private archival sources at home and abroad add their own insights. Moreover, the Jews of Ireland should not be examined in isolation: the numerous studies of Jewish populations in Britain and further afield offer useful comparative perspectives. While in certain respects the fortunes of Irish Jewry replicate those of so-called frontier Jewries in places as far apart as South Africa, Latin America, and northern Europe, Irish geography and history also lent them a certain uniqueness.[6]

The chapters that follow are thematic rather than chronological or narrative in structure. The plan of the book, briefly, is as follows. It begins by placing the immigration in context. Late nineteenth- and early twentieth-century Ireland was, to say the least, an unlikely destination for Jewish immigrants. Whether the choices of Ireland or Dublin as destinations were miscalculations or rational choices based on the relative status or skills of the small subset of migrants who settled there is an interesting issue. The immigrants settled in cities where, in contrast to rural Ireland, numbers were rising. Their skills and religious obligations account for why most of them opted for the larger towns and cities of Ireland; but why did Dublin receive more immigrants than the booming and (at this stage) bigger city of Belfast? Chapter 1 describes where most of the immigrants came from, why they left their homes, and why they came to Ireland.

Chapter 2 outlines the economic and social conditions faced by the immigrants between the 1880s and the 1930s, both in late Victorian and Joycean Dublin and elsewhere in Ireland. Its main focus is on Dublin, where a majority of the immigrants settled. There the small preexisting Jewish community, comfortably off and English speaking, sought to integrate the newcomers quickly "in accordance with Anglo Jewish ideas"; in due course, the immigrants adapted in their own way.[7] Despite the city's relative lack of industry, its evident poverty, and its disproportionately large casual laboring class, there was some improvement in living standards in this period. While Dublin had more than its share of substandard housing, its newer neighborhoods contained an ample stock of modest but well-built units that met the immigrants' needs. Moreover, in the late nineteenth century the market for rented housing was an active one, making it easier for the immigrants to cluster.

Chapters 3 and 4 describe how the immigrants made ends meet. Most first-generation males engaged in service occupations such as peddling clothes and house furnishings for credit, trading in secondhand goods, or petty moneylending. As so-called weekly men or credit drapers, they

offered many of the urban poor their first taste of borrowing on the installment system. Chapter 3 explores why peddling and moneylending
played such a key role in the economic life of the immigrant community
at the outset. Like other middleman minorities, the immigrants engaged
in work at which the natives were less adept or toward which they were
less inclined. Not all immigrants were middlemen, however, and as the
community grew in size, for a time the proportion of journeyman tailors
and cabinetmakers grew in tandem. Yet even the humblest wage earner
aspired toward self-employment or employer status; the canvasser or collector yearned to be a self-employed peddler, the peddler looked forward
to a less peripatetic means of survival, the tailor aspired to owning a clothing factory, and so on.[8] Chapter 4 chronicles the gradual shift from middleman minority to manufacturing and the professions. It also seeks to
account for the low proportion of "ordinary working men" among the
immigrants relative to, say, the proportions in Leeds, London, or even
New York.

Like immigrants everywhere, the Jews clustered in a particular area—
in Dublin this would become "Little Jerusalem"—on arrival. Within a
generation—and here, too, experience elsewhere offers strong parallels—
the more successful began to create another cluster a few miles south of
the original settlement. Chapter 5 devotes special attention to a selection
of streets in Little Jerusalem that were once heavily Jewish, and analyzes
their shifting ethnicity over more than half a century. It also describes
Jewish settlement in Belfast and Cork.

Surprisingly, perhaps, a significant minority of Ireland's pre-1914 immigrants were illiterate, or virtually so. However, like east European Jewish immigrants elsewhere, they were quick to take advantage of the educational opportunities available to their children. In Ireland a century ago,
schooling beyond the age of thirteen or fourteen was very much the exception for working-class or middle-class children, even in the cities. Yet almost from the start, the more successful of the immigrants were sending
their sons to fee-paying secondary schools, whether in Dublin, Cork, or
Belfast. Chapter 6 describes the schooling choices of first- and second-
generation immigrants—mainly Lithuanian Jews or "Litvaks"—and their
implications for acculturation.[9]

Chapter 7 addresses the historical demography of Irish Jewry. The demography of minority Jewish populations in Europe and America has
attracted considerable scholarly attention. Like the role of Roman Catholicism in delaying the demographic transition, the Jewish example seems
to give pride of place to the impact of culture and religion on demographic
trends. Jewish marriage and marital fertility patterns elsewhere have attracted considerable scholarly interest. Some Jewish populations have
been identified as forerunners or pioneers in the European transition to

low marital fertility, but the marital fertility of Jewish immigrants else-where on the eve of World War I is known to have been high.

The demographic impact of ethnicity has been widely noted.[10] In prac-tice, however, it is not easy to disentangle the relative importance of cul-ture and economics: in the case of Dublin a century ago, for example, there would be little point in comparing Jews living in modest comfort off the South Circular Road with, say, Catholics in the slums of the Coombe or inner-city Gardiner Street, or Protestants in the middle-class suburbs of Rathmines or Pembroke. Here I attempt to control for socio-economic and environmental factors by analyzing differences between Jewish and non-Jewish families living in the same neighborhoods. This helps isolate the impact of "culture," since both Jewish and non-Jewish households on the streets with a significant Jewish presence would have shared the same water and air quality, and the same access to public ser-vices (such as they were) and retail outlets.

Chapter 7 first describes the 1911 census of Ireland, the basis of the analyses of marital fertility and of infant and child mortality a century ago. The census contains household-level data on infant and child mortal-ity, on the duration of each marriage, and on age at marriage. It also reports proxies for household income such as housing quality, the pres-ence of domestic servants, literacy, and male occupations, and thus offers a guide to the influence of living standards on fertility and mortality. Sam-ples of Jewish and non-Jewish households in Dublin, Belfast, and Cork are used to analyze the variations in marital fertility by ethnicity and so-cioeconomic status in Ireland's Jewish neighborhoods. Was the fertility of Ireland's immigrants as high as the fertility of the native Irish, well-known for their half-hearted participation in the European fertility transi-tion? The answer is both yes and no. The marital fertility of couples living in rural Ireland was higher, but not that of Catholic and Protestant cou-ples living in the same neighborhoods as the immigrant Jews. The statisti-cal analysis reported in chapter 7 confirms Jewish exceptionalism in this respect, and variations in the socioeconomic conditions faced by native and immigrant couples fail to account for this fertility gap. While the 1911 census offers the basis for a detailed picture of fertility behavior at the level of the individual household, the decennial censuses offer useful snapshots of shifting fertility strategies. Chapter 7 also tracks fertility trends over time and assesses how immigrants' sons and daughters assimi-lated to a shifting Irish norm. The fertility strategies of other confessional groups also shifted over time, but the rapid transition of Jewish couples to low marital fertility in the 1920s and 1930s is particularly remarkable.

Also of interest is the seemingly universal or near universal pattern of lower mortality rates of Jewish infants and young children. Over three decades ago Israeli demographer U. O. Schmelz offered ample documentation that diaspora Jews succeeded in reducing their mortality sooner than the populations among whom they lived. Others since have added to the evidence.[11] Researchers have invoked a variety of cultural and socioeconomic factors in attempts to explain why Jewish infants and children fared better. These include greater attention to personal hygiene and housekeeping in Jewish households, the benefits of Jewish dietary regulations, differences in breastfeeding practices, better maternal care, lower illegitimacy rates, and the higher value put on children's education. The Jewish tradition of living in congested urban environments may also have lent them some immunity to certain infectious diseases. While the mortality advantage of Jewish infants and young children is well documented, it deserves further study, since both the advantage and the culture that underpinned it varied considerably across space and over time. Ireland and Dublin, where a majority of the Jewish immigrants settled, offer an interesting case study.

Social and economic historians debate the relative importance of cultural and economic factors in accounting for the relative success of immigrant Jewish populations. Chapter 8 describes some aspects of Irish Jewish culture—its politics, its tensions, its religiosity, its wealth of social capital—and how they might have influenced the health and material progress of the immigrants. Of particular interest are the possible roles of personal hygiene and diet in accounting for the Jewish mortality advantage.

Chapter 9 explores the social interaction between native and newcomer at the street and neighborhood levels. This remains a largely unexplored topic. To this day stereotypes inspired by the famous Limerick "pogrom" of 1904[12] and official reluctance to allow in would-be refugees from Nazi Europe, on the one hand, and the election of Robert Briscoe as lord mayor of Dublin in 1956 and 1961, on the other, still govern scholarly perceptions. However, popular impressions are more likely to be influenced by the nostalgia or, on occasion, the bitterness of autobiographical memoirs. In reality, attitudes on the part of both natives and newcomers shifted over time. Ireland's remoteness and poverty had long insulated it from significant immigration, while before their arrival in Ireland, the Litvaks' interaction with non-Jews had rarely strayed very far from the cash nexus. That followed from their status as a classic middleman minority. They and their children were determined to adapt to Irish society, however, to an extent that would have been undreamt of in pre-1914 Lithuania. The focus in chapter 9 is on adaptation and the degree of acculturation, and on how Dublin's Little Jerusalem (and its Irish satellites) in time became successful experiments in multiculturalism. Given the boundaries created by dietary requirements and by a preference on the part of both Jew and Gentile for "marrying in," in practice this meant that most intimate friendships, at least beyond childhood, were confined to one's own group. Chapter 10 concludes by offering an account of the decline of Jewish Ireland since mid-century and some comparative perspective on the immigrants' progress and acculturation.

Chapter 1

ARRIVAL AND CONTEXT

The circumstances in which my grandparents left
Lithuania meant that the connection was totally
severed in a dramatic and painful way. In my
imagination, Lithuania is a place of shtetls and
pogroms, in no sense a homeland.
—*Barbara Lantin, Irish-born Litvak*[1]

The most fundamental cause of emigration from
eastern Europe was the failure of the Jewish economy
to grow as rapidly as the Jewish population.
—*Todd Endelman,* The Jews of Britain[2]

IN *The Commonwealth of Oceana*, a political pamphlet first published in 1656, James Harrington described "Panopea" (Ireland) as "the soft mother of a slothful and pusillanimous people." Neither conquest by arms nor replantation with "a new race" of British colonists had made Panopea viable. If Harrington had his way, it would have been planted "with Jews, allowing them their own rites and laws, for that would have brought them suddenly from all parts of the world, and in sufficient numbers." There the Jews could have combined both trade and agriculture, in which they had excelled in the Land of Canaan. Panopea, thus peopled and transformed, would be worth "a matter of four millions dry rents."[3]

Harrington's fantasy was probably inspired by Oliver Cromwell's efforts in 1655 to allow a group of Marano Jewish merchants from hostile Spain to remain in England. His stance would make Cromwell, reviled in Irish nationalist memory for atrocities committed in Drogheda and Wexford in 1649, a champion for Jews everywhere. Harrington and *Oceana* were quickly forgotten, and in the following centuries Ireland would become a place of emigration, not immigration. During the century or so before World War I the Irish were the most emigration-prone people in Europe. Between the battle of Waterloo and the Great Famine of the 1840s, they made up about one-third of all permanent migrants from the Old World to the New. In the wake of the Great Famine, one million out of a population of 8.5 million left for Britain, North America, and further afield. Thereafter Irish emigration was great enough to make Ireland the only European country to lose population between the 1850s and the 1910s.

Irish emigration has marked the history of many lands and spawned a significant specialist literature.[4] This literature debates its causes and effects, and highlights its exceptional features, such as the high share of women and unmarried young people in the post-famine outflow and (until very recently) the small proportion of returning emigrants. This last characteristic is a reminder of what Ireland was *not* in this period: a place of significant immigration.

The number of foreign-born (i.e., non–United Kingdom) residents living in Ireland at any one time grew during the nineteenth century but remained a miniscule fraction of the total population. They numbered only 4,471 (0.05 percent of the total) in 1841; 10,420 (0.18 percent) in 1861; 11,210 (0.22 percent) in 1881; and 18,905 (0.43 percent) in 1911. In post-famine Ireland, moreover, two-thirds or more of the foreign-born had been born in "America" or in the United States, and their age distribution implies that most of them were the children of returning emigrants. In 1881 70 percent of the American born living in Ireland were aged less than twenty years, and in 1911 the proportion was still over 60 percent. By contrast, in 1881 only 15 percent of Ireland's European-born residents were aged less than twenty, and in 1911 only 14 percent of the French, 10 percent of the Russian, and 7 percent of the Germans were under twenty years. In assessing the reactions of Irish people to "strangers" a century ago, the tiny number of foreigners resident in the country at any one time should not be overlooked.

This brings us to a surprising feature of Ireland's Jewish immigration. If we set aside the inflow from America, which was made up mainly of people of Irish stock, then in their day the "blow-ins" from eastern Europe formed Ireland's biggest group of non–UK immigrants since the French Huguenots two centuries earlier. In 1911 Jews would have accounted for nearly all of the 1,985 Russian-born residents, who easily outnumbered natives of France (1,104), of whom over one-third were either fishermen or seamen who happened to be in the country on census night, and natives of the German Empire (963). Natives of Italy (417), the Low Countries (283), and Scandinavia (312) were few by comparison.

The immigrants from eastern Europe, mainly Lithuanians, who began arriving in the early 1870s dwarfed any previous Jewish settlement in Ireland. There had been a Sephardic presence in the seventeenth and eighteenth centuries, but few Sephardim settled permanently. They supported a synagogue on Crane Lane (linking Essex and Dame Streets), but theirs was an offshoot of London's Sephardic Bevis Marks community, and they preferred to be buried in London with their kin.[5] After about 1730 Ireland's Jewish community, such as it was, was mainly Ashkenazi. Its marginality is reflected in its difficulties in paying the rent on a newly acquired graveyard at Ballybough outside Dublin and keeping it in repair. Neither the date of foundation nor the exact location of its synagogue in Marlborough Green is known for certain, and in the late eighteenth century "attendance was meagre and the services irregular."[6] In the wake of legislation in 1816 allowing for the naturalization of Jews resident in Ireland, the number of immigrants rose, but the small size of the community before the influx from eastern Europe may be inferred from the number of burials in Ballybough: twenty-two in 1842–49, an annual average of three in the 1850s, five in the 1860s, and four in the 1870s.[7]

According to the decennial census of population, the Jewish population of Ireland (North and South) rose from 285 in 1871 to 5,148 in 1911, and to 5,221 in 1936/37. A peak was probably reached on the eve of the establishment of the state of Israel in 1947; the number of Jews on the island of Ireland fell to 3,592 in 1971 and there are about two thousand today. Dublin always accounted for the lion's share of the immigrants. The number living in Dublin city and county rose from 189 in 1871 to 352 in 1881, 1,057 in 1891, 2,169 in 1901, and 2,965 in 1911. The rate of growth slowed thereafter: Dublin had 3,150 Jews in 1926, and 3,372 in 1936. Belfast and Cork, the only other Irish cities with significant Jewish communities, contained 1,139 and 340, respectively, in 1911. By comparison, on the eve of the World War I London contained 180,000 Jews, Manchester 30,000, and Liverpool 11,000. Further afield, New York at this time contained about 1.1 million Jewish inhabitants, Chicago 200,000, and Boston 80,000, while Montreal had 35,000 and Sydney 6,000. The small size of the Jewish communities of Dublin, Belfast, and Cork relative to these other cities was almost certainly a reflection of Ireland's peripheral location and the more limited economic prospects facing both immigrants and natives there at the time. A century earlier, an English visitor reckoned that the small number of Jews in Dublin reflected the city's lowly economic status, since the presence or absence of Jews was "a barometer of poverty."[8]

The timing of Ireland's post-1870 Jewish immigration cannot be known with any certainty. Decennial census data suggest that it was mostly concentrated in the 1880s and 1890s.[9] Data on the numbers passing through or remaining only for a short time are unavailable, and civil unrest resulted in the absence of a census between 1911 and 1926. The lopsided age distributions of Russian-born residents in 1926 and 1936 also suggest that most had arrived before 1914. Thus, in 1926 82.5 percent of Russian-born Jewish males and 78 percent of Russian-born females in urban Leinster (mainly Dublin) were aged thirty-five years or over. A decade later, the percentages had risen to 93.3 and 85.2, respectively.[10]

Most of the newcomers were Litvaks. In other words, they had been born in Lithuania, then part of the tsarist empire. The first arrived, probably via London, in the early 1870s. It is possible that the London Jewish Board of Guardians rerouted a few of them to Dublin, since many in the long-settled Anglo-Jewish community were eager to be rid of the new arrivals from the east. Thereafter the migration to Dublin had all the characteristics of a classic chain migration. Many of the immigrants were related "by ties of blood and marriage."[11]

The immigrants had strong links with their coreligionists in English cities such as Manchester and Leeds. Several of the men enumerated in the Irish census of 1911 were married to English-born wives, and a smaller number of the women to English-born husbands. The community also had links with South Africa, which like Ireland was a destination favored by Lithuanian emigrants. The outbreak of the Boer War produced a temporary influx of Litvaks from South Africa into Ireland in 1899–1900. About three hundred returned there at the end of the war, and others left for South Africa later.[12]

LEAVING HOME: HISTORY AND MEMORY

Why did Ireland's Litvaks leave Lithuania? Presumably for much the same reasons as those bound elsewhere. An economist's answer would involve documenting a presumed widening gap between expected incomes in the home and host countries, and changes in the cost of moving from one to the other. The economist would also take account of the "friends and neighbors effect," whereby the stock of migrants in the host country at any point in time is an added influence on the flow at that time. While such an approach fails when the bulk of would-be migrants are either too poor to move or too rich to care about the financial gains, it explains much of the variation in the timing and size of nineteenth-century Irish and Italian migration to North America.[13] However, most accounts of Jewish emigration from the tsarist empire reject an analysis along such lines. Instead, they highlight the part played by anti-Jewish discrimination, typified by the so-called May Laws of 1882, and by pogroms, or the threat of pogroms, in the wake of the assassination of Tsar Alexander II in 1881.[14]

The decades between the 1880s and 1914 were punctuated by outbreaks of persecution and discriminatory legislation, notably the expulsion of thousands of Jews from Moscow in the early 1890s and major pogroms in Kishinev (Chişinău) in Moldova (1903) and Bialystok in northeastern Poland (1906). Legislation banned Jews from living outside the shtetls (as their towns or urban neighborhoods were known) and from buying land, and placed quotas on their entry into the professions and third-level educational institutions. The virtual annihilation barely half a century later of Lithuania's Jewish community by the Nazis, aided and abetted by local murderers, adds point to such accounts.

The appeal of an interpretation stressing political factors is clear. One extreme version is given in a memoir of a successful Dublin Litvak clan, *The Noyek Story*:

> Lithuania of the 1880's was subject to a tyranny more crushing that that which raged in Ireland. An entire people were being herded by the conquering Cossacks into slavery. Children were taken from parents for slave labour in the mines and to the labour camps of their Tsarist masters. Theirs was a life sentence and their parents preferred the ultimate risk of abandoning their children to the vagaries of an oceanic voyage in the hope that they would eventually arrive in the land of the free.[15]

More moderate versions of this theme are found in memoirs such as Cork-born David Marcus's *Oughtobiography*, which refers to "Jewish refugees fleeing the pogroms of their native Czarist-ruled Lithuania."[16] Dubliner June Levine, whose grandfather "came from Riga in Lithuania [*sic*]," claimed that "[h]e was conscripted into the Russian Army at the age of twelve but he ran away to escape a pogrom." Like him, most of the Jewish community in Ireland "came from backgrounds of terrible trouble." Levine's ex-mother-in-law "was one of two survivors of a family of thirteen who had been killed and raped in Russia. Her two sisters had been raped to death by soldiers." Levine's husband's surname "was taken for the town from which the Russian army chased his parents."[17] Long after the father of Israel Sieff, founder of the Marks & Spencer retailing dynasty, left Lithuania, "[e]ven in England, in Leeds, the pogroms were fresh in his mind."[18] The reminiscences of Glasgow-born Jack Caplan, whose parents were emigrants from Lithuania, are in the same vein. Jack's parents, "like thousands of other victims of anti-semitism, were compelled to flee from the pogroms, the burnings, the killings, and the rapings permitted and encouraged by the corrupt Russians."[19]

Such accounts both reflect and inform Jewish collective or folk memory of pre-1914 emigration from tsarist Russia. They also have colored many academic accounts of the outflow. Cases in point are Mark Wischnitzer's *To Dwell in Safety: The Story of Jewish Migration since 1800* and Samuel Joseph's pioneering study of Jewish emigration to the United States.[20] Joseph did not entirely dismiss what he dubbed "the forces of economic attraction exercised in the United States," but his main emphasis was on "the exceptional economic, social, and legal conditions in Eastern Europe," which were the product of "governmental persecution." More recently, the Jewish American historian Irving Howe has described the typical emigrant as having "[run] away from pogroms," and David Vital's account in *A People Apart: The Jews in Europe, 1789–1939* argues likewise, although he also lists as a factor the "steadily deepening loss of regard for the old habits and norms of Jewish life as well as for those who continued to uphold and teach them." In its 2003 Christmas issue, *The Economist* referred to "new restrictions governing where they could live and work in the Russian empire, plus pogroms, war and revolution [driving] more than 2m Jews out of eastern Europe." Closer to home, the account of emigration in Dermot Keogh's acclaimed *Jews in Twentieth-century Ireland* is heavily dependent on stories of pogroms and persecution for its account of the Litvak migration to Ireland.[21]

The May Laws and their aftermath undoubtedly affected the psyche of émigré Russian Jews and their descendants, most of whom remain convinced that those who left Lithuania were refugees or asylum seekers, rather than primarily economic migrants. The argument mirrors that of the nationalist historiography of nineteenth-century Irish emigration, which placed almost exclusive emphasis on "push" factors such as evictions by rapacious landlords and politico-religious persecution. In Ireland this line of argument no longer carries conviction. Whereas political factors undoubtedly left a minority no choice but to leave, most migrants were influenced by economic forces at home and in the host economies.

Specialists in the history of Jewish emigration from tsarist Russia reject an interpretation that places primary emphasis on persecution and discrimination. And they would accept that, whatever the validity of such an interpretation for other parts of the tsarist lands, it cannot account for the bulk of the pre-1914 Jewish outflow from Lithuania.[22] Lithuania, at the northern end of the Pale of Settlement, was not tsarist Russia. While there was no love lost between Jew and non-Jew in the Baltic provinces, over the centuries Jews had not been subject to the outrages perpetrated on their coreligionists elsewhere. Between 1881 and 1914, as for centuries before, Lithuania was virtually pogrom-free. One account lists as an exception "the sudden enforced baptism that began in 1495 and ended eight years later with the full rehabilitation of all the converts." As in the Irish case, a minority of engagé traditionalists are reluctant to accept new research findings that the emigrants' primary motivation was economic.[23]

Pogroms elsewhere in the empire in the wake of the May Laws may well have unsettled those living in the Litvak shtetls, but the collective memory of the emigrants' descendants is of direct rather than vicarious experience of pogroms. Why do pogroms and persecution feature so much in accounts of the post-1880 emigration? Why are they recurring motifs in Irish Jewish collective or social memory? The contextualization and function of these myths is really beyond the scope of this study, but

Figure 1.1. The Pale and its provinces.

the extensive literature on collective and social memory offers some clues.[24] It makes the point that such memory is prone to be partisan, simplistic, and subject to chronological confusion, making events in the distant past seem as though they happened yesterday. Collective memory, in this view, usually tells us more about the needs of the present than the past.[25] David Cesarani's study of Jewish migration to England provides an apt example. Cesarani, a leading specialist in Jewish history, documents several myths concerning the migration—the prevalence of pogroms, fear of military conscription, being cheated of one's money en route or on arrival, being tricked into disembarking in Britain rather than in America—and deems them all to be alibis for what he dubs "opportunistic migration." In an era of increasing hostility toward immigration in both the United Kingdom and the United States it helped to be seen as a political refugee and asylum seeker. Irish American collective memory of the Great Famine and the landlord-tenant system yields some points of comparison.[26] In the German American collective memory of migration, it is a similar story: the "1848-er" and the Great War draft dodger also play roles out of all proportion to their actual numbers. But there was a specifically Jewish aspect to this, too. It would be surprising if the subsequent catastrophic history of world Jewry did not also influence the collective memory of Jewish immigration to Ireland. But the meta-narrative of Jewish suffering goes back much further—consider the archetypal narratives of Exodus and the Passover Haggadah, with their themes of deliverance from destruction by hostile outsiders. Such narratives were endorsed by Zionism, which had a strong following in Ireland from the outset.[27]

Yet the lack of detailed and precise depictions of persecution or pogroms in firsthand accounts of emigration is striking.[28] It is instructive to compare the passage from *The Noyek Story* quoted above with the following account, based on the experiences of Myer Joel Wigoder.

> When my grandfather, Myer Joel Wigoder, left Lithuania in 1891, his destination was Holland. His motivations for leaving home and family to start a new life elsewhere were entirely economic. As I read through his works of memoirs, some written in Yiddish, some in Hebrew—in a beautiful copperplate script, sometimes naively but charmingly adorned—I find no reference to any anti-Semitic experience or to the atmosphere of pogrom and persecution which had been prevalent in Russia (to which Lithuania then belonged) for the previous decade. Various business ventures had not succeeded . . . so at the age of thirty-six he left his pregnant wife and four children and headed west.[29]

Myer Joel Wigoder also published his own autobiography in Leeds in 1935. There is no support there either for Dermot Keogh's claim that Wigoder's departure was the result of "the destruction of his house in a pogrom" in 1890. Wigoder's own account plainly describes the fire that destroyed his house as an act of God, which also swept away the Catholic church facing his house and much else in Wexna. Such fires were endemic in the shtetls of eastern Europe, where most of the housing stock was of wood; indeed, they are a recurring feature in the "railroad stories" of the great Sholem Aleichem. In July 1894 the *Jewish Chronicle* reported a "very serious fire in the town of Plumgany . . . by which eight hundred families were totally without any shelter—only fifty-seven small houses remaining." The fire had destroyed all the shops and killed several children.[30]

Lieb (or Levi) Berman also left for Ireland after a series of business failures. His brother-in-law had set him up as a brewer in Popalan, but "he made it so good that he lost heavily on every brew." When he switched to peddling "his horse ate up every groschen [he] had." The final straw was the spoilage of his cartload of smoked sprats on a sweltering day en route to Vecksna market. His exasperated wife, hearing glowing stories about a kinsman's success in "England-Ireland" (as the Litvaks called Ireland), prevailed on Lieb to try his luck there.[31] And Louis Wine's departure for Ireland in 1875 was also prompted by entirely economic considerations:

the spur was a letter home from his stepbrother who, "having found his way to Ireland, wrote glowingly of the country, saying he felt it was a land of great opportunity."[32] Louis Goldberg, father of the late Gerald Goldberg, one of Cork's best-known Jews, is another case in point. In its obituary of Gerald, the *Irish Times* described him as the son of a Litvak "who escaped from a pogrom in Russia in 1882 and landed in Ireland."[33] Given, however, that eleven-year-old Louis Goldberg was "at first sheltered by relatives who had settled in Limerick" and would marry into a Litvak family that had been in Cork since 1875, surely a straightforward economic interpretation of his migration is more plausible.

The May Laws would seem to have been mainly responsible for the departure of Lieb Berman's in-laws, the Zlotovers. A family memoir relates that they, petty gentry and the elite of the local Jewish community, were forced off their large farm (which included a toll bridge and a flour mill) near Popalan by "some of the shrewdest, most wide-awake amongst the peasants." But the Zlotovers were probably exceptional both in terms of their status and what happened to them.[34] The Zlotovers seem to have been particularly well-off, but even the average Lithuanian Jew was considerably better-off than the impoverished Lithuanian or Russian peasant. Perhaps this helps explain why IRA man turned businessman-politician Robert Briscoe, whose father came to Dublin from the shtetl of Zagar in northern Lithuania, made the point that Lithuanian Jews were relatively well-off and that there had been no pogroms against them.[35]

Though, as we shall see, most Irish "Litvaks" came from a small cluster of villages and towns in Lithuania, the term "Litvak" applies to Jews from an area much wider than present-day Lithuania, encompassing parts of Belarus and Poland. The population of this broader area grew rapidly during the nineteenth century, and by its end 1.5 million Jews lived in this wider region, sharing a common language (Yiddish) and a common religious culture. Most lived in villages, towns, and cities, where they often formed a majority. Their main interaction with the largely rural non-Jewish population (who were, by comparison, poor and unschooled) was economic; Jews formed a majority of middlemen (merchants, innkeepers, petty moneylenders, and so on) and skilled craftsmen throughout the region.

Unlike the peasants, the Jews had never been enserfed. At the outset most of them had lived in the countryside as traders or artisans, while a privileged minority worked for the ruling elite as clerks and agents. Others lived in small shtetls where they made their living as middlemen and self-employed craftsmen. Over time this urban component became the dominant one. Jews became disproportionately numerous in certain niche activities such as innkeeping and brewing, transport, and the corn trade.[36]

Tsar Alexander II's "revolution from above," which abolished serfdom on terms very unfavorable to the Russian peasantry, had taken place barely two decades before the beginnings of mass migration. Instead of increasing the occupational and geographical mobility of the peasantry, emancipation sometimes had the opposite effect. With the *mir* (or village commune) responsible for dividing up the contributions and obligations of the separate households, impediments to mobility remained. The ex-serfs and their children remained largely *adscripti glebae*, and were still overrepresented in menial jobs such as unskilled labor and domestic service at the century's end. Jews, on the other hand, were considerably over-represented in occupations requiring a modicum of physical and human capital. According to the 1897 census, in the tsarist province of Kovno (which covered most of Lithuania) Jews formed 18.6 percent of all those employed, but they accounted for 49.9 percent of those in crafts and industry, 51.8 percent of those in the free professions and the civil service, and 91.2 percent of those engaged in trade and credit. By way of contrast, they made up only 1.5 percent of the agricultural labor force.[37] While there were impoverished craftsmen and poor traders, Russian agriculture had its disproportionate share of the really poor.

There were economic pressures at work in these decades, driving out emigrants. The rapid growth of the Jewish population within the Pale was certainly a factor, particularly in the villages and small towns of the northwest, where population pressure was greatest and industrialization and economic growth slowest. The Jewish population of Kovno province rose from 81,500 in 1847 to 212,600 in 1897; that of Vilna from 64,800 to 204,700.[38] Edwin G. Burrows and Mike Wallace provide the following succinct summary of this "revisionist" view of the causes of emigration:

> Emancipation of the serfs in 1863 undercut Jews who had served as agents of the nobility. Railroads brought the products of urban (particularly German) factories to the Pale, supplanting rough-hewn artisanal output. Trains also brought cheaper grain from faraway markets, debilitating the peasant economy that sustained the shtetls. City-based commercial and financial enterprises grew, undermining shtetl merchants and moneylenders.[39]

Jewish contractors, traders, and craftsmen were hardly immune to these globalizing forces. The economy of the shtetl, long geared to service provision and artisanal production for local markets, was unequal to the challenge of mass production and mass marketing. It is also likely that emancipation enabled some former serfs to enter and compete in activities previously closed to them. On the other hand, the fact remains that the retail sector in Russia as a whole grew rapidly in these decades—by 3.5 percent or more annually between 1885 and 1913 according to economist

Paul Gregory—and average personal consumption also rose in real terms, though at the slower rate of about 1.6 percent.[40] Unfortunately, data on regional variations in these growth rates (e.g., Jewish Pale of Settlement versus non-Pale, north versus south) are lacking. It is also possible, indeed likely, that anti-Semitic legislation meant that Jews in the labor force suffered more, in relative terms at least, than non-Jewish subjects of the tsar. But the latter also emigrated in increasing numbers between the early 1880s and the 1910s. Jewish migration was spectacularly higher in proportional terms, but it shared a common upward trend with other migrations in this era.

Figures 1.2a and 1.2b point both to specificities in the Jewish outflow and to a common long-term pattern. Figure 1.2a shows the estimated annual outflows of Jewish and non-Jewish Russians between 1881 and 1910. The spike in the early 1890s may well reflect rumors of new restrictions on Jewish economic activities and the expulsions from Moscow, while the second peak in 1905–6 coincided with renewed pogroms; nonetheless, the broader trends in the Jewish and non-Jewish outflows were remarkably similar. Although the communal *mir* sometimes militated against movements out of the village in the wake of serfdom, there were powerful incentives to leave.[41] There were other, less specifically Russian, forces at work, too. The U.S. immigration data summarized in figure 1.2b are telling in this respect. Economist Simon Kuznets was the first to highlight the pattern shown here—"an insignificant trickle over decades, then more substantial but moderate levels, then high levels, both absolute and relative to the originating population"—for countries as different as Norway and Greece.[42] The close synchronicity between aggregate immigration flows from Russia (about half of which was Jewish), Italy, and Austro-Hungary to the United States in the three decades or so before the Great War suggests the dominant role of U.S. pull factors rather than country-specific push factors. All three outflows rose from a few thousand annually in the 1870s to very similar peaks, and short-term fluctuations in the three migration flows were also uncannily similar.[43] The correlations between first differences in the three series in the 1880–1914 period were strikingly high (see table 1.1).

The correlation between first differences in Jewish and non-Jewish Russian movements between 1881 and 1910 was also positive, though less strong (+0.33). Andrew Godley has shown more formally that in these decades Jewish emigration to the United States responded to the same forces as Italian, Irish, and British immigration. Godley's results highlight especially the role of employment conditions in the United States, and he concludes that "Russian Jews were principally economic migrants, not political refugees."[44] The economic-historical analyses of Kuznets and Godley run counter to—and effectively rebut—claims such as that of his-

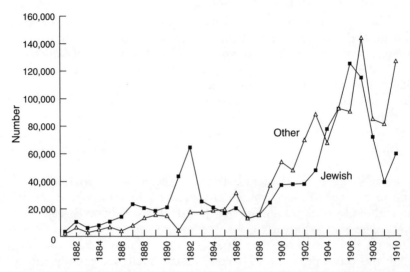

Figure 1.2a. Emigration of Jews and others from Russia, 1880–1914.

Figure 1.2b. Emigration from Russia, Italy, and Central Europe to the United States, 1880–1914.

TABLE 1.1.
Correlations between Migration Flows to the United States, 1880–1914
(First Differences)

	Italy	Russia	Austro-Hungary
Italy	1.00		
Russia	0.70	1.00	
Austro-Hungary	0.77	0.79	1.00

torian David Vital that "in Jewish cases strictly economic considerations were rarely preponderant."[45] They also argue against the likelihood that stories of pogroms in one part of the empire encouraged many of those living in other parts to leave.

THE MIGRATION IN CONTEXT

Pogroms in 1881 and the May Laws of 1882 may well have sparked an "emigration mania" in Jewish Russia, but other factors account for its persistence. Overemphasis on the events of 1881 and 1882 obscures the fact that less than 10 percent of all Jewish emigration to the United States between 1881 and 1914 occurred in the 1880s, compared to well over two-thirds from 1900 on.[46] Such considerations suggest that Ireland's Litvaks should perhaps be seen less as victims of persecution than as individuals and families—many of them poverty-stricken—bent on "bettering themselves." In this respect they were much like other south and east European emigrants to the United States in the same era, and indeed the Irish and German emigrants of a previous generation.

The various forces, general and specific, behind both the mass Jewish exodus of the pre-1914 era and its small Irish tributary need further research. The considerable international literature on this emigration leaves several questions about its regional spread and its socioeconomic character still unanswered, questions that also have a bearing on the origins and motivations of the Irish Jews. The rest of this account of the emigration that produced "Gaelic Golus" is devoted to a discussion of some of these.

1. If fear of persecution was the sole factor then, ceteris paribus, Jewish emigration rates from the southern provinces of the tsarist empire should have been much higher than from less-affected regions like Lithuania. But the opposite was the case. Jews in the tsarist provinces of Kovno (or Kaunus in Lithuanian) and Vilna (now Vilnius) accounted for only 8 percent of all Jews in Russia and Russian Poland in the decades before World War I, but voluminous impressionistic evidence suggests that they dominated

the pre-1914 flows to the United Kingdom (including Ireland) and South Africa. A recent analysis of Jewish archives in London and New York by economic historian Andrew Godley confirms the disproportionate share of the northwest and Russian Poland in the post-1880 outflow. Godley finds that the northwest (effectively Lithuania, Russian Poland, and Belarus) accounted for 29 percent of the population of the empire in 1897 but for 45.3 percent of emigration to London and 50 percent of migration to New York during the three decades or so before World War I.[47] Economist Joel Perlmann's identification of the "seven core provinces" supplying immigrants to the United States in 1900 puts Kovno province, broadly coterminous with present-day Lithuania, in the top three.[48]

More surprisingly, perhaps, these years also saw internal migration by Jews from the north, "where relations between Jews and Christians were relatively untroubled by pogroms," to the parts of Russia that were "at the centre of every anti-Jewish outbreak."[49]

2. For centuries the Baltic provinces (including those composing Lithuania) had led the Russian provinces in terms of virtually all indicators of economic development (e.g., industrial employment, grain yields, milk yields of livestock, literacy, and education). For this reason one might expect the pressure to leave to be lower in the Baltic region than elsewhere. On the other hand, economic growth seems to have been faster in southern Russia than in north in the second half of the nineteenth century, and the late 1860s and early 1870s were particularly hard years in the Baltic provinces.[50] This may partly account for the higher emigration rates from the region. But these generalizations apply to the population as a whole; Isaac Rubinow, for example, insists that the economic position of Jews was worse in the northwest than elsewhere.[51] Could it be that the lot of Lithuanian Jews was worsening while that of the rest of the population was improving?

3. In this period the cost of one adult steerage passage to the United States was about $25, while a second-class cabin passage cost $50 per adult and $25 per child. These sums may be compared to the "ordinary wage" of five rubles ($2.58) a week earned by Jewish factory workers in tsarist Russia in the 1890s, or the three hundred rubles (about $150) that it took to maintain a family in modest circumstances for a year.[52] Even a steerage passage for the average family thus cost at least several months' wages. This may explain why husbands as a rule emigrated first, and sent back the passage money for the rest of the household in a year or two. In the mid-1880s Ella Dina Rein left Lithuania for Dublin, where her husband had made a home for them. She traveled by boat and train, infant in arms and four more young children with "ropes round their middles which she attached to her own waist."[53] Perhaps, too, the lower cost of a passage to the United Kingdom meant that those who settled

there were marginally less well-off than those who ventured further west to the New World. On the other hand, their higher standard of living almost certainly helps explain the higher emigration rate of Jews over other subjects of the tsar.[54]

4. Social networks presumably played a role in producing concentrations in particular destinations of Jews from particular regions of Russia. This is certainly true in the case of Dublin. When Talmudic scholar Myer Joel Wigoder arrived in Dublin virtually penniless from Wexna (Viekšniai in Lithuanian) in 1890, a Litvak boy he encountered on the street took him to the house of a Dublin acquaintance, one Mr. Eppel, who gave him the addresses of other Wexna immigrants. In Jessie Spiro Bloom's home by the Grand Canal near Portobello "there was a constant stream of people passing through . . . and many of them would stop over at our home." While living in Athlone and Galway in the 1880s Hannah Berman's parents "were constantly visited by strange Jews." Her father originally chose Limerick because "Joseph Greenberg's older daughter, Esther Barron, was living there at the time, and [her father] would have someone to go to in case of need."[55]

Several of the immigrants who settled in both Dublin and Cork in the 1880s had come from the shtetl of Akmyan (Akmené in Lithuanian). In Joseph Edelstein's fictional account, Moses Levenstein of "Wexney" was met on arrival by "his townsman Chaim Weinblatt," who had preceded him fourteen years earlier, and "who was now living in Dublin in a big house, and who had a piano in the house." It is surely no coincidence that Wexna and Akmian, like several other towns mentioned in memoirs and elsewhere—such as Zhager (Žagaré), Kurshany (Kuršenai), Shavli (Siauliai), Papiljan/Popalan (Papilé), Yelok (Ylakiai), Telz (Telšiai), Zedick (Židikai), Klikul (Klykoliai), Plungyan (Plungé), and Pajurs (near Raisenai)—were *all* located in the same small corner of northern Lithuania (Kovno *gubernaya* in tsarist times), bordering the Courland region of Latvia. As figure 1.3 indicates, none of these places was more than fifty kilometers or so from any of the others.[56]

The towns and villages of origin of most of Ireland's Jewish immigrants, along with their Jewish populations, and the Jewish percentages of the total populations, are listed in table 1.2. The data are mostly taken from the 1897 Russian census, as reported in Schoenberg and Schoenberg's invaluable compendium.[57] Note the implication that most of the towns supplying Dublin's Jews were small and heavily Jewish. Akmyan—often singled out as the home place of many Irish immigrants—turns out to have been the smallest of the lot. Most likely, its relatively low Jewish population share was the product of heavy emigration in the previous decade or two. The 1897 census records for Akmyan bear the signs of this: a distorted age profile, a disproportionate number of absent hus-

Figure 1.3. The Litvak shtetls.

bands, and several elderly householders noted as dependent on emigrant remittances. The Schoenbergs report Akmyan's Jews as "engaged in small businesses, crafts and agriculture," Zedik's as small-scale traders and peddlers in the villages of Courland, and Klikul's as "peddlers, going out to neighbouring villages on Sunday and not returning until Sabbath eve." In Vexna "the market was in the center of the village and provided a livelihood for most of the Jews," and Plungyan was also mainly a market town. For most Telz Jews—small shopkeepers, artisans, peddlers, coachmen, and carriers—the late tsarist years were a hard period. But in the bigger towns such as Šhavli and Zhager Jews owned factories and exported considerable quantities of flax, hides, and grain to Germany. In Šhavli the tanneries owned by Chaim Freinkel and the Nurock brothers were substantial, technologically advanced concerns; the Nurocks also ran their own bank. In both these towns there must have been a considerable Jewish proletariat. Most likely, however, some of the Litvaks describing themselves as from these towns were from villages in their hinterlands rather than the towns themselves.[58]

5. Contingency also probably generated regional concentrations of immigrants. It has been suggested that South Africa's first Litvaks were diverted there in the 1860s, when for some reason—perhaps the outbreak

TABLE 1.2.
Shtetls of Origin

Village/Town	Jewish Population	Percentage Jewish
Vexna	1,646	56
Akmyan	543	36
Zhager	5,443	41*
Šhavli	9,847	71
Papiljan	1,000	—
Klikul	600	—
Plungyan	2,502	55
Zedik	914	73
Telz	3,088	51
Kurshany	1,542	48

Source: Schoenberg and Schoenberg 1991
* = 1923 (and higher earlier)

of the Civil War—their path to the United States was blocked. The decision of the Castle Shipping Line, which operated services to South Africa, to advertise widely for passengers in Lithuania when its traffic in emigrant Cornish miners dried up in the 1880s may also have diverted some migrants from the United States to South Africa. So for certain did the munificence of one Sammy Marks, a Lithuanian-born tycoon, regarded "as the chief pioneer of Lithuanian Jewish migration to South Africa."[59]

Similarly, the serendipitous transfer of some London immigrants to Ireland by the London Jewish Board of Guardians in the early 1870s may have been one of the spurs for the migration that followed. Oral tradition suggests that some of Ireland's Jews ended up there by accident or through ignorance. Ronit Lentin describes her grandfather-in-law as one of a group from Akmyan who arrived in Cobh on a ship from Hamburg "escaping forced conscription to the Czar's army"; they were "instructed to disembark in the South of Ireland, told that this is America." A U.S. descendant of Dublin Litvaks believed that "it was never my family's intention to settle in Ireland, but it was in fact an accidental landing point when they left Russia . . . a way station for some of the family, as most have made homes in other countries." Another memoir claims that some Jews believed they had landed in America when they "were dumped in England or Ireland." Gerald Goldberg, himself the son of an immigrant, described the Litvaks' arrival in Cork as "an accident." They were landed in the port of Cork and duped by the claim that "America is the next parish." Another, less plausibly, asserts that calls of "Cork, Cork" were mistaken for "New York," prompting "befuddled, bedraggled, wandering Jews" to disembark in the city by the Lee. Yet another version has the Jews staying in Cork because they ran out of kosher food; their ship was delayed there for repairs for several weeks.[60] Such claims—good examples of what David Cesarani dubs the myth of accidental arrival—are also a recurring feature of memoirs of Jewish emigration to Britain.[61]

6. If the May Laws militated most against better-educated and more skilled Jews, this, too, should have been reflected in the character of the outflow. On this issue the specialist literature is inconclusive. Samuel Joseph and Simon Kuznets point to the considerable occupational skills of those who left, but David Vital's comparison of Jewish occupational profiles in the Russian Empire in 1897 and among arrivals in the United States in 1901–6 implies an adverse selection bias in the outflow. In support of Vital, professionals and white-collar workers made up a significantly higher proportion of the Jewish population as a whole than of the substantial minority who left.[62] However, these were but a small fraction of the total Jewish labor force. Traders were also underrepresented. This is partly explained by the nontransferability of the skills of at least some of the traders who catered to the farming community in Russia.[63] Perhaps the life-cycle character of occupational status also played a part. Since many traders began their working life as craftsmen, craftsmen tended to be younger than traders. Their younger age profile meant that the craftsmen were more likely to emigrate. Skilled workers, on the other hand, were significantly overrepresented. The higher endowments of both human and physical capital in the shtetls than in rural Russia may help explain why Russian Jews were more alert to rising economic opportunities abroad than was the much poorer and numerically dominant Russian peasantry.

7. The 1897 Russian census revealed Jewish literacy rates to be twice those of non-Jews.[64] Lithuanian Jews were almost certainly more literate than Jews elsewhere in Russia. Jews from neighboring provinces considered the Litvaks as rather cerebral, characterized by "a certain emotional dryness, the superiority of the intellect over emotion, mental alertness, sharp-wittedness, and pungency."[65] In the nineteenth century, Lithuanian yeshivas (religious schools) attracted students from all over Russia, and Lithuanian rabbis were much sought after elsewhere for their learning. Vilna was famous for its publishing houses, which by no means confined themselves to religious books. If the evidence of other migrations is anything to go by, the higher human capital endowments of Lithuanian Jews may also have increased their propensity to emigrate.[66] As we shall see later, the trading and craft skills the Litvaks brought with them equipped them to take every advantage of economic opportunities wherever they went.

8. In her study of the Jewish immigrant community of Johnstown, Pennsylvania, Ewa Morawska has drawn attention to "the concentration of entrepreneurial employment . . . that Johnstown's Jews shared with their fellow ethnics in smaller American cities." She notes that while at the turn of the century three-fifths of gainfully employed Jews in the bigger urban centers in the United States worked in manufacturing industries, in smaller cities and towns over two-thirds worked in "middleman minority" occupations. For Morawska, this was no accident: Johnstown's immigrants had come mainly from rural shtetls, well equipped with the entrepreneurial skills and the group cohesion that would serve them well there, whereas the Jews who opted for the "large industrial ethnic enclaves" in New York and other major cities had the "group experience of urban living and industrial employment in the country of origin."[67] An account of Lithuanian Jewish emigration to South Africa argues along the same lines.

> The Jews of Lithuania were shopkeepers, itinerant peddlers, or petty craftsmen who labored in their own small workshops. It was only natural, then, that the latter should prefer the greater economic independence that South African settlement offered to those who were not wage earners.[68]

In order to clinch such claims, we would need to know more about how the origins of big-city (e.g., New York or London) Jews differed from those of Jews opting for Johnstown or South Africa. Meanwhile, the evidence from Ireland is supportive, since most Irish Litvaks had lived previously in small shtetls and would become traders of one kind or another in Ireland at the outset. In the longer run, the cities provided fewer outlets for the middleman activities in which the migrants specialized.

9. The fear of conscription into the brutal tsarist army has already been mentioned as a reason for Jewish emigration. Images of Jewish boy-soldiers being carried away at the age of twelve and of young draft dodgers fleeing across the border permeate Litvak folk memory.[69] Here again the documentary record clashes with collective memory. In 1827 Tsar Nikolai I extended the Russian system of military service to Jews and other minority groups, who had been traditionally exempted. Though recent research on the subject makes a strong case that the conscription of Jews was not the product of a specifically anti-Semitic agenda, features of this system discriminated against them, and some officers sought to convert Jewish recruits to Russian Orthodoxy, albeit with limited success. It was left to communal leaders to select those who would serve. The *kahals* (or community councils) tended to be dominated by the richer families in the community, so the poor and unlettered bore the brunt of the draft. Sometimes those chosen to fill the quota were

mere boys or adolescents, and service in the army lasted into late adulthood. Nikolai's integrationist measures left deep scars on the Jewish community.[70]

Flight would have been an understandable response to Nikolai's policies. The key point, however, is that the worst excesses of this recruitment system were removed after Tsar Alexander II's accession in 1855, more than two decades before the rise of mass migration.[71] There were further dramatic reforms in 1874. Thereafter, there was a large increase in the numbers recruited (amounting to about one-third of each male cohort), but the term served was much shorter. And the decision as to who would be recruited became less arbitrary. Instead of landowners or the village leaders deciding, the selection was made by ballot after central commissions excluded certain groups on the basis of health or dependency. The system as described by Hannah Berman—"a regular call-up before a tribunal"—was a much more humane affair. It exempted her father in 1874 because he was deemed to be "several years above the requisite age [of twenty-one], although he was almost exactly twenty-one," whereupon he was issued a valuable red passport that freed him from future duty. Lieb Berman's memories of the military tribunals were benign, and he was present when one very old man faced "some odd and amusing questions." The elderly peasant finally declared in tears that he had no desire to become a general, "only to be back home."[72]

In 1897 just over 1 percent (53,194) of a total Jewish population of 5.2 million was serving in the army or navy. The total size of the armed forces in 1897 (1,132,682 in a population of 125 million) implies that Jews were marginally overrepresented at this time.[73] Indeed, in the final decades of the tsarist regime, Jews were always overrepresented in the army, relative to both other male subjects of the tsar and to the non-Jewish urban population. By then they were deemed excellent soldiers. Collective memory of endemic evasion of the draft is not so easily squared with this mild overrepresentation of Jews in the tsar's forces. Emphasis on the connection between emigration and military service tends to conflate the excesses of the pre-1855 era and the post-1880 outflow. In a revisionist analysis of the social memory of Jewish migration, Cesarani has also raised "a question mark over the ubiquity of the threat of military service" as the motivation behind emigration.[74] In sum, although the threat of conscription surely prompted some to leave, it was never the paramount consideration.

10. In the 1880s and 1890s many of the immigrants who arrived in Dublin from Lithuania stayed only for a short time. Whether those who left differed in some systematic way from those who remained is a moot point. Jessie Spiro Bloom, who left, returned, and left again, opined much later, "Those that remained in Dublin seemed to be the type that were not

very ambitious to make a lot of money, but there was an atmosphere of learning in the place that the more temperate of the emigrants preferred, so though the opportunities for financial success [were] not very great, there was a feeling of ease."[75] Her claim is contradicted, however, by Myer Joel Wigoder's lament that in early twentieth-century Dublin "the predominant factor [was] money." To the devout Wigoder's regret, self-made men "rule the community, dominate the public institutions, and constitute the authorities in the Synagogues." Myer Joel Wigoder set high standards for devotion: in the late 1910s his daughter-in-law remembered being taken to his shop and seeing "this saintly, bearded man bent over the Talmud, deep in Jewish study . . . [a]nd around the walls were pictures of the Virgin Mary, the infant Jesus, Jesus on the cross etc.!" Yet the prominence of more worldly, status-conscious men in the leadership of the various *hevroth* and communal associations is indisputable. Joseph Edelstein's *The Moneylender* (1908), on which more in chapter 3, also supports Wigoder.[76]

11. The great majority of those who left the shtetls never returned. Nor did they leave, intending to return. Andrew Godley's estimates of gross and net outflows suggest that in the 1880–1913 period fewer than one in ten went back.[77] Irish emigration and Jewish emigration had this much in common. However, the Jewish immigrants' nostalgia for their Lithuanian shtetls seems not to have matched Irish emigrants' feelings for their homeland. The yearnings of the latter are highlighted in David Fitzpatrick's analysis of emigrant letters from nineteenth-century Australia, where the word "home" occurs 229 times in his database of 111 letters. While Jewish emigrants yearned for the company of their *landsleit* (friends from the same region or town), they certainly did not miss "home" in the way the Irish did. In his evocative memoir of Little Jerusalem Nick Harris wonders why his parents "did not talk to us about their *heim*." Most of the immigrants held on to their Jewish faith, but soon turned their backs on the Yiddish language and on the literature and music of the shtetls.[78]

Where the emigrants were numerous, they left a very lopsided age structure behind them. Akmyan, where so many Irish Litvaks claim their origins, is a good example. In 1897 this small town contained 554 Jews, of whom 123 were in their teens, but only 57 in their twenties, and 38 in their thirties; and women in their twenties and thirties outnumbered men of the same ages by a two-to-one ratio. The census also indicates that many Akmenites who remained relied on remittances from those who left.[79]

Chapter 2

"ENGLAND-IRELAND" AND DEAR DIRTY DUBLIN

There was little to lose by making a fresh start
in a country which I knew had attracted
some of my friends.
—*Myer Joel Wigoder*[1]

Ireland . . . the last place in the world anyone
would look for a Jew.
—*From* A Portrait of the Jews in Ireland (1971)

WHY DID the few thousand immigrants from the tsarist empire who emigrated between the 1870s and the early 1910s choose "England-Ireland" (as Ireland was known in *der heim* in the 1880s)? Why did a majority of them settle in Dublin? After all, the Irish economy was poor relative to, say, other destinations in this period, and its growth sluggish by comparison. On the eve of the World War I Irish GDP per head lagged far behind that of the United States, Great Britain, Australia, Canada, and Argentina.[2] Moreover, most post-1880 east European Jewish emigrants, no matter where they went, tended to opt for fast-expanding boomtowns. To take a few examples of cities with substantial east European Jewish communities by 1914: between 1891 and 1911 the populations of Toronto and Montreal nearly trebled, and that of New York doubled; Johannesburg grew from a miner's settlement to a city of 200,000 over the same period, and Buenos Aires leapt from less than 200,000 in 1870 to over 1.5 million by 1914.

By such standards, Dublin was hardly the most inviting or obvious destination for immigrants in this period. Its growth was proceeding at a snail's pace even by contemporary European standards. In mid-century it contained just short of 250,000 people. By 1881 the city and its middle-class suburbs contained just over 300,000, while by 1914 they had grown to 370,000. Belfast's population growth—from 98,000 in 1851 to 208,000 in 1881 and 387,000 in 1911—was headlong by comparison, but hardly spectacular relative to the destination cities mentioned above. By this yardstick Cork—with a population of 107,016 in 1831, 75,345 in 1881, and 76,673 in 1891—fared even worse. In the mid-nineteenth century Dublin was still in the top ten of European cities in terms of numbers; by the century's end it had dropped below the top twenty and had become Ireland's second city in demographic terms, temporarily ceding primacy to Belfast (see table 2.1).[3] Such comparisons explain why so few settled in Ireland, but what of those who did? Part of the answer must wait until chapter 3, but in the meantime an account of the economic conditions and trends in the Ireland of the era of Jewish immigration is warranted.

The contrasting population trajectories of nineteenth-century Dublin and Belfast are a striking reflection of the economic geography of early industrialization. Dublin was a city that the Industrial Revolution largely passed by. When English journalist Arnold Wright surveyed the scene from the top of Nelson's Pillar on Dublin's O'Connell Street in the wake of the labor unrest of 1913, he could count only "as many factory shafts as you can have fingers on your two hands."[4] The occupational profile of the city's labor force on the eve of World War I is revealing in this respect. More than half the 55,000 male Dubliners in "industrial" occupations were builders and decorators, unskilled mechanics, or laborers. The city's weak industrial base is also reflected in the kind of employment open to them. The female shares of the labor force in the two cities in 1911 were not very different—36 percent in Belfast, 32 percent of Dublin—but Belfast offered women workers more opportunities. In Belfast the textile sector employed two-fifths of working women, the same proportion as that in female domestic service in greater Dublin. Cork was closer to Dublin than to Belfast in this respect. After quite a precocious start in the late eighteenth century, post-famine Cork deindustrialized, so much so that automobile manufacturer Henry Ford (who set up a tractor factory in the city in 1917) could quip that "Cork had no real industry."[5]

Curiously, however, the relative progress of Dublin and Belfast is a poor guide to the relative size of their Jewish communities a century or so ago. In 1881, when Ireland's Litvak population was still very small, Dublin contained 352 Jews to Belfast's 61. By 1911 Belfast had made up ground, relatively speaking: the numbers then were 2,965 and 1,139, respectively. However, Dublin maintained its lead after the partition of the island in 1921; in the mid-1930s it still contained almost three times as many Jews as did Belfast. Meanwhile the Jewish population of Cork city and county rose from 26 in 1881 to 446 in 1911, before falling back to 366 in 1926 and 226 in 1936. Why did Dublin prove more attractive to immigrants than Belfast? Why did Cork's community fall back by almost half while those of Dublin and Belfast continued to rise? Was it because of the greater pulling power of the larger cities—their wider choice of schools or the better employment and marriage prospects afforded by their more elaborate social networks?

TABLE 2.1.
The Jewish and Russian-Born Populations of Dublin, Belfast, Cork, Ireland, and Great Britain, 1871–1936/37

Year	1861	1871	1881	1891	1901	1911	1926	1936/37
Jewish								
Dublin (city and suburbs)	335	189	352	1,057	2,169	2,965	3,150	3,372
Belfast		11	61	205	763	1,139	1,149	1,284
Cork (city and county)	0	6	26	217	447	446	366	226
Ireland	393	285	472	1,779	3,898	5,148	5,044	5,211
Britain (1,000s)						300		
Russian-Born								
Dublin		37	95	665	1,120	1,120	723 (*)	413 (*)
Belfast		8	18	102	371	424	—	—
Cork		4	28	145	182	183	84 (*)	45 (*)
Ireland		122	198	1,111	1,966	1,985	838 (^)	483 (^)
Britain (1,000s)		9.6	14.5	46.0	86.0	99.0		

Note: "Dublin" refers to the city and county combined. (a) is from Endelman (2002, p. 130); (b) refers to the number of Russian-, Polish-, and Romanian-born "aliens" as given in C. Bloom (1996, p. 31), citing Gartner (1960). The difference between (a) and (b) in 1911 reflects the high fertility of the Jewish community.

(*) urban Leinster and urban Munster

(^) Irish Free State only

It was not the strength of its preexisting Jewish community or culture that attracted the immigrants from the east to Ireland. Ireland as a whole contained fewer than three hundred Jews before the first Litvaks arrived. The Jewish population of Dublin and its suburbs was tiny, numbering only 335 in 1861 and 189 in 1871, and it was scattered thinly throughout middle-class Dublin, in areas beyond the reach of the immigrants. Dublin Jewry's status as a religious community was precarious: an English Jew who often visited the city on business in the early 1870s was more than once summoned from his hotel on the Sabbath to make up the necessary quorum (or minyan) of ten adult males.[6]

Judging from the addresses and occupations given in the congregation's birth and death registers, the pre-1880 Irish community was mainly commercial and middle class. It was also highly mobile. Although it felt duty bound to help the indigent among the newcomers, it did not welcome them with open arms. As explained in more detail later, there would be considerable friction between the "English" and the "Russian" Jews for some decades after the latter's arrival. The two groups would worship in different places, and intermarriage between partners form "old" and "new" communities would be the exception.[7]

MORTALITY

More than half of Ireland's Jews have always lived in Dublin. In the wake of the Litvak invasion Dublin's share of the island's total dropped but between 1901 and the mid-1930s it rose from 55.6 to 64.7 percent, and it has continued to rise since. Why Dublin? Paradoxically, perhaps, socio-economic conditions in the capital are part of the answer. A century ago "dear dirty Dublin" was notorious for its huge underclass of casual laborers and their families, and the appalling conditions in which they were housed. For Dublin's poor, housing in dilapidated tenements not only entailed dampness and inadequate hygiene; it also seriously constrained the benefits of investments in sewerage schemes, since the location of flush toilets in backyards and hallways made them prey to vandalism and effectively restricted their use to males. The city's notoriously high death rates were a measure of its poverty.[8] The immigrants experienced those conditions only vicariously, but the low incomes of many Dubliners and, consequently, their poor access to credit influenced how the immigrants made their living. As argued in more detail in the following chapters, it was the very poverty of so many Irish families that created a market for the trades in which the immigrant Litvaks specialized.

Explanations offered for Dublin's high mortality in the late Victorian era fall into three categories. First, social reformers and Unionist politicians tended to blame it on public squalor and municipal mismanagement. Certainly, there was venality and corruption aplenty. Many aldermen and councilors doubled up as property speculators. An official housing inquiry in 1913 revealed that sixteen of the city's eighty aldermen or councilors owned eighty-nine tenement houses among them, and named and shamed three of these as owners of property "unfit for human habitation." Whence the claim of the London *Times* that "the Dublin Corporation is in the grip of the slum landlord."[9] The poor were not entitled to vote. Yet not even the "Corpo," controlled by Irish nationalists uninterruptedly from the early 1880s on, was impervious to criticism. A start was made in the provision of low-cost housing in the 1880s, and a public health inspectorate under the long-serving Sir Charles Cameron vigorously pursued the owners of unsafe and unsanitary housing and the purveyors of contaminated and adulterated food. These campaigns seem to have yielded some dividends.[10]

Second, those on the political left pointed to the role of joblessness and individual poverty. As Cameron noted, diseases such as measles and whooping cough "rarely kill children who are well fed,"[11] but in Dublin outbreaks of infectious diseases, such as that of measles in 1899 and of smallpox in 1903, caused mortality rates to shoot up. The significant gradient in mortality by socioeconomic class and area is telling in this respect. In the 1900s the overall death rate in Dublin's North City No. 2 District, comprising part of the inner city north of the River Liffey, was 50 percent higher than in the city's relatively affluent southern suburbs. And in Dublin Registration District as a whole (i.e., the city proper plus suburbs) in the mid-1880s the death rate of a group comprising "hawkers," "porters," and "laborers" was nearly three times that of "merchants and managers, higher class."

A third interpretation of the high mortality rates emphasized the role of individual behavior. A case in point is Registrar General Thomas Grimshaw's broadsides against feckless and careless parents, which he supported with data describing the large proportion of children who died without medical certification. He revealed that during the first quarter of 1889 the percentage of children in the Dublin registration area who died in the first month of life without a medical certificate was 53.7. For those who died between the ages of one to twelve months, the percentage was 27.1. In London the respective percentages were 6 and 1.6. Grimshaw also held that a considerable proportion of deaths from noninfectious diseases were due to parental negligence. For example, "convulsions," which accounted for nearly one-quarter of all deaths of children under five years, could have been the result of "bad food, gross negligence, or injuries concerning which no particulars could be ascertained." Such deaths, Grimshaw asserted, reflected lax cultural or religious norms.

Filthy living conditions, negligence, hooliganism, drunkenness, feck-lessness: these were personal, not societal, shortcomings. Their impact on mortality in Dublin has not been quantified, though some suspected a link: "the Irish were held to be more dirty than the English and, lest there be any misdirected imputation, the Protestant cleaner than the Roman Catholic."[12] Be that as it may, in several respects the cultural gap between Catholics and others in Dublin was a wide one. They led separate, self-contained lives: schools, hospitals, charitable organizations, and political and social clubs were run along largely confessional lines. However, there was no residential segregation in Dublin of the kind found in Belfast and in many other Ulster towns, and mixed marriages were not unheard of: class rather than religion determined where one lived.

The contrast between housing conditions in Dublin and Belfast is obvi-ous, but the implications for mortality are not straightforward. Belfast City Council left the construction of housing for the poor to the private sector, which on the whole probably did a reasonable job of producing terraces of two-up two-down houses. There were scandals, however, and some of the main building contractors conveniently doubled up as city aldermen. These included Sir Daniel Dixon, an unscrupulous developer who served seven times as mayor and represented North Belfast as M.P. between 1905 and his death two years later. In 1900/1901 over one-third of Belfast housing still depended on the traditional combination of privies and ash pit. Belfast's shortage of water seems to have been partly responsi-ble for this.[13] Moreover, much of the housing built in the middle third of the century was already in very bad condition in the 1890s and 1900s. So even though its housing stock was newer and most families lived in purpose-built accommodation, Belfast faced its own housing problems.

Typhoid fever was a bigger problem in Belfast in the 1880s and 1890s than in Dublin and, indeed, in any other city in the United Kingdom. In the 1890s the disease, which was not confined to particular localities, was responsible for an annual average of 236 deaths, almost twice as many as in Dublin. Nor did newly built housing offer much of a defense against contagion: an analysis in 1900 by the registrar general of the addresses of victims of typhoid fever suggested that one-third of them lived in houses built after 1892. Presumably the poor quality of the city's water supply was responsible: an investigative report in the influential *Lancet* in 1899 placed the blame on the city council and its water commissioners.[14]

Trends in mortality in late Victorian and Joycean Dublin are also of interest. In Ireland the civil registration of births, marriages, and deaths began late (1864). As if to compensate, almost from the outset the regis-trar general produced a wealth of detail, including weekly data on births and deaths in Dublin for publication in the local newspapers. Beginning in 1880, cross-tabulations of deaths by age, gender, socioeconomic status, and district were also analyzed at length in the annual reports of the city's chief medical officer.[15] Unfortunately even in Dublin the registrar general's data for the early years suffer from considerable underenumeration. This is evident from the fact that until 1877 the total number of burials in the city's main cemeteries[16] exceeded registered deaths in Dublin Registration District. The ratio of registered deaths to burials jumped abruptly in 1879, when new legislation required the cemetery authorities to forward burial data to the registrar general. Between 1880 and 1914 the ratio of regis-tered deaths to burials hovered between 1.15 and 1.2. The ratio of infant to total deaths was also nearly constant over the same period (average 0.184, coefficient of variation 0.06). The president of the Dublin Sanitary Association was probably justified in claiming in 1890 that "probably at the present time the accuracy of the Dublin registration is as nearly perfect as care and labour can make it."[17] If that was the case, it means that the overall death rate in greater Dublin (i.e., the city and neighboring townships) declined in these years. Figure 2.1 draws on the cross-tabula-tions of deaths by social class in the 1880s and the 1900s produced by the Irish registrar general. The contrasting age distributions in Panels A and B highlight the steep socioeconomic gradient in mortality. The under-lying numbers also suggest an increase in life expectancy for all socioeco-nomic groups except the poorest between the 1880s and the 1900s (de-noted by an asterisk in both panels). In Panel A, for example, the I* schedule (representing professionals in the 1900s) crosses the I schedule (representing professionals in the 1880s) from below, and the same goes for the II* schedule, representing the middle classes.[18]

"Convulsions" and infectious diseases such as diarrhea/dysentery, whooping cough, and measles accounted for the high death rates. Regis-trar General Grimshaw noted with horror that convulsions accounted for 24.1 percent of all deaths of children under age five in greater Dublin in 1884–88, while mesenteric disease and tubercular meningitis accounted for another 5.9 and 5.1 percent, respectively. These numbers are worth comparing with data referring to the causes of death in three "high mor-tality" towns and three "low mortality" counties in England in 1889–91. The former had a combined infant mortality rate of 218 per thousand in those years, the latter of 97 per thousand. In the three towns convulsions, mesenteric disease, and tubercular meningitis accounted for 17.0, 2.6, and 1.7 percent of all deaths in the first year of life.[19] The difference high-lights the vulnerability of Dublin's infants and young children in the 1880s. However, it also highlights the vagueness of some of the categories used to describe the cause of death. The terms "convulsions" and "fits" are prime examples, describing symptoms consistent with a range of con-ditions. While Grimshaw characteristically attributed many of the deaths from "convulsions" to parental carelessness, U.S. demographic historians

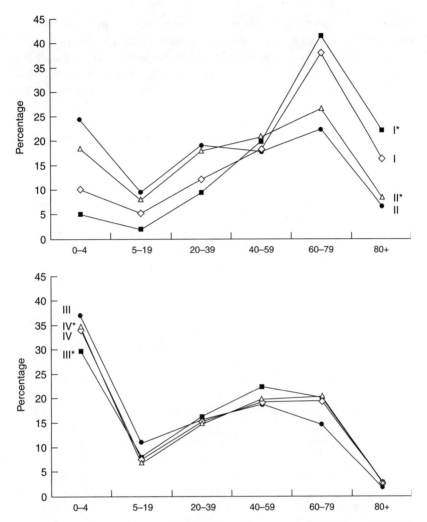

Figure 2.1. Age distributions of deaths (%) by socioeconomic group in Dublin Registration Area, 1883–87 and 1901–10. Note: I = professional and independent class; II = middle class; III = artisan and petty shopkeepers; IV = general service class (i.e., mainly unskilled and casual workers) and workhouse inmates. The asterisk refers to the 1900s. Source: *Weekly Returns of Births and Deaths* (yearly summary, 1883-87; BPP 1914, vol. 15 [.7121], "Supplement to the 47th Report of the Registrar-General Containing . . . Decennial Summaries," p. xlix.

Samuel Preston and Michael Haines note that such deaths were "usually only the final and fatal effect of infection or some other condition, often (though it was not widely acknowledged at the time) including dehydration resulting from gastrointestinal disturbances." Some historians associate such deaths with tetanus and infections resulting from teething.[20] Other imprecise, but numerically significant, causes of death in the Irish tables include "atrophy" and "croup."

Some causes of infant and child deaths fluctuated greatly from year to year.[21] And while deaths attributed to "local causes" were rather evenly spread throughout the year, those attributed to infectious diseases, in particular diarrhea/dysentery, were much more likely to occur in the summer months, when the risk of food infection was greatest. Thus the coefficients of variation of the weekly numbers of deaths from infectious diseases in the Dublin registration area were 0.91 for 1883–85 and 0.95 for 1900–1901, while those for deaths from local causes (mainly "convulsions," but also including meningitis and apoplexy) were 0.36 and 0.34.

There was little shift in the proportional importance of the main causes of childhood death in Dublin between the early 1880s and the early 1900s. In 1883–85 infectious diseases accounted for 19.5 percent of all deaths, and "local" diseases (mainly "convulsions') 46.6 percent. In 1900–1901 the percentages were 21.0 and 43.8. The infant mortality rate in the two periods was almost identical (170 per thousand). As noted earlier, the infant mortality rate fell in the 1900s, and the drop in the numbers succumbing to "convulsions" was partly responsible—accounting for 448 child deaths in 1900, but only 190 in 1908 and 130 in 1909. Clearly a better sense of what caused the convulsions responsible for so many deaths before 1900 would be helpful.[22] The marked difference in the seasonality of deaths attributed to "convulsions" and those due to infectious diseases (including diarrhea/dysentery) suggests that these are indeed separate categories. Unfortunately, cross-sectional differences and changes over time in the cause-of-death categories used make comprehensive comparisons of shifts in the causes of death difficult.

The trends in pre-1914 Dublin and Belfast infant and child mortality are described in table 2.2. They imply little improvement in either city before the turn of the century, and then a significant drop in the infant mortality rate in the 1900s.[23] The returns imply a narrowing in the gaps between Dublin and Belfast over these decades, particularly in the 1900s. Both aggregate and infant and child mortality trends c. 1880–1914 thus corroborate the impression gained from wage and housing data.

Normally when infant mortality declines, the share due to deaths in the weeks immediately after birth might be expected to rise. This is because a higher proportion of such deaths are due to congenital factors and acci-

TABLE 2.2.
Infant and Child Mortality in Dublin and Belfast

| Period | Infant Mortality | | Child Mortality | |
	Dublin	Belfast	Dublin	Belfast
1880/4	186.5	149.7	175.5	n/a
1885/9	176.6	148.1	167.6	n/a
1890/4	169.1	167.4	132.4	93.1
1895/9	175.0	161.6	157.0	122.7
1900/4	164.4	149.3	123.4	107.2
1905/9	146.6	139.1	104.6	92.8
1910/4	147.9	137.6	116.4	98.9

Note: These are rates per thousand. "Child mortality" refers to ages 1–5.
Source: ÓGráda 2004 ("Infant").

dents in childbirth. Thus in New York, where the infant mortality rate fell from 134 per thousand in 1885 to 81.6 per thousand in 1919, the proportion of infant deaths due to congenital factors rose from 30.0 to 45.6 percent.[24] For whatever reason, however, between 1883–85 and 1907–9 in greater Dublin the infant mortality rate fell from 178 to 148 per thousand, while the proportion of infant deaths occurring in the first month of life dropped only marginally, from 32.9 to 29.6 percent. More significant, and more in line with expectations, was the relative improvement between the age of one and four years: the proportion of deaths in the 0–4 year age group occurring after the first twelve months of life fell from 73.3 percent in 1883–85 to 63.5 percent in 1907–9.

More context may be useful here. In England and Wales the decline in early child mortality preceded that in infant mortality by several decades. The infant mortality rate dropped sharply in both urban and rural areas from 1899 on. The universal character of the fall suggests a common cause, and also argues against the specifics of water supply and sewage disposal in particular areas.[25] Robert Woods has stressed that the English pattern of a decline in early childhood mortality in the late nineteenth century, followed by a rapid drop in infant mortality from the beginning of the twentieth, was not unique.[26] In Dublin, too, the decline in child mortality seems to have preceded that in infant mortality. In sum, then, the civil registration data suggest that, as in Great Britain, infant mortality in Dublin seems to have fallen in the 1900s, preceded by some decline in the mortality of children aged 1–5 years.

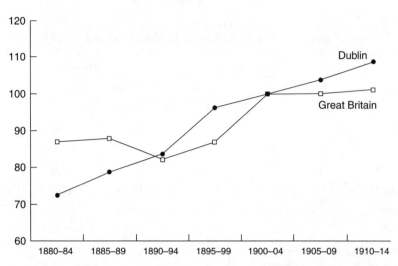

Figure 2.2. Wages in Dublin and Great Britain, 1880–1914.

LIVING STANDARDS

While the Ireland that greeted the Jewish immigrants was a relatively poor place, there were some signs of improvement for all but the poorest strata between the 1880s and the 1900s. During those decades, real wages rose more in Dublin (and therefore, presumably, in Ireland as a whole) than in Britain. The nominal daily wage in pence earned by (unskilled) Dublin building laborers rose by about one half between the early 1880s and the eve of the Great War, and the gap between British and Dublin nominal wages narrowed in the construction sector between 1880 and 1914.[27] In figure 2.1 both Dublin and British wages are set at 100 for 1900–1904. The data imply that while over the three decades nominal wages in Dublin rose by half, those in Great Britain rose by only a sixth. Since the cost of living probably fell somewhat over this period, an even bigger rise in relative living standards is indicated. By 1914 skilled workers in Ireland earned almost as much as their British equivalents, though unskilled laborers, both male and female, still earned perhaps one-fifth less when working and were more likely to be unemployed.[28]

Housing conditions also improved. The proportion of households living in one-room accommodation dropped from 46.7 percent in 1861 and 42.7 percent in 1881 to 33 percent in 1911.[29] The Dublin Corporation began to act in the 1880s, rehousing a total of 2,447 people in the Liberties, a long-settled area in the southwest part of the city. It did little in the 1890s but rehoused over four thousand more individuals between 1900 and 1913. This may not seem much for a city of over three hundred thousand people. And yet, for all the criticism of the corporation's neglect, its record in this respect matched that of any city in the United Kingdom. Meanwhile private speculators were also adding to the housing stock, particularly in the suburbs immediately to the south of the city proper. Their efforts were complemented by housing associations, which between the 1880s and the mid-1920s were responsible for building over six thousand housing units for the "respectable" working class.[30] The housing data surveyed above, however, ignore the expanding suburban areas and therefore underestimate relative improvement. A century ago over one in six of greater Dublin's 350,000 inhabitants lived in the middle-class townships of Pembroke and Rathmines-Rathgar, which would not be incorporated into the city proper until 1930.[31] In sum, Dublin's housing problem in the pre-1914 era stemmed less from the lack of improvement in the city area as a whole than from the persistence of thousands of one-room tenement units in its festering core.[32]

There was also some progress on other fronts. The use of flush toilets spread rapidly after 1880. Between 1880 and 1882 their number in Dublin rose from 743 to 15,000, and two decades later privies were almost a thing of the past. In order to minimize vandalism and the transmission of disease, corporation workmen set yard toilets in asphalt and rid them of all woodwork. The corporation also made strides in closing down dangerous housing, refuse removal, the control of slaughterhouses, and health inspections. Recalcitrant landlords were also fined and named.[33] Much more might have been done, had the corporation's tax base not been constrained by the retreat of so much of the middle class to the suburbs and by the reluctance of those remaining to pay more.

INTERWAR DUBLIN

For understandable reasons, historians of Dublin have tended to concentrate disproportionately on the architectural glories of the Georgian era and the social and economic miseries of the late Victorian era.[34] Social conditions in the postindependence decades, in particular, have received less attention. There is evidence of improvement in the 1920s and 1930s, albeit at a snail's pace. Take housing, the brunt of so much deserved criticism in earlier decades, first. The trends can be captured in different ways. For instance, the proportion of Dubliners living in tenement housing dropped from 29 percent in 1913 to 24 percent in 1938, and the proportion of people living in one-room dwellings in the greater Dublin area dropped from 20.6 percent in 1926 to 16.2 percent a decade later. Alternatively, the average number of people per room in Dublin fell from 1.55 in 1926 to 1.29 in 1936 and 1.14 in 1946, and the proportion of families with more than two people per room fell from 45.3 percent in 1926 to 27.3 percent in 1946.[35]

Second, infant mortality data are corroborative. Rates continued to be much higher in the capital than outside it, but in Dublin infant mortality dropped from 148 per thousand in 1910–14 to 115.4 per thousand in 1925–29 and 90.7 per thousand in 1930–34, before rising again to 99.1 per thousand in 1935–39 and 107.3 per thousand during the "Emergency" years of 1940–43.[36] Moreover, the significant increase in Dublin's population in the interwar period probably also implies amelioration. By the mid-1930s Dublin was once more the premier city on the island in terms of population. On the other hand, the story on the wages front was less cheerful: after the gains of earlier decades, there was little sustained increase in real wages between the early 1920s and the 1940s. And even though the impact of the Great Depression was less severe in Ireland than elsewhere, living standards in Dublin are likely to have fallen relative to those in the United Kingdom between the 1920s and the 1940s.

WATER AND SANITATION

In late nineteenth-century Europe improved water quality was deemed an important weapon in the campaign for better public health. Clean drinking water meant less typhoid fever, less cholera, less dysentery. Direct evidence on its impact has, however, been "surprisingly difficult to produce."[37] At first sight at least, the evidence from Dublin is also inconclusive on this score. By European standards the city was a leader in the public provision of clean water. The ambitious Vartry reservoir scheme ended Dublin's dependence on supplies from the Royal and Grand Canals in the 1860s. In Dublin (as elsewhere), however, it was claimed that mains water possibly exacerbated an already serious drainage and sewage problem for a time by prompting the spread of domestic flush toilets. Indeed the rich may have been affected more than the poor, to the extent that "their houses were rapidly converted into water-carriage systems of waste removal . . . while the poorer classes still depended on . . . ashpit and privy."[38] Occasional high-profile fatalities from typhoid fever such as that of the Jesuit poet-professor Gerard Manley Hopkins at the age of forty-four in 1889 lent credence to this view. This suggests that a proper sewerage system was a necessary complement to a clean water supply.

In the early 1890s Dublin possessed "an extensive and well-built system of street drains,"[39] but its house drains were of poor quality, and it still relied on the River Liffey as its main sewage outlet. Plans to provide a main drainage system had been mooted from mid-century, but a combination of factors—including resistance from adjoining suburbs, the refusal of the central government to underwrite municipal debt, ratepayer resistance to higher taxation, and reassurance from some quarters that the Liffey, though noisome, was not a health threat—delayed implementation for decades. The scheme eventually adopted was largely modeled on London's. Designed to carry the sewage of the city and outlying districts in large drains along the Liffey to the Pigeon House for treatment and disposal, it became operational in 1906.[40]

In 1880 a royal commission of inquiry found that "the existing system of sewerage, although a cause of nuisance by polluting the river, could not be made wholly answerable for the high rate of mortality." Two decades later another inquiry pointed again to poor housing conditions rather than inadequate public infrastructure as the reason for high mortality.[41] The city council, top-heavy with tenement owners who doubled up as aldermen or councilors, did little to improve the tenements, although (as noted earlier) it did achieve some progress on other fronts.

THE JEWISH COMMUNITY IN CONTEXT

The east European Jews who settled in Ireland would have witnessed the conditions described in the course of their daily travels. On arrival, some of them rented accommodation in poor, tenement-dominated parts of Dublin, but they did not remain in them for long. The worst of the conditions described above applied more to the immigrants' impoverished clients than to the immigrants themselves. They are relevant, however, because they help explain the demand for the skills and services provided by the immigrants. By the same token, improvements in health and living standards likely influenced the occupational opportunities open to the immigrants.

From the very start, Ireland's Jewish immigrants—unlike many other immigrant groups in other places—fared better than the poorest strata in the host community. In terms of housing, moreover, Dublin's Jews also fared much better than their coreligionists in Leeds or indeed in London. The square-mile area in Leeds known as the Leylands, which was almost completely Jewish by 1900, had more in common with Dublin's Coombe or north inner city than the area where Dublin's Litvaks settled. In Dublin the small preexisting community dwelt mainly in middle-class areas in the south of the city and in Rathmines; most of the newcomers lived in mixed, mainly artisanal, lower-middle and middle-class neighborhoods in the south city. As explained in more detail in chapter 5, these neighborhoods contained a range of housing stock, but all were purpose-built family units with good sanitation. Like most Dubliners at the time, the immigrants rented rather than bought their housing. The same held for the immigrants who settled in the little streets around the Carlyle Circus in Belfast and in or near Hibernian Buildings in Cork.

Chapter 3

"THEY KNEW NO TRADE BUT PEDDLING"

I did not scorn to carry a bag,
And deal in humble wares,
My back bent low, I carried on,
Heedless of stones and stares.
—*Myer Joel Wigoder*[1]

They used to put in panes of glass. They'd have the
sack with glass on their back. And some of the hard
chaws would throw a brick at them. Break the glass,
you know. . . . Then they came along and got into
clothes. But first of all they'd come with a picture of
Jesus. . . . Then they used to lend money. I remember
them coming around, always had ponies and traps.
Mostly Monday morning that would be . . .
—*An elderly Dubliner, 1980*[2]

FOR CENTURIES Jewish men everywhere have been disproportionately represented in trade and finance and in skilled craft occupations.[3] Some concentrated their business on the local marketplace or in retail outlets; others traveled around with their wares, selling to country people in their own homes. Already in the ninth century, the words *Judaeus* and *mercator* were almost interchangeable in Carolingian documents; in medieval times in the Near East Jews bartered manufactured goods for agricultural produce, which they then sold in the towns; in early modern Germany Jews became skilled horse traders; in eighteenth-century England, Jewish traders specialized in peddling cheap jewelry around the countryside; in early twentieth-century Bolivia east European Jews "appear[ed] in the most outlying villages, where hardly any Europeans have been, and manage[d] to eke out an existence, sleeping in their wagons under the stars." Often traders in goods doubled up as traders in money, or else graduated to the latter calling. Sometimes specialization by Jews in such niche activities led to their eventual domination of them. Why Jews have concentrated so heavily on commerce is a much-debated topic, to which we shall return in chapter 4. The most common explanation refers to occupational and property restrictions placed on Jews by host populations. The late Simon

Kuznets offered an alternative explanation in terms of the minority status of Jewish populations, while recent research by Maristella Botticini and Zvi Eckstein links its origins to the transformation of Judaism, almost two millennia ago, into a religion that required—in principle at least—universal male literacy. The debate about origins continues, but nobody disputes that for longer than anyone else the Jews have been history's archetypal middleman minority.[4]

Until the arrival of the railway, Jewish peddlers traveled by foot, on horseback, or by pony and cart. In the tsarist empire the iron horse produced the more long-distance trader immortalized in Sholem Aleichem's hilarious *Railroad Stories*, but it also brought increasing competition from foreign mass-produced wares. Lithuanian Jews were "such aggressive traders that they were known as *albe levones*—half moons—because they would even try to buy the dark side of the moon."[5] According to the tsarist census of 1897, in Lithuania that year nine-tenths of all peddlers, general merchants, and dealers in agricultural products, in building materials, and in fuel were Jewish. Competition between traders was often intense, and margins small. Novelist Hannah Berman likened peddling in Lithuania to "selling a *kopek*'s worth of needles and earn[ing] half a *groschen*, and at the same time, hav[ing] to swallow a rouble's worth of insults."[6] In the *Jewish Chronicle* "Halitvak" noted how the men of "Okmyan," whence several of Ireland's Litvaks came, had ever been "wanderers":

> It was characteristic of that town that for the greater part of the year it was left in the occupation of women and children, the men being away to all parts of the country, sometimes the farthest parts of the Empire, following their vocations as "Landkremers" (peddlers) and only coming home for the principal holidays at the end of each season in the year.[7]

By no means was all trading peddling, however, and in the towns and villages of eastern Europe Jewish traders spanned the range from the very rich to the very poor. Jews were also prominent in petty moneylending in eastern Europe and many took up this occupation when they moved west, especially in the first and second generation, so much so that the "Jewish moneylender became a typical stereotype."[8] On the basis of a careful review of occupational data in tsarist Russia and the United States, Joel Perlmann has argued that Jewish emigrants already "knew about petty capitalist ventures, about how to buy and sell, just as they knew how to use a needle and thread. Thus they came with two sorts of skills useful in an industrial economy."[9] On the other hand, such skills also reflected the relative economic backwardness of eastern Europe. For many peddlers from the shtetls, the struggle against the mail-order firm, the department store, the savings bank, and other financial intermediaries would prove an unequal one.

The histories of Jewish communities in Liverpool, Manchester, Glasgow, south Wales, and elsewhere testify to the importance of peddling to British Jewry outside London in the pre–World War I era. In Liverpool clothing and furniture sweatshops were numerous, but a majority of immigrants took up peddling. In Glasgow most of the early immigrants, also mainly Litvaks, made a living tailoring or peddling. A surprising number (61 out of 337 in the Gorbals in 1891) made and sold pictures and picture frames. In time some graduated to owning their own stores, but peddling continued to be an avocation in and around Glasgow long after it had ceased in Manchester or London. In Cardiff, where "even the poorest . . . preferred self-employment in which they could stop work on Sabbaths and holy days," Jews specialized in tailoring, jewelry, and furniture; in the valleys of south Wales there were Jewish miners and laborers, but the majority were traders of one kind or another. In the valleys of south Wales most Jews made a living from peddling, retailing household goods, and pawnbroking; a few also rented housing.[10]

THE WEEKLY MEN

Almost certainly, many of Ireland's new arrivals had also been traders of some kind before making their move. The historian of Irish Jewry Louis Hyman claimed that the post-1880 immigrants "[knew] no trade but peddling."[11] In the case of Akmyan, the dominant role of trading occupations is confirmed in surviving enumeration forms from the 1897 census. Shopkeepers, tavern keepers, sellers of small goods, and glaziers accounted for over one-third of the one hundred or so males reporting an occupation; the others included eight with religious occupations (rabbi, melamed, etc.), nine butchers, ten shoemakers, twelve cabmen/carriers, and six tailors.[12] Hannah Berman's father had previously been a peddler in Lithuania.

> His brewery having failed him, father resorted to the usual means of livelihood common to the place—peddling. He made up a huge pack of pieces of linen, sewing-cotton, needles, scissors, cereals and seeds, and let himself go along the thinly-populated countryside, in all weathers—in the rigorous winter, the torrential spring, when the roads were slippery with ice or deep in slush; and in the heat of the summer, when the dust lay knee-deep on the rough cart-tracks between the villages. Like all those who betook themselves to the roads with packs, he was kept going not by an even moderate measure of

success but his unquenchable Jewish optimism. Who knew if, at the turn of the long road, or tomorrow, or next day, a stroke of dazzling good luck would not fall his way?

The central role played by peddling and credit in the Litvaks' early decades in Ireland is undeniable. According to Hannah Berman, the newcomers "were almost without exception, weekly payment drapers, or as they were generally called, shilling-a-week men."[13] A draper meant a dealer in clothing and dry goods, including fabrics and sewing materials. Stanley Price, grandson of a Lithuanian-born peddler of religious objects, corroborates: "The common pattern was for . . . those with little money to become peddlers."[14] The numerical dominance of peddlers among the newcomers is also strongly hinted at in the warning of a Cork rabbi in the early 1890s: "Tomorrow is Monday, and the first day of *yomtov*. If any of you go collecting, I warn you that a curse will fall on you, and you will die."[15]

A resolution passed by the "free members" who constituted the managing committee of Mary's Abbey synagogue in Dublin in 1881 is also telling in this respect. Mary's Abbey, located off Capel Street north of the River Liffey, represented the preexisting Jewish community, small in size and mainly middle class, which now feared being overrun by poorer and socially inferior coreligionists from eastern Europe.[16] The resolution read: "That this board will for the future refuse to admit into Free Membership any person directly or indirectly engaged in the business of lending small sums on Bills of Sale to persons in the humbler ranks of society."[17] Note how the resolution singles out the petty moneylender; several more "respectable" moneylenders would figure prominently among the free members and council of the new "English" shul on Adelaide Road in the 1900s and 1910s.[18] Perhaps the Mary's Abbey resolution was an added reason for the establishment of the first southside *hevra* in the upper floor of a house on Saint Kevin's Parade in 1883.[19] However, moneylenders were also overrepresented in the Litvak *hevroth*. In Joseph Edelstein's fictional synagogue of the 1900s, presumably modeled on one of them, "the president is a moneylender, the committee are moneylenders, the members of the "shool" are mostly moneylenders."[20] Significant, too, is the account of Israeli president Chaim Herzog, who noted that in the Dublin of his youth (in the 1920s) "the community had the usual mix of *gevirim* (prosperous businessmen), intellectuals—who were regarded askance—and the rest of the community, who went about their business of peddling and moneylending."[21]

The occupational breakdown of Ireland's Russian-born residents (most of whom would have been Jewish immigrants) in the 1891, 1901, and

TABLE 3.1.
Main Occupations of Ireland's Russian-Born Residents, 1891–1911

Occupation	1891	%	1901	%	1911	%
Drapers	125	20	261	23	210	20
Dealers, shopkeepers	32	5	64	6	120	11
Tailors	8	1	72	6	128	12
Peddlers	227	36	223	20	124	12
Comm. Travelers	39	6	88	8	63	6
Other	195	31	402	36	406	39
Males aged 10–79 yrs.	626	100	1,110	100	1,051	100

Source: Census of Ireland, General Reports, 1891–1911.
Note: The bracketed percentages refer to males aged 10–79 years. The census tables provide data only on occupations employing over forty foreign born.

1911 censuses (table 3.1) are corroborative. Peddlers, drapers, shopkeepers and dealers, and commercial travelers accounted for 67 percent of males aged 10–79 years in 1891, 57 percent in 1901, and 49 percent in 1911. Details in a series of confidential memoranda compiled by the Dublin Metropolitan Police in the early 1900s for Sir Anthony McDonnell, permanent undersecretary in Dublin Castle, also corroborate the dominance of peddling. The police found that in Dublin in 1903 about 170 Jews were licensed as peddlers and another 46 registered as moneylenders. The same police report also noted, though it does not support in detail, the allegation that there were other unregistered Jewish moneylenders who lent mainly to the working classes, their only security being that the borrower was working.[22] These were significant numbers in a community numbering little more than two thousand. Moreover, the forty-six in Dublin alone represented almost one every four moneylenders licensed in the country as a whole up to the end of 1902.[23]

Outside Dublin the trades of peddler, draper, and traveler also dominated. A petition bearing the names and occupations of fifty-six Cork Jews in 1893 included twenty-one travelers, sixteen drapers, and four dealers.[24] There were only three tailors listed on the petition. Of the forty Jewish men living in Cork's Hibernian Buildings in 1901, thirty-two were described as peddlers in that year's census. The remainder included a butcher, a grocer, a rabbi, a house carpenter, a watchmaker, a huckster, and two teenage dentist's apprentices. In a database of married Jewish men in Cork's "Jewtown" in 1911 described in detail in chapter 5, peddler and kindred occupations alone accounted for half the total (nineteen

out of thirty-nine); in addition there were three rabbis, two master craftsmen, two moneylenders, a picture framer, a photo enlarger, a glazier, a
tailor, and nine dealers or shopkeepers. Some of these Jewish householders kept boarders, typically single men in their twenties; nearly all were
described as peddler or traveler draper in the enumeration forms. The
same holds for most householders' sons. In 1901 Harris Taylor of South
Terrace, for example, was a master cabinetmaker; his seventeen-year-old
son Lewis was a picture framer, and his daughters Jane (20) and Becky
(15) were, respectively, a dressmaker and a tailoress. Clearly the majority
of Leeside Jews found work as self-employed petty traders: in this list of
household heads in 1911 only the tailor, forty-year-old Maurice Taylor,
is likely to have been a wage earner. In the miniscule Jewish community
in Lurgan (County Armagh) it was likewise: only one of eleven Jewish
male household heads in 1911 was not described as a draper or the like:
thirty-year-old David Lewis was a "caretaker." The lodgers in Jewish
homes in Lurgan, all Russian-born young men, included a photographer,
a Jewish schoolteacher, a credit salesman, a collector and canvasser, an
antique dealer, and several drapers or travelers.[25]

The occupational profile that emerges from the 1911 Irish census (on
which more later) broadly corroborates the numerical importance of traders. The majority of the immigrants made their living as drapers, dealers,
or commercial travelers. Other traders were involved in selling jewelry, in
retailing, or in running secondhand, junk, or "marine" stores. Only one
of the 329 household heads in the Dublin database described more fully in
chapter 5—thirty-two-year-old Maurice Goldstein of almost exclusively
Jewish Oakfield Place—was described as a laborer. The total included
thirty-four tailors, however, and there were also several Jewish cabinetmakers and a few capmakers.

The alien naturalization files covering the 1914–22 period describe the
occupations of over five hundred Jewish immigrants.[26] These refer to a
significant minority of Jewish men in Ireland at the time, although longtime residents and the more comfortably off (who could have afforded
the hefty naturalization fee payable before 1914) are less likely to be included than recent arrivals. The five hundred or so with declared occupations included 186 dealers and merchants of various kinds, 104 tailors,
40 travelers, 35 peddlers, 24 cabinetmakers, and 12 jewelers/watchmak-
ers. The tailors and cabinetmakers were most likely to be employees,
though fifteen of the former declared that they were self-employed.
Doubtless, some of the travelers also worked for merchants and drapers.
The list includes one laborer, two machinists, two mechanics, four capmakers, a chauffeur, a chef, a cook, and two collectors, all presumably
working for somebody else. On the other hand, it also includes two opti-
cians, three dentists, a film agent, a bookmaker, and a cigarette maker,

presumably working on their own account. But the overall impression is of a workforce characterized by a high proportion of entrepreneurs.

Yet another source on Jewish occupations is Eugene Harfield's *Commercial Directory of the Jews of the United Kingdom* (1893). This extremely scarce compendium of the relatively well-off section of the community is by no means comprehensive, but it highlights the role of trade over manufacturing among Jewish businessmen, as well as the absence at this point in Ireland of businessmen who described themselves as tailors or master tailors. Business descriptions including the word "draper" dominated, particularly in the smaller cities, and it may be assumed that nearly all of these were credit drapers (table 3.2). Ireland differed considerably from the cities of Manchester and Liverpool in this respect. Traders other than credit drapers were relatively more important in both cities, as were tailoring and other clothing-related manufacturing (particularly capmaking and, in Manchester, the manufacture of rain-proof outerwear). At the outset, Ireland's manufacturers were mainly picture-frame makers.

In Ireland the peddlers were known as traveling drapers, travelers, tallymen (at least in Cork), tickmen (in Belfast), or weekly men (translated into Yiddish as *vekele*).[27] The drapers, peddlers, or packmen traveled from door to door with their wares, both in the city and further afield. A major advantage of the work was the freedom it allowed them to practice their religion; many would return home on Fridays in time for the Shabbat, and prepare for the following week's work.[28] Some peddlers worked on Sundays and on bank holidays, but never on Catholic holy days, at least in the countryside. Peddlers confined their business mainly to the woman of the house, and calling on the Feast of the Assumption or on the Feast of the Immaculate Conception risked an encounter with her husband.[29] Peddling also capitalized on the trading and risk-taking skills that the immigrants had brought with them. Another important consideration was that the work required only a rudimentary knowledge of English. When Jacob Elyan's grandfather arrived in Cork in 1881, other Litvaks taught him a few words of English, which "he wrote it down in Hebrew translation." They then told him to "go out and make a living for yourself."[30] Similarly his boss taught Moses Levenstein, the anti-hero of Joseph Edelstein's novella, a few phrases of English and the words for his stock in trade, which Moses thought he could learn in an hour. But so nervous was he on his first outing that he blurted, "Gut morning, do you vant blankets, quilts, seets, sorts, sawls, how is your husband?" all in one breath.[31] Another story concerns one Eli Schwartzman, who kept confusing his "pictures of Jesus" and his "little boys' jerseys." When asked to bring jerseys he brought pictures, and vice versa.[32] Lieb Berman, whose command of English was also rudimentary, devised an ingenious way of ordering goods from his Dublin suppliers. He would enlist the help of

TABLE 3.2.
Jewish Businessmen in Ireland, Liverpool, and Manchester in 1893

City	Draper	"Fin. Agent," "Banker"	Jeweler, Watchmaker	Other trade	Tailoring	Other Manufacture	Professional	Total
Belfast	13	1	1	5	0	4	0	24
Cork	17	0	1	2	0	2	3	25
Dublin	29	3	10	18	0	3	8	71
Limerick	10	0	0	0	0	0	1	11
Derry	2	0	0	0	0	0	0	2
Waterford	6	0	0	0	0	0	0	6
IRELAND	77	4	12	25	0	9	12	139
Liverpool	30	8	11	82	37	20	8	196
Manchester	11	1	10	82	33	52	1	190

Source: Harfield 1893
Note: "Draper" includes all businesses including the word "draper." "Professional" includes clergy and teachers.

a few country schoolchildren to whom he would patiently explain his requirements. They then would write them down in the form of a crude letter, stipulating the right railway station and sending payment in two separate mailings, each containing halves of torn pound notes.[33]

Most weekly men were self-employed or worked as a part of a family enterprise.[34] Becoming a weekly man required start-up capital, however. This was sometimes supplied as an interest-free loan from within the Jewish community, either informally or through an organization founded in 1900, the Hebrew Philanthropic Loan Society. In 1911, for example, the society made thirty-seven loans averaging £5 each.[35] In this respect, the Dublin community was replicating on a smaller and less formal scale what the London Jewish Board of Guardians did for budding entrepreneurs in London, what the New York Hebrew Free Loan Society did in New York, and what the Hebrew Friendly Society did in Liverpool.[36] A Hawkers Hebrew Society operated in the 1900s—it contributed £5 toward the burial of "Mr. Isaacson of Portobello" in 1902—though no other record of it seems to survive.[37] In later years, the loan society was described as "a group of businessmen" who would organize a loan for "anybody need-[ing] money to start something."[38] Before the creation of the loan society, informal loans within the community did the trick. Thus when Lieb Berman arrived in Dublin from Lithuania, Peisa Harmel, a prosperous businessman to whom he was related by marriage, "opened an account for him in a Dublin warehouse, and gave him £5 to start on his own," while a kinswoman put up another £5. Abram Cohen, who arrived with his wife in 1880, had been a baker back home; members of the community got together and helped them set up a small bakery in Dublin.[39]

The availability of this start-up capital within the immigrant community, free of interest, was another crucial consideration favoring peddling. This put the immigrants who arrived without any savings at a considerable advantage over any natives considering entry into the same calling. No Irish commercial bank in the 1880s or the 1900s would have lent the necessary capital to a would-be Irish credit draper. Nor was there any other financial institution equipped to do so. Part of the social capital of the Litvak community was the low probability of borrowers defaulting: if they did, they risked ostracism within the community and certain refusal in the event of future requests for loans.[40]

Nor, it seems, was there much squabbling among peddlers (or money-lenders) about territory. Their clients found them through word of mouth from friends, as one would find a doctor or a dentist. There was no need to advertise, and it was to the weekly men's advantage to be on good terms with one another and to be familiar with legislative and police procedures that might impinge on their livelihood. Peddling was a rather solitary avocation, but the peddlers certainly identified with their own community, and those working outside the city typically returned in time for the Sabbath.

In the cities the peddlers' *laptzies* (a somewhat pejorative Yiddish colloquialism for Gentile clients), to whom they sold mainly on credit, were mostly women of the poorer classes.[41] A recurring theme is the peddlers' fear of their clients' menfolk.[42] Typically payments were made in weekly installments. In the remoter parts of rural Ireland peddlers' sales had traditionally been for cash, and the visits of the packman less frequent and, probably, more welcome. Whether Jewish peddlers also sold for cash remains unclear. It seems unlikely, although if they restricted their business to credit and weekly collections, this would have excluded them from the remoter corners of the land. Either way, they, too, were apparently welcomed in rural areas. Lieb Berman liked to talk of "his happy encounters with every Irish man, woman, and child with whom he came into contact." He often described "their high-spirited cheerfulness and contentment—all high virtues in his own eyes."[43] The range of goods traded included items of clothing "neatly folded into an oilcloth cover to keep them dry and warm," framed oleographs or "holy pictures," slippers, ribbons and thread, sheets, tablecloths, tea, and so on. All were carried in appropriate backpacks. Sometimes the holy pictures were used as a way of canvassing reliable customers; if a client repaid the installments on the pictures regularly, then she might be offered clothes on credit or small loans. The peddler-drapers relied on wholesale drapers (dubbed *wholesaleniks*), of whom there were several on Lombard Street West in the 1900s, for their supplies.[44] Mr. Schorstein, Joseph Edelstein's fictional *wholesalenik*, held his premises there, and his customers exchanged news and trade gossip there as well. The *wholesaleniks*, former peddlers themselves, did not insist on immediate payment for goods supplied.

Presumably the peddlers worked according to some standard markup: 100 percent is plausible, though direct evidence for it is lacking.[45] In Joseph Edelstein's detailed account,

> Mr. Greenblatt told Moses that he would begin on Tuesday next by traveling with a pack; that he would have to go to Mr. Schorstein in Lombard Street and get from him four blankets at 4s 3d; four undersheets at 10½d; two shawls at 6s 6d; six pair sheets at 1s 4d; six petticoats at 1s 5½d; four table sheets at 1s 2d; two "ladies" skirts at 4s 4d; that he should note down all he got; and that on Tuesday morning he would take the pack containing these articles, neatly folded, and place it on his back; and hold one end of the strap, which would be wound round the leather, in his right hand; and he would buy a penny pocket-book and go out to travel, and would knock at each house and ask the residents if they required skirts, blankets,

quilts, shawls, petticoats, sheets, boots, suits, and everything in the drapery line.

One assumes that these are the retail prices: if so, in aggregate the goods in a backpack might fetch £5 or £6.[46]

No written contracts between peddler and purchaser have been un-earthed so far, but they probably resembled that given in an unlikely source: James Joyce's *Ulysses*. The anonymous narrator in the Cyclops chapter, a "collector of bad and doubtful debts" for Moses Herzog of Saint Kevin's Parade, has been on the trail of one Michael Geraghty. Ger-aghty had reneged on his debt to Herzog, knowing that Herzog, an unli-censed peddler, could not pursue him in the courts. Joyce rendered the contract between Herzog and "that bloody big foxy thief" as follows:

> For nonperishable goods bought of Moses Herzog, of 13 Saint Kev-in's Parade in the city of Dublin, Wood quay ward, merchant, herein-after called the vendor, and sold and delivered to Michael E. Ger-aghty, esquire, of 29 Arbour hill in the city of Dublin, Arran quay ward, gentleman, hereinafter called the purchaser, videlicet, five pounds avoirdupois of first choice tea at three shillings and no pence per pound avoirdupois and three stone avoirdupois of sugar, crushed crystal, at threepence per pound avoirdupois, the said purchaser debtor to the said vendor of one pound five shillings and sixpence sterling for value received which amount shall be paid by said pur-chaser to said vendor in weekly instalments every seven calendar days of three shillings and no pence sterling: and the said nonperishable goods shall not be pawned or pledged or sold or otherwise alienated by the said purchaser but shall be and remain and be held to be the sole and exclusive property of the said vendor to be disposed of at his good will and pleasure until the said amount shall have been duly paid by the said purchaser to the said vendor in the manner herein set forth as this day hereby agreed between the said vendor, his heirs, successors, trustees and assigns of the one part and the said pur-chaser, his heirs, successors, trustees and assigns of the other part.[47]

The weekly payments involved were typically small, sixpence or a shil-ling a week. So common was this calling that it paid at least one immi-grant to print special cards for the weekly men.[48]

There is no obvious way of knowing precisely how much the typical weekly man earned. Lieb Berman, who relied on family connections both for his passage to Ireland and the capital that started him off as a peddler, had made enough after about eighteen months in business to send for his wife and children in Lithuania.[49] Joseph Edelstein's fictional Moses Levenstein began as a traveler for Chaim Greenblatt in November 1899

at the modest weekly wage of fifteen shillings, out of which he paid 6s 6d
for "board, lodging, and washing." On his first day in the city's Liberties
he made five sales. Within a year he was drawing £2 12s weekly in return
for collecting a weekly £8 10s for Greenblatt. On Christmas Eve 1900 he
bought out his employer for £85, which Greenblatt deemed a fair price
for outstanding business of £364, after allowing £100 for bad debt and
£100 for the effort of collecting the remainder. After some haggling,
Moses, who possessed £45 in cash, agreed to pay £40 immediately and
to sign promissory notes for two later payments of £25 and £20. Moses
Levenstein, who had arrived in Ireland with only one shilling and four
pence, prospered thereafter.[50] If he and Greenblatt were at all representative—and the prices and initial wage level cited by Edelstein are realistic
enough—then their form of peddling on the installment system, though
hard work, was indeed a lucrative one. Levenstein's wages just before he
bought out Greenblatt were more than double the weekly wages of the
average unskilled Dublin laborer.[51]

THE OLD AND THE NEW PEDDLING

The immigrants who became traveling salesmen occupied a niche well
suited to the skills they brought with them and for which there was evi-
dently a demand. In so doing, they increased the range of choice available
to the poor and dented the monopoly power of rural traders. Rural people
"seem[ed] to like this system of dealing."[52] To trade in holy pictures was
an inspired choice, both because the interiors of Irish Catholic homes at
the time were lined with them, and because this trade led to trade in other
items. It is said that some of the early arrivals took to selling holy pictures
after seeing immigrant Italians producing them; one story mentions a Jewish family finding a shed full of pictures and statues in the backyard of a
newly occupied house in the South Circular Road area, and starting off
in the trade in that way. The previous occupants, an Italian family, had
produced the pictures.[53] But political pictures were popular, too, and in
Belfast the peddlers soon learned not "to dispose of a King William in the
Pound district, or a Robert Emmet in Sandy Row."[54] The evident success
of the immigrant Jewish traders corroborates Mark Duffy's claim that the
choice of peddling reflected "an adaptation to regional demand and market niches rather than economic retardation."[55]

For centuries itinerant peddlers had been an important link between
industry and agriculture, and between the city and the remote countryside. Their customers were mostly rural householders with a little discre-
tionary income. Their stock-in-trade tended to be exotic, novel, and
mildly luxurious products, which they could offer at a better price than

the sedentary shopkeeper located at a distance. Hence the association between peddling and products such as books, jewelry, leather goods, hardware, medicines, textiles, tobacco, and tea. Most traveled on foot, which placed limits on the kinds of goods sold, but some also carried heavier wares by horse and cart. Some served the same customers year after year. The spread of the country store, cheaper travel, mail-order shopping, and rising living standards proved the undoing of the old-style peddler. By the early twentieth century he was very much on his last legs throughout most of Europe, but he still survived on the margins in southern and eastern Europe. In post–Civil War America, with the spread of the rail network, the South remained the last redoubt of the peddler.[56]

The history of peddling in Ireland remains obscure. In the eighteenth century, as Niall Ó Ciosáin has inferred from licensing data, peddlers were as common in Ireland as across the Irish Sea. But in post-famine Ireland, they were fighting a losing battle against the increasing mobility of country people and increasing competition from retail outlets in the towns and cities. The decline in Ireland's rural population did not help: between 1841 and 1914 the proportion of the population living in rural districts (generously defined as living outside towns of two thousand or more people) dropped from 7.0 million to 2.9 million. In the nineteenth century only the census offers an indication of aggregate numbers of peddlers;[57] its evidence, perhaps inevitably, is confusing. In 1831 there were 7,569 "hawkers, peddlers, and duffers." The 1841 census did not report peddlers separately, but the 1851 census listed 4,147 of them. A decline between 1831 and 1851 is plausible, given the impact of the Great Famine and of increasing commercialization, but Ó Ciosáin suggests that the decline may also have been due in part to the different timing of the two enumerations. The 1831 census was conducted in June, at the height of the traveling season, whereas that of 1851 was taken on 31 March.[58] Peddlers are not listed as such in the census thereafter, though their decline is almost certainly reflected in the increasing access to retail outlets throughout Ireland. The census is not unambiguous on such outlets either, but by one broad definition[59] the number of shopkeepers of various kinds rose from about 13.1 per thousand in 1881 to 15.2 per thousand in 1911. In Connacht, the poorest of Ireland's four provinces, the ratio rose from 7.8 to 9.9 per thousand over the same period. This takes no account of the increasing range and volume of goods stocked by the average retailer.[60]

Nonetheless, memories of peddlers and peddling were still fresh in the minds of many of those providing material to the Irish Folklore Commission in the 1930s and 1940s. Informants from all over the island offered both general accounts of their activities and stories about individual traders. In Irish *peidléara* and *mangaire* were the most common words for peddler, but *gáinéar* and *lucht gáineála* were also used in the west; variants of *joultaer* referred to traveling fishmongers and others traveling in wheeled vehicles, while the *cliabhaire* (from *cliabh* = basket) dealt in poultry. In Corca Dhuibhne in west Kerry there were stories of peddlers with old carts and of women who sold pigs' trotters and sausages, white bread and soap, candy and sweet cakes. In Roscommon there were peddlers selling tea, in east Galway sugarcane, in west Cork stockings. Around Kiltartan in southeast Galway they exchanged tea, tobacco, snuff, and soap for eggs; no money was used. In Dromintee in south Armagh "pahvee" referred to "men or women in our parish who are peddlers of cloth so that a man who has to hawk or peddle anything is said to be 'pahveeing.' " In south Kerry an elderly woman exchanged needles and pins for old rags. In the same area Siobhán a' tSaighdiúra lent money to farmers, who repaid her in kind in due course with eggs. Country people were used to itinerant traders.[61]

Remarkably, the immigrants from Lithuania, where peddling was still important, made a success out of this declining trade for a time. Their version of peddling differed in three important respects from that described above, however. First, it usually involved weekly repayments, whereas the traditional Irish packman—like most peddlers historically elsewhere—would have sold mainly for cash. The new version represented one aspect of a credit revolution that would characterize consumer spending in the developed world in the twentieth century. It was in effect a form of installment payments for the poor.[62]

Just how novel this form of hire purchase—the "never-never" by another name—was in late nineteenth-century Ireland remains unclear. In England and further afield itinerant "Scotch drapers" had been using virtually the same system for a century or two to sell items such as tea and soft goods to the poor. In the nineteenth century their business grew in tandem with working-class spending on clothing, inexpensive cutlery and jewelry, and the like. In the mid-Victorian period hundreds, if not thousands, of expatriate Scotsmen were serving hundreds of thousands of customers at any one time. Their significant contributions to "the routine provision of plebian credit and then in the routine collection of plebian debts" have been documented by Gerry Rubin and by Margot Finn.[63] The concentration of their business south of Hadrian's Wall has been linked to the ease with which they could sue for small debts through the county courts: in Scotland such a remedy was no longer open to them. The credit drapery business and its associated trade associations were notable for being Scottish fiefdoms. Presumably some of these Scotsmen crossed over to Ulster, though evidence of their presence further south is elusive. In the second half of the nineteenth century the Scots were joined by increasing number of German and, later, east European Jews.[64]

Nor were peddlers the only sellers on credit to the poor; homegrown shopkeepers and petty traders in the villages and towns had been doing it for generations. In an account of conditions in the west of Ireland a decade or so after the Great Famine, journalist Henry Coulter described as "usurers" and "harpies" retailers who preyed on the poor, charging interest rates in the 50–100 percent range. Such rates, Coulter claimed, were out of all proportion to the risks involved. In the following decades increasing competition forced down the rates charged by these "gombeenmen."[65] For the gombeenman and the city shopkeeper who sold dry goods on hire purchase or some other form of credit, the traveling Jewish draper was another form of unwelcome competition. As the writer Standish Hayes O'Grady put it, "If there were no Jews in Ireland, our own Christian usurers . . . would be at just the same bad work, only without competitors."[66] Thus, in Limerick Jewish weekly men and moneylenders represented only a minority of those offering credit in the late 1890s and early 1900s. Judging by the number of cases brought before the city's circuit court in the years just before the boycott of 1904 (on which more in chapter 9), the moneylending businesses of Stephen F. Dowling and William Humphreys dwarfed that of the brothers Hyman and Bernard Graff. The Graffs often appeared as plaintiffs, but typically only a few times per session, whereas Dowling and Humphries between them brought twenty-eight defaulters before the court in the session preceding the boycott. By the same token, the likes of Solomon Ginsberg, Simon Spiro, and Philip Toohey were really small-time traders compared to Cannock & Co., William Todd & Co., John Daly & Co., Richard Smith & Co., Mary Carmody, or William H. Owens.[67] In Belfast, too, established traders outnumbered the Litvak credit drapers. In response to a charge in the *Belfast Telegraph* in 1894 that these "born hustlers" were becoming more powerful "with each succeeding day and week," one of the Litvaks declared that they sold as cheaply as anyone in Belfast, that no alien "tickman" had so far made a fortune, and that two of them had failed in the previous few years.[68]

A second difference between the new peddling and the traditional Irish version is that the stock-in-trade of the new peddling was less exotic. The Jewish peddlers specialized in dry goods worth more (and hence requiring credit) than the trinkets associated with the Irish peddler. A third difference between the Jewish traders and their Irish counterparts is that the former seem to have focused primarily (though by no means exclusively) on the main cities (Dublin, Belfast, Cork, Limerick) and their rail-linked hinterlands, whereas the traditional Irish variant concentrated on more remote rural customers. Ireland was a poor and unpromising location for immigrants in general, and peddling carried the attendant risks of nonpayment, physical abuse, and robbery.[69] For those with the skills and

resourcefulness of the Litvaks, the very economic backwardness of Ireland may have helped. This may also explain why Dublin was a more
important destination for Litvaks skilled in peddling than booming Belfast. Myer Joel Wigoder explained how in Dublin "it was very difficult to
get customers in the better districts."[70] In this respect Dublin may have
had more in common with some of Britain's poorer provincial towns and
cities than with Ireland's northern Linenopolis.[71]

In rural Ireland, then, the recent immigrants had to compete with long-
established traders, some of them also itinerant packmen. In the towns
and the cities they competed with shopkeepers, hucksters, and dealers in
secondhand clothing. This presumably constrained the newcomers" ability to overcharge. Competition also required the new peddlers to create a
base of repeat customers, and be accepted by the host community.[72] Those
involved in the weekly system had an added incentive to ensure that the
goods offered were of acceptable quality and durability; exacting repayments for goods that failed to pass muster would surely have been more
difficult. For the poor, the niche carved out by the immigrant peddlers
meant a new source of (albeit expensive) credit; for existing traders, the
peddlers meant increased competition.

Peddling or "traveling" was the main way of making a living at the
outset. The data on the occupational spread of Russian-born residents,
most of whom would have been Jewish, in the census reports of 1891–
1911 hint at the declining role of what was dubbed peddling in that period. The combined share of peddlers and commercial travelers in the
Russian-born population dropped from 24 percent in 1891 to 9 percent
in 1911, with a more or less corresponding rise in other forms of trading.
Peddlers are also surprisingly few among the naturalized aliens mentioned
earlier; by the 1910s they were far outnumbered by sedentary dealers and
merchants of various kinds. However, many, if not most, of the drapers
and tailors listed as such in 1911 were really peddlers by another name.
Instead of buttons, cutlery, or tea, they sold dry goods and clothes on the
weekly system.

The trade thus lingered on in different guises. Older residents of the
South Circular Road area remember the last of the Jewish peddlers, often
bearded and in heavy, dark clothes, doing their rounds on foot. An elderly,
dapper Bennie Bloom (1881–1966), sometimes mentioned as a model for
his Joycean namesake Leopold Bloom, was still canvassing for business
in the 1960s. Bennie would head off for poorer suburbs such as Crumlin
by tram, holy pictures under his arm. At that stage, some of his mainly
female clients probably took pity on this octogenarian in his slouched hat.
Bloom's goal in selling holy pictures was to identify reliable customers,
whom he would then "sell on" to a credit draper or moneylender. In the
1950s and 1960s his pictures, obtained perhaps from Yanks Marcus on

the South Circular Road, might have cost the amiable but enigmatic Bloom five shillings each; the "fee" for "selling on" a customer might have been twice that.[73] In the 1950s and 1960s Benny Bloom was already an anachronism in his reliance on travel by foot and by tram and bus. By then the credit draper or moneylender, operating from a downtown office, would employ car-driving agents or collectors to fulfill orders received by post or to make weekly collections. The last of the Jewish credit drapers ceased business in the 1970s.

"THE JEWMAN MONEYLENDER"

Some of the more successful weekly men, like Moses Levenstein, quickly graduated to moneylending. The higher economic status of moneylenders is apparent from a list of Jewish moneylenders prepared by the Dublin police in 1905. The average valuation of a moneylender's residence, which sometimes doubled as a business office, was about £22. Compare this to the £9 average valuation on a house on Oakfield Place or £13–£15 on Saint Kevin's Parade. However, there was quite a range between the small-time operators living off Lower Clanbrassil Street and the likes of Nathan L. Levin, Esq., with addresses at 88 Heytesbury Street (valuation £15) and at Goldenbridge House, Inchicore (valuation £50).

At the outset most major Jewish moneylenders hailed from the "English" community, but in the 1900s the fictional Moses Levenstein, newly arrived from Lithuania, "heard that most of the L—Yidden were rich because they were in that business"; presumably "L—" refers to the more successful of the early Litvaks.[74] Some moneylenders doubled as merchants. As a licensed moneylender Simon Watchman owned the United Loan and Discount Bank, but he also ran the Talbot Furnishing Company and S. Watson and Company. The last two concerns sold goods on the hire purchase system. In 1912 Watchman lived at 72 Leinster Road, Rathmines (valuation £40).

The overlap between trading in goods and trading in money is also seen in accounts of one Julius Goodman, who in the late 1880s took over premises at 51 Great Brunswick (later Pearse) Street, occupied since 1878 by "financial agent" (i.e., moneylender) Baron J. Cohen and his "Advance Bank." The firm of Lipson, Jacob & Co., financial agents and drapers, then operated from the same address. In 1901 *Thom's Directory* describes the householder as "Goodman & Co., insurance and financial agents, furniture dealers, drapers and factors," and in 1910 as "Goodman & Co., jewellers and watchmakers, antique dealers." In both years they list owner Julius Goodman's residence as 79 Lower Mount Street (valuation £36). By the 1890s Goodman was one of the "English" community's most influential members; in October 1896 he was elected president of the Hebrew Society for Visiting the Sick.[75] The main shifts in tenancy at 51 Great Brunswick Street were as follows:

Year	Householder
1875	Cathcart, dressmaker
1878	Anthony Sage
1879	B. J. Cohen, Advance Bank
1881	Baron J. Cohen, financial agent
1884	Baron J. Cohen, financial agent
1889	Lipson, Jacob & Co., financial agents and drapers
	Julius Goodman, agent
1890	Lipson, Jacob & Co., financial agents and drapers
1895	Goodman & Co., financial agents
	Julius Goodman, agent
1901	Goodman & Co., insurance and financial agents, furniture dealers, drapers, and factors
	Goodman, Julius, residence 79 Lower Mount Street
1910	Goodman & Co., jewelers and watchmakers, antique dealers
	Goodman, Julius, financial and insurance agent

Becoming a *percentnik* (or moneylender) required more capital than did peddling dry goods on one's own account. The wealthiest among the first generation of Litvak immigrants were moneylenders; they dominated communal institutions and were "the effective ruling class."[76] The sums they lent were bigger, typically between £5 and £20, but repayment was also generally on the weekly installment basis. In the 1900s several of the moneylenders in the police listing operated under names like the Union Loan Bank, the Private Loan Bank, the Abbey Loan and Discount Bank, and the Central Loan Office in special business premises. Four were located on Great Brunswick Street and several others in other locations close to the city center.[77] However, most *percentniks* economized by operating from an office in their own home. Often they paid a commission to canvassers or local shopkeepers who identified or introduced reliable borrowers.[78] Some moneylenders advertised for rural customers in the newspapers and sent agents by train to the homes of potential borrowers. In such cases, the cost of the trip was an added expense for the borrower.

Typically, like their non-Jewish counterparts, these Jewish moneylenders exacted promissory notes from borrowers stipulating the amount and number of weekly installments. Sometimes land or other property was offered as security.[79] The promissory notes were crucial in the event of litigation about nonpayment. The effective interest rate charged was typically high: a loan of £1 might be repaid in twenty-five weekly installments of a shilling, or one of £20 might involve receiving only £15 or £16 in cash followed by twenty weekly repayments of £1. The interest on such a loan might be described as four shillings in the pound in advertisements, but the effective annual interest rate was about 120 percent rather than 20 percent.

The petty moneylender's costs were high, too. In 1932 a representative of such moneylenders, worried by the implications for business of a reduction in the maximum permitted rate, reckoned that £1 loans cost about a shilling to manage, and that another shilling represented "dead loss."[80] The weekly calls to clients for repayments were costly, and the court system was no guarantee against deceitful practices on the part of some borrowers. Among borrowers, there was a sense that Jewish lenders were easier to shake off than their Gentile competitors. In Dublin a woman might get a man to play the role of an irate husband to ward off a "Jewman," or employ local children to tell the "Jewman" that the woman had gone out for the day. In Drogheda a woman reputedly got rid of "Jack the Jewman" (who was well liked in the community) by tearing her blouse on one of his weekly visits and threatening to blame him. Others, more desperate, simply vanished by moving. One woman who had borrowed the price of a confirmation dress fell behind in her repayments. Her unlicensed moneylender, Mr. Glick, could not bring her to court, but nonetheless persisted in demanding his money until her son "waylaid him one night and the poor man never knew what hit him."[81]

No Jewish moneylenders' ledgers have been unearthed, and it seems unlikely that any will be uncovered. In the absence of business records, some sense of the size of clientele and the typical sums involved may be obtained from the addresses and professions of defaulters proceeded against in civil bill cases in the Dublin circuit court.[82] Sensible creditors presumably opted for extralegal accommodation if some unforeseen circumstance such as unemployment or death was the reason for nonpayment. In other cases, the courts offered traders a quick and inexpensive, if very public, means of enforcing contracts: they could force "contumacious" debtors to repay by installments or, in extremis, face a jail sentence.[83] Here we focus on the 1909–14 period, during which nearly two hundred defendants faced over twenty different Irish-based Jewish plaintiffs. The bulk of the cases concerned five major players—Julius Goodman, Julius Solomon, Michael Mofsovitz, Simon Watchman, and Oscar White. The notoriety attendant on frequent court appearances did not deter these operators. Mofsovitz, Watchman, and White were Litvaks, while Goodman and Solomon were members of the English community. Four of the five ran "Loan Banks"; the fifth, Oscar White, is listed as a draper in the 1911 census. Most cases concerned dishonored promissory

notes. The average value of the sum claimed from 171 defendants on the
eve of World War I (1908–13) was £6.6; the median was £5.4. Alas, in
most cases, neither the address nor the employment of defendants is given.
About one borrower in six (or 30/171) was a lone female defendant. The
male defendants included seven "gentlemen," five clerks, a professor of
music, two policemen, a foreman at Guinness's, two car owners, and two
cabinetmakers. At the other end of the scale there were two porters, a
gardener, and a van driver.

There was a continuum between the credit drapery business and moneylending. Judging from the civil bill data, the clientele of Jewish merchants and credit drapers who sold goods on the weekly system was quite
similar to that of the moneylenders. The mean claim in 342 cases involving credit drapers, household furnishers, and the like in the same year was
£5.2, with a median of £3.5. However, differences in the average size
of transactions between individual lenders are also discernible: Hyman
Barron sought an average of £7.9 from fifty-seven defendants, while Arthur Newman sought an average of less than half that from forty-one
defendants (see table 3.3). Again—and more surprisingly, given both
contemporary commentary and oral tradition—only a small minority
(about one in ten) were lone female defendants. But perhaps this is because judges were unlikely to side with creditors who had lent to women
without their husbands' knowledge.[84] Male occupations are given in fifty-
seven cases. They represent a wide spectrum of occupations, including a
medical practitioner and a barrister, thirteen "gentlemen," ten clerks, two
pensioners, three commercial travelers, five traders/dealers, two priests,
two carpenters, two pensioners, a tailor, and four laborers. This occupational profile is also perhaps somewhat unexpected, given the presump-
tion that the weekly men's clients were the very poor. However, chasing
working-class defaulters through the courts was less likely to yield dividends for the weekly men, and this probably biases the client profile
gained from civil bill data. The women included ten widows, seven spin-
sters, and five married women. Some of the details of these returns are
summarized in table 3.3.

As noted above, lenders relying on the court system for redress relied
on the evidence of the promissory note. Many loans were transacted without any formal paperwork, however. The poor who needed a small loan
in a hurry and the humble street trader who needed to replenish stock
relied on moneylenders who knew them to tide them over. A caveat is
necessary here: the above data refer only to licensed, legal moneylenders.
Unlicensed moneylenders like James Joyce's Moses Herzog could not pursue defaulters through the courts. The typical loan made by an unlicensed
moneylender was probably less than the average of £5 indicated above,
and the smaller the loan the less worthwhile an appeal to the courts

TABLE 3.3.
Average Size of Loans Made by Jewish Moneylenders and Traders c. 1910–13

Name	Trading as	Address	Avg. (£)	Med. (£)	N
Moneylenders					
Julius Goodman	Brunswick Loan Bank	57 Gt. Brunswick St.	5.5	6.0	12
Simon Watchman	Union Loan & Discount Bank		5.6	4.0	59
Julius Solomon	Dublin Loan & Discount Bank	4 Fleet St.	5.9	5.5	36
Michael Mofsovitz	National Loan & Discount Bank	43 Dawson St.	5.7	6.0	21
Oscar White		17 Victoria St.	6.8	6.2	20
Moses Grinspun		42 Synge St.	5.5	5.5	1
William Allaun	Trading as Jas C. Walshe	15 Anglesea St.	8.3	8.3	2
Traders					
Abraham Briscoe		9 Adelaide Road	8.5	8.5	2
Jacob Barron	Clothier	14 Harcourt Road	2.2	2.7	7
Hoseas Weiner	House furnisher	33 Talbot St.	4.1	3.5	6
Peter/Lewis Cohen	Diamond Coal Co.		2.4	2.2	15
Abraham Elkinson		26 Victoria St.	3.7	3.1	7
Arthur Newman	The City Tailors	4 South Frederick St.	3.5	3.0	41
Simon Watchman	Talbot Furnishing Co./ Watson & Co.		7.0	5.8	18
Benj. Rosenberg	Celtic Tailoring Co./ Bernard & Co.		2.2	2.3	11
Bernard Glick		3 Wolseley St.	5.0	5.0	5
Hyman Barron	Munster Furnishing Co.	24 Lr. Camden St.	7.9	5.6	57
Joseph Hesselberg	Dublin Furnishing Co.		7.6	4.8	5
Joseph Levitt	Eclipse Furnishing Co.	6 Lr. Ormond Quay	5.9	5.8	16
Louis Levitt			4.3	3.8	9
Louis Lewis	Tailor	28a Wellington Quay	3.6	3.0	9
Mau. and Jos. Block	Block Bros.		5.6	5.0	5
Morris Newman	People's Own Tailors	8 Eustace St.	3.3	3.5	5
Samuel Isaacson	British & Irish Furnishing Co.	169 Gr. Brunswick St.	21.6	21.6	2
Solomon Sevitt		21 Greenville Tce.	2.9	2.9	2
Solomon Ginsberg	Irish House for Tailoring		2.2	2.1	8
Louis Orlik			2.0	2.0	2
Joseph Isaacson	B. Hyam	28 Dame Street	4.5	3.8	3
H. Weiner/J. Lipson	House furnishers	33 Talbot St.	2.7	2.7	2
Abraham Barron		21 Wolseley St.	7.6	7.6	2

Source: National Archives, civil bill books 1911–14; *Thom's Directory 1912*.

against a defaulter. The nature of the unlicensed moneylenders' operations almost certainly entailed higher interest charges. They operated outside the law in an equilibrium involving higher costs, higher interest
charges, smaller loans, and higher default rates. Most Jewish moneylenders lived within the law, however, and relied on the courts to enforce
their contracts. They did not resort to the violent tactics used by some
illegal operators.[85]

In the late nineteenth century moneylending was a sensitive issue for
the Jewish community in both Britain and Ireland. In March 1893 a London rabbi, A. A. Green, lamented how "notorious money-lenders . . . men
of sullied commercial morality, or little personal character, and absolutely
no caste whatever" were presiding as *parnassim* (or leaders) over provincial congregations, but he reserved his strongest condemnation for "the
dealers on the hire system . . . who block the County Court every court
day with summonses and judgement summons by the hundred at a time."
He declared, "I would rather see the synagogue closed on the Day of
Atonement than the County Court thronged as I have seen it." Rabbi
Green's letter led to a correspondence in the *Jewish Chronicle* that extended over several weeks. His views were strongly contested by some
provincial moneylenders and their supporters.[86] In 1898, when legislative
controls on moneylending were imminent, Sir George Henry Lewis testified to a parliamentary inquiry.

> I know that the Jewish community despise and loathe these men and
> their trade; they are not allowed any public position in the commu-
> nity; they are utterly ignored; the Jewish clergy preach against them
> and their usury in the synagogues; and I may say this because I know
> it of my own knowledge. I am myself a Jew.

Lewis continued with remarks that reflected the hostility of many in his
own anglicized community to its immigrant coreligionists:

> It is impossible that the community can do anything with these men,
> who come over from Poland, Jerusalem and other places, and start
> themselves up in this way, but they would be only glad to see them
> put down and abolished altogether, and imprisoned.[87]

Joseph Edelstein's controversial and scurrilous *The Moneylender* was
first published in Dublin in 1908 and reprinted in 1931.[88] This short
novel—certainly no masterpiece—offers an insider's very unflattering
portrait of the fictional immigrant packman, Moses Levenstein, and his
circle. Moses and his greedy friends prey on impoverished and gullible
clients. There is no love lost on either side. Part of the story concerns
Moses' only son, Abrom, who, articulating Edelstein's own position, re-
jects his father's avocation. By the time Abrom arrives in Dublin from

"Wexney," "his father was president of a 'Shool,' lived in a large house in Rathmines, and . . . was a rich moneylender." In *cheder* Abrom meets young Moses Horwitz, who "cordially disliked the sons of those parents who were engaged in moneylending." Abrom quickly comes to the view that the condemnation of usury in "the twenty first of Exodus, chapter xxii"—which exempted lending to Gentiles from the prohibition against usury—had been "wrongly interpreted and understood" and applied equally to *all* lending, be it to Jew or Gentile. Abrom succumbs soon thereafter to a fatal fever, despising his father, who goes "collecting" even on the day of the funeral. In his will a repentant Moses Levenstein bequeaths the bulk of his ill-gotten wealth to Dublin charities, "mainly Gentile." Edelstein, at this time a Home Ruler, believed that the moneylending, or at least the behavior of some moneylenders, poisoned relations between the immigrants and the host community.[89] Both Myer Wigoder's poem and Edelstein's novel refer to the verbal and physical abuse faced by the immigrant packman on his rounds, and indeed Dublin folklore describes instances of innocent traders being assaulted and robbed by young hooligans. But Edelstein saw the moneylending and the abuse as mutually reenforcing each other.[90]

Some within the Litvak community shared the sense that at least some of the weekly men and moneylenders exploited the poor. Jessie Bloom's father "might have fared better in the 'weekly payment' business, but the idea of taking a shilling a week from poor Irish people who were hardly able to pay it repelled him." In private, Louis Hyman, too, confessed that his father was opposed to making a living from the weekly payment business, though he questioned Jessie Bloom's decision to air such self-doubts in public.[91] The chief rabbi of the United Kingdom, Herman Adler, repeatedly raised the issue on visits to Ireland in the 1880s and 1890s. In August 1888 he urged Limerick Jews "to conciliate the goodwill of their Christian fellow countrymen by adopting the vernacular and dealing with them fairly and honestly," and in Cork "accentuated the importance of having . . . children trained in handicrafts so that they might not be dependent on trade for their livelihood."[92] Four years later he asked the Limerick faithful to "be honest in their dealings with their fellow countrymen," and at the opening of the new Adelaide Road synagogue in Dublin asked his audience to "rigidly abstain . . . from everything that could conduce to the hurt and harm of your fellow-citizens," and to be "scrupulously fair and honest in your dealings with them." Adler returned to this theme in 1898.[93] His remarks on that occasion led Louis Goldberg and some others in Limerick to form their own shul, "the principal reason [being] not to associate ourselves with moneylenders."[94] There is a hint of more of the same in the plea of Rev. L. Mendelsohn to his Adelaide Road congregation in 1895 "to act honourably, fairly, and kindly towards their fellow-citizens of all creeds and classes, and thus assist in being the means of ennobling the Jewish race, and securing the respect of those amongst whom they are destined to live."[95] Later Geoffrey Wigoder, a noted advocate of Jewish-Christian dialogue, editor of the *Encyclopedia Judaica*, and grandson of Myer Joel Wigoder, mused whether "the frequent obligation to meet weekly payments owed to Jewish pawnbrokers and moneylenders did not help the Jewish image."[96] In a poem in memory of his dead father, Leslie Daiken thanked him for not bequeathing him "the usurer's black blood, nor legacy of bawdry or disgrace."[97]

The issue made the headlines again in the mid- and late 1920s when the IRA waged a short-lived campaign against moneylenders. For a few weeks during the summer of 1926, IRA volunteers raided the offices and took away the account books and promissory notes of several moneylenders in Dublin and of two in Limerick. Several volunteers were arrested in the wake of the raids, including Fiona Plunkett, sister of 1916 martyr Joseph Mary Plunkett. Although nearly all those attacked were Jewish, the IRA explicitly and repeatedly denied any anti-Semitic intent.[98] The campaign ended in an agreement between representatives of some of the moneylenders and the IRA in January 1927. The agreement did not end the trade; instead, moneylenders agreed not to pursue clients through the courts and to allow them time to settle debts. A list of lenders agreeing to these terms was to be deposited "in a safe place."[99] Robert Briscoe, Dublin Jewish businessman and Republican activist, supported the IRA actions in *An Phoblacht*, and expressed his admiration for the campaign to end "this rotten trade."[100] Three years later Briscoe introduced a private member's bill to control moneylending. The bill, which Briscoe helped pass in 1933 after Fianna Fáil had assumed power, was almost identical to one passed in the United Kingdom a few years earlier.[101]

The age-old antipathy toward moneylenders is founded on the belief that they strive to maintain a lasting hold over vulnerable and sometimes desperate borrowers. Briscoe singled out the lenders who went "from house to house offering and inducing the wives of working men to borrow money, for the purpose of getting them into their power, and keeping them paying perpetually certain sums weekly, without any regard to original amount lent, or any morality with regard to reasonable rates of interest." In folklore, in literature, and in populist discourse, the term "moneylender" seems almost inseparable from such expressions as "extortion," "prey on," or "in the clutches of." The loans tend to be "unproductive," in the sense that they meet consumption rather than investment needs. In backward economies, where competition is lacking and information imperfect, and where both informal and institutional supports for the poor are lacking, the relationship between borrowers and lenders is often an unequal one. The effective interest rates charged are far from obvious, even to the well-informed observer. This imbalance has prompted—and still prompts—ideological injunctions and legislative controls against moneylenders.[102]

Attitudes toward moneylenders have evolved over time. In late eighteenth-century Cork moneylenders were held in such "contempt and infamy . . . [that their] offspring was . . . despised and deserted on matrimonial and upon every other honourable connexion, as much as they deserted the felon's or the murderer's offspring."[103] Attitudes in Ireland are much more relaxed today, but even now the moneylender's reputation is darker than, say, that of the bookmaker, the licensed vintner, or the slum landlord.[104] Nor is that reputation *entirely* unearned. In the past, some moneylenders certainly engaged in deceitful practices. Some took advantage of the ignorance of their clients; others encouraged reckless and undue credit, and pursued a strategy of relying on the custom of oppressed serial borrowers. Moses Levenstein, the future moneylender, saw the game as a *"dam kluger schwindel."*[105] In the decades that are the focus of this study, the widespread sense that moneylending involved exploitation and deception was sustained by Thomas Farrow's influential *The Money-lender Unmasked* (1895) and by official inquiries that exposed several instances of unscrupulous behavior and sky-high interest charges.[106] In the Dublin slums a century or even half a century ago, there were many housewives and families like the unfortunate Redmonds in Edelstein's novel. The frequent appearances in the civil courts of moneylenders seeking redress against recalcitrant and demoralized debtors hardly helped their reputation.

Edelstein's aim was to integrate the Jewish community and protect it from the hostility and suspicion facing moneylenders. However, in the attempt he painted an unduly dark portrait of his compatriot moneylenders. The rates they charged, though high, were certainly no higher than those charged by non-Jewish moneylenders before their arrival, and probably not much higher than those by pawnbrokers, another major source of credit for Ireland's poor.[107] A few years after the publication of *The Moneylender*, Jacob Elyan, himself the son of a peddler, noted in the *Jewish Chronicle* that long-established traders were also adopting "the method which ensures the permanence of the customer." The weekly system was far from being "the worst of modern evils," since its "leniency" enabled the poorest to avail of necessities otherwise utterly beyond their reach.[108] Moneylenders, then as now, responded to an age-old demand: they were more a symptom than a cause of poverty. The widespread demand for the services of both the weekly man and the *percentnik* in Dublin tells its own story. There is evidence, too, that in later years at least some customers deemed the weekly men "the poor man's friend," or "fair" and understanding.[109]

In nineteenth-century Ireland, the moneylender's power to exploit was constrained by growing competition and increasing legislative scrutiny and control. The borrower was not as helpless as before. Recognizing this, the Catholic Church had effectively jettisoned its traditional teachings on usury long before the arrival of the Litvaks. The tribulations of one Cork curate, Rev. Jeremiah O'Callaghan, reflect the shift. In 1819 O'Callaghan refused to absolve a dying Roscarberry gombeenman (i.e., a shopkeeper who charged high interest on credit purchases) of his sins unless he amended his will to compensate those he had wronged. Dr. William Coppinger, Catholic bishop of Cloyne and Ross and thus O'Callaghan's superior, promptly suspended the troublesome priest and sought to reassure the gombeenman that his passage to heaven was secure. However, the elderly usurer replied that "he had always heard from the old priests that usury was against the law of God and that he looked on Mr. O'Callaghan's advice as the safest with regard to eternity." The unfortunate O'Callaghan was banished, but he would publish a spirited and learned defense of his views in a monograph published in London in 1825. This won him the enthusiastic support of another radical romantic, William Cobbett, who republished it in 1828. An embittered O'Callaghan accused Bishop Coppinger of being a usurer himself, having been informed by his lordship's ex-chaplain that he "often was the bearer of interest from his debtors to him." O'Callaghan also held that not long ago moneylenders (*úsairí* or *breiseoirí* in the local vernacular) were despised in rural Cork, whence they would "pass . . . every Easter to Cork (City), in the next diocese, for fulfilling their religious obligations." After a series of unsuccessful visits to Rome, the Cork priest eventually secured a parish in faraway Vermont in the United States, where "his pastoral zeal radiat[ed] far and wide."[110]

Gombeenmen were still active in Ireland in the late nineteenth century. In 1880 an American correspondent of *Harper's Magazine*, waiting for a boat to the Aran Islands in a Connemara village, encountered "a dignitary styled a money-lender" who lent money at an "exorbitant rate of interest," adding that "there are few Irish villages which do not possess one or more of these cormorants."[111] Liam O'Flaherty's *House of Gold* (1929) offers a scathing portrait of another "cormorant" at work in south Connemara in the 1870s or 1880s. O'Flaherty's depiction of conditions in the west of Ireland at the time rings true but neglects the fact that the moneylender's hold over such communities was already on the wane. Rising living standards and competition were reducing the exorbitant interest he could exact.[112]

The days of ecclesiastical fulminations against usury were already almost over.[113] However, others, such as the writer George Russell (better known by his nom de plume, AE) and fellow activists in the co-operative credit wing of the Irish Agricultural Organisation Society, would keep the campaign against moneylenders alive.[114] Even a century ago, however, a majority of policymakers and commentators in Ireland still regarded moneylending as a necessary evil. Others saw it in more positive light, as a means of extending invaluable credit to the poor in a world in which every sector of the economy relied on credit. In this view, the poor would have been worse off without the credit provided by the moneylender and the pawnbroker. However, social respectability in the wider community and moneylending did not mix, and few sons and grandsons of successful moneylenders—and in this respect the Litvaks were no exception—followed in their fathers' footsteps.

Chapter 4

SELF-EMPLOYMENT, SOCIAL MOBILITY

"Arbeiter far yennem was for a goy, nicht far a Yid."
—*Yiddish saying*[1]

Artisans

The claim in a confidential 1903 police report that Dublin's Jewish immigrants "do [not do] any manual labor" was true in the narrow sense that they did not engage in the dominant proletarian occupations of servant, gardener, casual laborer on the docks, or in transport or construction. But that is not to say that there were no wage earners—"ordinary working people"—in the immigrant community a century ago. Several—including recent arrivals, the so-called greeners—found work as tailors, cap-pressers, machinists in clothing sweatshops or factories, cabinetmakers, brushmakers, glaziers, shoe repairers, or collectors of rags or old furniture. All such jobs also embodied skills that were common in *der heim*.[2] Some of the tailors would have been members of the small but grandly named International Tailors Machinists and Pressers Union, founded in Dublin in 1908. That union was modeled on its Glasgow namesake, which joined the Glasgow Trades Council in 1890, and soon became part of the British Amalgamated Jewish Tailors, Machinists and Pressers Union.[3] Some of the cabinetmakers were probably members of the Jewish Cabinetmakers Trade Union, which was involved in the walkout c. 1909 against the Jewish-owned Dublin firm of J. F. Kelly & Co. Kelly & Co. supplied furniture to a number of downtown department stores.[4]

Census data summarized in table 3.1 imply an increase in the share of tailors in the Jewish labor force between 1891 and 1911. Other evidence described later corroborates this. The rise is plausible: the community was initially too small to leave room for masters and workers, but the progress of some of the early arrivals from peddler to tailor/draper would have placed them in a position to employ more "greener" tailors. This suited the workers, too; it was easier in that way to observe the Sabbath and the Jewish holidays and, at the outset, to work through the medium of Yiddish. By the 1910s several immigrants also worked for non-Jewish firms such as Brown Thomas, Switzers, and Kapp & Peterson. However, the small size of most the workshops and the ease with which workers could switch from tailoring to peddling made union organization difficult.[5] In sum, while the laboring element among the early immigrants should not be overlooked—after all, the Irish socialist revolutionary James Connolly issued an election notice to Jewish workers in Dublin in 1902[6]—they were a marginal rather than a central presence.

In the United States, neither German Jews who traveled the countryside before the advent of mail-order firms nor the Lower East Side pushcart trader regarded peddling as a lifelong avocation. Instead they saw it as an occupation for younger men, an avenue to a more sedentary livelihood. The number of peddlers plying the streets of New York or Chicago at any one time was only a fraction of those who had served their time as peddlers.[7] In Ireland, too, the differing age distributions of some of the main occupations in the 1911 census hint at a shift from skilled artisan (tailor, brushmaker, bootmaker, cabinetmaker) to trader over the life cycle. According to the census, in 1911 only 17.4 percent of the tailors in our database were aged forty years or over, compared to 44.3 percent of the drapers and 66.2 percent of the dealers, shopkeepers, and merchants (see table 4.1). The tailors, who were more likely to have been recent arrivals, would have found work with Yiddish-speaking Jewish employers. Nick Harris's father, who had received excellent training as a tailor in Lithuania, is a good example of the transition. Israel Chachanoff (renamed Harris by a confused immigration officer) arrived via England with his own patterns and immediately got a job in a tailoring establishment belonging to a fellow Jewish immigrant. He worked there for a wage until he had enough money to start his own business. Like father, like son: Nick Harris also set up his own factory after several years of working for his father.[8] Another example is Abraham Sevitt, one-time trade union activist, who later established his own clothing business on Harcourt Road.[9] Moses Levenstein's progress from a credit draper's employee to prosperous moneylender also fits the pattern. In this respect most men in the community would eventually conform to the Yiddish dictum that "*arbeiter far yennem* was for a goy, *nicht far a Yid.*"[10]

OCCUPATIONAL MOBILITY

In Great Britain and the United States one's religion has long been regarded as a private matter, and the population census has always steered clear of the issue of religious affiliation. In Ireland, however, the census contains data on religion since 1861, and the size of the Jewish population can thereby be ascertained decennially. Unfortunately, no census between 1861 and 1911 disaggregates its occupation and religion tabulations sufficiently to offer separate data on Jews. Occupational breakdowns are

TABLE 4.1.
Age and Occupation in the Dublin Jewish Community, 1911

Occupation	Under 40	40+	Total	% 40+
Brushmaker	4	0	4	0.0
Cabinetmaker	7	1	8	12.5
Tailor	38	8	46	17.4
Bootmaker	3	1	4	25.0
Cap maker	3	3	6	50.0
Draper	34	27	61	44.3
Traveler	30	34	64	53.1
Dealer	24	47	71	66.2
Rabbi	4	14	18	77.8
Total	147	135	272	54.0

Note: "Rabbi" includes Hebrew teachers; "dealer" includes grocers, merchants, and jewelers; "traveler" includes peddlers, hucksters, and hawkers.

given for Catholics, Anglicans, Presbyterians, and Methodists, but Jews are grouped together with other minority religions. The 1926, 1936, and 1946 Irish Free State censuses list Jews separately, offering some sense of the occupational trajectory of the Jewish labor force in the Irish Free State. Here, let us focus on 1926 and 1946. There are minor differences in coverage. The 1926 data refer to all those aged twelve and above, while the 1946 data include only those aged fourteen and above; in 1926 there are detailed data for Dublin County Borough, while in 1946 comparable data refer to Dublin plus the southern suburb of Dún Laoghaire. Tables 4.2a and 4.2b report numbers in the main occupational categories for 1926 and 1946. The data compare the occupational distributions of the Irish Free State as a whole, of Dublin city, and of the Jewish population. The concentration of the Jewish labor force in manufacturing, commerce, and the professions (Sectors IV, VI, and VIII) stands out. These sectors accounted for 91.3 percent of Jewish male employment and 69.1 percent of Jewish female employment in 1926. They accounted for 92.2 percent and 62.3 percent, respectively, two decades later. The combined shares of these sectors in the Irish Free State labor force as a whole were 24.6 (25.1) percent for males and 26.4 (30.4) percent for females in 1926 (1946). In Dublin, obviously, the same sectors accounted for higher percentages of employment than in rural Ireland—53.2 (47.1) percent of males in 1926 (1946), and 48.7 (41.0) percent of females in 1926 (1946)—but still far less than in the Jewish community. The "commerce, finance, insurance" sector alone provided half of the Jewish jobs in 1926, though only 38.5 percent two decades later. The more-or-less compensatory increases in the male shares of Sector IV from 27.1 percent to 35.3 percent and of Sector

TABLE 4.2a.
The Occupational Profile of Jews and Others in Ireland, 1926

Sector	Total Labor Force				Dublin Borough				Jews			
	Male	%	Female	%	Male	%	Female	%	Male	%	Female	%
I. Agriculture	550,172	57.1	121,957	35.5	1,262	1.3	100	0.2	4	0.3	5	1.6
II. Fishing	5,736	0.6	17	0.0	0	0.0	0	0.0	1	0.0	0	0.0
III. Mining	2,590	0.3	9	0.0	0	0.0	0	0.0	0	0.0	0	0.0
IV. Other producers, repairers	154,016	16.0	32,601	9.5	35,386	37.7	10,376	24.2	334	27.1	62	20.0
V. Transport and communications	63,686	6.6	1,266	3.7	17,831	19.0	456	1.0	13	1.1	0	0.0
VI. Commerce, finance, insurance	56,520	5.9	28,488	8.3	10,575	11.3	6,783	15.3	649	52.7	131	42.3
VII. Public administration/defense	33,348	3.5	3,985	1.2	6,266	6.7	769	1.7	6	0.5	1	0.3
VIII. Professional (excl. clerks)	25,936	2.7	29,505	8.6	3,929	4.2	4,082	9.2	142	11.5	21	6.8
IX. Personal service	18,381	1.9	109,461	31.8	3,575	3.8	15,114	34.0	10	0.8	20	6.5
X. Clerks (private sector), typists	17,206	1.8	12,801	3.7	5,300	5.6	4,390	9.9	34	2.8	58	18.7
XI. Other	36,177	3.8	3,803	1.1	11,114	11.8	2,074	4.7	39	3.2	12	3.9
Total occupied	963,708	100.0	343,894	100.0	93,986	100.0	44,404	100.0	1,232	100.0	310	100.0
Unoccupied	193,012		783,183		19,721		82,533		248		1,085	
All aged 12+	1,156,780		1,127,077		113,707		126,937		1,460		1,395	

Source: Saorstát Éireann, Census of Population 1926, vol. 3, Religions and Birthplaces (Dublin, 1928), pp. 24–25, 28–29, 93, 112–13. These data do not include Northern Ireland.

TABLE 4.2b.
The Occupational Profile of Jews and Others in Ireland, 1946

Sector	Total Labor Force				Dublin and Dun Laoghaire				Jews			
	Male	%	Female	%	Male	%	Female	%	Male	%	Female	%
I. Agriculture	512,127	53.2	81,526	24.3	3,397	2,3	171	0.2	3	0.2	1	0.3
II. Fishing	3,643	0.4	4	0.0	128	0.1	0	0.0	0	0.0	0	0.0
III. Mining	3,113	0.3	16	0.0	40	0.0	0	0.0	0	0.0	0	0.0
IV. Other producers, repairers	152,369	15.8	35,252	10.5	42,031	28.4	16,355	18.4	492	35.3	62	18.0
V. Transport and communications	57,837	6.0	1,342	0.4	21,526	14.5	579	0.7	7	0.5	1	0.3
VI. Commerce, finance, insurance	56,263	5.8	31,734	8.9	16,787	11.3	10,290	11.6	562	40.3	107	31.0
VII. Public Administration/defense	36,146	3.8	7,721	0.9	13,097	8.8	3,869	4.3	8	0.6	2	0.6
VIII. Professional (excl. clerks)	34,092	3.5	36,806	11.0	10,979	7.4	9,790	11.0	232	16.6	46	13.3
IX. Personal service	20,934	2.2	101,901	30.4	7,021	4.7	26,639	30.0	18	1.3	19	5.5
X. Clerks (private sector), typists	19,822	2.1	23,898	7.1	9,834	6.6	13,562	15.3	25	1.8	99	28.7
XI. Other	68,159	7.1	14,662	4.4	23,160	15.6	7,594	8.5	49	3.5	8	2.3
Total Occupied	963,505	100.0	334,862	100.0	148,000	100.0	88,851	100.0	1,394	100.0	345	100.0
Unoccupied	138,482		746,500		26,689		138,288		190		1,221	
All aged 14+	1,101,987		1,081,362		174,689		227,139		1,584		1,566	

Source: Saorstát Éireann, *Census of Population 1946*, vol. 2, *Occupations* (Dublin, 1953), pp. 92–108, 196–97. These data do not include Northern Ireland.

VIII from 11.5 percent to 16.6 percent bespeak the upward mobility of the Jewish community. They also capture the ongoing shift from middleman to manufacturer. The protectionist tariff regime introduced by the Fianna Fáil party, which ruled uninterruptedly between 1932 and 1948, was a boon to clothing manufacturers, and Jewish immigrants with tailoring skills capitalized. Nick Harris reckons that in Dublin in the early 1940s "Jewish firms dominated . . . by as much as 75 per cent."[11] The near absence of Jews in the public sector, in personal service, and in "transport and communications" is also noteworthy.

Jewish women were much less likely to be in the labor force than non-Jewish women in these years. In 1926 22.2 percent of Jewish women aged twelve and over were reported as "occupied," as against 35 percent of Dublin women, and 30.5 percent of all Irishwomen; two decades later the percentages of women aged fourteen and over were 22, 39.1, and 31, respectively. This is partly accounted for by earlier marriages and the lower proportion of never-married women in the Jewish community. The high number of domestic servants in the city—hardly any of whom would have been Jewish—also played a role. Another interesting difference is the much higher proportion of Jewish female workers employed as typists and clerks (18.7 percent of Jewish women aged twelve and above in 1926, versus 9.9 percent of Dublin women and 3.7 percent of women in the Irish Free State; and 28.7 percent of Jewish women in 1946, versus 15.3 and 2.1 percent, respectively).

Another perspective on the shifting occupational profile of Irish Jewry is offered by a database on Jewish schoolchildren recently compiled by genealogist Stuart Rosenblatt. The database, drawing on the surviving records of all the main schools attended by Jews in Dublin, Belfast, and Limerick between the 1880s and the 2000s, includes the occupation of the male parent at the time of admission. Obviously many parents feature more than once, but the outcome reported here is based on a reduced data set that includes each parent listed only once.[12] The data provide a very interesting overview of the upward mobility of the Jewish population. Five in six of the four thousand or so of the parents fit into one of the following occupational categories:

- Manufacturer, company director, manager
- Moneylender, financier
- Tailor, machinist, presser, capmaker
- Peddler, traveler, hawker
- Commercial traveler, agent
- Dentist, doctor, surgeon
- Lawyer
- Dealer

- Cabinetmaker, carpenter
- Shop/store/grocery owner
- Butcher/poulterer
- Jeweler/watchmaker
- Merchant
- Shoemaker
- Furniture/furnishing
- Rabbi
- Other white collar

The heterogeneous "other white collar" category includes accountant, engineer, civil servant, chiropodist, chemist/pharmacist, artist, teacher, musician, designer, diplomat, scientist, and professor/lecturer. Some features are not so surprising. In the 1880s and 1890s peddlers, drapers, and travelers accounted for over three-fifths of all occupations reported, shopkeepers for 6.2 percent, tailors for 3.3 percent, and house furnishers a further 2.9 percent. By the 1960s occupations that might be termed middle class—manufacturers, company directors, workers with professional qualifications, artists, and so on—accounted for half of those occupied. The broad peddling category still accounted for 5.9 percent, and tailors 3.9 percent. The trends in the shares of the main occupations are set out in figures 4.1a–p. Tailors were very prominent between the 1910s and the 1940s, while those working with and/or dealing in furniture were well represented into the 1950s. The share of dentists and doctors rose over the decades, from less than 1 percent before the 1930s to nearly 6 percent in the 1970s. Medical men have long loomed large in the Jewish community—notably Leonard Abrahamson, acknowledged lay leader of

Figure 4.1a–p. Shifting shares of several occupations or occupational groups.

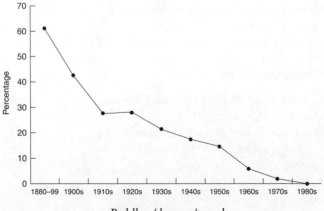

a. Peddlers/drapers/travelers

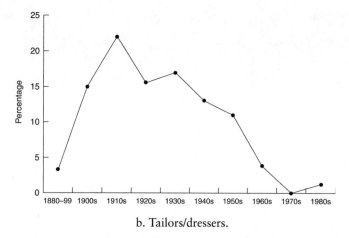

b. Tailors/dressers.

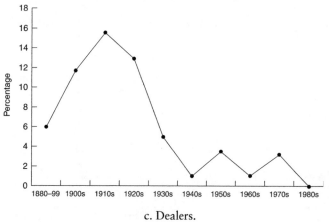

c. Dealers.

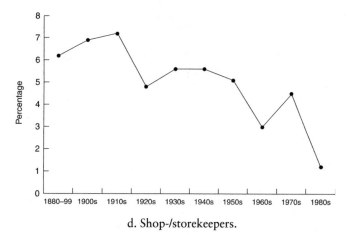

d. Shop-/storekeepers.

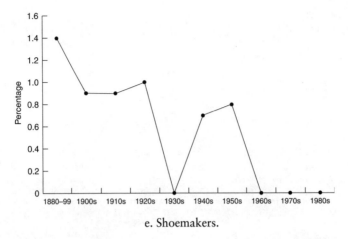

e. Shoemakers.

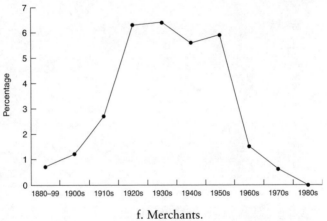

f. Merchants.

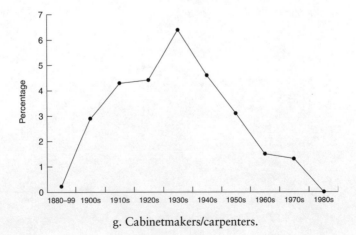

g. Cabinetmakers/carpenters.

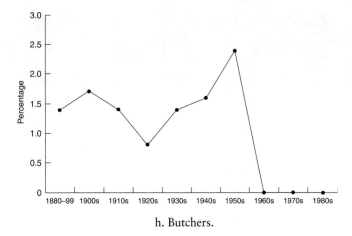

h. Butchers.

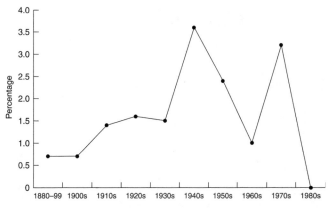

i. Commercial travelers/agents.

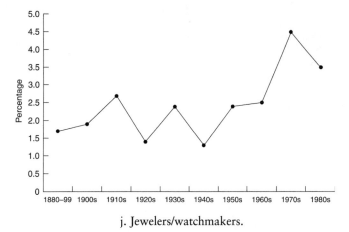

j. Jewelers/watchmakers.

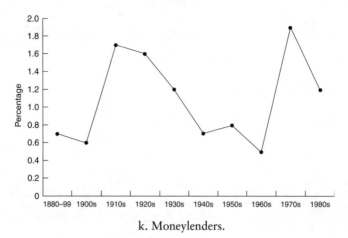

k. Moneylenders.

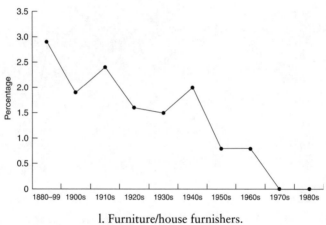

l. Furniture/house furnishers.

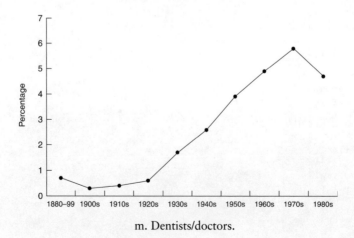

m. Dentists/doctors.

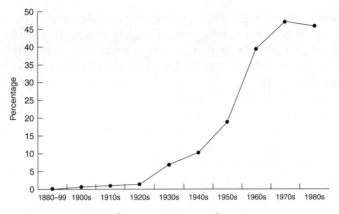

n. Manufacturers/company directors, etc.

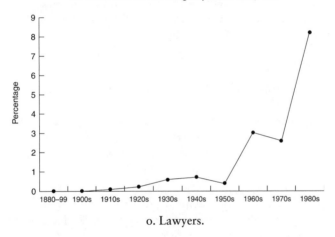

o. Lawyers.

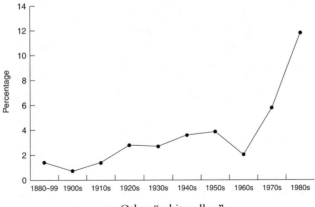

p. Other "whitecollar."

the community for some decades, and Bethel Solomons, rugby international and first Jewish master of the Rotunda Hospital—and the rise in their proportional contribution is a measure of the community's rising affluence. By the early 1930s four Jewish dentists had rooms on Dublin's Harcourt Street, while in the mid-twentieth century seven of Cork's forty dentists were Jews.[13] Some categories—moneylenders, watchmakers/jewelers—always represented a small share of the total, but they proved more resilient than might have been expected. For all their prominence in the stereotyping of Jews, moneylenders always constituted less than 2 percent of Jewish occupations—though the likelihood that some moneylenders described themselves otherwise should be borne in mind.[14] Overall, the embourgeoisement of Irish Jewry also took several decades; the share of "middle-class" occupations was only 2 percent in the 1880s and 1890s; in the 1920s it was 5 percent; in the 1930s 12 percent; and in the 1940s still only 17 percent. Thereafter it rose quickly, reaching over 70 percent in the 1980s.

IMMIGRANTS AS ENTREPRENEURS AND WORKERS

I neither smoke nor drink and believe in everything
that will make me better off.
—*Angor Wilchinski, Jewish immigrant in
London, 1902*[15]

We noted the tendency of Ireland's Jewish community to opt for self-employment rather than wage labor in chapter 3. We have seen how the first generation consisted mainly of self-employed middlemen: peddlers, credit drapers, glaziers, picture-frame sellers, retailers, and petty moneylenders. By and large they shunned trade unions and political activism. As the community grew in size, there was more scope for wage labor, so the numbers of journeyman (i.e., wage-earning) tailors and cabinetmakers grew, too. So too did the number of employers, but self-employment probably still dominated. Later generations of Litvaks maintained their own distinctive occupational profile but it was no longer that of a middleman minority. Those who could afford to do so steered their children toward business, medicine, dentistry, and the law rather than, say, the civil service careers favored by many in the indigenous population. Thus, although Ireland's immigrants produced no super-rich millionaires, they seemingly "brimmed with the Smilesian virtues . . . enterprise, drive and technical expertise" that economic historian E. H. Hunt attributed to their brethren in contemporary Britain.[16]

The employment pattern of Ireland's immigrants bears comparison with those of Jewish immigrants in Britain and in the United States. Hunt's summation echoes a long line of similar claims about Britain's immigrants. John Burnett, a Board of Trade official, reported from London's East End in 1888 that it was "the desire of every man who works under the system to become as soon as possible a sweater of other people and to get into business on his own account." Bernard Susser, historian of Jewry in southwest England, attributed the quest for independence to the expense of maintaining self-respect in the Jewish community. According to Stephen Aris, "whereas the English workman was content for the most part to remain an employee the over-riding desire of the majority of the emigrants was to control their own destiny by becoming their own masters."[17]

That used to be the standard view on Britain's Jewish immigrants. Two recent studies take issue with it, at least insofar as London is concerned. First, David Feldman has claimed that for many of London's East Enders immigration in the late Victorian and Edwardian eras meant proletarianization in tailoring sweatshops rather than upward mobility through self-employment. His census-based calculations suggest that four in five Jewish immigrants were engaged in manufacturing, mechanical, or laboring occupations at the turn of the century, and that the great majority of those were wage earners. Feldman's account finds corroboration in Andrew Godley's recent comparison of the Jewish labor forces of London and New York a century or so ago.[18] Godley found that the proportion of entrepreneurs in London's Jewish labor force rose gently from 14.4 percent in the 1880s to 18.0 percent in 1907, while in New York the proportion shot up from 18 percent in 1880 to 35 percent in 1914. The share of "blue-collar" workers (mainly tailors and cabinetmakers) was correspondingly higher in London. Godley's occupational breakdown is based on marriage registration data, and therefore on the evidence of relatively young men, but the decennial census broadly corroborates. Three "artisanal" occupations—tailoring, shoemaking, and cabinetmaking—accounted for nearly half of all occupied Russian-born (and therefore mainly Jewish) males in England and Wales between the 1880s and World War I (see table 4.3).[19]

Given the similar origins and skills of the London and New York Jewish communities—and that of Dublin, too—the stark difference in occupational profiles a century or so ago is striking. Godley attributes the Anglo-American difference to cultural rather than economic factors, arguing that both groups of immigrants quickly assimilated to the aspirational norms of their host communities. In "anti-entrepreneurial" Britain this meant becoming a skilled worker or journeyman, but in the United States it entailed climbing the socioeconomic ladder as a self-made entrepreneur.

TABLE 4.3.
Occupations of Russian- and Russian-Polish-Born Males in
England and Wales, 1881–1911

	Year	Total (%)
All males	1881	6,967 (100)
	1891	21,271 (100)
	1901	37,994 (100)
	1911	43,135 (100)
Tailors	1881	2,728 (39.2)
	1891	8,303 (39.0)
	1901	15,282 (40.2)
	1911	17,877 (47.1)
Hawkers, etc.	1881	168 (2.4)
	1891	547 (2.6)
	1901	1,275 (3.4)
	1911	1,320 (3.1)
Cabinetmakers	1881	168 (2.4)
	1891	1,081 (5.1)
	1901	3,011 (7.9)
	1911	3,217 (7.5)
Shoemakers	1881	637 (9.1)
	1891	2,515 (11.8)
	1901	3,432 (9.0)
	1911	2,550 (5.9)
Commercial travelers	1881	269 (3.9)
	1891	746 (3.5)
	1901	683 (1.8)
	1911	555 (1.3)
Painter, glazier	1881	449 (6.4)
	1891	533 (2.5)
	1901	583 (1.5)
Med. practitioner/dentist	1881	13 (0.2)
	1891	26 (0.1)
	1901	28 (0.1)
	1911	54 (0.1)

Source: Population Census, England & Wales, 1881–1911. "All males" refers to those aged ten and over in 1891–1911 and those aged five and over in 1881. Seamen (mainly from Russian ports) are excluded from the total.

For Godley, immigrant culture is endogenous: it adapts quickly to conditions in the host economy. This distances him from both sociologist Stephen Steinberg, who argues that migrants' culture was endogenous to conditions in *der heim*, and cultural determinists who hold that Jewish shtetl culture was a product of a specifically Jewish moral code and worldview, or "God-given."

Godley's argument is less compelling when Dublin and the rest of Ireland (and indeed some provincial U.K. cities such as Liverpool and Glasgow) are brought into the reckoning. Dublin's culture was not especially "entrepreneurial," yet a lower proportion of its Jewish population were wage earners than those of either London or New York. Jewish "costermongers," "hawkers," and "commercial travelers," who were relatively few in England and Wales, were numerous in Ireland. Most of Ireland's weekly men, it is true, were "fringe" capitalists. They would have mixed uneasily with those deemed entrepreneurs by Godley.[20] Nonetheless, whatever about their poverty and social status, they were traders and therefore risk-taking entrepreneurs in the classic economic sense of the word. The same goes for the mainly self-employed Jewish labor forces of Liverpool and Glasgow in these decades. Nor did differences between the occupational distributions of Dublin and Belfast Jews in 1911 reflect the more entrepreneurial character of the northern capital. Tailors were proportionately more numerous in Dublin than in Belfast, but so were dealers and merchants of all kinds.

Insofar as the assimilation of Yankee values meant "to be an American, dress like an American, look like an American," then surely Godley is right to argue that the assimilation of U.S. Jewish immigrant communities was "both rapid and pronounced."[21] And the same might be said, mutatis mutandis, of British Jews. No matter where they landed, the immigrants compromised their east European ways in order to achieve material success. Compulsory schooling for their children usually entailed shedding the clothing, the learning, the language, and (for men) the hairstyle of the shtetl. And because the economic benefits of the culturally self-sufficient middleman minority were less obvious in the modern city, in time the Jewish community became more outward-looking and less distinctive. But does the assimilation of late nineteenth-century values account for the different occupational trajectories of New York and London Jews? The anomaly of Dublin's heavily entrepreneurial immigrants suggests not.

There are other ways of reconciling the apparent contrast between the East End and the Lower East Side. First, the seemingly slower embourgeoisement of London Jews may also reflect the relative attractions of being an employee or a "market man" in London in the 1900s. Bernard Susser notes that "as the nineteenth century progressed there was a marked decrease in the number of Jewish men engaged in commercial pursuits and a corresponding increase in the number who were engaged in manual trades."[22] The network of ten thousand miles of railway had made the peddler "largely redundant." This was more so in London than in the provinces: a century or so ago the opportunities for trading were still better in outlying towns and cities. To that extent, the immigrants' skills were less attuned to modern industry than sometimes claimed in the literature. Second, the dichotomy between entrepreneurial New York and laboring London also occludes the extent to which Londoners saw themselves as operating on the margin between age labor and self-employment. According to Jerry White, chronicler of Jewish working-class life in the East End, "many workers moved in and out of street trading, trying their hand at it when normal trade was depressed."[23] Willie Goldman's account of life in the East End at the turn of the century writes of his father "always harping on the stability of people with a 'real trade in their hands' [while] the sweat-shop worker talked perpetually of 'the adventure of trading.' "[24] In New York the fictional David Levinsky switched from peddler to helper in a tailoring sweatshop, which he soon regarded as "a temporary round of dreary toil, an unavoidable stepping-stone to loftier occupations."[25] In New York 89 percent of an admittedly small sample of elderly Jews embarking on their first entrepreneurial venture early in the twentieth century had served time as employees in the same industry; in London in 1906 a Jewish trade unionist claimed that 90 percent of masters in the mantle trade had formerly been members of his union.[26] And in fin-de-siècle Germany, too, there was a good deal of switching to and fro between peddling and wage work. Indeed, in Germany the occupational profile of east European Jewish workers became more proletarian in the two or three decades before 1914.[27]

An important feature of both tailoring and cabinetmaking in London was the small scale of plants. As Beatrice Potter's survey of coatmaking workshops in the East End in the late 1880s shows, only 15 out of a total of 901 employed over twenty-five workers; 201 employed between ten and twenty-five, while the remainder employed fewer than ten hands. Given that her count omitted many small workshops, it is clear that most employees were to be found in workshops employing ten men or fewer.[28] Moreover, new workshops were being continually started up and shut down. According to Robert Wechsler, "the ease with which one could set up as a small manufacturer was legend in the Jewish community."[29] A striking indication of how common it was to set up on one's own is the thirty thousand interest-free loans averaging £7 made by the London Board of Guardians between 1898 and 1909 to Jews seeking start-up capital.[30] Given that London contained thirty-six thousand adult Jewish males at the turn of the century, this means that about five loans were granted for every six workers in the East End in this twelve-year period.

TABLE 4.4.

Percent of the Jewish Male Labor Force in Selected Occupations in London,
Lancashire, Yorkshire, and the Rest of England and Wales

	London	Lancashire	Yorkshire	Rest of E&W
Tailors	41.9	32.3	59.1	25.7
Cabinetmakers	7.8	12.8	4.6	4.1
Shoemakers	12.0	3.2	6.5	2.5
Painters/Glaziers	0.9	2.4	2.0	3.1
Medical	0.1	0.0	0.0	0.0
Waterproof goods, etc.	0.3	6.0	0.2	0.1
Hawkers	1.9	5.3	4.5	7.6
Drapers	0.8	2.2	1.9	1.1
Comm. travelers	1.3	2.1	1.9	4.1
Total	24,043	6,048	3,660	4,243

Source: Population Census, England & Wales, 1881–1911.

Such an environment discouraged class solidarity and trade union membership, and induced people to think of climbing the ladder from greener or apprentice to the top. It is significant that in the East End most Jewish trade unions were short-lived and attracted small memberships.[31]

We have seen how the census confirms the importance of tailoring in the economy of English and Welsh Jewry in 1891–1911. The 1901 census also provides data on a small number of English counties with a considerable immigrant population. These (see table 4.4) reveal a higher proportion of self-employed traders outside London, and significant variation in the importance of tailoring outside the capital. Presumably part of the reason tailoring bulked larger in the East End than in smaller provincial communities is that East End tailors were better paid. Though estimates of the average earnings of East End tailors range widely—a survey of conditions in "the lower branch of men's coat making" in 1887 put a presser's daily wage at 7s, a principal machinist's at between 6s 6d and 7s 6d, and a plain machinist's at 4s, while one factory inspector claimed in 1902 that "a good worker earns 70s to 80s weekly"—they were far from the starvation wage alleged by critics. Moreover, a master's income in the lower-quality shops differed little from that of the better machinists and pressers.[32]

Third, the choice between self-employment and wage labor depended on age. Godley's London database consists of workers predominantly in their twenties: indeed 57.7 percent of them were aged 20–24 years. Correcting for age differences in occupational structure fails to allow for how

the shifting margin between wage labor and self-employment also depended on one's place in the life cycle. Younger workers in all sectors
were much more likely to be employees.[33]

A sample of just over one thousand Yiddish-speaking males culled from
the 1910 U.S. census public use sample is instructive in this respect.[34]
Those in the sample were born in eastern and central Europe, and resident
in New York City; 957 of them reported an occupation. Their average
age was just over thirty-two years, and their average residence in the
United States was ten years. Average age differed significantly by occupation. Focusing on the main occupations, the average Jewish "manager,
occupier, or proprietor" was 37.3 years old, the average tailor 36.2 years,
the average "operative and kindred worker" 30.1 years, the average
painter and decorator 29.3 years, and the average salesman or sales clerk
only 25.6 years. Alternatively, 32.1 percent of "managers, etc.," were
aged less than thirty, 36 percent of tailors, 56.2 percent of "operatives,"
71.4 percent of painters and decorators, and 75 percent of salesmen and
sales clerks. Or, again, 14 percent of those aged 20–24 years and 28 percent of those aged 25–34 years were in the "professional" category (which
includes those identified as self-employed), as against 36 percent of those
aged 35–49 and 50 percent of those in their fifties.

When all is said and done, the parameters of social mobility in New
York and London were broadly similar in the longer run, with the gradual
dispersal of the East End ghetto beginning in the 1900s, and the move to
the suburbs "well under way by 1929 and complete by the 1950s."[35] Insofar as suburbanization is concerned, Dublin replicated London. The rate
of upward mobility was by no means uniform, but many of those who
did not manage to become self-employed or to move to the suburbs at the
outset ensured that their children would.

In sum, the Jewish propensity for entrepreneurship might be seen as the
product of life in the shtetls, where trading and self-employment were so
important, rather than as a litmus test of assimilation. The same might be
said of the tendency of most Jewish wage earners in Ireland (and seemingly
in Britain, too) to work for Jewish employers. The greater resilience of the
peddler in Ireland and in provincial Britain was less a reflection of the
entrepreneurial ethos of such locations than their relative backwardness
and peripherality. And the higher propensity for wage labor in London
might be seen as a reflection of fewer openings for self-employment there.

The weekly system offered the newcomers a foothold in their new home.
It offered few psychic rewards, however, and became increasingly dis-
agreeable as the immigrant community became acculturated and prospered. When Cork-born Larry Elyan's father died young in the 1900s, his
sister had no option but to give up her education and take over the fami-

ly's weekly business. So ashamed was she to be seen by her former fellow students and teachers that she hid whenever she saw one of them at a distance. A retired weekly man, one of Dublin's last in the business, listed three reasons for the decline of the business: a preference for white-collar professions, the decline in the size of the community, and the fact that those engaged in the trade "did not like it."[36] The big drop in the share of peddlers, travelers, and drapers in the Jewish labor force beginning in the 1890s was also probably the product of economic modernization: more competition from settled traders, alternative credit facilities, and rising living standards.[37] Another elderly Jewish businessman told of selling off the moneylending business he had inherited from his father-in-law, having no stomach for it himself.[38]

Some second- and third-generation Litvaks continued to specialize in petty moneylending, but most opted for more respectable occupations requiring a good education or considerable start-up capital. Many, if not most, of the sons and grandsons of the immigrants thus graduated to owning their own businesses and to the professions, whether in Ireland or abroad. A memoir of the Eppel and related families describes a common progression, noting that "at one stage in his life time [moneylender] Avrom Behr [Eppel] had two sons and eleven grandsons, all doctors, not mentioning four or five in-laws who were also doctors."[39] Arthur Newman, son of the *shochet* of Saint Kevin's Parade shul, began as a credit draper but eventually graduated to the retail clothing business, and his sons ran a number of shops on some of Dublin's best shopping streets. In the 1920s and 1930s Newman was a devoted and inspirational leader of the Litvak community. Having made the transition from Litvak *hevra* to the respectability of Adelaide Road, he played a leading part in the establishment of Zion National School.[40] Max Nurock, another moneylender's son, was the first Jew to win the University Studentship at Trinity College. Had Chaim Herzog, future president of Israel, remained in Dublin, "like many boys in the Jewish community, I would undoubtedly have studied medicine."[41] Some families made the leap to middle-class respectability very quickly. In September 1898 Cork's lord mayor was present at the marriage of Mr. M. L. Goodman and Miss R. Levi. In 1908 the *Jewish Chronicle* reported the "elation" of the Jewish community at the appointment of Philip Sayers as a justice of the peace.[42] Stanley Price's paternal grandfather had been a peddler, his father a general practitioner. Myer Joel Wigoder's shortcomings as a businessman were more than made good by his talented son Harry, who helped educate or settle the rest of the family. The transition from peddler/moneylender to respectable businessman and professional within a generation is also a dominant theme in *Zlotover Story*, a family history. A similar pattern is observable in Glasgow, in Liverpool, and in south Wales in the same period.[43]

Technical Appendix: More on Age and Occupational Choice in the United States

THE IPUMS-derived sample described above invites a closer look at the impact of marital status, age, and number of years in the United States on occupational choice. The sample offers a breakdown of occupation by broad category in 1910. Four of these categories are relevant here. Estimation is by logit regression. Table 4A.1 reports the marginal effects of age, marital status, and years in the United States on being in the professional, unskilled, skilled, and clerical categories, respectively. In the case of New York's Jews, the first of these categories consisted overwhelmingly of managers, officials, and proprietors. Not being married increased the likelihood of being a clerk, which was mainly a young man's occupation; it reduced the likelihood of being a professional or a skilled worker. The impact of age on the likelihood of being a professional was strongly positive and of being a clerk strongly negative.

Table 4A.2 reports the impact of age, marital status, and years of residence on SEI and OCCSCORE, using ordinary least squares regression. These are constructed IPUMS variables seeking to capture occupational status. They suffer from the drawback that they refer to 1950 data; nonetheless, the strong positive impact of age on both variables is striking.

TABLE 4A.1.
Impact of Age, Marital Status, and Years in United States on Occupation: Marginal Effects

Dependent variable	Professional	Unskilled	Skilled	Clerk
EVER MARRIED	0.052	0.028	0.069*	−0.064**
AGE	0.009*	−0.004*	−0.001	−0.007**
YRSINUS	0.005**	−0.014**	−0.002	0.008**
N	957	957	957	957
No. in occ. Category	273	373	227	109
LR chi2 (3)	85.91	54.42	4.68	102.44
Prob > ch2	0.000	0.000	0.197	0.000
Pseudo R^2	0.077	0.043	0.004	0.151

Note: ** significant at 1 percent, * significant at 5 percent.

TABLE 4A.2.
Impact of Age, Marital Status, and Years in United States on
Occupational Status: Marginal Effects

Dependent variable	SEI	OCCSCORE
YRSINUS	0.675**	0.223**
AGE	0.201**	0.129**
EVER MARRIED	−0.126	0.808
N	887	887
F (3, 987)	21.56	24.47
Adjusted R^2	0.065	0.074
Root MSE	21.25	8.78

Note: ** significant at 1 percent, * significant at 5 percent. Only men under 60 years included.

Chapter 5

Settling In

At what period and by what devious ways the . . .
settlement came into being, it would be
impossible to determine.
—*Hannah Berman, Litvak novelist*[1]

FOR CENTURIES, Jews have been more urbanized than any other ethnic or religious group. For observant Jews, living close together in clusters was a prerequisite for religious practice: the ten-man minimum needed for communal prayer (the minyan), the requirement that the faithful proceed to shul on foot on the Sabbath and on holy days, and the need to sustain even a part-time minister—who might also serve as butcher (*shochet*) and circumciser (*mohel*)—presupposed a community of ten or more households for viability. Their urbanization may have had noneconomic origins, but it lent itself to occupations as traders and skilled artisans, which in turn presupposed commercialization and specialization. By the mid-nineteenth century the Jewish population of eastern Europe was overwhelmingly shtetl-based, and most of those who emigrated from the shtetls became town or city dwellers.

HOUSING AND SETTLEMENT

Virtually all of Ireland's Jewish immigrants settled in urban areas. On the eve of World War I nearly nine in ten lived in one of the three main cities: Dublin, Belfast, or Cork. There were also small settlements in Limerick (119), Waterford (62), Derry (38), and—most surprisingly—in the Armagh linen town of Lurgan (about 75).[2] While Lurgan's Jewish presence lasted for several decades, neither Galway nor Kilkenny, both bigger towns, ever sustained a viable community. In Derry, according to one account, "religious orthodoxy was carried to a point of fanaticism in many cases. . . . Life . . . revolved around the shool . . . until it was demolished in the 1920s." Derry's Jews included several credit drapers, an art dealer, and "a man who sold ice-cream."[3] Most of those who plied their trades outside these cities tended to return for the Sabbath, or at least for the most important of the Jewish holy days.

The newcomers began arriving in the early 1870s. The big rise in the number of Russian-born residents in the 1880s (from 198 in 1881 to 1,111 in 1891) was almost matched by the rise of 855 in the 1890s. Thereafter the Jewish population relied on natural increase rather than immigration for further growth, since the number of Russian-born was only marginally higher in 1911 than in 1901. Stricter controls on immigration into the United Kingdom in the 1900s, particularly in the wake of the United Kingdom's Aliens Act (1906), may be partly responsible for this. The arrival of the Litvaks increased the geographical dispersion of Irish Jewry for a time. Dublin's share of the all-Ireland total fell from 74.6 percent in 1881 to 55.6 percent in 1911, but increased steadily thereafter. In 1926 it was 62.5 percent; in 1936, 64.7 percent.

The small preexisting Jewish community was wary of the newcomers. The tension between "English" and Litvak Jews, replicated wherever east European Jews settled, was based largely on class. The huge cultural gap between recusant Catholics and Irish immigrants in mid-nineteenth-century England, and the tensions between Irish and Italian Catholics in the late nineteenth-century United States, offer useful parallels. Ireland's small "English" Jewish community was mainly middle class and English speaking, its workplaces and residences well dispersed across the city. It was inconspicuous and bent on integration. Its leader, Lewis Harris (1812–1876), was elected a Dublin alderman in 1874 and would have become lord mayor in 1876, had he lived; he left an estate valued at the enormous sum of nearly £160,000.[4] His community regarded the Litvaks as rather ignorant and uncouth, and overzealous in religious orthodoxy. According to novelist Hannah Berman, "an old man in Dublin, Davis the glazier, often told father how, soon after he appeared in Dublin carrying his case of glass on his back, he was told by the self-appointed leaders of the community . . . [that] he was a disgrace to Jewry, and they offered him the then colossal sum of £40 to betake himself elsewhere, America or wherever he liked, only to vanish from the Dublin horizon."[5] Nonetheless, as more indigent Litvaks arrived, the preexisting Jewish community did help them. In 1878–80 an annual average of about forty households received relief in kind, worth about £1 per household. In 1878 one Jacob Davis of Chancery Lane (perhaps the same Davis mentioned above or, more likely, his son) received 10s (£0.5) worth of matzos, meal worth 4s 4d (or £0.22), sugar worth 1s 4d (£0.07), and tea and coffee worth 1s 9d (£0.09). In 1880 Davis also received five shillings (£0.25) in cash.[6]

What would "Davis the glazier" have looked like? Irish playwright Seán O'Casey (1880–1964) has left an unflattering pen portrait of somebody like him, doing his rounds in Dublin in the late 1880s or early 1890s. His distinctive dress and lowly status would certainly have set him apart from his settled coreligionists:

The Jew was short and stocky; bushy-headed, and a tiny black beard, tinged with grey, blossomed meagrely on his chin. A pair of deep black eyes stared out of a white fat face. Long locks of jet-black hair straggled down his forehead. The trousers of a shabby black suit were well frayed at the bottoms; his boots were well worn down at the heels; his head was rasped with a high and hard and shining white collar, set off by a gallant red, green, and yellow patterned tie. The Jew's arms were held out in front of his body to strengthen the resistance to the heavy weight on his back. His body was so much bent that the back of his head was sunk into the back of his neck to enable him to look to his front and to see any possible need for his services. The sweat was trickling down his cheeks, and glistening patches showed where it had soaked through his clothes near his armpits and the inner parts of his thighs.[7]

The Dublin Metropolitan Police, it seems, found accommodation for some of the earliest arrivals next to the police station in Chancery Lane off Bride Street, about halfway between Dublin Castle and St. Patrick's Cathedral. They lived "in a little square wherein stood the police station, Chancery Lane, joining the other foreigners—Italian organ-grinders, bear-leaders, one-man-band operators, and makers of small, cheap plaster casts of the saints of the Catholic church." Originally a small but elegant street of three- and four-story buildings, by the 1870s Chancery Lane was in a state of dilapidation.[8] Two houses on the lane were featured on a list of tenements condemned as unfit for human habitation, and were therefore closed, between 1879 and 1882.[9]

Some of the first immigrants to arrive can be named. The register of births covering the pre-1880 period records children born to Jacob Davis of 28 Chancery Lane (29 September 1874), Marks Isaacs of 78 Bride Street (10 September 1875), and L. Rosenberg of Moore Street (18 November 1875). The last-mentioned is probably Levin Rosenberg from Tels, who arrived via Edinburgh in 1873,[10] and Jacob Davis is probably the aforementioned glazier or, more likely, the glazier's son. The visiting missionary who met "two glaziers from Russia" in Dublin in 1868 and befriended them by addressing them in Yiddish may have been referring to the Davises. This would seem to be the first reference to "Russians" settling in Ireland. The glaziers were impoverished, "being obliged to labor hard for their bread."[11] Jacob Davis is listed as a painter in the marriage register of Mary's Abbey, where he married on 2 October 1873, and his father is listed as a glazier. Jacob's address then was given as 14 Chancery Lane. His next child was born while he was living at 12 Chancery Lane (26 August 1876), but by December 1878 he had moved to Peter Street, a few blocks away (see figure 5.1). A Jacob Davis would later

become *shammas* (beadle) of Oakfield Place shul. These details corroborate Hannah Berman's remark that the pioneers moved first to "streets
and laneways not far from Jervis Street, Mercer Street, and Bride Street."
Molly Harmel Sayers, whose uncle would become for a time the richest
man in the immigrant Jewish community, was born in a tenement house
on Jervis Street; "a delicate child, [she] survived only because of the tender
care bestowed on her by a drunken applewoman." She is presumably the
Miriam Harmel recorded in the Jewish birth register as having been born
on 6 February 1878; if so, her family moved to 20 Upper Mercer Street
around this time. Nos. 18 and 19 Upper Mercer Street were among the
"ruinous, deserted and uninhabitable" houses listed by the Dublin corporation in 1883. Jervis Street was not far from Moore Street where L. Rosenberg lived, or from Mary's Abbey where the city's only synagogue was
located. Perhaps the presence, albeit temporary, of the Rosenbergs and
Harmels in the Jervis Street area indicates the drawing power of a place
of worship to these very observant Jews. The Church of Ireland national
school on Bride Street, next to Chancery Lane, was the first to receive
immigrant children. It is estimated that the Lithuanian Jewish population
numbered about twenty-five in the late 1870s.[12]

The newcomers did not remain in the tenements for long. The earliest
movers to the complex of small streets off Lower Clanbrassil Street and
the South Circular Road on the southern edge of the city, where most of
the community would soon settle, can be guessed at from *Thom's Directory*.[13] The 1881 directory, referring to tenants resident in the city before
the end of 1880, lists two Jewish householders living on Oakfield Place
(the highly mobile Jacob Davis at no. 15 and Harris Lipman at no. 16),
where there had been none in earlier directories. The 1884 directory lists
only two (at nos. 16 and 17), but there were four by 1886 and six by
1890. Nearby Saint Kevin's Parade contained one Jewish householder
(Meyer Schindler) by 1882, two by 1886, and four by 1890. These two
streets would soon become heavily Jewish. Located in an area populated
by semi-skilled and clerical workers, they were particularly favored by
recent arrivals or greeners. Around the same time Micha (or Michael)
Harmel settled at 57 Lombard Street West. Meanwhile, the Spiros arrived
from Cork and settled at 20 Windsor Terrace by the Grand Canal in 1879
or so, and the Rubinsteins took up house at 7 Walworth Road.

The housing stock, mainly roadside one-story terraced units, was new
or almost new. Most units, however modest, contained outside flush toi-
lets and running water. On streets off Lower Clanbrassil Street such as
Saint Kevin's Parade, Peyton's Cottages, Arbutus Place, and Oakfield
Place, dwellings containing three or four small rooms were typical. Lower
Clanbrassil Street, which ran north-south, would become the heart of the

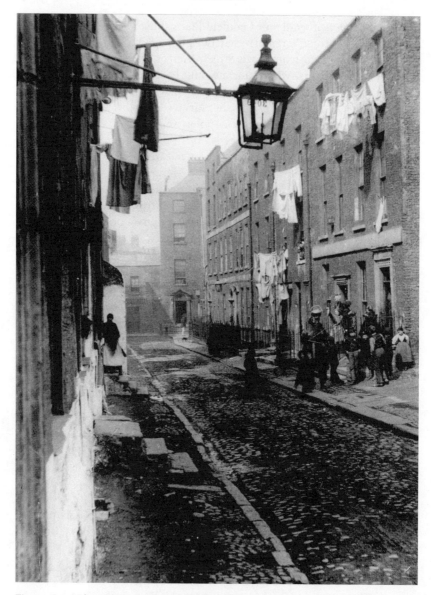

Figure 5.1. Chancery Lane 1913. This is where the Dublin Metropolitan Police found accommodation for Litvak immigrant Jacob Davis on his arrival in Dublin, probably in the late 1860s. Courtesy of the Royal Society of Antiquaries of Ireland.

community; the South Circular Road, which ran from east to west, crossed it at Leonard's Corner.

Much of the housing that would constitute Little Jerusalem was built in the 1870s and 1880s (see figures 5.2a–d). In the late 1870s several small speculative builders were at work in the streets off Clanbrassil Street, building blocks of terraced houses, sometimes as few as two or three at a time. Their work is still evident in the streetscapes of Saint Kevin's Parade, Oakfield Place, and Lombard Street West. The minor variations in house types along these streets, a by-product of their builders' lack of capital, are a pleasing architectural feature.

Just a few years later, the Dublin Artisans Dwelling Company (DADC) embarked on a substantial building project on the other side of the South Circular Road, in Portobello. The DADC was run by a group of high-minded and energetic citizens interested in improving housing conditions in the city. They married profit and philanthropy, and the weekly cost of a DADC dwelling was high enough: 3s 6d to 5s per week for a single-story, and 6s to 8s for a two-story unit. As its name implies, the DADC catered to "respectable" households who could be relied upon to pay their rents regularly.[14] Their somewhat genteel reputation would quickly become part of their appeal. The brand-new houses in Portobello came on the market at exactly the right time for clusters of Jewish immigrants ready to pay the 6s to 8s weekly rent. Though more monotonous aesthetically than the housing on the other side of the South Circular Road, the DADC housing was of a very high standard.

The area that would soon come to be known as Little Jerusalem included most of the streets between Saint Kevin's Parade and the Grand Canal. At the turn of the century there were two small clusters with very heavy concentrations of Jews: one around Saint Kevin's Parade/Oakfield Place/Lombard Street West, and the other across the South Circular Road, around Kingsland Parade/Walworth Road/Martin Street by the Grand Canal. In the following decade the concentration of Jewish families further west, between Raymond Street and Greenville Terrace, would become much denser. There was a hierarchy of streets within the ghetto: newcomers might opt for a street like Oakfield Place, while on Dufferin Avenue or Longwood Avenue "the tone was one of middle class assurance." William (or Wolve) Nurock and his family thus started off in modest circumstances in Oakfield Place (1892–95), whence they moved to 8 Emorville Avenue (1895–1908), and then to the relative affluence of 79 South Circular Road. These houses were valued at £7 10s, £20, and £34, respectively. Wolve Nurock's different homes, within a short stroll of one another, all doubled as moneylenders' premises.[15] Moneylender Oscar White[16] moved from 1 Kingsland Parade (valuation £15) to 11a Saint Kevin's Road in 1906 (£15), then to 17 Victoria Street (£24) in 1908,

Figure 5.2a. Dufferin Avenue. A prosperous middle-class street;
the Mirrelsons lived at no. 25.

Figure 5.2b. Greenville Terrace. Author and businessman
Nick Harris grew up here in no. 14.

Figure 5.2c. Longwood Avenue. Community leader Joseph Zlotover and his family lived here in no. 42.

Figure 5.2d. Oakfield Place. Nos. 15 and 16, probably the first houses in Little Jerusalem to be occupied by Litvaks.

and finally across the canal to the upper-middle-class respectability of 57 Kenilworth Square (£46) in 1918. Hyman Barron, who operated a thriving business on Camden Street selling house furnishings on credit, moved from a comfortable house at 7 Emorville Avenue to the more salubrious 38 South Circular Road in 1902–3. Jacob Davis, whom we described earlier as starting off in Dublin as an itinerant glazier/painter and living in a tenement house in Chancery Lane, might be the Jacob Davis listed in the 1912 *Thom's Directory* as "contractor, 8 Wynnefield Road, Rathmines" (valuation £30). Similarly Nick Harris's parents moved from Greenville Terrace to Victoria Street on the other side of the South Circular Road in 1929, and Hannah Berman's household moved in rapid progression from sharing a small house with the Price family at the corner of Lombard Street West and Oakfield Place, to renting a room in one of the old houses on Upper Clanbrassil Street, to having houses to themselves, first at 25 Arnott Street and then, in 1894, at 37 Lombard Street West.

Non-Jewish residents of Greenville Terrace got along well with their Jewish neighbors, but considered those living on nearby Dufferin Avenue "a different breed" and "arrogant" or "higher up."[17] The Jews sensed these class distinctions, too. The "rather snobbish Peisa Harmel, who was living in great style in Upper Clanbrassil Street," and who "drove behind a prancing horse, a beautiful dapple-grey, in a grand car," "had not much use for [his] naïve unkempt greenhorn of a brother-in-law." Peisa and his family were "snobbish, uppish, even towards their own relative."[18]

The social gap between the old and most of the new Jews was also marked, although some of the more successful among the new were quick enough to bridge it. When the Dublin Hebrew Congregation moved south of the Liffey in 1892, it chose "a respectable, quiet, well circumstanced neighbourhood" not far from the Little Jerusalem area. Many of the "foreign Jews" continued to worship in their own small *hebroth*, however. The most upwardly mobile were more than willing to move out and switch to Adelaide Road, however.[19] Though the area north of the South Circular Road contained some middle-class streets, on the whole the Jews who lived there were less well-off than those living south of the South Circular Road. Jewish-tenanted houses to the south were roomier and more likely to house a live-in domestic servant. Jessie Bloom describes housing conditions in Dublin as follows:

> The . . . social strata of the children that played the streets of Dublin might best be described by the type of home in which they lived. The children who lived in a house, and did not share that house with any other family, but had their own backyard and front garden, were on the highest level. Then there were those that lived in the "shut-door"

tenement, and the last were those that lived in tenements that always had the front door open.[20]

In fin-de-siècle Dublin it was unheard of for a Jewish family to live in any kind of tenement accommodation, though the poorest lacked a back or front garden. It was also very unusual for a Jewish household to rent lodgings in a house owned by non-Jews. On the other hand, it was not uncommon for poorer Jewish households to keep a Jewish boarder, or for prosperous Jewish households to include a Catholic domestic servant.[21] Only four Jewish households (out of 329) in the database described in detail in chapter 5 lived in one-room accommodations in 1911. Three of these were elderly couples and the fourth a recently married brushmaker with one child.[22]

An indicator of the material progress made by the immigrant community on the eve of World War I was its ability to collect, within a matter of months, over £2,000 in subscriptions toward the purchase of the site of the future Greenville Hall shul in 1913–14. Apart from £100 from Lord Rothschild and a few other much smaller foreign contributions, this sum was made up of the subscriptions of 264 members of the *hevroth* constituting the United Hebrew Congregation. Subscriptions ranged from a few shillings to three of £100 or over. The median contribution of five guineas, a sizable sum at the time, is a measure of both the community's piety and its material progress.[23]

At the outset the Litvak community was too small to sustain a kosher butcher. For a time two Gentile butchers, Byrne's of Camden Street and McDonnell's of Wexford Street, paid *shochtim* 10s to 12s weekly to slaughter livestock and poultry according to Jewish ritual. The *shochtim* were also supposed to attend while Jewish customers were being served. In 1895 the Jewish Meat and Provisions Company opened at 73 Lower Camden Street,[24] but this attempt at founding a cooperative kosher butchery failed. Then one Naphthali Cristol opened a butcher shop at 1 Walworth Road c. 1900, and soon after Myer Rubinstein and L. Barron opened shops on Lower Clanbrassil Street. By that time Clanbrassil Street had already become Little Jerusalem's main shopping artery. Buckleys and Eastmans, two of the main Gentile butchers on Camden Street, continued to employ their own *shochtim* for a time and competed with Clanbrassil Street butchers, but by 1928 the communal Board of Shechita had accumulated sufficient funds to spend £215 on a poultry slaughtering house on Vincent Street.[25]

The occupational and settlement profiles of Dublin's Jewish immigrants as given in the 1911 census imply that they were in better circumstances than their coreligionists in London's East End. Many East Enders had also arrived penniless. Unlike their Dublin brethren, however, they had chosen one of the poorest parts of their adopted city to live in.[26] Their occupational profile was also different: many were employed as wage workers in the sweated trades of tailoring and shoemaking. A factory inspector described conditions in the East End thus in 1903: "The alien is imprisoned day and night and kept in a semi-nude state for a semi-starvation allowance. Family and all sleep in the same room. . . . The effect of this is found in the anaemic and lifeless state of the workers."[27] Though peddling remained an option, fewer than one in three of the immigrant labor force earned their living as small traders. There was also more social differentiation within East London Jewry than in Dublin's Little Jerusalem.[28] Such factors may help explain why left-wing political activism was more characteristic of London's Jews than of Dublin's.

Dublin's immigrants included many very poor families, but on average they were also relatively well-off compared to the city's large underclass of casual unskilled laborers and their families. As Thomas Finlay S.J. noted in 1893, "nor are they given to the occupations of the 'sweated' Jew of London. They are respectable in their way, well dressed and well fed, not at all likely to compete with our poor tradesmen for the 'jobs' on which they depend for a livelihood."[29] Even within Little Jerusalem, as we shall see, they had the edge economically on their Gentile neighbors. The same was true in Belfast and Cork.

Little Jerusalem was always a compact area. To the south it was bordered by the Grand Canal, which separated the city proper from the municipality of Rathmines and Rathgar. The rectangle defined by Camden Street to the east, Donore Avenue to the west, and Pleasants Street and the Meath Hospital to the north, contained virtually all the streets that were, to a greater or lesser extent, Jewish between the 1890s and 1930s. Most of the streets within this rectangle are included in our database. As noted earlier, some were almost completely Jewish at one point, while others never contained more than a minimal Jewish presence.

The immigrants' settlement patterns are of interest. Their determination to live close together is hardly surprising: ghettos have always been a key feature of immigrant life. Though the long-run economic advantages of ethnic neighborhoods or ghettos are debatable, in the short run they confer several advantages on the recent immigrant. They reduce the costs of adjusting to life in a setting very different from home by providing less expensive lodging, friendship, and recreation. They offer better opportunities for finding work or starting a business quickly, as well as some security against prejudice and crime. In addition, living close to places of worship and scriptural learning would have weighed heavily with many in a very religious community like that of the Litvaks.[30] All these factors influenced the choices made by Dublin's Litvaks. Because the community

was relatively small and lived in a mixed neighborhood, clustering did
not retard host language acquisition.

Six Streets in Little Jerusalem

As noted earlier the newcomers selected where to settle wisely. When
they began to move into the little streets and lanes off the South Circular
Road and Lower Clanbrassil Street in the early and mid-1880s, most of
the housing stock in the area was newly or very recently built. Its quality
was good; most units, however modest, had running water and an outside toilet. Moreover, the housing varied in size and cost, allowing the
poor, the less poor, and the comfortably off to be part of the same community. Another crucial factor was the high turnover of tenancies in the
early 1880s.

Here I focus first on the settlement of Jewish immigrants on six streets
in the Little Jerusalem area: Oakfield Place, Saint Kevin's Parade, Longwood Avenue, Greenville Terrace, Saint Kevin's Road, and Dufferin Avenue. These streets housed a broad cross-section of the immigrants and
their descendants. Four are located north of the South Circular Road,
two to the south of it. All six streets still contained significant, if already
declining, Jewish populations in the 1930s and 1940s. To some extent
my choice of streets was constrained by the information given in *Thom's
Directory*: since *Thom's* usually did not report the names of individual
householders on streets where the average house valuation was less than
£7 or so, this ruled out heavily Jewish streets such as Peyton's Buildings
and Arbutus Place.

1. Oakfield Place, a compact cul-de-sac of twenty small, one-story
units, located off Lombard Street West at the Lower Clanbrassil Street
end, is where some of the earliest immigrants settled. Built in the mid-
1870s, it was the most modest of the six streets selected. As far as can be
ascertained, it was the first street in what would become Little Jerusalem
to house immigrants. The first reference to Litvaks in Oakfield Place is to
Jacob Davis and Harris Lipman, who are listed as living next door to each
other in nos. 15 and 16 in 1880. Before long Oakfield Place would become
one of the most Jewish streets in Dublin, favored in particular by greeners
or recent arrivals. The average valuation of houses—a useful guide to
their relative size and comfort—was just over £9. Each unit, terraced and
fronting on to the street, contained three or four rooms. In the early 1890s
Wolve Nurock ran a moneylending business from no. 20; in the early
1900s "Barron and Green" operated as *wholesaleniks* from no. 1A. In
1911 the Jewish male householders present on Oakfield Place included

three tailors, a laborer, a cap-presser, a traveler for a draper, a huxter, a dairyman, an illiterate antique dealer, two general dealers, a bootmaker, and a draper. In addition three husbands were away from home on census night, presumably traveling either on their own account or for someone else. Several household heads would have been wage earners. Several households supplemented family income by taking in boarders. The Jewish presence on Oakfield Place remained considerable until the 1940s; today only one of its houses remains in Jewish hands.

2. Saint Kevin's Parade is a labyrinth of modest terraced houses, mostly single-story, linking Lower Clanbrassil Street and Lombard Street West. A century ago all units on the Parade were valued at between £13 and £15, except for nos. 10 and 11 (valued at £9 and £8, respectively) and no. 19 (£28). The typical house, again fronting on to the street, contained five rooms. The street's occupational profile in 1911 reflected its somewhat better housing relative to nearby Oakfield Place. Three-quarters of those living on the street were Jewish. Jewish male household heads included two Hebrew teachers and a clergyman; two butchers; two retired peddlers; a "general marine dealer"; a coal merchant; a bookseller; two tailors; and a traveler for a draper. The last three of these would have been wage earners.

The street and several Jewish residents are mentioned in *Ulysses*. Moses Herzog, the one-eyed, bibulous peddler who features in the Cyclops chapter, lived at no. 13 between 1894 and 1906. In chapter 4 ("Calypso") Bloom muses about pleasant evenings in the company of "poor Citron" in Saint Kevin's Parade, with Molly Bloom seated in Citron's basket chair. Louis Hyman identified Citron as Israel Citron, a peddler who lived at no. 17 between 1904 and 1908. His next-door neighbor in no. 16 was Philip Maslansky, identified by Louis Hyman as "Mastiansky [*sic*] with the old cither" in the same passage in "Calypso." "Maslansky" was incorrectly rendered as "Mastiansky" in *Thom's Directory*, and Joyce perpetuated the error.[31] The first southside shul was established there at 7 Saint Kevin's Parade in 1883 at the instigation of Robert Bradlaw, Peisa Harmel, and some others. According to an unfriendly report in the *Jewish Chronicle*, Bradlaw had broken away from the Dublin Hebrew Congregation when his application to become a free member was refused; he then persuaded "some very important persons and some others having business relations with him" to spend £300 on a new *chevra*.[32] Peisa Harmel was president of the *hevra* for many years and "was presented with a silver snuff box" by the congregation when he was leaving for South Africa.[33] This was where in 1890 some representatives of the long-established Mary's Abbey community "found about two hundred persons assembled in a room in the upper part of a house, not more than 250 feet square, and of a height not exceeding eight or nine feet."[34]

3. Longwood Avenue is located south of the arterial South Circular Road. Its fifty houses, built between the late 1840s and the late 1850s, ranged in ratable value from £12 to £26, but most were valued at about £20. Longwood Avenue was a relatively affluent place. Its houses had gardens to the front and rear. More than half of its Jewish householders had domestic servants in 1911, whereas none on Oakfield Place had one. The first Jewish resident of Longwood Avenue, Israel Leventon, was a representative of the old community. Originally minister to the Mary's Abbey congregation, he moved south to minister to the newcomers, occupying no. 43 Longwood Avenue in 1889. The first Litvak tenant, Israel Ellis, settled on the street in 1895, making his living as a draper. Louis Levitt followed in 1896, and Louis Mendelson, M. Copman, and T. Fridjohn in the following year. Joseph Zlotover's house (no. 42) was one of the focal points of the Litvak community for many years.[35] By 1911 more than one in four of Longwood Avenue's inhabitants was Jewish.

The occupational profile of Longwood Avenue's Jews in 1911 reflected its better housing stock. They included five drapers, two travelers, a merchant, a financier (Michael Mofsovitz), a furniture dealer, the minister in charge of Adelaide Road shul (Rev. Abraham Gudansky), a musician (Marks Rosenberg, one of several talented musical brothers), and a house painter (thirty-seven-year-old Isaac Rubin).

4. Greenville Terrace is off the South Circular Road across from Portobello Barracks. It is another street of modest one-story terraced houses, but with small railed-in fronts and more substantial rear gardens. It was built in the 1870s. This is where Nick Harris, author of *Dublin's Little Jerusalem*, grew up. The Solomons took over no. 14 from Nick Harris's parents in 1928. The Solomons were poor; Mrs. Solomons supplemented the family income by putting cloth covering on buttons. Mr. and Mrs. Solomons later died tragically from accidental gas poisoning.[36] Jewish occupants in Greenville Terrace in 1911 included a cabinetmaker, three tailors, two general dealers, four drapers, two commercial travelers, a painter, a Hebrew teacher, and a dry cleaner. They included Abraham Eppel, a draper, and Joseph Eppel, a general dealer.

5. Saint Kevin's Road is located next to the Portobello complex of streets constructed by the DADC in the 1880s, next to the Grand Canal, and about half a mile from the original core settlement area around Saint Kevin's Parade and Oakfield Place. The housing on Saint Kevin's Road consisted of thirty-five mostly identical on-street terraced two-story units. Jews began settling on the road in the 1900s. Here, too, they were mainly self-employed in 1911: traveling salesmen (4), drapers (3), tailors (3), or dealers (4), but they also included another Hebrew teacher and a cap manufacturer. Henry Gilbert at no. 9 was listed as an auctioneer.

108   CHAPTER 5

6. Dufferin Avenue, at the western end of Little Jerusalem, was the most middle-class street north of the South Circular Road to be settled by Litvaks. The first family to settle there were the Weiners in 1901; Levi Berman followed in 1902. The street was almost brand-new then. The Jewish households living in its six-roomed homes on the night of the 1911 census were prospering: over half employed a live-in domestic servant (compared to two out of twenty-seven non-Jewish households). The seventeen Jewish male household heads included seven drapers, three general dealers, a master tailor, two tailors, a jeweler, a factory manager, a commercial traveler, and a capmaker. Talmudic scholar Myer Joel Wigoder, whom we encountered in chapter 1, lived for a time at no. 53.[37] Myer Joel's son Harry was an able businessman, and "Wigoder" would become synonymous in Dublin with wallpaper and house decoration; in due course two Jewish families also well known in the broader community—the Mirrelsons (at no. 25) for their cab service and weekly business, the Mushatts (at no. 8) for their pharmaceutical remedies—settled in the avenue.

WITHIN-STREET CLUSTERING

Ar scáth a chéile a mhaireann na daoine
[people rely on each other in times of need].
—*Irish proverb*

Only fleetingly, once or twice, did the Jewish community have a whole street to itself. What of within-street clustering? Here, using data taken from *Thom's Directory*, I describe settlement patterns on six streets in Little Jerusalem between the 1880s and the 1960s (see figures 5.3a and b). These streets represent a socioeconomic and geographic spread. On Saint Kevin's Parade and Oakfield Place, among the first to house Litvaks, the housing stock was very modest. Longwood Avenue and Dufferin Avenue were affluent by comparison, while Greenville Terrace and Saint Kevin's Road occupied an intermediate position.

Figures 5.4a–f show the density of Jewish settlement from the late 1870s to mid-century and beyond on the six selected streets. The Jewish presence was strongest on Oakfield Place and Saint Kevin's Parade, where it topped 80 percent for a time. Figures 5.5a–f compare the actual percentage of Jewish households having a Jewish next-door neighbor in each year, with the expected percentage if Jewish households had been randomly distributed on the street.[38] This is a crude measure: for example, comparing the actual and expected proportions living within two houses of another Jewish household would almost certainly accentuate the clustering. There is also evidence of such clustering in Cork, at least in the

Figure 5.3a, b. The streets of Little Jerusalem.

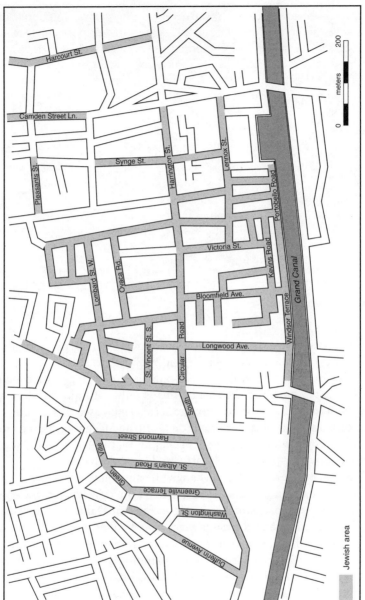

a.

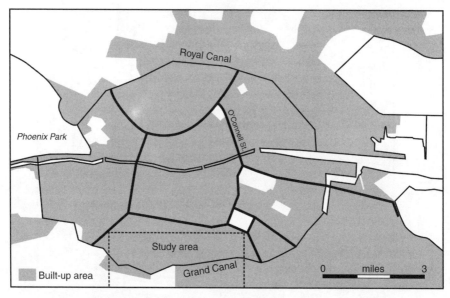

b.

early days. Half of the Jewish-occupied houses in Hibernian Buildings in 1893 were numbered between 79 and 93.[39] Jewish households also lived in nos. 30, 32, and 34. For households used to living in an exclusively Jewish environment in the shtetls, this is only natural. The close family ties between so many of the immigrants also increased their desire to cluster. In assessing claims of mutual friendship and neighborliness from both Jew and Gentile (on which more in chapter 9), the understandable preference of Jews for Jewish neighbors should be borne in mind.

Houses on these six streets changed tenants quite often, particularly in the early years. In the early 1880s, around the time when the first Jewish families moved in, about one house in four on Oakfield Place and Saint Kevin's Parade changed tenants every year. Houses were rarely vacant for long. In this fluid market it was easy for the immigrants to make their mark in a relatively short time. Neither landlords nor existing tenants seem to have resisted the arrival of the Litvaks. Immigrant families already in residence kept an eye out for vacancies on behalf of friends and relations.

When a sitting tenant decided to move on, custom dictated that he had the right to select the incoming tenant.[40] This urban version of "tenant right" inevitably led to offers and payments of key money. However, when Nick Harris's parents passed their house on Greenville Terrace to the Solomons, they took no key money because the Solomons were poor. Shifts in tenancies in Little Jerusalem, as reflected in *Thom's Directory*, clearly

Figure 5.4a–f. Density of Jewish settlement on six streets.

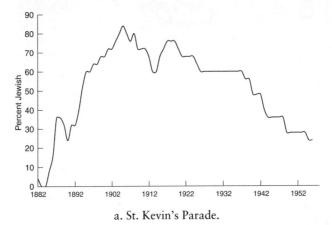

a. St. Kevin's Parade.

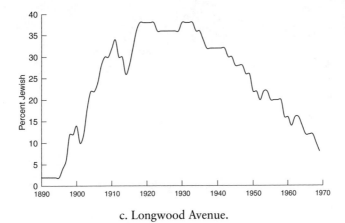

b. Oakfield Place.

c. Longwood Avenue.

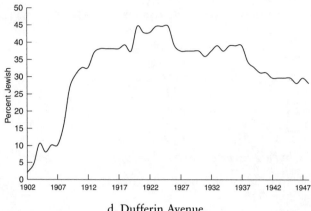

d. Dufferin Avenue.

e. Lombard Street West.

f. St. Kevin's Road.

Figure 5.5a–f. Within-street clustering.

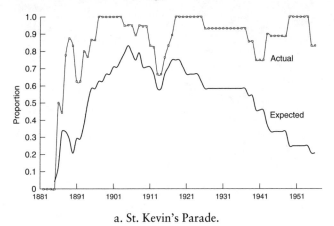

a. St. Kevin's Parade.

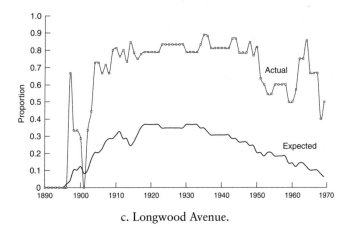

b. Oakfield Place.

c. Longwood Avenue.

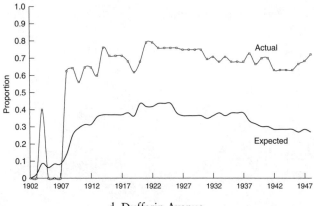

d. Dufferin Avenue.

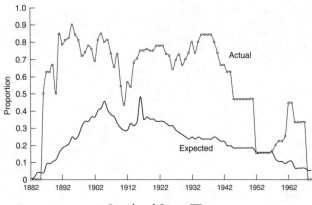

e. Lombard Street West.

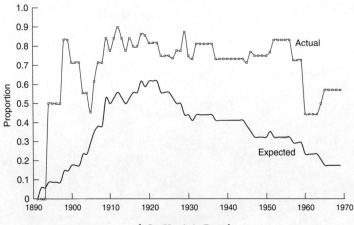

f. St. Kevin's Road.

indicate that Jewish tenants gave first call to coreligionists. When a Jewish-occupied house became vacant, the incoming tenant was very likely also Jewish. In many cases, the new arrivals were related to a family already on the street: for example, three of the Jewish families living in Greenville Terrace in the 1920s and 1930s (the Whites, the Orkins, and the Gudkins) were related by marriage.[41] The rapid turnover of tenancies on Oakfield Place and Saint Kevin's Parade in the pre-1914 era is another indication of Jewish upward mobility. Over half of the Jewish households settling in either of these streets before 1914 stayed four years at most.

The Little Jerusalem area would remain the epicenter of the Jewish community for over half a century. Already in the 1880s three in five of Dublin's Jewish schoolchildren lived in the area.[42] Between the 1890s and the 1910s the ratio was over four in five. Some of the more affluent families were already drifting south, however, and by the 1920s one schoolchild in four lived "over the bridge," a proportion that would rise to over 70 percent by the 1950s and over 90 percent in the 1970s. At the outset significant numbers also lived in the inner-city area, where the household's business premises might often double as housing. Between the 1890s and the 1930s 8 percent or so of children lived in the inner city, but by the 1950s that proportion had dwindled to less than 1 percent. Figure 5.6 shows the gradual suburbanization of Dublin Jewry. "SCR" refers to the area straddling the South Circular Road; "Over the Bridge" to Ranelagh, Rathmines, and beyond; and "City Centre" to the inner city. The beginnings of suburbanization in the 1910s are evident.[43]

CORK AND BELFAST JEWRIES

Cork-born Jessie Spiro traced the origins of the Cork Litvak community to "Uncle Jackson," a Zachs from Akmené who landed in 1876 or 1877. He was followed to Cork by a nephew, who prospered and returned to Akmené a few years later to find a bride. He married Jessie's aunt from Shavl, and that was how her uncle came to join Uncle Jackson in Cork in 1880. Two years later he sent for his wife and Jessie's older brother. Thus Cork's earliest Litvaks were a tight-knit group: "most of them came from Akmian. They all knew each other. They grew up there. Figuratively speaking, they called them *pferd gonovim*. That was horse thieves. . . . They were all right but they were squabbling all the time."[44]

Cork's Jewish community would never be big: it rose from only 10 in 1881 to 155 in 1891 and 359 in 1901. Then, despite an influx of some Limerick Jews in the wake of the "pogrom" of 1904, it fell back to 340 in 1911. Thereafter it dropped to 290 in 1926 and 125 in 1936; in the late 1950s it was still able to maintain a nightly minyan and three services

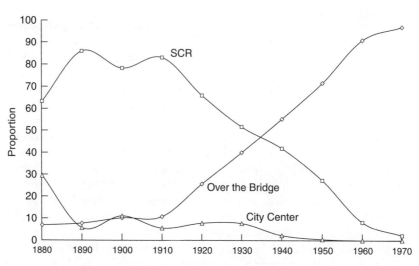

Figure 5.6. The suburbanization of Dublin Jewry.

on Shabbat, but today it is down to single figures and no longer viable. The community was initially concentrated in a small area south of the River Lee, not far from the city center: it never made the leap to middle-class suburbia that occurred in Dublin and, to a lesser extent, Belfast.

At the outset the community's focus was on a recently built housing complex called Hibernian Buildings and on nearby streets, within earshot of the Albert Road railway station and the city docks.[45] Much of the streetscape today is as it was more than a century ago when the first Litvaks arrived. Hibernian Buildings itself was a triangular development of one hundred or so compact yellow-brick on-street dwellings. Each unit consisted of four rooms, including a bedroom up in the loft. Monarea Terrace nearby had small two-floor redbrick houses with a tiny garden space in front. One side of Eastville, another street containing many immigrant households, replicated Hibernian Buildings, while the opposite side contained larger and more respectable two-story units. All units had a privy in the back. Today the area still has a 1870s–1880s feel to it. Its housing stock represents the better kind of improved working-class housing favored by Litvak immigrants in Dublin and Belfast. The smaller units were a terraced urban version of the rural laborers' cottage of this period, but the range of housing also encompassed the very lower fringes of the middle class. The synagogue was located on South Terrace, one of the main routes into the city from the south. Close to the city center, it was within easy walking distance of the area known locally as "Jewtown."

The Cork community had close links with those of Dublin and Limerick. All had originally emigrated from the same small cluster of shtetls in northwestern Lithuania, mainly in the 1880s and 1890s. When Larry Elyan's very *frum* grandfather arrived in Cork in 1881 he expected to find a vibrant Jewish community, but there was not even an active synagogue in the city: "They had a room in the house in which they were supposed to hold services . . . but they never used it at all." Instead of observing the Sabbath his coreligionists went off to wherever there was a fair, selling "all the Catholic things . . . Catholic emblems . . . Catholic pictures." And they taught Jacob Elyan a few words of English and told him that he would have to do likewise himself. Elyan began a weekly payment business, and "barely made a living with it." In time, he cajoled his coreligionists into observance, though they were very reluctant at first.[46] The story is surprising, given the ultra-orthodoxy and confessional factionalism for which Cork Judaism was noted in the 1880s and 1890s.

At the outset the community's focus was on Hibernian Buildings. On a square in front of the complex, most of the elderly men would assemble on Friday evening before sundown and on Saturday after shul services. Esther Hesselberg, who grew up in Cork in the 1900s, remembered one Captain Levy "who must have been nearly a hundred years old" regaling youngsters with tales of the hardships endured by the Jews under the reign of the kaiser, "stories our parents would never talk about."[47]

Cork Jewry was notoriously fractious. Larry Elyan, whose grandfather had been a minister in Cork in the early days, reminisced in 1972

> Going through my grandfather's papers who died in 1928 I saw a letter addressed to him by the chief rabbi Nathan Adler. . . . "Dear Mr. Elyan, I am very happy to hear that there is a *shalom* [written in Hebrew characters] in your community, but I regret that I am unable to [meet] your request to supply a *sefer torah* [again written in Hebrew], in view of what happened to the last one." They hit each other over the head with it.[48]

For years the community was divided between two parties, one led by the Jacksons and the other by the Cleins. The two factions buried their differences in 1895. Esther Hesselberg's brother, who ghostwrote the shul minutes for a fee of a shilling per meeting, was present at the historic meeting when Chief Rabbi Dr. Adler paid a pastoral visit to inaugurate the united shul in South Terrace.

> The celebration was graced by the presence of the Cork High Sheriff whom Dr. Herzog [*recte* Adler] asked for an English speaker after the initial Yiddish orations. One noted member welcomed the "extinguished" guest and hoped he would continue to work "with his soldiers at the wheel," which caused the chairman to tell him to con-

tinue his oration in his best King's Yiddish and to keep his Litvak English for the shul meetings.[49]

Cork had the reputation of vying with Cardiff and Gateshead in its orthodoxy. Nobody was allowed to carry even a handkerchief on Sabbath, and according to Esther Hesselberg,

> the only facility (now happily discontinued) was the provision of spittoons in the synagogue for bronchitic *baila batim*, and my brother used to tell me that those kosher hillybillys wee "dead eye dicks" and never missed their target. One proud boast of the Cork community in my early years was the export of its surplus *kihila* talent to Dublin in the persons of Arthur Newman, Jacob Elyan, Philip Sayers, and the Shillman family and many others who were destined to form a nucleus of Dublin's every successful effort.[50]

Apparently for the want of adequate premises, the community continued to worship in two different places until South Terrace was refurbished in the early 1910s, and in 1911 there were still three clergymen to serve a community of 340 souls.[51] Although the community for a time could support two rabbis, it was never big enough to support a kosher butcher. Instead, in the early days one of the local butchers provided a special table where the *shochet* would kill twice a week and supply the community's kosher meat.[52]

A family memoir suggests that the first Jews to arrive in Cork aroused keen curiosity from passersby. Reassured that the new arrivals were ordinary mortals like themselves, some of the local people "came back with gifts of food and some stools to sit on and small ornaments and an old mattress—and one woman even brought a framed picture of Jesus!"[53] Within a few years, however, it was a different story, when the perceived threat to "honest labor" from Jewish immigrant workers provoked a unanimous demand from the local trades council that the immigrants "be hunted out of the city on the ground that they were ruining honest trade." Some delegates made blatantly racist speeches. Calm was restored when the Katz brothers, who employed several Jewish cabinetmakers, were arrested for frauds committed in England.[54] There are signs of communal harmony later. In late 1894 the corporation, prodded by the mayor and the aldermen, granted the community "a piece of ground in the best part of Cork" for the construction of a synagogue and school; in the summer of 1896 the mayor invited the rabbi of the recently united community to the traditional "throwing the dart" ceremony in the city's harbor.[55]

Cork was hardly an auspicious destination for immigrants in the 1880s or 1890s. The nineteenth century had been one of stagnation and deindustrialization for the city. Population had peaked at 107,016 in 1831; it was only 75,345 in 1881, and 76,673 in 1891. However, as in Dublin and Belfast, Jewish immigrants' niche as peddlers provided a living in a poor city for the small number of immigrant household heads.

As in Dublin a century ago, Jewish households in Cork's Jewish quarter were somewhat better-off than their non-Jewish neighbors. Thus eight of the thirty-nine Jewish homes in a database culled from the 1911 census[56] could afford a domestic servant, compared to only fourteen of the 148 non-Jewish homes. The Jewish households with servants included four drapers, a furniture dealer, a herring exporter (Solomon Birkahn, Esther Hesselberg's father), a jeweler, and a metal merchant. The average Jewish household also had more space at its disposal than its non-Jewish neighbors. In Cork the numbers were 5.54 rooms per household for Jews and 4.49 rooms for others. The respective standard deviations, 2.12 and 2.62, are consistent with less within-group inequality in the Jewish community at this juncture—by this criterion at least. Still there was a clearly defined socioeconomic pecking order within the community. This is reflected in an unlikely place: a petition, dated October 1893, to establish a "tent" (or branch) of Chevovei Zion in Cork. In the petition, which captures the ardent Zionist feelings of Cork Jewry, the *machers* in the community were listed first; travelers and peddlers mostly last. A block of names at the bottom of the list is penned in the same hand. This could indicate the illiteracy of those concerned or possibly their absence on their rounds in the countryside. The near absence of residents of Hibernian Buildings in the list of traders in Harfield's *Commercial Directory*, also published in 1893, is also noteworthy.[57]

The small size of the Cork community meant a higher degree of self-employment than even in Dublin.[58] The thirty-eight married Jewish men in Jewtown in 1911 included eighteen peddlers/travelers/drapers, eight dealers or merchants, three rabbis/clergymen, a glazier, a photo enlarger, a master cabinetmaker, a picture framer, two moneylenders, a master cap-maker, a tailor, and a "commercial agent." Only the last of these is likely to have been in the employ of someone else.

Belfast had no settled Jewish community in the mid-nineteenth century. In October 1845 an English rabbi was invited to give a series of lectures in Belfast, but "a rabble gathered at the place, and with drums, noises and riots prevented the lectures from proceeding."[59] In 1871 the number of Jews in the city numbered only twenty-one. Thereafter its population grew in tandem with Dublin's and experienced similar tensions between earlier settlers and Litvak immigrants. Before the arrival of the Litvaks, Belfast's Jews numbered no more than a few dozen; by 1911 there were 1,139 Jews, mostly east European immigrants or their children. By 1879 there was a philanthropic loan fund and regular religious services. However, as in Dublin the newcomers set up their own place of worship, and

TABLE 5.1.
Median Year of Enrollment by Grid Area

↓ GRID →	F		G	
7			1898	(4)
8			1900	(4)
9	1903	(161)	1906	(76)
10	1933	(24)	1930	(36)
11	1945	(21)	1937	(19)
12	1940	(5)	1954	(33)
14			1955	(6)

Note: Enrollments refer to the eldest child only. The number of enrollments is given in parentheses.

resentments between the older-established and more integrated German Jews, on the one hand, and the poorer and more Orthodox recent arrivals, on the other, persisted well into the 1900s. As in Dublin, there were tensions about doctrine and ritual, and about the Litvaks' business practices. When some of the Litvaks began to use the boys' school on Regent Road, opened in 1898, for prayer, the synagogue authorities closed it by force. Even the grand new synagogue—financed in part by wealthy linen merchant Sir Otto Jaffe, a Mecklenburger who had arrived in 1856—which opened in 1904 was not enough to unite the two factions. In November 1912 the defeat of the "English" *Mitanglim* in an election for the vice president of the new synagogue (which had been under "English" control from the outset) prompted enthusiastic celebrations by the Litvak *Haredim*.[60] Eventually, however, the new synagogue would serve the entire community. Most of the newcomers lived on streets located north of the Carlisle Circus and by the Cliftonville Road and the lower end of the Antrim Road, in purpose-built artisanal and working-class housing.[61] This was a largely Protestant part of the city. Jews were four or five times as likely to have a non-Catholic Gentile family as neighbors as a Catholic one.[62] As in Dublin and Cork the immigrants lived as close to other immigrants as they could. Thus in 1910 on Dargle Street there were no Jewish families on the even-numbered side of the street, but nos. 29, 35, 37, 45, 49, and 51 were occupied by Jewish drapers and travelers. On Glenravel Street, the only Jewish households occupied nos. 5, 7, and 9. On Groomsport Street there were no Jews in odd-numbered houses, but Jews lived in nos. 16, 20–24, 34–40, 46, and 58–62.[63]

As in Dublin, the suburbanization of the Belfast community can be mapped through school enrollment records. Table 5.1 describes the distribution of students by median year of enrollment to mid-century, based on the grids in a modern Belfast street map.[64] The grids range north and east from F7 (near the city center) to G12 and G14 (Fort William and beyond). For example, 161 boys and girls enrolled from street addresses in the F9 grid between 1891 and 1939; the entry in table 5.1 refers to the median pupil, who enrolled in 1903. The heavy concentration in F9 and F10 in the early years is seen to gradually give way to one in the F11–G12 quadrant in the northern middle-class suburbs.

Chapter 6

Schooling and Literacy

Max Nurock (elder son of Mr. and Mrs. W. Nurock,
South Circular Road) has been elected First Classical
Scholar of Trinity College, Dublin, on the results of the
examination held in May. This distinction is the more
noteworthy as he was still in his Junior Freshman year
when presenting himself as candidate.
—Jewish Chronicle, *7 June 1912*

I had the greatest hopes of Philip, and when he passed
his first examination and gained the first prize, I felt
my cup of joy filled to overflowing.
—*Myer Joel Wigoder, referring to his son*

JEWISH CULTURE in the late nineteenth-century shtetls valued learning, both religious and secular. For generations, most boys had received a form of schooling in the Holy Law that put a premium on "mental agility, close attention to the meaning of words, and lively criticism."[1] In the late nineteenth century shtetl Jews also increasingly valued secular schooling, so much so that they were greatly overrepresented in the best schools, whereupon the authorities sometimes imposed quotas on them. The bookish Litvaks particularly valued schooling. The Litvak author Israel Kasovich was not alone in having to face many frustrations in trying to get his children an education. In his case, it cost him half his income; "The Russian Jew was used to that." Parents' expectations of their children's ability and success were commensurate.[2]

East European Jewish emigrants saw the classroom, rightly, as a vehicle of both acculturation and upward mobility. They made the most of opportunities available, more so than other immigrant groups.[3] Their children were overrepresented everywhere in second- and third-level educational institutions. In New York in the 1920s, for example, Jewish students were twice as likely to finish high school and college as other students. The high propensity of Jews to invest in schooling eased their passage from middlemen and craft workers to manufacturers and professionals.[4]

Given the Jewish reputation for learning, Jewish literacy levels in Dublin in 1911, as reflected in table 6.1, are perhaps lower than expected.

TABLE 6.1.
Literacy and Age Heaping in Dublin in 1911

[a] Literacy

Level	Jewish Male	Female	Catholic Male	Female	Other Male	Female
0	.243	.399	.007	.013	.000	.003
1	.053	.043	.004	.013	.000	.000
2	.705	.558	.989	.974	1.00	.997

[b] Age heaping

Age	Jewish Male	Female	Catholic Male	Female	Other Male	Female
30–34	.250	.319	.244	.291	.306	.194
40–44	.383	.424	.308	.434	.256	.294
50–54	.385	.400	.414	.400	.222	.360
60–64	.667	.400	.417	.391	.333	.300

The census did not report educational levels; its data on literacy are self-reported. Household heads were asked to describe all those under the same roof as illiterate (coded 0 below); able to read only (coded 1); or able to read and write (coded 2). The data in table 6.1 refer to husbands and wives in our database of Dublin Jews and non-Jews living in the Little Jerusalem area (on which more in chapter 7). Only 70 percent of Jewish husbands and 56 percent of their wives claimed that they could read and write. Older men and women were less likely to be literate. Forty percent of Jewish women (and a striking 62 percent of women aged forty years and over) declared that they could neither read nor write.[5]

This high female illiteracy rate squares with impressionistic evidence,[6] but it bears emphasis that some respondents who were literate in Yiddish or Hebrew are likely to have interpreted the question on literacy as referring to literacy in English only. In that event, literacy as measured here might be seen as a measure of another kind of human capital: knowledge of the English language.[7] At the same time, it is worth noting that while in Dublin more than one in four of those declaring illiteracy or partial literacy had "proletarian" occupations, only one in nine of those declaring literacy did. Alternatively, only eighteen of the thirty-nine tailors in the database professed to be able to read and write, compared to fourteen out of sixteen rabbis or Hebrew teachers. The illiteracy of *any* rabbi or

Hebrew teacher is hard to credit, however. Either way, the Dublin literacy rates largely mirror socioeconomic status.

Other evidence also suggests that literacy among Russian Jews was far from universal. Joel Perlmann's reappraisal of the 1897 tsarist census, for example, suggests that between 20 and 30 percent of males "could not read by whatever vague criteria respondents use when they answer census takers."[8] It also bears noting that the literacy rates for men and women reported in table 6.1 (panel A) are higher than those recorded for Russia's Jewish population in the 1897 census.[9] And in Belfast and in Cork, the patterns found in Dublin were replicated.

The information on ages in the census can be used to generate a simple index of age heaping, which is a good proxy for innumeracy and presumably correlated with illiteracy. The index used here is simply the proportion of those aged 30–34, 40–44, 50–54, and 60–64 years giving their ages as 30, 40, 50, and 60 years, respectively. Table 6.1 (panel B) reports illiteracy and age-heaping levels for males and females by religious affiliation (Jewish, Catholic, and other). Both male and female Jews were more likely to age heap than either of the other two groups.

In Ireland elementary schooling until the age of twelve had been compulsory since 1868. In Dublin, until the foundation of Zion Schools in the middle of the Jewish neighborhood in 1934, most of the immigrants' children were sent to primary schools managed by the Church of Ireland (at first St. Peter's National School on Bride Street, then St. Catherine's on Donore Avenue) or else to the interfaith (but Unitarian-run) and coeducational Damer School on St. Stephen's Green. The Jewish elementary school operated in conjunction with the Adelaide Road shul from 1892 on never attracted the support anticipated by its founders, despite the support of Chief Rabbi Adler, and it closed in the 1920s.

The speed and eagerness with which the immigrants availed of the opportunities offered by the post-primary schools in their vicinity is remarkable. In Dublin the main schools in question were the high school, funded by the Erasmus Smith Trust and under Church of Ireland management, which had been operating on Harcourt Street since 1870; Methodist-run Wesley College, located on St. Stephen's Green, and taking in students from 1845; St. Andrews, founded by members of the Presbyterian faith in 1894 and located at 21 St. Stephen's Green North; the Diocesan School for Girls (on Adelaide Road); and Alexandra College, offering (mainly Protestant) girls quality schooling since 1864. None of these schools ever imposed quotas on the number of Jewish students (nor did any third-level educational institution), though at times the priority given to Protestant applicants meant that not all Jewish (or Catholic) students could be admitted.[10] The establishment of Stratford College, a Jewish secondary school, in 1952 eased the pressure on places in the fee-paying Protestant sector.

Stratford owed its existence mainly to the enthusiasm of Rabbi Immanuel Jakobovitz (who had arrived in Ireland in 1949) for Jewish education, but the new school never received the support of the entire community.[11]

Wesley, St. Andrew's, and the High School were all conveniently located within a mile or so of Little Jerusalem. All were fee-paying; in the pre-1914 era a year's tuition without meals or board would have cost £6 to £10, depending on the school and the range of subjects taken. Such a sum represented one-fourth to one-third of an unskilled worker's annual wage.

Jewish boys attended the High School almost since immigrants began arriving. The earliest Litvak admissions included Jacob Greenberg of 20 Windsor Terrace, a street abutting the Grand Canal; Abraham Spiro of the same address (and brother of Jessie Spiro Bloom); and Edward and Abraham Harmel of 57 Lombard Street West. Abraham Spiro would become the first Litvak to sit the Intermediate examination set by the Department of Education; the Latin paper, which had been set for a Saturday, was rescheduled to suit him. Others who enrolled in the 1890s and the 1900s were Hyman Edelstein, brother of the controversial Joseph Edelstein and future poet; and members of the well-known Briscoe, Noyk, Nurock, Zlotover, and Wigoder families. These were all children of some of the earliest Litvaks to arrive in Ireland; the speed with which their parents enrolled them is remarkable. Thereafter the High School received a few boys from Little Jerusalem every year. The average valuation of the houses sending these boys was a relatively modest £22. Litvaks were also quick to enter Wesley; the first clear example is Moses Green of Lombard Street West, who enrolled in 1891; four more would enter in 1898, and by 1930 about 250 had done so. Most of Wesley's Litvaks in these years lived in Little Jerusalem, though by the late 1920s one-third commuted from "across the bridge" in Rathmines or Rathgar.

St. Andrew's College enrolled thirty Jewish boys between 1894 and 1913, and another 105 from 1914 to 1927. In early 1894 at most ten out of St. Andrew's three hundred boys were Jewish, while in early 1913 the number exceeded twenty; in 1924 Jewish boys accounted for forty-two out of 260 (16 percent) of all boys in St. Andrew's (or "Andrew's," as it was widely known).[12] Thereafter the introduction of classes on Saturday mornings probably deterred some Jews from attending the school and prompted a few more to leave. Nor did the headmaster of the day allow alternative arrangements for those who remained when exams fell on Saturdays and on Jewish holidays.[13]

Within the Jewish community, access to such high school education was unequal. Few from the poorer streets in Little Jerusalem made it as far as Andrew's or Wesley during the period considered here. The occupational background of Andrew's boys in the early and mid-1920s testifies both to the progress made by the immigrants and to the underrepresentation of Jewish boys from poorer households. Most fathers were either in the clothing or house furnishing business, or else professionals. The most obvious exceptions were Abraham Goldstone, a cap-cutter from 25 Saint Kevin's Parade, and Leo Coleman of 127 Parnell Terrace, Dolphin's Barn (a modest address), whose son Tobias entered in September 1924 on an open scholarship. The ratable valuation of the houses in which Andrew's Jewish boys lived offers some indication of the students' background. The average valuation in 1894–99 was £82.4; in the 1900s it was £53.2; and in the 1910s and 1920s it fell to about £35, still a considerable valuation. This suggests that only the very well-off were represented in Andrew's in the 1890s; even in the 1920s the average valuation reflected the middle- and upper-middle-class background of Andrew's boys. Socioeconomic background was also important in the case of Wesley; none of the Jews admitted there up to the early 1930s came from poorer streets such as Saint Kevin's Parade or Martin Street; Oakfield Place supplied only one.

Some boys from poorer households attended the Christian Brothers' Schools on Synge Street[14] and Westland Row, where fees were nominal and the standard of education was "considered as high as that received in the private schools." After a family consultation, Louis Wigoder entered Westland Row Christian Brothers School in 1907. In an unpublished memoir he later described his three years with the Christian Brothers as "very happy" and free of anti-Semitism. His contemporaries there included Barney Shillman, lawyer and historian of Irish Jewry. Jewish boys were exempted from prayers and allowed to leave early on Fridays during the winter months. Louis Wigoder was a star pupil; he became a regular contributor of prize money to Westland Row, and received special mention in the school's centenary brochure in 1964.[15] Nick Harris was one of three Jewish lads at Westland Row in the late 1920s and early 1930s; he remembers discipline being strict there, but none of the Jewish boys in his day endured the infamous leather strap.[16] In Cork the second-level school of choice for Jewish boys was a fee-paying Catholic one, Presentation Brothers' College on the Western Road; in Belfast, Belfast Royal Academy fulfilled the same role. The academy's location on the Antrim Road in the north of the city was ideal.

A century ago Jewish women were expected to marry young, so in general they were less likely to benefit directly from schooling (though they would benefit indirectly through marriage). In Wesley, which admitted girls from 1914, there were twice as many Jewish boys as girls between then and the early 1930s. In the late 1920s Alexandra College contained an average of only two Jewish girls at any one time. They were mostly the daughters of wealthier families; they included daughters of Oscar White (shoe trade), Bernard Eppel (a contractor), L. H. Rosenthal (a lawyer), and Joshua Orgel (a jeweler). The Diocesan School for Girls (known colloquially as Diocesan), a fee-paying Church of Ireland institution offering both regular and commercial subjects, also attracted girls from better-off Jewish households. Between 1902, when the records begin, and 1936 Diocesan admitted seventy-seven Jewish girls. The first to enter, in autumn 1904, were eleven-year-old Dora Barron of 38 South Circular Road and fourteen-year-old Annie Nurock of 8 Emorville Avenue. The next three girls admitted were the daughters of a dentist, a wholesale clothier, and the owner of house property. These girls lived in comfortable houses on either Victoria Street or Longwood Avenue (average valuation £22). By the time Annie Nurock's younger sister Tillie enrolled in 1908, the upwardly mobile Nurocks had relocated to 79 South Circular Road (valuation £34). Diocesan accepted girls of all school-going ages; the average age at admission of the Jewish pupils was eleven, and the average stay just under four years.[17] Comparing the intake of Alexandra, Diocesan, and Wesley (girls) with the intake of Andrew's, the High School, and Wesley (boys) suggests that Jewish boys were three or four times as likely to obtain a secondary education as girls before World War II.

Many of the Litvaks distinguished themselves as students. In the early years, Max Nurock (brother of Annie and Tillie), Abraham Spiro, and Hyman Edelstein stood out. In 1929 Wesley's headmaster gave the whole school a holiday when it ranked first among "Protestant schools in Ireland, with Exhibitions to Sevitt, Levinson, and Isaacson."[18] Several of the best pupils progressed to third-level education. In the 1890s and 1900s reports in the *Jewish Chronicle* highlighting the scholarly achievements of both "Russian" and "English" Jews in third-level institutions in Dublin, Belfast, and even Cork were frequent. Most of those concerned came from the more prosperous households in the community. One of the first was Jacob Jaffe of Limerick, who won a literary scholarship worth £30 yearly for two years at Queen's College, Cork, toward the end of 1895, and who in due course became "an associate of the Queen's College, Cork by virtue of passing exams in three successive years."[19] In the following few years students singled out in the *Chronicle* included the son of A. Bradlaw ("prince" of the Litvak community, president of an independent Dublin shul, the Chevra Kadisha, and a moneylender), who passed his final medical examinations in 1899;[20] Abraham Spiro, son of the proprietor of the Dublin Guide & Daily Programme of Events, a pupil of St. Andrew's who distinguished himself in exams in both the Royal University and Trinity College Dublin (TCD); and Miss Eda Copeland, who obtained first prize in third grade at Dublin's College of Music. I. Goldfoot, son of S. L. Goldfoot, leading light in the Cork Hebrew Congregation and Commandant of the Cork "tent" of Chevovei Zion, was one of the first Jewish pupils at the Cork Grammar School, and "passed into the College of Surgeons" in late 1893. Somewhat later two of Goldfoot's sons passed medical exams in Dublin and Edinburgh.[21] We have already seen how Goldfoot père had paid out of his own pocket for the subsistence of Jewish ship passengers stranded in Cork for some weeks in 1895. A namesake, Mr. L. Goldfoot of 6 Saint Kevin's Parade (as we have seen, a modest address), passed his final exam in the Dental Hospital in July 1901, while Mr. I. Siev passed first arts at the Royal University. In 1908 Philip Wigoder obtained prizes in descriptive and practical anatomy from the Royal College of Surgeons, while Solomon Levy was the first Dublin Jew to obtain a medical degree from the Royal University of Ireland. Louis Wigoder passed the entrance examination to the newly founded National University of Ireland (NUI) c. 1911, but opted instead for the College of Surgeons and, later, Trinity College, because NUI "had not any tradition."[22] He was the first Jew to qualify as a dentist in Trinity. However, the star among the first generation of Litvak students was probably Hyman Edelstein, who "after examinations lasting a month" in 1908 won prizes worth £400.[23] Fewer of the first Irish-born generation opted for the legal profession, although in 1910 Charles Spiro left Dublin to practice at the South African Bar, and Louis Barron (38 South Circular Road, brother of Dora Barron, mentioned above) qualified as a solicitor. Of course, the achievements of members of the "English" community were also reported. Thus Edwin Solomons, son of Maurice Solomons (manager of Adelaide Road National and Hebrew Schools), passed the entrance exam to Dublin University in June 1896; Nat Allaun, son of William Allaun of 148 Leinster Road, a moneylender, passed the entrance examination to the Royal College of Surgeons in his fifteenth year; and Julius Leventon, son of the Reverend Israel Leventon, passed the final examination in dentistry at the Royal College of Surgeons a few months later. In 1901, Myer Cohen, son of moneylender David J. Cohen and grandson of the late Reverend Leventon, passed the entrance exam to the Royal College of Surgeons.[24]

Chapter 7

The Demography of Irish Jewry

> [Jews] are better husbands than we are, better
> fathers, and better sons.
> —James Joyce[1]

FOUR FEATURES of Jewish demography stand out: the contrasting marital fertility rates of secular and non-Orthodox Jews, on the one hand, and Orthodox and Hasidic Jews, on the other; the increasing incidence of "marrying out" among diasporic Jews; the relatively high life expectancy of Jews; and the decline of Jewish populations everywhere outside Israel. A century ago, as noted at the outset of this study, it was the low infant and child mortality of Jewish populations that struck observers most. We now take a closer look at that aspect of Jewish demography in Ireland, as well as the fertility of married couples. Our main focus will be on household-level rather than grouped data. Most of our attention will be devoted to Dublin, although, as we shall see, most of the patterns found there were replicated in the Jewish neighborhoods of Belfast and Cork.

Historical demography is an inherently interdisciplinary field. Sociological, economic, and biological interpretations complement and compete with one another in accounting for variations in demographic behavior, both over time and across groups and nations. In the analysis of, for example, Jewish mortality or Catholic fertility, cultural explanations usually bulk large. Disentangling economic and noneconomic factors is typically difficult, however. Here, by concentrating on the differences between Jewish and non-Jewish couples living in similar housing in the same neighborhoods in Ireland in the decades before World War I, we will be seeking to control (or allow) for socioeconomic and environmental factors. Jewish and non-Jewish households in Dublin's Little Jerusalem area shared the same water and air quality, and had access to the same medical facilities and public services. The same held for the smaller Jewish communities of Belfast and Cork. Household-level data on housing quality, literacy, domestic servants, and male occupations offer a guide to the influence of living standards on mortality and fertility. By accounting as best we can for economic and environmental factors, we hope to better isolate and understand the impact of "culture."

Another feature of demographic inquiry worth noting is the role of social interaction and social networks. Modern research into the spread of
fertility control in less-developed countries emphasizes how women often
obtain their information about contraceptive technologies informally from
their neighbors. Neighbors can also offer reassurance and validation. Typically, the denser the social networks in which women participate, the
quicker the diffusion of new information. Demographic behavior and outcomes depend on living standards and cultural factors, but they also respond to the transmission of such information. An early study of family
limitation in South Korean villages in the 1960s showed that socially iso-
lated individuals (or couples) were significantly slower to use contraceptives; the more members of an individual's network were using contraceptives, the more likely that individual was to use them also. More recent
research highlights the importance of gossip about family planning in societies as different as northeastern Thailand and a Luo-speaking area in
Kenya. The precise mechanism whereby networks help diffusion is not
always clear. Sociologist Hans-Peter Kohler distinguishes between social
learning and social influence. The former is about reducing uncertainty
and helping the individual make the appropriate choice; the latter is more
about how the behavior of others generates copying and conformity.[2]

The forces governing the diffusion of information about birth control
should also apply, broadly speaking, to the spread of information about
new health-improving technologies and personal hygiene. They may be
less influential, however, since agents find it easier to identify the mechanisms resulting in an averted birth than those preventing the death of a
child or infant. On the other hand, taboos of the kind possibly surrounding birth control are less likely to hinder the spread of information
about, say, soap or pasteurization.

The dense social networks operating within the Irish Jewish community, fortified by blood ties, are described in some detail in chapter 9. They
are consistent with the faster spread of contraceptive knowledge and of
new health-enhancing medical practices within that community. Gaps between Jewish and non-Jewish fertility and mortality in Dublin or urban
Ireland would therefore have depended in part on how, and how quickly,
new information or habits specific to one group were transmitted to another. It would be nice to know how much contact there was, since this
would have affected the extent of mutual influences on mortality and
fertility. The degree of social integration or isolation of a minority group
may matter in another respect: it may affect their exposure to infectious
disease. A recent study of religious differentials in infant and child mortality in the Netherlands suggests that in the second half of the nineteenth
century the isolation of the children of Jews and of members of minority
Christian denominations may have increased their life chances, though

the particular diseases and social mechanisms at work are not clarified.[3]
I return to the issue of intra- and intercommunal networking and social
learning below and in chapter 9.

THE 1911 POPULATION CENSUS

I begin with Dublin a century or so ago. The data used to analyze the
variation in marital fertility and child mortality across households, Jewish
and non-Jewish, are the manuscript enumerators' forms of the 1911 Irish
census of population.[4] As elsewhere in the United Kingdom, in Ireland the
census was the responsibility of the registrar general, who relied on the
police to act as enumerators. The diligence of the Irish registrar general's
office ensured an end product that was delivered quickly. Throughout the
United Kingdom the census of 1911 was held on the night of 2 April 1911;
in Ireland the registrar general forwarded a preliminary report to the government on 18 May 1911. The detailed volumes followed a year later.

The 1911 census, though largely modeled on its immediate predecessors, differed from them in one important respect: it required all coresident couples to answer questions about marriage duration, the number
of children born to them, and the number still alive.[5] In this respect the
Irish census was modeled on those conducted simultaneously in England
and Wales, in Scotland, and on the U.S. censuses of 1900 and 1910. The
new questions were prompted by an increasing eugenics-inspired concern
in official quarters that the decline in the birth rate was unevenly spread
across socioeconomic and ethnic groups.[6] The resultant data are a rich
source of information on marital fertility patterns and trends. Though the
ages at death of nonsurviving children are not given, these data, taken
together with data on marriage duration, also allow an analysis of infant
and child mortality. The data are subject to the limitation that the reporting of infant and child deaths was retrospective and supposedly confined to the deaths of children of couples cohabiting on census night. Still,
demographers and historians deem them sufficiently accurate for both
cross-sectional and time-series inferences.[7]

The census offers a snapshot of the community at one point in time.
Had the 1891 census enumeration forms survived they might describe a
less prosperous community in which very recent immigrants or greeners
figured more. Thus our 1911 snapshot may present an overly optimistic
picture of the community's history in its infancy. Mark Duffy's analysis
of the 1901 returns argues against bias on this score, however, since it
reveals that Jews were already the "premier socio-economic group" in the
South Circular Road area by then.[8]

The database producing the results described here consists of 329 Dublin Jewish households containing 2,112 people, and 856 non-Jewish households containing 4,668 people. This means that there are enough data for an analysis of variation both within and between different confessional groups. For consistency, it excludes "grass widows" such as Annie Riskin, Bessie Wolfe, and Annie Share of Oakfield Place, or Anna Zachs of Saint Kevin's Parade, whose husbands were away, presumably on their rounds, on census night. Even so, taking into account the 98 (all non-Jewish) domestic servants resident in these households, the database still contains over two-thirds of all Jews living in greater Dublin at the time.

The data used are not ideal in a number of respects. In most cases, neither the year of birth nor the age at death nor the parity of dead children can be derived from the data. Thus, in the case of long-duration marriages, a dead child could as easily have been the victim of tuberculosis in adolescence as of a difficult high-parity birth late in marriage. A second problem is that the occupations listed in 1911 were not necessarily the same as those held when the decisions about having children were made. As noted in chapter 4, some occupations, particularly in the Jewish community, were more likely to be chosen by younger men. Third, quite apart from this life-cycle aspect, the descriptions of some occupations are uncomfortably vague. A baker or a tailor might be a journeyman or a self-employed businessman; an engineer might be a skilled craftsman or a professional; while "clerk" and "civil servant" cover a wide range of occupations.[9]

Only 18 percent of Jewish husbands present in 1911 could be found in census forms filled in the same or neighboring houses a decade earlier. The proportions for Catholics (16 percent) and all others (17 percent) were essentially the same, however. This is a reflection of the high turnover of tenancies described in chapter 4. The birthplaces of coresident Jewish children bespeak an immigrant community. While most children were born in Dublin, 53 of the 290 couples on which there is information in the database had coresident children born in "Russia," while 44 had children born in Great Britain. About 40 Jewish children were listed as born elsewhere in Ireland. Twelve of these had been born in different counties in Leinster, 10 in Cork, 8 in Armagh, 3 in Limerick, 1 in King's County (Offaly), and 6 in Sligo. Many of these were the children of travelers and drapers. Curiously, none was listed as born in Belfast.

The database contains several mixed marriages between Catholics and other Christians but none involving Jews. Ninety-four percent of the Jewish husbands and 83 percent of the wives in the database had been born either in the Russian Empire (i.e., Lithuania) or Poland. Sixteen Jewish wives and three husbands were Irish born, while nine husbands and twenty-seven wives had been born in Britain.

My strategy will be to compare Jews and non-Jews living in the same small districts of Dublin, Belfast, and Cork. This helps control for or neu-

TABLE 7.1.
Housing and Occupations: 1911 Dublin Database

[a] Housing	Jews	Catholics	All others
Avg. no. rooms	5.4	4.4	5.2
Std. deviation	1.9	2.4	2.7
Density	1.29	1.63	1.16
% w. dom. servant(s)	27.7	9.3	15.5

[b] Occupations (%)	Jews	Catholics	All others
Unskilled	0.6	21.0	12.5
Commercial	64.4	7.2	9.8
Artisan	20.1	30.3	24.3
Professional	2.4	2.9	13.2
Clerical, white collar	5.5	11.5	16.6
Police	0.0	5.6	5.1
Other	7.0	21.5	18.5
N	329	558	296

Source: 1911 database.

tralize the impact of factors such as water and environmental quality, access to hospitals and other medical facilities, and so on. Only streets on which there was at least a minimal Jewish presence are included in the database. The streets that make up the Dublin database are the shaded streets in figure 4.1. The total number of households in the database is 1,185, of which 329 are Jewish, 558 Catholic, and 219 Episcopalian, and the remaining 79 either belonged to other Christian denominations or were mixed marriages involving one Catholic partner. Given the small number in the last two categories, in some of the cross-tabulations reported below they are included with members of the Episcopalian Church of Ireland. The exclusion of families headed by single parents and of children born outside of wedlock means that our measures of fertility are not comprehensive, though they are comparable with measures derived from enumeration forms in the United States and in Great Britain.

The census also reports the birthplace of everybody enumerated. Occupations are also given, although here account is taken only of the occupations of husbands since it was quite exceptional for a married woman to work outside the home. Table 7.1 reports on housing and occupational status in Dublin: again, in Belfast and Cork the patterns were analogous. The census data on housing quality is quite detailed: here we rely on the number of rooms as the best indicator of quality. By this yardstick, Jewish households had significantly more living space than Catholic households and marginally more than other residents.[10] The higher percentage of Jewish households with one or more live-in domestic servants is also significant. Note, too, based on the standard deviation of rooms per household, the implication that the gap between rich and poor was smallest in the Jewish community in 1911. Other data point to a social pecking order within the community, however. For example, none of the twenty Jewish couples on working-class Martin Street had a domestic servant, while nine of the seventeen on middle-class Dufferin Avenue had one.[11] The occupational profiles of the three communities were quite distinct. Most striking is the dominant role of trade in the Jewish community. Jews were least likely to be found in professional or white-collar occupations, or working in the public sector (represented by the police). Catholic men were most likely to be unskilled, and most likely to be artisans.

THE FERTILITY TRANSITION

Fifteen children he had. Births every year almost.
That's their theology. . . . Increase and multiply.
—James Joyce, *Ulysses*

Today the control of births within marriage is virtually a worldwide phenomenon. By a recent reckoning only about a dozen of the world's poorest economies have yet to embark on a "fertility transition." Yet for most of recorded history it is reckoned that *homo* and *mulier sapiens* did not control fertility within marriage. Though some groups began to control their fertility earlier, the decades that are the primary focus of this study—the 1870s to the 1940s—were central in this regard. These were the years of the so-called European fertility transition, when an increasing proportion of married couples throughout western Europe began to limit family size. Between the late 1960s and mid-1980s, the transition was the focus of a famous research project by a team of scholars led by Princeton University's Ansley J. Coale and of an extensive, interdisciplinary literature. Coale and his colleagues offered both new measures of the timing and extent of the transition, and a theoretical framework for describing it. The monographs that flowed from their Princeton European Fertility Project highlighted the role of sociological and cultural factors; they could find little correlation between economic backwardness or economic growth, on the one hand, and the onset or intensity of the transition, on the other.

They found that Catholic populations almost everywhere, regardless of the economic context, were more reluctant to embark on birth control. So, it seemed, were certain categories of workers, such as coal miners. They also found that the comfortably off (the aristocracy, the bourgeoisie, the professional classes) were most likely to pioneer family limitation, perhaps in response to an increase in the survival prospects of their progeny. In the Princeton view, the spread of contraception owed more to culture and to social networks and who-met-whom than to strictly economic considerations. Subsequent research has placed more emphasis on economic factors such as urbanization and shifting occupational opportunities for women, but the relative importance of "culture" and "economics" is still debated.[12]

In this literature, the Irish are well-known for having been unenthusiastic participants in the fertility transition. Ireland's low rates of industrialization and urbanization and the dominance of the Roman Catholic Church are the explanations usually invoked to explain this. Nonetheless, scrutiny of published data reveals that in Ireland a significant minority of married couples were already controlling births by 1914, and estimates of the standard Princeton measure of marital fertility (I_g) suggest considerable variation across the counties of Ireland even before the turn of the century. I_g measures marital fertility against a maximum age-specific fertility schedule, based on the fertility of married women professing the Hutterite religion in the 1920s. The Hutterites, an Anabaptist sect, settled in the north-central United States and south-central Canada in the late nineteenth century: their fertility was extremely high because they rejected contraception, their lifestyle was healthy, and their women breastfed for relatively short periods after birth. Few historical populations have matched Hutterite marital fertility levels for any sustained period.[13] Hence observed I_g—in effect the ratio of observed to Hutterite fertility—is almost invariably less than one. In Ireland in the 1880s I_g was about 0.8; it fell gently thereafter. Analyses of 1911 household-level data confirm that Catholic couples were slower to adjust their behavior and that the decline in fertility was fastest in urban, middle-class Ireland. Studies of households in the relatively well-off Dublin suburbs of Rathmines and Pembroke yield evidence of birth "spacing" early in marriage, of a socioeconomic class gradient to fertility, and of higher fertility in Catholic households.[14]

Shifts in Irish fertility after 1911 have been less scrutinized, but the drop in marital fertility was modest: according to the Princeton survey I_g in the two Irelands, north and south, fell slowly from 0.610 in 1926 to 0.570 in 1936 and 0.548 in 1961. Non-Catholics and the middle classes were more likely to make the transition. The Catholic Church's ban on artificial methods of birth control and the legal and social sanctions against the possession and marketing of prophylactic devices are important parts of the story. Still, a U.S. Jesuit sociologist studying Dubliners in the late 1940s and early 1950s was informed by "several priests" and a medical doctor that the Catholic middle and lower-middle classes were increasingly resorting to birth control. This most likely entailed sexual abstinence, not reliance on contraceptives. Be that as it may, by the 1940s there was a sizable gap between the marital fertility of Catholics, who formed the overwhelming majority of the population, and that of non-Catholics.[15]

West European Jews, on the other hand, were precocious participants in the fertility transition. The marital fertility of Italy's small Jewish community had already fallen significantly before the fertility decline reached other groups. In the kingdom of Bavaria the Jewish birth rate fell by half, from 32.7 per thousand in 1876–80 to 16.3 per thousand three decades later, while the Catholic birth rate fell by only a sixth, from 43.3 to 36.0 per thousand, over the same period. The mainly urban character of Bavaria's Jewish population only partly accounts for this. Between 1875 and the early 1890s the marital fertility of Munich's Jews fell from 0.522 to 0.299 on the Princeton I_g scale, while that of Munich's Catholics registered a gentler decline from 0.660 to 0.532. In late nineteenth-century Berlin the confessional gap was narrower: I_g was 0.337 for Jews, 0.393 for Lutherans, and 0.446 for Catholics. Demographic historian John Knodel, who supplied these numbers, suggests that the closeness of family and cultural ties within the Jewish community "provided a situation in which changing norms regarding family size and family limitation could spread rapidly and relatively independently of the rest of German society." Given these signs of fertility control among German and Italian Jews, it is hardly surprising to find that already in the mid-nineteenth century English Jewry was showing some signs of embarking on the fertility transition.[16]

JEWISH AND GENTILE FERTILITY

When I think of my mother coming to Dublin with
three young children and then having five more,
she obviously had her hands full.
—Nick Harris, *Dublin's Little Jerusalem*[17]

How did Litvak fertility in Ireland compare with that in *der heim*? The demographic history of tsarist Russia remains largely unwritten. Taking the empire as a whole, there is little evidence of any significant decline in marital fertility before the 1890s: the mean age at marriage remained very

TABLE 7.2.
Births, Deaths, and Natural Increase in Vilna and Kiev Provinces, 1858–69

(a) Vilna

Year	Jewish population	Births	Births per 1,000	Deaths	Deaths per 1,000	Rate of natural increase
1858	75,802	3,873	51.1	3,315	43.7	7.4
1862	81,832	3,081	37.7	2,396	29.3	8.4
1865	103,958	3,000	28.9	2,991	28.8	0.1
1869	108,191	2,554	23.6	2,756	25.5	1.9

(b) Kiev

Year	Jewish population	Births	Births per 1,000	Deaths	Deaths per 1,000	Rate of natural increase
1858	222,074	9,112	41.0	6,072	27.3	13.7
1862	247,842	8,816	35.6	6,259	25.3	10.3
1865	258,525	8,692	33.6	6,934	26.8	6.8
1869	267,867	9,792	36.6	6,427	24.0	12.6

Source: Freeze 2002, p. 61.

low and the birth rate high. However, some regional and confessional variation in rates and trends is likely: in the Baltic provinces, in particular, marriage age was higher and the marriage rate lower than elsewhere. Moreover, the proportion of all Jewish marriages involving women aged less than twenty-one years plummeted from 60.7 percent in 1867 to 23.9 percent in 1902.[18]

In her important study of Jewish marriage and divorce in late imperial Russia, historian ChaeRan Freeze has identified important adjustments in the nuptiality and fertility of the Jewish populations of both Vilna province and the Ukraine. She finds that the mean female age at first marriage in Vilna province rose from 18.0 years in 1837 to 21.3 years in 1870 and 23.2 years in 1895. Given the fecundity of women in their late teens and early twenties, such a rise could have been enough to cut completed family size by two. The mean male age at marriage rose from 19.8 to 23.1 to 26.3 years over the same period.[19] Freeze also reports the estimates of births, deaths, and rates of natural increase in the Jewish populations of Vilna and Kiev provinces reproduced in table 7.2. The decline in the Jewish birth rate in Vilna over such a short period is much greater than the increase in the mean age at marriage over the period—20.1 years in 1860,

21.3 years in 1870—might imply. Nor are the very different trends in Vilna and Kiev explained. In addition to the rise in marriage age, Freeze suggests that the control of births within and outside marriage may have also been partly responsible for the declines.[20] Even allowing for the added possibility that one or more of the four years chosen in table 7.2 was an outlier, the implication that there was demographic adjustment in Vilna province remains. Freeze also reproduces data concerning nuptiality and fertility by confessional group in European Russia in 1896–1904. These show that the Jewish birth rate (30.7 per thousand) was lower than that of any other confessional group except Protestant (29.2 per thousand), and not much more than half the Orthodox rate (51.1 per thousand).

Nonetheless, east European Jewish marriages remained highly fertile in the late nineteenth and early twentieth centuries. One of the surprising results of the Princeton study of Russian fertility was that in the census year of 1897 there was little variation across provinces in the marital fertility of *urban* Jews, and that Jewish marital fertility was higher than that of the rest of the *urban* population in all but one of fifteen provinces. Ansley J. Coale and his coauthors found corroboration for this outcome in "an odd place": the 1910 U.S. census revealed that the average parity among Russian-born (and thus mainly Jewish) women aged 45–49 and married at least twenty years (7.5) was exceeded only by that of French-Canadians (7.9) and Poles (7.6).[21] In this respect the Jews of eastern Europe differed markedly from those of western Europe, whose fertility had already been declining for a century or two, and was lower than that of most, if not all, other confessional groups.[22] The high fertility of the east European Jews, like that of Catholics, had an ideological component: the biblical injunction "to be fruitful and multiply" (Gen. 1:28) was to be taken literally. And even today, among both Orthodox Jews and Catholics fertility is a function of religiosity.[23]

So what of Ireland's Litvak immigrants? In Dublin a century ago immigrant Jewish women married young and few of them remained unmarried. As noted earlier, they rarely worked outside the home, even before marriage. In Dublin's case the mean age at marriage of Jewish women was very low by local standards before 1911, four years lower than that of other women living in the same part of the city (table 7.3). In Cork and in Belfast the gap in a woman's age at marriage was also nearly four years (21.7 versus 25.5 years in both cases). Jewish men married young, too, though the gap between Jewish and non-Jewish males was about a year less. A tendency toward later marriage is implied: the average age of Jewish wives of less than five years was 23.2 years, whereas for brides of 5–14 years it was 21.5 years, and just over 20 years for those already married fifteen or more years in 1911.

TABLE 7.3.
Average Age at Marriage in Little Jerusalem

Mean	Jews	Catholics	Others
Male	24.8 (5.0)	28.9 (7.3)	29.0 (8.0)
Female	20.9 (3.5)	24.9 (5.3)	25.7 (6.7)
Female, duration 0–9	21.8	25.9	26.0
Female, duration 10–19	20.9	24.7	27.0
Female, duration 20+	20.2	23.8	24.3
Median			
Male	21	28	27
Female	24	24	24
Average duration	17.1 (12.1)	14.9 (11.4)	16.2 (12.2)

Note: Standard deviations in brackets.

Earlier marriages account, at least in part, for the higher marital fertility of Jewish couples. But was age-specific marital fertility also higher? The great care that Jewish women took of their young, the religious restrictions on sexual intercourse for several weeks after giving birth and for seven days after menstruation, and the prevalence of breastfeeding might argue for longer intervals between births.[24] However, table 7.4 suggests that, for more recent marriages at least, age-specific Jewish marital fertility was higher than that of Catholics living in the same part of south Dublin. For marriages of less than twenty years' duration, the difference is striking. Note, too, however, the implication in table 7.4 that the Jewish fertility advantage did not persist for longer marriage durations.[25] This probably means that Jewish mothers ceased having children at an earlier age than non-Jewish mothers. If so, they bore a higher proportion of their children when they were younger and healthier.

Another remarkable feature of Jewish fertility in Dublin a century ago is the much lower incidence of childless marriages. It held across all marriage durations (table 7.5); it also held for Jewish couples in Belfast and Cork (table 7.6). The lower incidence of Jewish childlessness is partly due to Jews marrying younger, though it also holds true when the age at marriage is controlled for.[26] To some extent the gap may reflect the better health status of Jewish couples and the lower incidence of sexually transmitted diseases, but it is also evidence that fewer of them wanted to limit family size. In Dublin a significant minority of both Catholic and Protestant couples were already spacing births early in their marriages on the eve of World War I.[27] There is no evidence here of spacing on the part of Jewish couples, however.

TABLE 7.4.
Duration and Average Number of Children

DUR = 0–4	Jews		Catholics		All Others	
	Average	N	Average	N	Average	N
AAM15–19	1.71	7	1.25	8	0.75	8
AAM20–24	1.10	29	1.18	39	0.75	20
AAM25–29	0.60	5	1.02	48	0.67	21
AAM30–34	—	0	1.00	16	0.64	11
DUR = 5–9						
AAM15–19	3.44	18	2.71	7	3.20	5
AAM20–24	3.11	37	2.96	45	2.91	23
AAM25–29	3.00	7	2.50	34	1.50	4
AAM30–34	2.67	3	2.10	20	1.50	10
DUR = 10–14						
AAM15–19	5.31	13	3.86	8	—	0
AAM20–24	4.59	39	4.26	39	3.58	12
AAM25–29	4.14	7	3.44	27	2.00	10
AAM30–34	4.00	1	0.90	10	2.00	5
DUR = 15–19						
AAM15–19	6.11	18	6.18	11	4.80	5
AAM20–24	6.00	21	5.76	33	4.43	14
AAM25–29	8.00	1	3.94	17	2.75	12
AAM30–34	—	0	3.71	7	2.50	8
DUR = 20–24						
AAM15–19	7.47	17	9.20	10	1.67	3
AAM20–24	6.76	17	6.05	21	4.88	8
AAM25–29	3.75	4	5.20	10	5.50	4
AAM30–34	—	0	3.80	5	3.33	3
DUR25–34						
AAM15–19	6.76	17	8.50	22	8.00	9
AAM20–24	6.48	23	5.08	26	6.04	27
AAM25–29	4.33	6	5.56	18	5.00	15
AAM30–34	5.00	1	2.38	8	2.67	3

Source: 1911 database.

TABLE 7.5.
Percentage Childless by Duration

Duration	Jews	Catholics	All others
0–4	24.4 (41)	34.2 (117)	52.4 (63)
5–9	4.6 (65)	17.9 (112)	12.2 (49)
10–14	3.3 (60)	21.1 (90)	30.0 (40)
15–19	9.8 (41)	11.4 (70)	12.8 (39)
20–24	2.6 (38)	6.4 (47)	17.4 (23)
25–29	3.6 (28)	11.5 (52)	10.7 (28)

Note: Number of observations in parentheses.

Table 7.6 reports the average number of children born by marriage duration in Belfast and Cork. The outcomes for 15–19 years and for 20–29 years in panel A are consistent with more "stopping" late in marriage among Jews than among Catholics or members of the Church of Ireland. The "Other" group, consisting mainly of Presbyterians and other Dissenters, also seems to have been following a strategy of "stopping."[28]

Econometric estimation corroborates the impressions gained from the cross-tabulations above. The details are described in a technical appendix at the end of this chapter; only the main points need be summarized here. The goal is to account for at least some of the variation in the number of children born to couples. After controlling for economic (occupation, literacy, the number of rooms in the house, the presence of domestic servants) and biological (duration of marriage) factors to the extent allowed by the data, the importance of religious affiliation remains. Being Jewish is associated with an extra child per couple. Another feature of the results bears noting. Couples who planned their families had a target number of children in mind. Some such couples might be expected to have replaced an infant or child who died. Indeed the strength of the replacement effect is one measure of the prevalence of family planning. The econometric results indicate that the replacement effect was present in all three communities, but was much stronger for both Catholics and members of the Church of Ireland in the South Circular Road neighborhood than for Jews. This outcome suggests that along the South Circular Road other Christian couples were further along the fertility transition in the 1900s than Catholic and, especially, Jewish couples.

One more outcome of the econometric analysis bears noting. As the "Jewishness" of a street (measured by the proportion of its inhabitants who were Jewish) increased, the fertility of its Jewish couples also rose. It is not clear why this should have been so; perhaps the more devout in

TABLE 7.6.
Marital Fertility in Belfast and Cork

A. *Average Number of Children by Marriage Duration: Belfast*

Duration	Jews	Catholics	Church of Ireland	All others
0–4	1.13	0.50	0.73	0.76
5–9	2.33	2.82	3.24	2.50
10–14	4.11	3.00	2.70	3.97
15–19	6.18	4.00	3.31	5.04
20–29	5.69	6.75	6.57	4.69

B. *Average Number of Children by Marriage Duration: Cork*

Duration	Jews	All others
0–4	0.75 (4)	1.18 (33)
5–9	3.86 (7)	2.00 (23)
10–14	4.83 (6)	3.27 (15)
15–19	6.00 (4)	4.21 (24)
20–29	6.73 (10)	5.94 (31)

C. *Percentage of Childless Couples by Marriage Duration: Belfast*

Duration	Jews	Catholics	Church of Ireland	All others
0–4	0.29 (7)	0.67 (9)	0.60 (15)	0.46 (24)
5–9	0.08 (12)	0.18 (11)	0.12 (17)	0.21 (24)
10–14	0.07 (28)	0.33 (12)	0.30 (10)	0.18 (28)
15–29	0.03 (30)	0.14 (14)	0.09 (34)	0.14 (63)

D. *Percentage of Childless Couples by Marriage Duration: Cork*

Duration	Jews	All others
0–9	0.18 (11)	0.30 (56)
10–19	0.00 (10)	0.26 (39)
20–29	0.10 (10)	0.13 (31)

the Jewish community—who were also least likely to limit births—were concentrated in the more heavily Jewish streets.

The rapid fertility transition of the Jewish population is one of the strongest signs of its acculturation. With acculturation came the attenuation of traditional religious beliefs and the desire to raise better-educated children. It also entailed increasing hopes of living in middle-class suburbia and increasing opportunities for women working outside the home. The acculturation was toward an urban rather than a rural, a Protestant rather than a Catholic, Ireland, however.[29] In Ireland in the 1930s and

TABLE 7.7.
Marital Fertility by Confessional Group in 1946

Religion	Ireland	Dublin
All	1.88	1.60
Catholic	1.92	1.65
Church of Ireland	1.27	1.03
All others	1.33	1.04
Jewish	0.99	—

1940s the marital fertility of Jewish couples was less than half that of Catholic couples and also significantly less than that of Church of Ireland couples (though not of Dublin-based Church of Ireland couples). This statement is based on an admittedly rather crude but serviceable measure of marital fertility, taken from the Irish census of 1946.[30] The outcomes for the Irish Free State and for Dublin in 1946 are given in table 7.7. The census does not report a separate estimate for Dublin Jews, but this hardly matters, since most Jews lived in the capital.

This measure makes no allowance for infant and child mortality, but since (as explained below) Jewish mortality was almost certainly lower than non-Jewish mortality, it probably underestimates the marital fertility gap between Jews and others.[31] The calculations surely imply that the marital fertility of Ireland's Jews was lower than that of any other significant confessional group in the 1940s. Ireland's Jewish community thus shared the enthusiasm with which other immigrant Jewish communities from eastern Europe participated in the fertility transition in the 1920s and 1930s.[32]

INFANT AND CHILD MORTALITY

Funny sight two of them together, their bellies out.
Molly and Mrs. Moisel. Mothers' meeting.
—James Joyce, *Ulysses*[33]

Dublin's chief public health officer in the pre–World War I era, Sir Charles Cameron, and others repeatedly pointed to Dublin's poverty as the main cause of its high mortality. The sharp contrasts in death rates between rich and poor neighborhoods and between professional and unskilled occupational groups, already outlined in chapter 2, support such claims. Research on infant and child mortality in Europe a century ago also stresses the importance of socioeconomic factors.[34] This comes as no surprise, since not only did the rich consume healthier food and live in healthier neighborhoods, they also had more resources to devote to childcare in general. In the first days and weeks of an infant's life, the role of genetic defects and the trauma of birth bulked large, but thereafter socioeconomic factors mattered more. The impact of such factors was even greater during early childhood than in the first year of life. Yet as noted at the outset, the infant and child mortality rates of Jewish communities throughout Europe and North America a century ago were low, and this achievement has been linked less to their socioeconomic status than to cultural factors.

Several scholars have focused on the higher survival prospects of Jewish infants and children in the past. Nearly a century ago, the American author Madison Peters accounted for the low mortality rates of Jewish populations as follows:

> Perhaps the great immunity of the Jew from zymotic diseases and many other kindred evils which afflict the Gentiles may be attributed to cleanliness. . . . The Jew is extremely fond of soap and water under all circumstances; especially has he a fondness for the latter. Whenever he gets an opportunity to take he bath he takes one. During the summer months the public baths are patronized by no people so much as by the Jews. . . . At home if at all possible, the Jew has his bath. No matter how small his apartments, he reserves a space for his ablutions. . . . The orthodox Jew also cuts his finger nails and toe nails once a week, for according to Rabbinical teaching, the dirt beneath contains evil spirits . . . he must also wash his hands before and after each meal, and also rinse his mouth. These habits are very sanitary and doubtless go a long way to ward off sickness.[35]

In 1917 William Guilfoy, New York City's registrar of records, produced the data cross-tabulated in table 7.8. Jewish infants and children are represented by those of mothers born in either Russia or Austro-Hungary. Guilfoy's data are marred somewhat by the high proportion of deaths attributed to "other causes," but they seem to imply that Jews were at lower risk from *all* causes listed. Such was the impact of Jewish immigration that excluding Jewish children from both numerator and denominator in 1915 would increase the infant mortality rate in the city from 98 to 105 per thousand.[36]

In R. M. Woodbury's classic study of infant mortality in eight American cities in the 1920s, the Jewish advantage over other ethnic groups (alas, the Irish are not included separately) is also highlighted. Woodbury emphasized the role of breastfeeding, but his cross-tabulations also allow some scope for other factors. He instanced the lower marital fertility of Jewish women and the higher average income of Jewish families. Noting

TABLE 7.8.
Mortality Rate per Thousand Births of Children under Five Years by Mother's Nationality, Manhattan, 1915

Nationality	All causes	Infectious diseases (%)	T.B. (%)	Acute respiratory diseases (%)	Diarrheal diseases (%)	Accidents	Syphilis	Other (%)
United States	400	38 (9.5)	21 (5.3)	79 (19.8)	80 (20.0)	8	6	168 (42.0)
Ireland	368	57 (15.5)	19 (5.2)	61 (16.6)	72 (19.6)	10	2	147 (39.9)
Germany	323	34 (10.5)	14 (4.3)	51 (15.8)	48 (14.9)	13	3	160 (49.5)
Italy	425	58 (13.6)	16 (3.8)	176 (41.4)	70 (16.5)	7	5	93 (21.9)
Russia	249	30 (12.0)	11 (4.4)	61 (24.4)	30 (12.0)	11	2	104 (41.8)
Austro-Hungary	263	36 (13.7)	11 (4.2)	61 (23.2)	52 (19.8)	6	2	95 (36.1)
All	370	43 (11.6)	17 (4.6)	97 (26.2)	66 (17.8)	8	4	135 (36.5)

Source: Meyer 1921, table IX, citing Guilfoy.

the low mortality of the infants and children of Jewish immigrants to the United States in the early twentieth century, Samuel Preston, Douglas Ewbank, and Mark Hereward put it down to "unmeasured child care practices, having mostly to do with feeding practices and general hygienic standards."[37] Invoking Woodbury's classic study, Preston and his colleagues point in particular to the low incidence of Jewish infant and child deaths from "gastric and intestinal diseases" as evidence that the Jewish diet was particularly "pure." They also speculate on the possible roles of community support systems, the care with which Jewish citizens upheld sanitary laws, the long experience of Jewish communities with urban living, and the likelihood that Jewish mothers were healthier. The point that Jews had become adapted to city life over the years, generating a selection process that increased their resistance to diseases such as tuberculosis, and that the shtetl was a good preparation for life in the slums of New York, Boston, or London, goes back at least a century.[38] The same holds for claims regarding the curative properties of the Jewish diet.[39]

In a pioneering study of Latin American Jews, Judith Elkin attributes their low infant mortality rate to their high urbanization rates, earlier adoption of birth control, low illegitimacy rates, better access to medical practitioners, and to "the existence of Jewish religious observances that are supportive of good health."[40] In the case of Irish Jews, only the last of these factors can have counted for much. The search for explanations continues. Closer to home, English medical historian Lara Marks has also pondered the issue. In her study of Jewish mothers in London's East End a century ago, she put the healthiness of their children down to behavioral factors such as inspections by the Jewish Board of Guardians and the ritual washing of hands before meals. Demographer Alice Goldstein and her coauthors conveniently isolate six factors that might explain the lower Jewish mortality: racial and biological differences; religious practices; personal cleanliness and housekeeping; socioeconomic status; family and childcare practices; and better access to scientific care.[41] The first of these may be dismissed: there is no evidence that race per se influenced mortality.[42] And the last is less compelling when one is comparing Jews and non-Jews living in the same or adjoining neighborhoods (as we shall be doing here), since in that case the same medical practitioners, chemists, dispensaries, and hospitals were available to all—as long as one was prepared to pay. However, if Jewish culture valued medicine more than non-Jewish cultures did, then Jewish children may have had better access to medical facilities for cultural rather than locational reasons. Given the marked gradient in infant and child mortality rates in Dublin, socioeconomic status presumably mattered, although its impact within the South Circular Road neighborhood remains to be seen. The other factors noted by Goldstein and her colleagues are tied up with culture.

A century ago a significant share of the high infant mortality in urban areas was due to deaths from diarrhea/dysentery during the summer months (July, August, and September). Was this the key to the Jewish mortality advantage? If so, this should be reflected in the different seasonality patterns of Jewish and non-Jewish infant mortality. The relevant Irish data are lacking, but data on births and infant deaths for London in the 1900s should have a bearing on the issue. Comparing London as a whole with three East End registration subdistricts—Spitalfields, Goodman's Fields (both of which were heavily Jewish at the time), and Bethnal Green (which was not)—we find the following. The infant mortality rate in London (102.8 per thousand) was higher than in either Spitalfields (85.4 per thousand) or Goodman's Fields (95.0 per thousand), but lower than in Bethnal Green (132.8 per thousand). However, all four had roughly similar mortality peaks in the third quarter of the year.[43] In London as a whole 29.3 percent of all infant deaths occurred in July–September. In Spitalfields the percentage was 32.1, in Goodman's Fields it was 30.2, and in Bethnal Green 27.3. Had diarrhea/dysentery been mainly responsible for the higher mortality of non-Jewish infants, the percentages in London and Bethnal Green would have been significantly higher than in the Jewish areas of Spitalfields and Goodman's Fields. The finding that they were not suggests that a lower incidence of diarrhea was just one of a range of factors responsible for lower Jewish mortality in the 1900s.[44]

Mortality in Jewish Ireland

Table 7.9 compares the marital fertility and infant/child mortality levels of Dublin Jews and others. Note first how infant and child mortality in the Dublin Registration Area (or greater Dublin, including the suburban townships) exceeded that in Ireland as a whole by a considerable margin. Within Dublin, the life chances of Catholic infants and children were presumably considerably worse. In the South Circular Road area that supplied my database, the Jewish advantage is clear. Catholics lagged behind both Jews and other non-Catholics. For example, table 7.9 shows that while 89.8 percent of the children born to Jewish couples in our database who had married 15–19 years earlier were still alive in 1911, the percentages for Catholics and all others in the same neighborhood were 79.6 and 84.9 percent, respectively. In greater Dublin the percentage was 76.1 percent, and in the mainly middle-class suburban township of Pembroke it was 79.9 percent. Note, too, the implication that the mortality rates of children born of recent marriages (less than ten years) in greater Dublin were twice those of Jewish children. Moreover, Jewish fertility was high, and completed family size higher than for either of the other groups. This

TABLE 7.9.
Marriage Duration, Fertility, and Mortality in Ireland and Dublin before 1911

	Ireland		Greater Dublin		Pembroke	
Duration	Avg. number children born	Percent dead	Avg. number children born	Percent dead	Avg. number children born	Percent dead
0–4	0.98	8.4	0.95	10.9	0.93	8.2
5–9	2.81	11.2	2.62	16.8	2.47	11.2
10–14	4.17	14.0	3.93	20.8	3.79	16.6
15–19	5.20	16.0	4.91	23.9	4.91	20.1
20–24	5.87	17.9	5.61	27.3	5.59	21.2
25–34	6.57	20.3	6.24	30.4	7.26	25.1
	SCR Catholics		SCR Jews		SCR "All Others"	
Duration	Avg. number children born	Percent dead	Avg. number children born	Percent dead	Avg. number children born	Percent dead
0–4	1.07 (117)	15.1	1.12 (42)	0.0	0.64 (64)	10.0
5–9	2.52 (112)	15.6	3.17 (65)	6.3	2.31 (49)	16.8
10–14	3.51 (91)	20.4	4.68 (60)	9.6	2.28 (40)	19.2
15–19	5.06 (70)	20.4	5.98 (41)	10.2	3.56 (39)	15.1
20–24	6.26 (47)	24.8	6.76 (38)	13.2	4.13 (23)	10.5
25–34	5.83 (77)	27.4	6.41 (49)	19.4	5.47 (55)	21.9

Note: In the case of South Circular Road couples, the number of couples is given in parentheses.

was at least partly a product of early age at marriage, since Jewish age-specific fertility was highest at most durations and age groups. Note, too, the implication that the better survival chances of Jewish infants and children were not the product of lower fertility.

In the South Circular Road area all 42 infants born to Jewish mothers married for four years or less on census night in 1911 were still alive. This is indeed an impressive outcome: in the same area 15.1 percent of Catholic infants and 10 percent of all other infants born to mothers married for four years or less had died. The gaps for marriages of 5–9 years duration are proportionately narrower, but still striking: only 6.3 percent of Jewish infants and children had died, as against 15.6 percent of Catholic and 16.8 percent of all others. The record of this artisanal, lower-middle-class area was little better than that of the city as a whole in this respect.

Smaller Belfast and Cork databases, constructed along the same lines as that for Dublin, broadly replicate the patterns found in Dublin. The Belfast database contains 88 Jewish households (containing 532 people) and 339 non-Jewish households. All households in the Belfast database lived on the same clusters of streets, mainly located north of the Carlisle

TABLE 7.10.
Child Survival Prospects in Belfast and Cork

A. Proportion of Children Alive by Marriage Duration: Belfast

Duration	Jews	Catholics	C. of I.	All others
0–4	1.00	1.00	0.91	1.00
5–9	0.96	0.84	0.85	0.90
10–14	0.97	0.81	0.96	0.87
15–19	0.96	0.75	0.84	0.86

B. Percentage of Children Alive by Marriage Duration: Cork

Duration	Jews	All others
0–4	100.0	92.3
5–9	85.2	91.3
10–19	86.8	78.0
20–29	84.6	77.7

Circus and by the Cliftonville and Antrim Roads. This was a largely Protestant part of the city. Twenty-one percent of couples in the database were Jewish, 23 percent were members of the Church of Ireland, 43 percent belonged to other non-Catholic (mainly Presbyterian) faiths, while the remaining 13 percent were Roman Catholic. The housing stock in this area was relatively new in 1911 and quite similar to that found in Dublin's Little Jerusalem.

Panel A in table 7.10 reports the proportions surviving at different durations in Belfast. Survival prospects in the Jewish streets of Belfast were better than in Little Jerusalem, but otherwise the implications for infant and child mortality mirror those found for Dublin. Jewish children in their teens, in particular, seem to have been at less risk than those of any other group. The Cork database consists of 39 Jewish households (composed of about 200 Jews and some servants) and 135 non-Jewish households living in the same neighborhood in the south of the city. Of the latter, 117 were Catholic, and 6 had mixed marriages. In Cork, too, the survival chances of Jewish infants and children were higher than those of non-Jews. This may be seen from cross-tabulating the percentages surviving by duration of marriage (see panel B).

Nevertheless, the gap between Irish Jews and non-Jews is perhaps not so striking when compared to rates recorded elsewhere around the same time. In Frankfurt-am-Main in the 1890s and 1900s, the infant mortality rate of Jews was 73 per thousand live births and that of the general population 155 per thousand live births; in Amsterdam in 1900–1913 the rates were 77 per thousand for Jews and 102 per thousand for non-Jews; in

Montreal in 1931 the rates were 43 per thousand for Jews and 113 per thousand for the general population. The evidence for mortality in early childhood suggests comparable gaps. Thus in Montreal in 1931 the mortality rates for children aged 0–4 years were 13.6 percent for Jews and 36.7 percent for the general population; in New York six years earlier the rates were 14.7 and 24.5 percent; in Berlin in the mid-1920s, 10.3 and 25.5 percent. In Amsterdam the mortality rates of children aged 1–4 years in the 1900s were 11.2 percent for Jews and 18.2 percent for the general population. For first-generation urban Irish immigrants in the United States c. 1900 the probability of dying before age five was 24.6 percent; for first-generation urban east European (and so disproportionately Jewish) immigrants it was 20.6 percent.[45]

These data compare non-Jewish mortality in cities as a whole with that of its Jewish community. Obviously, such comparisons ignore likely gaps due to location and socioeconomic status. Our strategy of comparing Dublin's Jews with other residents of Little Jerusalem is a way of controlling for environmental factors: the air breathed and the water consumed by everybody in the neighborhoods was presumably very similar. As table 7.9 indicates, the focus on different groups living in the same area reduces the Jewish mortality advantage, but there is still a considerable gap to account for. The technical appendix summarizes an attempt to account for this gap using a range of econometric models. The impact of most variables is broadly as expected. Thus mortality was negatively correlated with housing quality and the number of domestic servants, while having a professional occupation, being a policeman or an artisan, or being engaged in trade also reduced the risk of death. Similarly, female illiteracy and early marriage increased the risk, while the infants and children of women born in Dublin or in Great Britain were at less risk. Most striking of all, perhaps, is the big coefficient on being Jewish. Being the infant or child of Jewish parents reduced the mortality risk significantly.

An interesting feature of the results is the implication that, controlling for other factors, Catholic mortality was lower on "Jewish" streets. This is not easily explained. That Catholics learned habits of hygiene and healthy eating from their Jewish neighbors seems unlikely. Perhaps there was a lower incidence of infectious disease on heavily Jewish streets. Perhaps, too, there was an element of selection bias at play here: some Catholics may have chosen to live on or to remain living on such streets because they were culturally closer to their Jewish neighbors to begin with. But it is less obvious how precisely that should have been so.

The birth and burial records of the small "pre-Litvak" Dublin Jewish community suggest that it, too, was characterized by low infant and child mortality. Given the changing size and high mobility of this community, the data must be considered indicative rather than conclusive. The register recorded 299 births between 1838 and 1879. Among the deaths recorded in these years were five of children aged less than three months, seventeen of children aged between three months and a year, and fourteen of children aged between one and five years.[46] With one exception, all these deaths were of children also included in the birth register. The deaths of children and infants who left the country immediately or soon after birth are excluded. Presumably these were a small fraction of the total. The implied infant mortality rate was therefore almost certainly under 100 per thousand, and the mortality rate of children aged 1.0–4.9 years considerably less than that. Though the lack of reliable civil registration data for this period rules out a formal comparison with rates in Dublin as a whole, the gap between Jewish and non-Jewish rates can only have been substantial, since the rates reported in table 7.3 were almost certainly exceeded in earlier decades. Data on Jewish infant mortality elsewhere in western Europe before 1900 are scarce, but a rough guess at Ireland's rate compares favorably with, for example, Westphalia's (96 per thousand in 1819–70), Glasgow's (about 90 per thousand c. 1880–1900), Berlin's (about 170 per thousand in 1816–66), and Florence's (139 per thousand in 1818–47).[47]

Finally, evidence from gravestone inscriptions in the Jewish cemetery at Dublin's Dolphin's Barn offers a hint at the life expectancy of Irish Jews born about a century ago. The data refer to burials in the cemetery between its opening in the autumn of 1898 and 2004. In order to minimize bias, I focus only on those born between late 1898 and the end 1903: 121 males and 118 females.[48] One apparent shortcoming of the data should be noted: very few of those dying in infancy or early childhood are commemorated in Dolphin's Barn. However, it may be assumed that most others in the Jewish community are commemorated, in imitation of Rachel whose husband Jacob "set a pillar upon her grave." The data suggest that those who survived infancy and early childhood were long-lived: the average age at death of recorded males in this cohort was 62.4 years and that of females 70.7 years. Nineteen percent of the males and 42.3 percent of the females reached the age of 80 or above.[49] Figure 7.1, which describes the proportion of deaths by age group for males (m%) and females (f%), shows that females were more likely to die in their eighties than in any other decade. The modal decade for male deaths was 60–69 years. This wide gender gap is a sign of demographic modernity: in Ireland a century ago, there was no such gap favoring women. In Ireland as a whole, expectation of life at birth (e_0) was about fifty years for both males and females in 1900–1902, which would be consistent with an expectation of about sixty years at age ten ($e_{10} = 60$). These averages reflect what was then a mainly rural Ireland. In greater Dublin, calculations already reported in chapter 2[50] suggested expectations of life in the

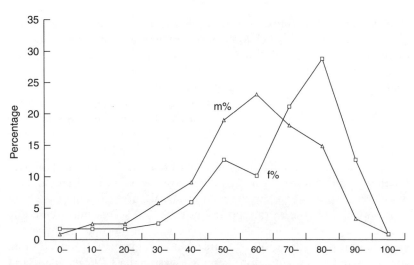

Figure 7.1. Ages at death of Dublin Jews born 1899–1903.

1900s ranging from 32.3 years for the "general service class" (mainly unskilled and casual workers and workhouse inmates) to 42.1 years for the "middle class" and 60.3 years for the "professional and independent class." Such numbers accentuate the Jewish advantage.[51]

Culture Mattered

The Jewish population of early twentieth-century Dublin was concentrated in a particular part of the city. Though the community was separated from its neighbors by history, religion, and language, at the same time it was much less a strictly segregated community than, say, London's East End or New York's Lower East Side. The analysis reported here shows that, nonetheless, its demographic characteristics were quite distinct from those of Dublin at large and those of its south city non-Jewish neighbors. The most striking difference is that the infants and children of Dublin's Jews were much more likely to survive than non-Jewish children growing up in the same neighborhood. The higher socioeconomic status of their parents only partly explains their better survival prospects.

Nor had differential fertility much to do with it. This may seem surprising, given that throughout Europe Jewish couples were in the vanguard of the marital fertility transition, deciding early on to invest their parental resources in the "quality" rather than the "quantity" of children. Yet the fertility of our first generation of Jewish immigrant women, nearly all of them born in Lithuania, was largely unaffected by the transition. Age-specific Jewish marital fertility was higher than that of either Catholics or other Christians in the same neighborhood. And Jewish couples were less likely than others to have another child in order to replace any infants or children who died. Their high fertility was undoubtedly one part of their culture or belief system that this first generation of Ireland's Jewish immigrants had not left behind in Lithuania. At the same time there is a hint in the data that the age at which Jewish women "stopped" having children was lower. In the following generation, as the occupational status and aspirations of the Jewish community shifted, so did their marital fertility.

The dramatic contrast between the situation in 1911 and that in 1946 suggests that Irish Jews replicated a pattern described by Barry A. Kosmin for Great Britain. There over four-fifths of Jewish couples marrying in the 1920s relied on artificial methods to control births. "The important point here," notes Kosmin, "is that the majority of these Jewish women were the daughters of women from a natural fertility regime." Kosmin mentions two other features of Jewish demography that survived this remarkable transition in both Britain and Ireland: a low illegitimacy rate, and a low percentage of childless couples.[52] In their rapid transition to low marital fertility Irish Jews had much more in common with their English coreligionists than with their non-Jewish neighbors.

Technical Appendix: Accounting for the Variation in Fertility and Infant/Child Mortality

ECONOMETRIC estimation corroborates the impressions gained from cross-tabulations in tables 7.6–7.9. Here we include the bulk of the occupations listed into one of five groups: unskilled, artisan, commercial, professional, and police. Table 7A.1 summarizes the results of estimating four versions on a multivariate model of fertility variation. The dependent variable is *chborn*, a non-negative count variable. All regressions estimate a zero-inflated negative binomial (ZINB) maximum likelihood distribution of *chborn* on a range of independent variables. The choice of ZINB reflects the possibility that the number of couples with zero births include those who choose that level of *chborn*, and those have no children because they cannot have any. The large positive values of the Vuong test statistic in all versions of the model (reported in table 7A.1) suggest that ZINB is the appropriate choice.

The second and third regressions attempt to take some account of the endogeneity of infant and child mortality. This refers to the likelihood that some couples will seek to replace a child who dies. Indeed, this replacement effect is a measure of the prevalence of family planning. The available data make taking account of this very difficult.[53] In these regressions *chdead* was first regressed against the ages of marriage of the husband and wife (*aamw, aamh*), *cmr* (as defined above), and the number of domestics (*doms*), and the expected value of the dependent variable, *xb*, then interacted with religion dummies in the second stage.[54] The outcome is reported in the second and third set of results in table 7A.1. In these, our preferred specifications, being Jewish was associated with an extra child being born (the coefficients on *jewish* being 1.27 and 1.12). The father having a professional occupation reduced the number of children born by about 0.4, while being a policeman increased it by over 0.5 and being an artisan also increased it by 0.43. The coefficient on *rooms* also had the right sign. Economic considerations therefore mattered. A father's being a Dubliner increased fertility; fertility was positively correlated with housing quality (measured by the number of rooms) and negatively correlated with mothers being aged over thirty at marriage (*othirty*) and the

TABLE 7A.1.
Accounting for the Variation in Fertility: Marginal Effects

	[1]		[2]		[3]		[4]	
Estimation method	ZINB		ZINB		ZINB		ZINB	
Number of obs	1180		1076		1079		1079	
LR chi2(16)	882.42		703.73		705.13		764.93	
Prob > chi2	0.0000		0.0000		0.0000		0.0000	
Log likelihood	−2395.8		−2160.2		−2166.6		−2136.7	
variable	*dy/dx*	*z*	*dy/dx*	*z*	*dy/dx*	*z*	*dy/dx*	*z*
dur	.310	19.43	.474	18.31	.478	18.63	.931	14.59
dur2	−.005	−14.57	−.010	−14.05	−.010	−14.07	−.042	−10.04
dur3							.001	7.83
jewish*	1.17	3.43	1.221	2.90	1.386	3.30	1.025	2.58
cath*	.151	0.27	.252	0.79	.351	1.11	.238	0.77
prot*	−.040	−0.12	−.300	−0.83	−.189	−0.52	−.249	−0.72
cdjew	.366	7.20						
cdcath	.516	12.71						
cdprot	.452	7.26						
xbjew			.203	0.67	.128	0.43	.437	1.50
xbcath			.495	2.90	.458	2.71	.618	3.85
xbprot			.623	2.41	.586	2.27	.748	3.04
prof*	−.301	−1.54	−.329	−1.16	−.246	−0.91	−.283	−1.10
police*	.493	1.62	.381	1.21	.399	1.26	.370	1.22
unskilled*	.191	0.94	.160	0.77	.102	0.51	.125	0.67
artisan*	.404	2.59	.418	2.95	.391	2.82	.298	2.27
hdub*	.237	1.88	.388	2.59	.373	2.49	.235	1.54
wdub*	.152	0.56					.052	0.36
rooms	.066	2.34	.034	1.18				
jethos	.774	2.82	.371	1.27	.338	1.16	.300	1.09
hgb*							−.051	−0.22
wgb*							−.173	−0.84
Inflate								
agediff	−.010	−2.33	−.010	−2.27	−.010	−2.27	−.009	−2.26
othirty	−.015	−7.60	−.015	−7.79	−.015	−7.77	−.015	−7.95
Vuong Test (ZINB vs. NB)	5.39		5.84		5.86		6.05	

* dy/dx is for discrete change of dummy variable from 0 to 1.
Variables: *agediff* = age difference between husband and wife; *othirty* = age of wife if 30+, zero otherwise; *cdjew* = chdead*jew, *cdcath* = cdead*cath, *cdprot* = cdead*prot; *dur2* = duration squared.
Note: [2], [3] and [4] include only marriages of years duration.

TABLE 7A.2.
Mean Values of Variables

variable	n = 1180	n = 1076
dur	15.82	13.44
dur2	389.7	266.3
jewish*	.2788	.2732
cath*	.4720	.4768
prot*	.1847	.1831
cdjew	.1839	
cdcath	.4314	
cdprot	.1398	
xbjew		.2031
xbcath		.2946
xbprot		.1097
prof*	.0517	.0539
police*	.0390	.0409
unskilled*		.1372
artisan*	.2593	.2584
hdub*	.3466	.3513
wdub*	.3907	.3996
rooms	4.872	4.869
jethos	.2246	.2772
agediff	3.782	3.795
othirty	4.901	5.158

age difference between husband and wife (*agediff*). Note too how in the third specification the "Jewishness" of a street increased Jewish fertility but reduced that of Catholics. It is not clear how this result should be interpreted. However, the most interesting result concerns the coefficients on the interaction variables *xbjew, xbcath,* and *xbprot.* These are intended to capture how the replacement effect varied by religion. Both specifications indicate that the replacement effect was much stronger for both Catholics and members of the Church of Ireland in the South Circular Road neighborhood than for Jews. Note, too, how the effect is much weaker for Jews and Catholics when *chdead* is endogenized. Since the strength of the replacement effect is a measure of family planning, this outcome suggests that along the South Circular Road other Christian couples were further along the fertility transition in the 1900s than Catholic and, especially, Jewish couples.

Table 7A.3 reports the results of an analysis of the variation in infant and child mortality. Here, as earlier, our strategy is to compare Dublin's Jews with other residents of Little Jerusalem as a way of controlling for environmental factors. In modeling infant and child mortality, the number of children dead in a household (*cdead*) or the proportion of children dead (*pdead*) are probably the most obvious candidates for the dependent variable. One of the results reported in table 7A.3 uses *pdead*. The other two rely instead on the mortality index devised by Michael Haines and Samuel Preston[55] for their classic study of infant and child mortality in the United States a century ago. It is defined as the ratio of actual child deaths (as given in the census for all mothers in the database) to expected deaths. Expected deaths are obtained by multiplying the number of children born to a mother by an expected child mortality level for the relevant marriage duration group (0–4, 5–9, 10–14, 15–19, 20–24, 25–29, and 30–34 years). The use of marriage duration categories controls for the number of years children have been exposed to the risk of dying. Here the expected averages are based on the Coale-Demeny Model Life Table Level 13.5, which is consistent with $e_0 = 49.8$ years. This, close to the average for Ireland as a whole at the time, seems reasonable for the South Circular Road area. The choice of level is not crucial, however, since the index values are proportional. The index (dubbed CMI for child mortality index in table 7A.3) is normalized at a value of one.

Two variables are included as measures of exogenous pressures at the stage when infants and children were most at risk. The first is the gross emigration rate during the first four years of marriage (*emr*), which rose from 10 per thousand in 1876–80 (for marriages of 30–34 years duration) to 16.9 per thousand in 1881–85, and fell thereafter, reaching 7.2 per thousand in 1906–10 (for marriages of 0–4 years duration). Our second background covariate is the child mortality rate in greater Dublin during the first four years of marriage (*cmr*); this is included to capture the shifting incidence of risks such as the prevalence of infectious diseases. This measure also fell over time, but with a blip in 1896–1900. In the estimation we also include the interaction term, *rcjethos*, which measures the impact of living on a more Jewish street on Catholic mortality.[56]

The outcome of our estimation is given in table 7A.3. Including economic variables reduces the Jewish mortality advantage, but there is still a considerable gap to account for. The coefficients measure marginal effects. Thus, for example, being a policeman reduced the CMI mortality index by one-third, as did the wife being a Dubliner. The signs on most of the coefficients are as expected. More rooms and more domestic servants[57] meant less mortality; being a professional, a policeman, an artisan, or

TABLE 7A.3.
Accounting for the Variation in Mortality: Marginal Effects

	[1]	[2]	[3]	
Depvar	CMI	CMI	PDEAD	
Estimation	OLS	Tobit	Tobit	
F (18, 872)	4.78			
Pseudo R^2			0.1726	
LR chsq (17/18)	139.1	227.0		
N	891	891	985	
variable	*dy/dx*	*dy/dx*	*dy/dx*	*mean value (***)*
rooms	−.089**	−.243**	−.030**	4.94
doms	−.020	−.603	−.034	.192
jewish*	−.570**	−2.40**	−.232**	.309
cath*	.260	1.55**	.058	.461
rcjethos	−1.03	−4.29**	−.354**	.077
prof*	−.085	−2.37	−.049	.046
police*	−.344	−.574	−.092	.040
comm*	−.320**	−1.52**	−.087**	.250
artisan*	−.280**	−.829**	−.085**	.273
wlit	−.051	−.663	−.004	1.71
aamw	−.053	−.680	−.010	23.2
aamw2	.001	.011	.000	558.
hdub*	.178	.190	.032	.346
wdub*	−.373**	−.692	−.096**	.385
wgb*	−.364**	−.680	−.093	.099
cmr	.004	.076**		142.
emr	.007	.004		10.2
chborn			.042**	4.74
dur			.008**	16.9

* dy/dx is for discrete change of dummy variable from 0 to 1
** significant at 1 percent; ^ significant at 5 percent
*** mean values for n = 985; those for n = 891 similar

Variables: rooms = number of rooms; hdub = husband Dublin born; wdub = wife Dublin born; wgb = wife British born; aamw = wife's age at marriage; aamw2 = wife's age at marriage squared; hlit = husband's literacy (see text); wlit = wife's literacy; jethos = jewish ethos (see text); rcjethos = cath*jethos; prof = professional; comm = commercial; mixed = rc-prot marriage engaged in trade also reduced the risk of death. Our background variables *emr* and *cmr* have the expected signs, but pack very little punch. Being the infant or child of Jewish parents, as opposed to one of the control group of mixed or nonconformist families, reduced the mortality risk by 76 percent. Catholics were no different than the control group, while Church of Ireland households were in an intermediate position, though closer to the Catholic than the Jewish average.

Chapter 8

CULTURE, FAMILY, HEALTH

And right behind the workshop, shining.
The kitchen!
The kitchen shining as with the Shekinah, shining
 with my mother,
Golden Sabbath-candlelight of my home . . .
 my holy mother
                    —*Hyman Edelstein*[1]

It was in the food that I could see the difference
between Jews and Catholics. I could see it
in the attitude to food.
                    —*June Levine*

The goyim are really different. Their mothers don't
shout at their children as much as Jewish mothers
do, and I don't think they care so much if their kids
get good marks or bad ones. I mean, they care,
but not as much as our mothers.
                    —Journey to the Dawn

TRADITIONALLY, economists have been more skeptical of cultural approaches to human behavior than other social scientists. The economists' assumption that human beings are endowed with stable, exogenous preferences leaves little room for differences or changes in tastes when accounting for relative economic performance, at either the macro- or microlevel. Adam Smith believed that tastes across individual consumers were broadly similar. Other economists insist that while some individuals may be born with more acute or less sophisticated tastes than others, the spread of tastes across different communities is more or less the same. Either way, the main point is that tastes are "given." In the economic sphere, prices and incomes account for variations in consumption: to invoke differences in culture or taste is a lazy substitute for an exhaustive search for possible economic interpretations.

In the late 1960s and the 1970s a new wave of young economic historians took the message to heart and proposed economic explanations for a range of historical outcomes previously attributed to culture. Most famously, perhaps, they held that economic rather than cultural or sociological factors were responsible for the alleged "failure" of the British economy in the late Victorian era. Further research in this vein has restored the reputations of economic agents ranging from the habitants of Quebec to the slave owners of the U.S. South.[2] Other economic historians, equally well versed in economics, have long been more sympathetic to a tradition that allows culture a role. Here I am thinking of culture as defined by economic historian Peter Temin: "the distinctive attitudes and actions that differentiate groups of people." Studies that incorporate culture in this sense have addressed topics ranging from the "work psychologies" of fifteenth-century Mendip miners and nineteenth-century textile mill workers to the contrasting medieval Muslim and Christian attitudes toward science and nature and the Chinese Qing dynasty's rejection of Western technology.[3] More recently, the increasing attention devoted to institutions and to "irrational," "herd," and "altruistic" behavior in economics and the focus on social capital in sociology and political science all argue for paying more attention to culture.

Over a century ago political arithmetician Sir William Petty declared that "Trade [was] not fixt to any Species of Religion as such; but rather . . . to the Hetrodox part of the whole." Some of his examples—Jews and Christians in the Ottoman Empire, Jews and "Non-Papist Merchant-Strangers" in Venice—were minorities, but for Petty not belonging to the state religion was more important than minority status per se. Petty offered no convincing reason for this pattern. Others since have produced economic rationales for certain features of the economic behavior of Jews and other ethnic minorities, deeming them to be defenses by such communities against discrimination or persecution. For instance, the propensity of middleman minorities to invest in (inalienable and mobile) human capital and to maintain "a portable or easily liquidated livelihood"[4] has been seen as a way of ensuring against predatory exploitation by the host population, while the overrepresentation of Jews in moneylending has been linked to their exclusion from other professions in medieval and early modern Europe.

Economists Werner Sombart (in the nineteenth century) and Simon Kuznets (in the twentieth century) have argued that although the propensity of Jewish communities to cluster in urban ghettos may have had noneconomic origins, it yielded economic benefits. In a similar vein, Maristella Botticini and Zvi Eckstein have recently pointed to the requirement that Jewish males be literate in order to study Judaism's sacred texts, enforced by rabbinical authority since early in the Christian era, had as its by-product a species of human capital that steered them toward urban occupations, in particular commerce and moneylending.[5]

The very fact of being a minority in some host community, hostile or otherwise, can also have economic pluses. The distinctive cultural values of ethnic minority communities such as Jews, Parsees, or expatriate Japanese, Chinese, and Mauritanians and their need to maintain group identity are associated with resource pooling and mutual trust, and the existence of strong sanctions against those who freeload or abuse the system.[6] The minority is rather like an extended family. A recent contribution to this literature by economists Samuel Bowles and Herbert Gintis formalizes the costs and benefits of the combination of cooperation and exclusion, which they dub "parochialism." Cultural affinity minimizes conflict and opportunistic behavior within an ethnic or religious group, and the benefits gained from the informal enforceability of contracts within the group outweigh the costs of interacting less with outsiders. Clearly, though, there is a limit to the optimal size of such a group.[7] Moreover, the advantages associated with kinship might be greater in undeveloped economies, where access to credit is more limited, information of all kinds costlier, and contracts more costly to enforce; indeed, in advanced economies ties that bind, like the family firm, may be counterproductive. The mutual antipathy between majority and minority may also lead the latter to engage in certain middleman activities such as moneylending that are frowned on by the majority (or even by both parties). In such cases, antipathy toward the "other" reduces the psychic costs of an unpleasant occupation.

Students of Jewish history often point to features intrinsic to Jewish culture in accounting for Jewish economic success and, in particular, the upward mobility of immigrant east European Jewish communities. These include "bourgeois" virtues such as sobriety, a desire to succeed, a dislike of violence, an emphasis on education and learning, and high self-esteem. In a classic study, sociologist Stephen Steinberg has criticized what he deems to be this overemphasis on culture, arguing that U.S. ethnic historians have exaggerated and romanticized its role. Such accounts, by treating culture as God-given or exogenous, neglect how the economic status of U.S. immigrants in their land of origin influenced their relative success in urban industrial society. In this sense, Steinberg argues, the Jews were fortunate. Despite the disabilities facing them in tsarist Russia, the craft and trading skills of Jewish immigrants and their high literacy levels meant that they were well placed to climb the socioeconomic ladder in the United States quickly. The attitudes and skills of, for example, impoverished *contadini* from the Italian *mezzogiorno*, or black ex-sharecroppers from the rural U.S. South were less suited to social structures in industrialized New England than those of east European Jews or northern Italian industrial workers. Black (and, though at an earlier stage and to a lesser extent, Irish) attitudes toward schooling were also influenced by discrimination in the job market. For Steinberg class is everything: "cultural factors have little independent effect on educational outcomes." Against Steinberg, critics like Joel Perlmann hold that regardless of the origins of such cultural attributes, the main point is that they mattered.[8]

Economic interpretations can be pushed only so far: most of those who have studied the field would concede that there remains an irreducible cultural component to the enduring specifics of Jewry and Judaism. The religious training undergone by most Orthodox Jewish boys went much further than learning Hebrew and knowing passages of the scriptures by rote. Like Calvinism, it entailed literacy and abstract reasoning, skills that might well translate into creativity and the ability to think laterally in a secular environment. Even in less advanced economies, literacy is useful in business and particularly so, perhaps, in the service sector. Jewish religious morality is less ascetic than certain versions of Christianity, but it encourages traits that engender success in business: good decision-making skills and a willingness to work hard. Moreover, the Jewish yearning for a vicarious afterlife by marrying within the community may help explain why Jews discount the future less and are more eager to invest in their children's educations.[9] When economic historian W. D. Rubinstein argues persuasively for a distinctive economic role for minorities (like the Jews) with a high degree of marginality and high self-esteem, he is pointing to aspects of Jewish culture that are difficult to separate from religious belief.[10]

The economic historian of Jewry has all the more reason to invoke culture in accounting for the fortunes of his subjects. The striking differences in the past between Jew and non-Jew in language, dress code, diet, alcohol consumption, occupational profile, literacy and educational levels, and core ethical beliefs are obvious. What the *Jewish Chronicle* described almost a century ago as "the natural ability of the Jew to rise in the social scale, and his determined ambition"[11] are also cultural constructs. Culture, however, is not a constant. The tensions between western and eastern Jewry a century ago in both England and Ireland about what constituted ethical business behavior and respectable business pursuits are an obvious case in point.

Much in the literature about the economic history of minorities fits Ireland's Litvaks very well. Ireland's Jewish immigrants brought their own beliefs and culture with them. Settlement and marriage patterns were influenced by religion, and before long Little Jerusalem had its rabbis and its shuls, its burial society, its ritual slaughterers or *shochtim*, and its welfare and educational infrastructure. To what extent did the immigrants' culture influence their demography and their health? Did their culture constrain the choice of career, or did it adapt to Irish conditions?

LITVAK CULTURE

The immigrant Litvaks were very Orthodox. We have already seen how long after the establishment of the grand Adelaide Road synagogue in 1892 many of the faithful continued to support their own small shuls and minyans.[12] Jacob Greenberg, who died in 1910, gave Talmudic expositions at Saint Kevin's Parade *hevra* every evening, and presumably it was the same story in other *hevroth*. All economic activity ceased at sundown on Friday. Many refused to handle money on the Sabbath, as stipulated in the Talmud, and *shabbas goyim* from the neighborhood, who lit and stoked fires and boiled water in Jewish homes, were left their few pence under the tablecloth or else collected it later.

There was religious controversy, too, and not only between "old" and "new" Jews, although divisions in Dublin never matched those besetting its sister communities in Cork and Limerick in their early years. In Limerick in 1889 the police were notified when "the Chazan was knocked down, and the book used for the service was carried off."[13] As already noted in chapter 5, Cork Jews were reputed for orthodoxy, and many of the early leaders of Dublin's Litvak community were products of the city by the Lee. In Dublin it was "considered . . . a sin to tear paper on Sabbath,"[14] and this applied to toilet paper, too. The newcomers were probably more observant than the "English" of Mary's Abbey and Adelaide Road. In the 1900s the Adelaide Road synagogue had difficulty in operating its minyan room, and year after year its annual report referred to the lack of decorum in the synagogue during the long services. In 1912 a shul subcommittee demanded that the cantor "be asked to avoid too much singing and that the work of the Readers be solemn and impressive"; in February 1914 the Reverend Gudansky was asked to keep his monthly sermons to under fifteen minutes.[15] June Levine remembers that in Greenville Hall "everybody talked because the service was very long. It wasn't like a church. The men would talk and clap until the rabbi got irritated; he would then look up at the gallery and bid them be 'Quiet.' He wouldn't disrespect the men by telling them to shut up."[16]

Clearly, there were gradations of *frum*-ness. Members of the second generation were less devout than their parents. "The back-to-the-wall boys [in] the proletarian pew" would pencil in or chisel out all manner of irreverent slogans on the book rests, and "the callow Bar Mitzvah youth . . . following page by page of the spidery text," would soon "hear between the lines all those jests and half-hints about commerce; conversation whispered between the *alioth* . . . a vocabulary based on mercenary words like *fùnt* and *vìfill* and *sechàyrah* and *schmàttes* and *ferlòren*."[17] In the 1920s and 1930s many Portobello Jews attended the Lennox Street shul, "which was rife with discussion about such spiritual matters as the horse races at Phoenix Park—especially among the gurriers in the back rows who would be warned by the *shamas* to be quiet ('You veldt henimels of de strits') and [who] were quite likely to respond by enquiring whether the official might enjoy 'a good belt on the snot.' "[18] Nevertheless in those decades most Irish Jews observed the dietary laws and attended shul weekly.

A story told by an elderly non-Jewish native of Little Jerusalem is worth relating here. My informant described encountering a Jewish teenager "going down Stamer Street one Saturday afternoon and she saw a sixpence on the ground but there was an hour to go before sunset so she put her foot on the sixpence and waited for an hour before she picked it up." She was eighteen at the time. "*I* would have done that," added my informant, "but *she* was rich." He even gave me the girl's name. However, for all the detail, the story seems to be an urban legend. A Jewish friend supplied the following version of the same story, which was doing the rounds in Dublin when he was a child, and which, indeed, circulated widely: "On a Saturday A meets B who is standing still in the street and asks him what he is doing. B does not reply, whereupon A hits B on the head. B sees three stars. As seeing three stars was accepted as a sign of nightfall B exclaimed that it was 'Out Shabbes' (or something similar), lifted his foot, and picked up the sixpence."[19] Although the story serves as a reminder of the pitfalls of oral history, both versions attest to the orthodoxy of the community.

A more poignant indication of religiosity concerns Bob Bloom, a young Dublin-born Litvak prospecting for gold in the Klondike at the beginning of the last century. The Klondike "at that time was as far removed from civilization as one could get." At the approach of Passover a letter from Bloom's father arrived, with the advice that "if only he took some flour and water and made some dough even if it be as thick as thick could be, it would be considered alright for Passach, since it was no trick to be a Jew in Vilna, but making the effort in the far flung frontier of the frozen North was sufficient evidence to show his good intentions."[20]

That there was a link between Mosaic Law and the healthiness of Jewish populations has been recognized for centuries. The religious orthodoxy of the Litvak immigrants probably entailed higher standards of personal hygiene and cleanliness than was the norm in Dublin a century or so ago.[21] Laundresses and charwomen were employed to wash and iron and, as we have seen, Jewish households were much more likely to include domestic servants than those of their non-Jewish neighbors. This could have been a factor in curbing infectious diseases. Jewish dietary laws emphasized clean food, clean cooking utensils, and personal cleanliness. Hands were routinely and ritually washed before and after meals and after visits to the toilet. In Dublin, no less than elsewhere, attention to hygiene entailed particular care with poultry and meat. Kosher meat was probably less liable to infection in any case. Not only did the excision of the blood vessels reduce the likelihood of contamination, carcasses with any signs of pulmonary disease were deemed unfit for consumption. Properly koshering meat meant immersing it in water for half an hour, salting and placing it on a slanted drainer for another hour, and then rinsing it three times.[22] There was also an element of communal quality control. In the 1940s an elderly Mr. Levi was wont to wander into the *shochet*'s slaughterhouse on Dublin's Vincent Street and put stickers on the legs of chickens to indicate when they were slaughtered. The stickers, a useful form of quality control in the days before refrigeration, had different colors and Hebrew letters for each day. Moreover, meat held in store had to be washed down anew after three days. In London the Board of Shechita's inspectors rejected a much higher proportion of meat samples than officials at the city's main markets, enough to convince the *Jewish Chronicle* that "clearly kosher meat . . . is far safer as food than even that sold in the strictly inspected markets of London."[23] At home, food was again steeped in saltwater for half an hour or so, and then the salt washed out of it before it was cooked.

Another feature of a viable Jewish community is its communal bathhouse or mikvah: apart from the scriptural obligation on women to immerse themselves after "the seven clean days," the bathhouse reflected the importance of bathing and hygiene in Jewish culture, and served as a place of relaxation and community networking. In the early years Dublin lacked a Jewish bathhouse, but Jewish women availed of special mikvah facilities provided at Tara Street municipal baths. The plunge bath, which began operations in 1897, was kept open even during six weeks in 1914 when a water shortage closed down all other facilities at Tara Street.[24]

The annual ritual of spring cleaning in Orthodox households at the approach of Pesach also bespoke a respect for hygiene. This was accompanied by meticulous searches behind cushions and under stoves for any crumbs or traces of leavened material (*chametz*). Koshering cooking utensils was part of the ritual: for example, Esther Hesselberg, born in Cork at the turn of the century, remembered that "all the glasses they had used to be put into a big bath for three days and then . . . the pottery used to be dipped . . . three times in boiling water."[25] Some residents of Martin Street in Portobello improvised by washing their pots and pans in the Grand Canal at the top of their road. Another custom was to stick cutlery in the earth overnight as a means of cleansing it. This was an acceptable way of ritually cleaning a meat knife if used when a dairy knife was appropriate, or vice versa. However, even very poor Jews tended to have a completely separate set of cooking and eating utensils for Passover.

In late nineteenth-century Europe there was an increasing awareness of the link between better housekeeping and the increasing use of soap, detergents, and clean clothes, and a reduction in the risk of illness and death. The findings of scientists Robert Koch and Louis Pasteur led to an increasing stress on the link between cleanliness and hygiene. Recently Robert Fogel has stressed the impact of huge investments in public health in late nineteenth-century Europe and America on morbidity and life expectancy, while Joel Mokyr has highlighted how the growing realization that the health of household members depended on the amount of housework done resulted in "more work for mother."[26] In Ireland these changes were reflected in both private and public action directed at instilling habits of cleanliness in the less well-off. The Dublin Sanitary Association (founded in 1872) and the Women's National Health Association (founded in 1907) reflected the voluntary side; the activities of Dublin Corporation's public health supremo, Sir Charles Cameron, and of the Local Government Board, the public side. The public health campaign against tuberculosis a century ago pointed to the risks of spreading germs through spitting, kissing, and the sharing of eating and cooking utensils; in the mills of Belfast the old practice of "kissing the shuttle," that is, extracting the thread in the shuttle by sucking it, was increasingly frowned upon. Dublin's famous Rotunda maternity hospital furnishes a well-documented example of how improvements in personal hygiene mattered. For decades the cavalier attitude of medical personnel toward washing their hands had led to many unnecessary maternal deaths from puerperal fever, until a reforming Rotunda master, Arthur Macan (1882–89), insisted on the practice. In that case well-educated and wealthy medical men were to blame but, more generally, receptiveness to health-enhancing hygiene is considered to be a function of education and literacy. Today soap and laundry detergents are widely available in less developed countries, but through poverty or lack of health education only a minority of households use them.[27]

How prevalent were the practices of taking a bath, washing one's hands, using soap and detergents, and the like in Dublin a century ago? Hard evidence is lacking, but given that in Britain even today only half of British mothers wash their hands after changing a diaper, and only one person in three does so after visiting the toilet, the answer is presumably "not very."[28] In Jewish households, by contrast, the likelihood is that hands were routinely washed, albeit not necessarily with soap, before meals and after visits to the washroom according to Jewish law. Jewish homes are also likely to have been cleaner; as already noted, they were more likely to contain a domestic servant, whose main duties entailed scrubbing and washing rather than cooking. Several Irish Jewish memoirs refer in passing to habits that must have enhanced hygiene and health.

Jessie Bloom remembered "nice, clean, comfortable beds [being] part and parcel of our daily life" and the soaking of glasses in time for Passover. Nick Harris recalled a large tin bath used for bathing his younger siblings and trips to the Iveagh Baths with his brothers; his parents would go there in the evening. Like all Orthodox Jewish women, his mother also visited the mikvah once a month, while his father went there weekly before the Sabbath service. In Athlone Hannah Berman remembered the huge bath that stood in a corner of the kitchen, which her father had acquired from the local military barracks.[29]

The prevalence of breastfeeding is another well-known, important influence on infant mortality. Jewish mothers breastfed their children.[30] Whether they did so to a greater extent than non-Jewish mothers living in the same area cannot be known, though that seems unlikely. Statistics collected by Sir Charles Cameron's lady sanitary subofficers for his public health report for 1911 are relevant here. The ladies' duties included visiting less well-off mothers who had recently given birth in their homes. They recorded 3,974 infants fed exclusively on breastmilk, 111 fed partly on cow's milk, and 126 wholly on cow's milk. The prevalence of breastfeeding is partly explained by the low labor force participation rates of married women. Cameron's visitors found that while 2,582 of the fathers were in regular employment and 1,519 in casual employment, only 219 of the mothers worked regularly while another 158 were in casual employment. The totals include the 940 mothers visited by nurse Elizabeth M. Byrne. Eight of the children she visited were stillborn, 43 had died almost immediately, 24 were "very delicate," 880 were being breastfed, 30 bottle-fed, and 2 spoon-fed.[31] Since both Jewish and non-Jewish mothers breastfed their children, the issue therefore is when infants were weaned, and what they were weaned on.[32] The high marital fertility of Jewish women (on which more below) makes it unlikely that they breastfed their children for longer than other mothers. However, the dairy milk and the feeding bottles they used may well have been cleaner.

Here a degree of inference based on what is known about Jewish communities in the same era must be allowed. Comparative assessments are revealing, especially when most or all argue in the same direction. Witnesses before two parliamentary inquiries in the early 1900s—the Select Committee of Physical Deterioration (1903) and the Royal Commission on Alien Immigration (1903–4)—were almost unanimous in their view that the mortality advantage of Jewish infants and children was due to their mothers' care. London's medical officer of health summarized: "In the end, the only conclusion I could come to was that the difference in the death rate was due to the better care the inhabitants took of themselves and their mode of life." She instanced their abstemiousness, the care they took of their children, and their "more regular lives." Her counterpart in Liverpool declared that the women were "very good mothers"; "they devote a great deal of care and attention to their children, and their children are well fed and well clothed."[33] A representative of the Jewish community mentioned the impact of the mikvah on the "extraordinary health and fecundity of the race, seldom found in any other people," while an English clergyman surmised that "their laws require a great deal more cleanliness than ours" and health-wise "they are distinctly better than the average of that class in the east of London." Witnesses appearing before the Select Committee on Physical Deterioration in 1904 were unanimous in their claims that Jewish children were better fed than Gentile children.[34] In the same vein, a Glasgow medical practitioner referred a few years later to "the greater care taken by Jewish mothers of their children, and to the activities of the many Jewish associations and societies." Foreign-born Jews, he found, were not particularly "cleanly in their habits," nor were they immune from infectious diseases, but when it came to caring for children, other Glasgow mothers "might learn a good deal from Jewish mothers."[35]

A recent comparative study of the mortality of the infants and children of immigrants to the United States in the early twentieth century highlights the low rates of infant mortality achieved by Jewish parents. Given their concentration in unhealthy northeastern cities, their achievement was all the more remarkable. Samuel Preston and his coauthors put it down to "unmeasured child care practices, having mostly to do with feeding practices and general hygienic standards." Invoking Woodbury's classic study, they point in particular to the low incidence of Jewish infant and child deaths from gastric and intestinal diseases as evidence that the Jewish diet was particularly "pure." They also speculate on the possible roles of community support systems, the care with which Jewish citizens upheld sanitary laws, the long experience of Jewish communities with urban living, and the likelihood that Jewish mothers were healthier. But these remain no more than plausible hypotheses, unsupported by firm evidence.[36]

It is true that in Dublin in the 1890s and 1900s Sir Charles Cameron's public health inspectorate won convictions against a number of Jewish traders whose clients would also have been mainly Jewish. The Jewish Meat and Provision Company of Lower Camden Street was twice found guilty of "having sold or intending to sell diseased or otherwise unsound food," and there were nine other convictions for selling watered down or adulterated milk. Two dairy proprietors, Max Sigman of Saint Kevin's Parade and Mark Froedman of Arbutus Place, were fined twice. But these constituted a very small proportion indeed of all convictions. This is presumably in part because Jewish grocers and butchers served a demanding and closely knit clientele of repeat purchasers. Traders' success depended on their reputations for hygiene and observance of the dietary laws.

In cases of illness, Jewish households were also probably more likely to rely on medical expertise than were their non-Jewish neighbors. Medical practitioners were few among the first generation of immigrants, but the high status of doctors in the Jewish community is reflected in the eagerness of many in the second generation to pursue a medical career. Henry Samuel Misstear's pharmacy, located at Leonard's corner at the junction of the South Circular Road and Upper Clanbrassil Street, was central in this respect.[37] Misstear, who dispensed both medicaments and sage medical advice for four decades, came to be known as "a friend of the Jews."[38] Other evidence of a Jewish propensity for seeking medical advice and attention is corroborative. A recent study of elderly Italian and Jewish women finds that Jewish women were more likely to avail of the services of doctors and pharmacists.[39] However, the impact of medical remedies on health in the pre-antibiotic era should not be exaggerated.

Largely for religious reasons, first-generation mothers-to-be tended to shun the maternity hospitals that catered to a significant proportion of Dublin's poor and not-so-poor at this stage.[40] Jewish mothers relied instead on midwives and home deliveries. The best known of the midwives was Ada Shillman (Bernard Shillman's mother), who delivered a few thousand infants (including future lord mayor Robert Briscoe) over four decades.[41] Shillman's clients were exclusively Jewish at the outset; her "business book" suggests a woman familiar enough with the community in the 1890s to charge those better-off (including Mrs. Briscoe) three or four times as much as the poorest.[42] Shillman was also behind the creation in 1913, with Bethel Solomons, of a free medical dispensary for Jews, operating first at 1 Stamer Street and from 1917 at 43 Bloomfield Avenue. Given Shillman's and Solomons' skills the dispensary catered mainly to women. Located next to a minyan room, it opened twice weekly for many years.[43] Solomons, a skilled surgeon, would later become master of the Rotunda Hospital.

The role of the mother within the Jewish household was paramount.[44] Harold Mushatt claimed that before his mother arrived in Dublin from Zhager in 1886 at the age of twelve, she had already been taught sewing and the rudiments of "Latin"—presumably meaning the Latin script—by her own mother in preparation for Ireland. Though her first job was to look after children for her Dublin aunt, she never left the house with them in case neighbors mistook her for a domestic servant. Instead, she supplemented her income by sewing children's dresses for shops in Camden Street at four pence per dress.[45]

Whatever the reasons for Jewish women not working outside the home, the consequences for child welfare can only have been beneficial. But this hardly accounts for any Jewish advantage in infant or child mortality, since the great majority of Dublin women of all faiths gave up work outside the home after marriage. Even in the part of Belfast where most immigrant Jews lived, it was very much the exception for a married woman to work outside the home. In my 1911 Belfast database (described in chapter 5), 2 out of 87 Jewish women reported an occupation; 1 of 53 Catholics; 7 of 97 members of the Church of Ireland; and only 4 of 189 of other faiths (mainly Presbyterians). Both occupations reported by the Jewish women (dressmaker and tailoress) were consistent with working at home. Another supposed characteristic of Jewish mothers is that when food was scarce they put their children before themselves and their husbands, whereas in Ireland the husband as breadwinner got priority.[46] This might explain any mortality differential in the case of very poor children. However, in the Dublin of Little Jerusalem the kinds, or quality, of food consumed probably mattered more than the quantity.

Food, Drink, and Health

We're not a pub-crawling people by any means.
—A Dublin Jewish woman in 1990[47]

More important than attitudes toward medicine and medical expertise was the attitude toward food. Hasia Diner's monograph on the adaptation of nineteenth-century Jewish, Irish, and Italian immigrants to life in the United States, as reflected in their different attitudes toward food and the rituals of communal eating, is pertinent in this context. She shows that while Jewish and Italian immigrants "retained a commitment to foods emblematic of their culture," food played almost no role in the cultural legacy that Irish emigrants brought with them to the New World. That nineteenth-century Irish emigrants did not miss the foods they ate in the old country is reflected in the lack of references to matters of the table in letters home. In David Fitzpatrick's close study of dozens of letters between Ireland and Australia, only one refers nostalgically to any aspect of the Irish diet.[48]

Dublin Jewish households almost certainly had the edge over their non-Jewish neighbours in terms of nutrition. The local staples of white bread, tea, sugar, bacon, dripping, and potatoes were no match for a diet emphasizing such items as vegetable oil, dairy products, cocoa, fish, eggs, poultry, and some fresh fruit and vegetables. Cabbage and turnips were the only vegetables, other than potatoes, widely consumed in Dublin a century ago. Elderly present-day residents of Little Jerusalem point to the importance of boiled fowl, fish, and oil in the Jewish diet, and to the presence of exotic items such as cucumbers, gherkins, and raw herring. In Jessie Spiro's house there were "potatoes in their jackets," too, "both boiled and baked, the latter commoner at our house in the winter, as the kitchen range was going all the time."[49] Clanbrassil Street was where one got "peppercorns, all-spice, bay leaves, smoked salmon orange-coloured and fatty, laid out on a board; and swimming in the acids of glass containers, sour cucumbers and pickled herrings."[50] In Cork city poachers sought out Jews as the most likely purchasers of their salmon.[51] The dietary divide is also evident in the memories of an eighty-two-year-old non-Jewish man born in a flat on Lower Clanbrassil Street next to the Ordmans and the Rubinsteins:

> My mother used to work for a lot of the Jews, cleaning their houses, and she also worked for Ordmans and she used to get a lot of food and chickens from the sisters, Sophie and Edie Ordman. We used to get a lot of chicken, because Jews wouldn't eat a fowl if it had a pin or something in its craw. I often wondered did my mother put these things in the chickens. I know I was the only kid on Clanbrassil St who tasted fowl. My mother also got work at weddings in the Synagogue on the Circular Road, and we at home would have a feast of left overs, cakes and desserts.[52]

Other non-Jewish residents of the area also remember Jewish food as different and exotic. Elaine Crowley remembered Clanbrassil Street for "the lovely smells, smells that were different, that were gorgeous, foreign smells," mentioning Ordman's shop with its barrels of pickled cucumbers, which some of the Christian women "became very fond of." There was smoked salmon—"you'd see it and it looked lovely"—but she never tasted it until she was older.[53] Olive Sealy, an octogenarian resident of Martin Street, also mentioned cucumber, and remembered how the fish dealer who came on Fridays relied on Jewish households for most of his business. The Jewish women, unlike the rest, tended to bargain for their fish.[54] Jessie Bloom recalled,

> Fish was plentiful and always fresh . . . a fish we called bream . . . was popular with the Jews, and at the wholesale fish market the auctioneer would call out, when he had bream on the auction block, "how much for this bunch of Jewmen." . . . The Jews . . . used fish extensively so much so that when some Jewish boys showed evidence of superior intelligence in some competitive public examinations one Gentile remarked, "No wonder they are always eating fish."[55]

An elderly resident of Greenville Terrace recalls bringing some empty jam jars to buy gherkins (pickled cucumbers) and raw salted herrings on Clanbrassil Street "for the novelty of it"; their mother "would smell [the unusual food] from them" when they got home, and her reaction was, "if I put it up to you wouldn't eat it." She also remembered the sour rye bread, which their mother and one of her sisters loved, the annual ritual of being given matzo bread at Passover, and gifts of delicious poppy-seed cakes from a neighbor across the street at the Jewish feast of Purim. Most depictions by non-Jews highlight the novelty of Jewish food items.

The dietary restrictions meant that Jewish children tended not to accept food from non-Jewish neighbors.[56] The only trouble young Olive Sealy of Martin Street remembered having with a Jewish playmate was when she innocently stuck her fork in Gertie Bennett's kosher steak. Olive and Gertie would have been eleven or twelve at the time. Two elderly residents of Greenville Terrace remember a little Jewish boy from across the road accompanying them on trips to places such as Ballinteer and the Three Rock Mountain in the 1930s, or to the Crumlin Road to pick blackberries, and he partaking with relish of their picnics. But he "was the only Jew we remember eating Gentile food."

Though data on working-class diets in pre-1914 Dublin are not entirely lacking,[57] comparative analyses of diets across neighborhoods and socioeconomic groups are limited. Such an analysis was conducted in Glasgow in 1911–12, and its database included five foreign-born Jewish families living in the Gorbals. Clearly, a nonrandom sample of five has its limitations. It is still worth considering, however, given the common Litvak background of Glasgow and Dublin Jews. The eating habits of the Glaswegian Jews probably offer a fair picture of Little Jerusalem diets on the eve of World War I. The study's author, Carnegie Research Fellow Dorothy Lindsay, observed her subjects' eating and spending patterns over a week. The Jewish families in her database were better circumstanced than average, and Lindsay noted the tidiness of their homes and their "wonderful" parlors, "with full suites of furniture, photographs, crystal or china ornaments, antimacassars, &c."[58] She could just as easily have been referring to Dublin, because accounts of the interiors of Jewish homes in Little Jerusalem are very much in this vein. An elderly resident of Dufferin Avenue, a street once heavily Jewish, remembers as a boy lighting fires in Jewish homes on the Sabbath and finding them "sparkling and full of good furniture and the dining room always seemed to me to have big tables covered with beautiful table cloths and eye-catching menorahs." On neighboring Greenville Terrace the Cunningham sisters remember as children peering through the windows of Jewish homes on Dufferin Avenue and seeing wine decanters on the table for the Sabbath dinner. An informant (JB) who grew up on Victoria Street off the South Circular Road remembered Jewish houses as "dark and cold, with wonderful furniture."

Lindsay's Glasgow study deserves a closer look. We are not informed how the sixty households subjected to analysis were selected, although presumably they were deemed representative. There are detailed schedules of the income and expenditure on food and rent of sixty families, ranging in status from the very poor living on less than £1 weekly to the reasonably comfortable living on three times as much.[59] Some of these households were Irish but they were not identified separately since "they presented no national features."[60] Lindsay's analysis of diet, modeled on an earlier study of Edinburgh, would seem to have been carefully done; each household's consumption of twenty or so items is reported, as are the resultant intakes of protein, fat, and carbohydrates, and the average daily caloric intake per adult male equivalent. How different were its five Jewish households from the rest? Did they differ from other households earning roughly the same income?

Some of the detail in Lindsay's survey is summarized in table 8.1. The five Jewish households in the sample were better-off than the average; they were better housed (an average of 3.6 rooms per household versus 2 per household for others) and earned higher incomes (£1.93 versus £1.37 weekly). Setting aside income differences for a moment, some of the contrasts between Jews and non-Jews are striking. The Jewish households consumed an average of 53 grams of poultry per adult male equivalent, while *none* of the fifty-five other households consumed any poultry. Most households consumed some fish, but average Jewish consumption (163 grams) was over three times that of non-Jewish consumption (52 grams). Jewish households consumed less beef (107 versus 121 grams per male adult equivalent) and fewer vegetables (309 versus 399 grams) than their non-Jewish neighbors, but their consumption of eggs was well above the average (31 grams versus 19 grams). Jews were also more likely to consume oil and cucumbers. They spent more on food than the average, though this must have been due in part to the higher cost of kosher meat.

Even after allowing for income differences by comparing Jewish consumption with that of the top twenty non-Jewish households, the distinctiveness of the Jewish diet remains. Jewish households still spent more on food, and consumed more fowl, fish, milk, and eggs. They also consumed more calories and came closer to the recommended norms of protein (120 grams) and fat (100 grams) than the sample of the more affluent Glasgow working class. According to this evidence, however, Glasgow's Jews ate little fresh fruit. Note, too, how Jewish households living on about £2 weekly chose more spacious accommodation—and therefore paid considerably more in rent—than non-Jewish households on the same income.

It seems safe to assume that the dietary differences so carefully documented by Lindsay were also found in Dublin. How might such differences have affected infant mortality? In her study of Jewish mothers in

TABLE 8.1.
Working-class Diets in Glasgow in 1911–12

	Jews (n = 5)	Others (n = 55)	Others (top 20)	Others (bottom 35)
Household size	7.40	6.64	7.60	6.09
Adult male equivalent	5.60	4.41	5.29	3.90
Weekly expenditure (sh.)	30.37	18.68	24.52	15.34
Poultry *	52.60	0	0	0
Fish *	162.6	52.2	46.1	55.73
Vegetables *	308.5	399.0	413.3	390.9
Beef *	106.6	120.8	111.3	126.3
Pork *	0	22.6	32.7	16.9
Eggs *	31.4	19.0	26.9	14.5
Av daily expenditure *	9.14	6.99	7.61	6.63
Av energy *	3381.4	3145.2	3220.5	3102.2
Av protein *	122.7	109.8	112.3	108.4
Av fat *	98.5	81.9	86.5	79.2
Av milk *	304.3	206.2	208.8	204.7
Av buttermilk *	71.2	48.5	65.1	38.5
Rent (shillings)	5.57	3.60	3.99	3.37
Rooms	3.6	2.0	2.2	1.9
% on food	80.7	70.8	63.3	75.1
% on rent	14.8	14.7	10.7	17.0
Income	1.93	1.37	1.95	1.03

Source: Derived from Lindsay 1913. * grams per adult male equivalent.

the East End of London a century ago Lara Marks notes the low incidence of rickets, a disease associated with vitamin D deficiency, in Jewish children. She argues that a Jewish diet rich in fish oils, eggs, cheese, and milk was an effective preventative. Rickets, unpleasant in itself, also apparently weakens the immune system against measles and whooping cough, and these were major causes of early childhood mortality in Dublin. However, according to the authoritative Charles Cameron, "rickety children" were not often seen in Dublin in this period, and Lindsay's Glasgow study found little connection between food intake and the incidence of rickets.[61] The fish and fresh vegetables in the Jewish diet also guaranteed an ample intake of vitamin A, and there is evidence that vitamin A offers some protection against respiratory diseases and measles.[62]

But the main infant killer in Dublin—and the main reason that infant mortality was greater in urban than in rural areas generally—was diarrhea. In accounting for the incidence of diarrhea, the type of food mattered less than its quality and the level of hygiene associated with its preparation and consumption. Here, too, Jewish ritual almost certainly helped: kosher meat was subject to careful inspection, and kosher cooking entailed the meticulous cleansing of cooking utensils. The Glasgow Jewish women studied by Lindsay "made a strong point" of how they washed their food before cooking it; all meat was steeped in cold water for an hour, and then placed in saltwater for another half an hour.[63]

The immigrants also differed from the natives in their attitude toward alcohol. Redcliffe Salaman, a scholar best known in Ireland for his expertise in the history of the potato, wrote as follows about Jews and alcohol:

> The Jew, no matter in what part of the world, is free from alcoholism, and this freedom has been less affected by his assimilation with the west than any other major trait peculiar to the race. It is only necessary to note that in the London Hospital a Jewish alcoholic is one of the rarest events of the year, whilst the record of the Board of Guardians which deals with some 1100 new cases a year, finds it unnecessary to make the smallest provision for destitution arising from alcoholism.[64]

The reputation of the Irish both at home and abroad was very different, and is amply supported by statistical evidence. Judicial, military, and hospital records highlight the overrepresentation of the Irish among the inebriate and the alcoholic in the United States a century ago. In the Borough of Manhattan in 1915, for example, 9.1 percent of the deaths of twenty-five to forty-four-year-old Irish-born men and 4.0 percent of the deaths of same-aged women were due to alcohol-related diseases. For Russian-born (and therefore mainly Jewish) men and women of the same age group the rates were 0.7 and 0.4 percent; for Austro-Hungary (also mostly Jewish) the rates were 0.9 and 1.1 percent.[65]

Leopold Bloom's and Moses Herzog's fondness for convivial drinking in public houses notwithstanding, few of Dublin's Jews frequented such places. Alcohol plays a central part in Jewish ritual: it is essential for the Shabbat Kiddush (blessing over wine) and the drinking of four glasses of wine during the Passover seder. Yet the Litvaks, though rarely teetotalers, consumed alcohol sparingly. Non-Jewish natives of Little Jerusalem corroborate the impression of Jewish abstemiousness. Dominick Casey of Dufferin Avenue "never met a Jewish man in a bar." Drink had its ritual, ceremonial function, however. Olive Sealy of Martin Street enjoyed a taste of their sweet Passover wine, though her parents did not care for it.[66]

An incident described by a Dublin-born Litvak offers an apt summing-up of the cultural difference between Jew and non-Jew in this respect. Abram Bloom was returning home with a Gentile friend from the celebrations marking the twenty-fifth anniversary of the Adelaide Road synagogue in 1917. There had been plenty to eat and drink, and everybody had been congratulating everybody else. Abram casually asked his friend, "What did you think of it?," whereupon his friend answered, "There were two bottles of whisky unopened." Abram kept a straight face but on reflection "felt it was a sort of sizing up of Jewish life in general as compared to the Irish."[67]

Philanthropists highlighted the connection between drink and poverty: the secretary of the Dublin branch of the Royal Society for the Prevention of Cruelty to Children declared it "an undoubted fact that drink is the cause of nine-tenths of [poverty]." In an address to the Dublin Sanitary Association in 1886, T. W. Grimshaw drew attention to the strong association across urban areas in the United Kingdom between the death rate and the incidence of drunkenness.[68] Grimshaw's numbers placed Dublin in the unenviable first place for the arrest rate for drunkenness in his league of fourteen cities. Drink was just one factor of several in accounting for poverty: if one in five of Dublin's street-trading children had a parent who drank heavily, nearly one-third of them had lost a parent, and several more had sickly, disabled, absent, or unemployed parents.[69] Moreover, it bears noting that both alcohol consumption and drunkenness seem to have declined in late Victorian and Edwardian Ireland. Still, drink mattered. Although *how much* the difference in drinking habits affected the health and living standards of the immigrant and native communities must remain a moot point, it almost certainly played a role.

Chapter 9

NEWCOMER TO NEIGHBOR

The smallest of the three groups, the Jewish
community, at least in the twenties, exhibited the
same sort of syndrome that was characteristic of the
two larger groups, that is to say loyalty, orthodoxy,
piety and the fiercest intolerance.
—*Niall Montgomery*[1]

My mother said, "When you go to Saint Peter's
school don't have anything to do with that rough
crowd from the back streets." But I could not
find anything bad about them.
—*Leslie Daiken, Dublin Litvak*

TODAY OVER one in every ten residents of the Republic of Ireland was
born outside the country. Great Britain and Northern Ireland still account
for a majority of these but may not do so for much longer. Between May
2004 and April 2005, over eighty-five thousand personal public service
(PPS) numbers were issued to nationals of countries admitted into the
European Union in 2004, or over ten times the number of work permits
issued to nationals of the same countries in the previous twelve months.
Poles accounted for half of the total in 2004–5, and Lithuanians a further
one-fifth. Ireland is also home to some thirty thousand Asian-born residents, and similar numbers of Africans and Eastern Europeans now live
in Ireland. This pattern, unprecedented in Irish history, is a product of the
rapid economic growth of the Irish economy since the late 1980s. Early
in 2004 a report titled *Building Solidarity across Communities* lamented
the lack of social interaction between immigrants and the native population in a section of Dublin's south inner city. The area surveyed contained
the highest concentration of recent immigrants and asylum seekers in Ireland. It was far from being a classic ghetto, however: the newcomers,
who remained a minority in the area, represented a mosaic of thirty-two
nationalities from places as far apart as Poland and Trinidad. *Building
Solidarity* attributed the lack of contact between native and newcomer to
language barriers and cultural differences, and recommended the creation

of an "intercultural working group" and anti-racism training for local community representatives.[2]

The low levels of communal interaction or identification described in the report are depressingly commonplace in areas where immigrants have recently settled. Was the same true of host and recently arrived Litvak communities in Ireland over a century ago? How did attitudes shift over time? Today, hard evidence on these questions is elusive. Replies often invoke high-profile events such as the infamous Limerick boycott of 1904 (on which more below), the recognition of Judaism in the 1937 Irish constitution, the failure of the Irish authorities to do more for Jews seeking to flee from Nazi Germany, and the election of Robert Briscoe as Dublin's lord mayor in 1956 and again in 1961. Other sources at the historian's disposal, albeit often fragmentary and fallible, such as contemporary impressions, autobiographic memoirs, or evidence drawn from other broadly comparable contexts, are rarely consulted. My own main interest is in the interaction between Jewish and non-Jewish neighbors and between Jewish traders and their non-Jewish customers, insofar as these may have affected demographic characteristics and trends, but the issue is of more general interest. Much more has been written about native attitudes toward the newcomers than vice versa.

In the Beginning

The Jews understand the Irish little; the Irish
understand the Jews less.
—"Halitvac," *Jewish Chronicle*, 1906[3]

"Oh," said the Jewman, "this woman standing so near,
A fine pair of blankets she bested me fair";
Said she, "you're a liar, you dirty old Turk,
You tried to insult me while my husband's at work."
—From "The Jewman," a Waterford song[4]

The first, much-cited mention of Jews in Irish sources was not an auspicious one. In the Annals of Inisfallen the entry for A.D. 1079. Includes, "*Coicer Iudaide do thiachtain dar-muir and aisceda leo do Thoirdelbach and a n-dichor doridise dar muir* (Five Jews come from across the sea with gifts for [King] Toirdelbach [Ó Briain] and they are driven back to sea again)."[5] As explained in chapter 2, for eight centuries after this abortive visit the Jewish presence in Ireland was minimal. Jews did not feature much in Irish folklore or folk song nor, it seems, in sermons from the altar, although an anti-Semitic undertow in the attitudes of some of the local clergy was probably inevitable.

Before the arrival of the Litvaks it is safe to say that most Irish people knew little or nothing of Jews. Nor were the early arrivals always identified as such. The young priest who befriended an almost destitute Louis Wine in Kilkenny in the mid-1870s had never before met a Jew. Nobody in the village of Tullow had encountered a Jew before Israel Khan established a business there, but Mrs. Khan was "a great favorite" at the local Brigidine convent, and taught her children to respect the nuns and their prayers. The Catholic mother superior in the Irish midlands town of Clara, who treated the recently arrived peddler Lieb Berman so kindly and canvassed for customers for him, may have mistaken him for a Catholic "from one of those districts in Italy where red-haired people are frequent." Given his lack of English, "he could not have corrected her view even if he had known it." Lieb's daughter, Hannah Berman, imagined that "not even the mother superior herself had ever met a Jew in her life." In Athlone, Lieb was also taken for an Italian.[6] As noted in chapter 5, Cork's earliest arrivals were greeted with gifts of household goods, including "even framed pictures of Jesus."[7] The newcomers probably elicited many similar reactions elsewhere in the 1880s, since the preexisting Jewish community was tiny, comfortably off, and mainly resident in Dublin. Soon, however, all foreigners in the remoter parts of Ireland were taken to be Jews.

Some of the immigrant traders were agreeably surprised by the reception they received from Irish country people.[8] But there is plenty evidence, too, as noted in chapter 3, of peddlers being roughly treated or sneered at on their travels. The perpetrators (including the apocryphal Waterford woman cited above and the young Seán O'Casey) were more xenophobic than strictly anti-Semitic.[9] The same might be said of the reaction of Dublin and Cork cabinetmakers and tailors to the threat of competition from Litvak artisans.[10] A century ago, the outlook of most Irish people of all persuasions was blinkered, parochial, and prejudiced by today's standards.

Of course, there was classic anti-Semitism, too. Presumably the oft-cited utterances—all dating from about a century ago—of Limerick preacher Father John Creagh (who sparked off a boycott against Jewish traders in Limerick in 1904, and on whom more below), nationalist leader Arthur Griffith, Westminster M.P. F. H. O'Donnell, and writer-politician and surgeon Oliver St. John Gogarty (model for Buck Mulligan in Joyce's *Ulysses*) represented something much broader. The same goes for William Bulfin's nasty, anti-Semitic depiction of a Jewish peddler encountered on his *Rambles in Eirinn* and for cartoons such as that printed in the satirical *Leprecaun* in 1907.[11] Until mid-century at least, the Irishism "Jewman" (compare Chinaman, Corkman, and so forth) was often used pejoratively and insultingly, particularly as a synonym for moneylender, even in the

Dáil.[12] Militant Catholicism embodied or promoted anti-Semitism at various levels: some of its adherents saw Jews and Freemasons (often coupled together) as part of an anti-Catholic conspiracy, while others were convinced of the age-old smear that "Jews killed Jesus Christ." There was also—almost certainly there still lingers—a degree of "economic" anti-Semitism, a native "begrudgery" stemming from the relative affluence of the immigrants and their descendants. And, as in Britain, there was middle-class and elite anti-Semitism, epitomized by the blackballing of Jews in several of Dublin's social and golf clubs.[13]

The Litvak *mentalité* or mind-set on arrival is also of interest. "Otherness" tends to be a two-way street. It is inconceivable that attitudes toward non-Jews back in *der heim* did not color initial feelings toward the Irish. So how did the inhabitants of the Lithuanian shtetls regard their Gentile (and mainly peasant and anti-Semitic) neighbors? With a combination of superiority and suspicion is the likely answer. Charles Liebman and Steven Cohen, authors of a much-cited sociological study of how American Jews see themselves and others, explain.

> Jews harbored many unflattering images both of Gentile individuals and Gentile culture. These negative images were constituent elements in traditional Jewish identity, reinforcing Jewish notions of their own individual and collective superiority, and contributing to the sense of Jewish familism (the belief that Jews were all part of one extended family) and Jewish chosenness. Most Jews regarded themselves as spiritually superior to non-Jews. . . . The contempt of traditional Jews for Christianity was paralleled by a disdain for Christians as individuals.[14]

Liebman and Cohen refer to Mark Zborowski and Elizabeth Herzog's famous anthropological study of the mentalité of east European shtetl dwellers, which also highlights how Gentile and Jewish perceptions of each other differed. Zborowski and Herzog describe the children of the shtetl (a Yiddish term that largely owes its broader currency to them) as growing up "to regard certain behavior as characteristic of Jews, and its opposite as characteristic of Gentiles." Gentile traits included "emphasis on the body, blind instinct, sexual licence, and ruthless force"; the peasant "gets drunk, he beats his wife, he sings a little song." And, add Zborowski and Herzog, "reality" buttressed such stereotypes, since "the neighboring peasants [were] illiterate, uninterested in the values that the Jews hold highest, and more prone than the Jews to excesses of drinking and violence."[15] Yuri Slezkine offers several unpleasant examples of the anti-Gentile ethos of the shtetl: a grandmother covering a child's eyes at the approach of a Christian procession and remarking, "May your clear eyes never see this filth"; the use of words ordinarily reserved for animals when

182   CHAPTER 9

describing Gentiles eating and drinking; and in Lithuania the development of a special linguistic code to refer to Gentile (as opposed to Jewish)
sisters, weddings, and deaths.[16] Again, according to Ewa Morawska, who
has studied Jewish immigrants in small-town America a century ago, "in
the eyes of the shtetl, the *goyim*-peasants represented everything a Jew,
including members of the *proste* or uneducated strata of Jewish society,
did not want to and should not be, and this value-laden distinction was
inculcated in children from infancy." Such attitudes were longstanding.[17]

In the shtetls most contact with non-Jews was through the cash nexus.
A French memoir of the Litvak shtetl notes, "what is incredible and para-
doxical is that Jews and Gentiles lived together, but did not socialize."[18]
The *Encyclopedia Judaica* entry on Lithuanian Jewry corroborates.

> Lithuania was a poor country, and the mass of its inhabitants, con-
> sisting of Lithuanian and Belorussian peasants, formed a low social
> stratum whose national culture was undeveloped. The Jews who
> had contacts with them as contractors, merchants, shopkeepers, inn-
> keepers, craftsmen, etc. regarded themselves as their superior in
> every respect.

This superiority complex permeates the writings of even the good-na-
tured Sholem Aleichem, the giant of Yiddish literary fiction: his goyim are
remote and rather stupid and gullible. Attitudes undoubtedly varied
across space and over time, however. Particularly in the remoter villages
and towns, anti-Gentile elements in the the Babylonian Talmud may also
have influenced attitudes toward outsiders.[19] On the other hand, in the
second part of the nineteenth century a certain globalization of both ideas
and economic activity led to increased contact between Jew and non-Jew
in eastern Europe.[20] Integrated schooling, increased migration, the spread
of socialist ideas of brotherhood, secularization, the abolition of serfdom,
and tsarist policies of centralization all played their part. Yet in the pre-
1914 era cultural self-sufficiency remained an important feature, as did
an abiding contempt for the peasantry.

In 1891 the London *Jewish Chronicle* described east European immigrants in England as "our principal care"; in the same breath it declared
them "uninviting in appearance and sometimes also in character, they are
what their surroundings have made them." The *Chronicle* anticipated
some difficulties in indoctrinating them with "English habits" yet nonetheless believed that would soon "enjoy the Anglican peace."[21] In the
event, acculturation took a little longer than the *Chronicle* predicted.

Modern sociological research suggests that even today Jewish attitudes
toward non-Jews in the United States still contain traces of an anti-Gentile
prejudice formed by the east European experience. Liebman and Cohen
found that as many as half of U.S. Jews still clung to negative images of

their Gentile compatriots in the late 1980s. Such images have been much attenuated by contact and familiarity over the years with non-Jewish neighbors and work colleagues, however.[22]

A recent account of South African Jewry in the years before World War I is also worth citing in this context, since South African Jews, like Ireland's, were mainly of Lithuanian origin.

> It is likely that the feeling of superiority, at times even of contempt, which characterized the Litvak Jews' view of the Lithuanian peasants facilitated the adoption of similar attitudes toward the equivalent farm laborers and urban workers of black and colored pigmentation whom the immigrant now encountered in South Africa. . . . Thus every African, no matter what age, was addressed as "boy"; even white children called an adult African "boy." An African woman was referred to as a *shikse*. The word *kaffir* was adopted into Yiddish. . . . As it happens, the Yiddish term *poyer*, applied to the peasants in Lithuania, is etymologically related to the Afrikaner word *boer*. But in South Africa, not the Boer but the African was the equivalent of the Lithuanian peasant.[23]

If anti-Gentile attitudes persist in attenuated form in some quarters in the United States even today, it surely stands to reason that Ireland's immigrants' sense of superiority over non-Jews stayed with them for a time and conditioned initial interaction with the host community. There are scattered hints that such was the case, though hard evidence is scarce. One example is the unpleasant piece of Yiddish doggerel current during Leslie Daiken's childhood in Little Jerusalem in the 1900s and 1910s, and certainly imported from Lithuania: "*Yaski Pandre likt in drerd, Kush mein tokkes vee a ganze ferd*" (Jesus Christ lies in the earth [i.e., dead], kiss my arse the size of a horse). *Yaski* (or *Yoshke*) *Pandre* also crops up in an unpublished version of Hannah Berman's memoir of her father's family, where she refers to their drunken Galway neighbors in the 1880s as "horrible—all Yoshke Pandres."[24] Another Yiddish expression in the same vein, common in the early twentieth century, was "A cholera *auf die* Goyim" (a cholera on the Gentiles). Sometimes "cholera" was replaced by *gedochas* (plague) or some similar fate.[25] Noteworthy, too, is the currency in early twentieth-century Dublin of the Yiddish term *laptzies* (or *laptseh*), a derogatory way of describing gullible Gentile clients. Joseph Edelstein's weekly men employed it in the 1900s, and in the 1920s and 1930s it "applied generally to gentile women of lower social class as in 'factory *lapze*' (or *lapzie*) and it was pejorative." It was still current at least among some of the older generation in mid-century, as witnessed by the following snippet of conversation about a fish purchase between two Jewish housewives recorded on Lower Clanbrassil Street in the early 1950s.

"Three for three-and-six! I don't want them . . . I really don't need them!" She pays, takes her fish, and walks away, contented. "Ah! Good morning to you Mrs. 'Q' ". (She has just met our old friend). "I've just got a real bargain off the old *laptseh* (non-Jewish woman selling at stalls) at the corner. Three plaice, beauties, for three-and-six. Enough for three. A *metziah* (bargain)!"[26]

No doubt, some of the language in common usage a century ago—on all sides—sounds harsher to modern ears than it did then. By the same token, in some quarters expressions such as *goy* and *shikse* have lost some of the unpleasantness they undoubtedly possessed in the past. When Princeton-based Irish poet Paul Muldoon, whose wife is Jewish, refers to himself as "the goy from Moy," we smile with him. Yet in Jewish Dublin the terms *goy* and *shikse* were employed in the demeaning sense that they still retain elsewhere.[27] In households that could afford an (almost invariably Catholic) domestic servant, she was often referred to as "the *shikse*." Sometimes, it is true, *shikse* meant simply "an unmarried Gentile woman": "she is such a nice *shikse*" might be kindly meant. Yet Jessie Spiro Bloom's mother deemed the word offensive a century ago and prohibited its use in the Spiro home by the Grand Canal in the 1890s and 1900s.[28] Also in widespread use was the Irish Yiddish slang term *baitz* (pronounced "bates"), linguistic code for Irishman (or *baitzke* for Irishwoman and *baitzimer* in the plural). This had its origin in the Hebrew word for "egg," and derives from the Yiddish pronunciation of Ireland— *Eier*-land or "Eggs"-land. During Leslie Daiken's Dublin childhood there were weekly "scraps with the batezmir": "a bates is an enemy of a yid. No rocks are the condition today."[29]

As noted in chapter 5, Irish Jewry lived cheek by jowl with its host community from the outset. The lack of residential segregation did not exclude a sense of separateness on both sides, however. One indication of this is the way Catholic and Jewish children taunted each other on the streets of Little Jerusalem from time to time both in verse and prose. Catholics would respond to "Catty, Catty go to mass, riding on the divil's ass" with catcalls of "Buy a vatch! Buy a vatch" or "Holy Moses, King of the Jews, bought his wife a pair of shoes." There were fights, too. Louis Wigoder always bore the mark of a glass object thrown at him in childhood by a passing butcher boy, against whom "one of our boys passed some remark." Michael Brennan of Martin Street (whose father Wolf Brener arrived from Akmijan in 1893 at the age of three) was taunted with "Ay Jewman, where diju ever ger a name loik Brennan?" which elicited the response, "Dja wanna do sumtin abowrih?" and perhaps a fistfight. The late Ellard Eppel remembered the corner where Heytesbury Street met the South Circular Road being the danger spot, where shouts of "Go back to Poland!" and a school cap thrown on the footpath were the usual provocations.[30] Such sectarian slanging matches and bullying owed more to sectarian socialization through the schooling system than to any deep racial antipathies. They long preceded the arrival of the Litvaks and were not unique to Dublin.[31]

A. J. Leventhal and Leslie Daiken grew up in Jewish households off the South Circular Road in the 1900s and 1910s. Later, the two recalled different verses of a song current during their childhoods as evidence of each community's stereotypical view of the other. The bits pieced together here seem to be of mixed, Jewish-Gentile provenance. The mocking repartee contains a degree of self-deprecation as well.

"Two shillies, two shillies," the Jewman did cry,
"For a fine pair of blankets from me you did buy;
Do you think me von idjit or von bloomin' fool,
If I don't get my shillie I must have my wool."

"Von shilly, von shilly," the Jewman did cry
When a big red-nosed Bobby just then did pass by,
"What's the row here, what's the row here, d'ye think ye're at shul?"
"If I don't get my shilly I must get my wool!"

"Two pennies, two pennies," the Christian did shout,
"For a bottle of porter or Guinness's stout;
My wife's got no shawl and my kids have no shoes,
But I must have my money, I must have my booze."

Next Monday morning the Jewman called round
He knocked at the door but he heard not a sound,
"Are you in Missus Murphy?," he cried, with a shout,
"If I don't get my shilly you won't get your stout!"[32]

To an extent, the religious orthodoxy of the Jewish community constrained interaction with the indigenous community. Religious observance was a time-intensive activity; many adult males attended prayers daily, and Hebrew and religious instruction were obligatory for younger males. On weekdays other than Fridays, most boys received instruction from Yiddish-speaking tutors after attending regular schools.[33] Fear of assimilation and intermarriage was a real worry, and very religious couples frowned on their children even playing soccer with their non-Jewish neighbors. They also discouraged soccer for another reason: many of the most important games were played on the Sabbath. Chaim Herzog's parents would not "hear of" young Chaim joining the local scout troop, despite his protestations.[34] The seven "rabbis" or "ministers" and dozen Hebrew teachers living in the South Circular Road area in 1911 served a very observant community. Dietary restrictions also reduced neighborly contacts, since they meant that Jews concentrated much of their business on Jewish-run shops along arterial Lower Clanbrassil Street or on the few smaller Jewish shops in Portobello. Clanbrassil Street was "the *kosher* street where we go to do our shopping . . . [with] foodstuffs that you cannot buy in O'Connor's, Burke's or Purcell's."[35] The dietary restrictions also meant that Jews rarely ate in non-Jewish homes.

The Jewish community was close-knit and caring. It was rich in what economists and sociologists dub "social capital," quickly establishing its own vibrant and exclusive network of clubs and support groups.[36] In part this was a replication of what had existed in *der heim*, but some of the new associations reflected the immigrants' desire to adapt to new surroundings.[37] Thus, the early communal ventures in Dublin included the reading and lecture rooms established at 21 Curzon Street in late 1889 by Litvaks of "the poorest class," "extremely anxious to raise their educational status" and welcoming gifts of books in English, German, and Hebrew; and the Dublin Young Men's Hebrew Association, which organized a "successful concert" in its rooms in the Portobello Hotel two years later.[38] The long list of organizations created in the early decades included the Board of Shechita (a kosher slaughtering society); the Jewish Board of Guardians; the Hebrew Philanthropic Loan Society[39]; the Limerick, Dublin, and Cork Chovevei Zion branches; the Belfast Literary and Social Society; the Dublin Jewish Chess Society[40]; the Belfast and Dublin Hebrew Societies for Visiting the Sick; the Dorshei Zion Societies of Belfast and Limerick; the Belfast Hachnosas Orchim; the Cork and Dublin branches of B'nouth (or Bnot) Zion (the Daughters of Zion); the Limerick and Cork Hebrew Young Men's Association; the Dublin Jewish Athletic Association (Adelaide Football Club); the Cork Jewish Young Men's Literary Association; the Cork Hebrew Philanthropic and Burial Society; the Cork Board of Guardians (established in 1910); the Adelaide Girls' Friendly Club; the Adelaide Cricket Club; the Literary, Debating and Social Club (Dublin); the Dublin Young Men's Reading and Debating Association (77 Lombard Street West)[41]; the Jewish Mutual Benefit Society; the Passover Relief Fund; the Hebrew Foreign Ladies' Benevolent Society; the Belfast Foreign Ladies' Benevolent Society; the Jewish Lads' Brigade; the 16th Dublin Jewish troop of Baden Powell Boy Scouts; the Dublin Jewish Boxing Club; Agudath Yisroel (founded 1913); and the Jewish Bride's Aid Society (founded in 1894). The "English" community had its Montefiore Musical and Dramatic Club, its Hollymount Amusement Club, and its annual all-night dance organized by the Hollymount Dancing Club.[42] Cork's Litvaks were the first (in 1890) to establish their own state-funded primary school, which combined Jewish ethos and national curriculum. Irish Jewry's charitable activities received a huge boost in 1906, when a bequest of £15,000 by millionaire Samuel Lewis, a Dublin-born London moneylender, for the relief of Dublin's Jewish poor was distributed among the several Jewish charitable societies. Lewis's gift was worth about €2 million in today's money.[43] Significantly, there were no self-defense or vigilante organizations.

The societies and clubs noted above catered to the religious, welfare, sporting, and cultural needs of the community. Their number and vibrancy certainly reduced contact with non-Jewish Ireland. No wonder a police report dating from the early 1900s noted, "They only associate with themselves . . . always trading when possible with one another."[44] Chaim Herzog, future president of Israel and resident of Little Jerusalem (where he was known to his friends as Hymie) between 1919 and 1935, concurred. "Physically and psychologically," he remembered, "the Jewish community was closed in on itself. . . . Very few Jews mingled socially with non-Jews."[45] Exclusivity sometimes bred misunderstanding and resentment. In Cork in 1888, at a time of heightened communal tension, a trades council delegate appended an anti-Semitic tirade with the complaint that local Jews "would not eat with or shake hands with a Christian."[46]

Not all the Jewish clubs, however, excluded ongoing contact with non-Jews. This was particularly so in the case of the Carlisle Cricket Club, founded in 1908. Carlisle, which changed its name to Carlisle Athletic Union in 1918 and became the Dublin Maccabi Association in 1954, was a focal point of Jewish social life for many decades, but it often fielded a few non-Jewish players, and its competition always came from non-Jewish teams.[47] Similarly with boxing: only five of the twenty-four boxers featured at the Dublin Jewish Boxing Club's annual tournament in 1939 were Jewish.[48] Sport fostered communal pride, but it also undoubtedly narrowed the cultural divide between native and immigrant, and in time many Jews joined and supported non-Jewish rugby and football clubs.[49]

And at the outset at least, there was also the barrier of language. Courtship and marriages between Jews and non-Jews were frowned on by both sides and were very much the exception. Though mixed Catholic-Protestant marriages were not unheard of along the South Circular Road area a century ago—about 2.3 percent of non-Jewish couples living there were in this category[50]—for a Jew to marry a Gentile was far more unusual. Jews who married out ran the risk of being permanently cut off from their own community. Occasionally the children or grandchildren of immigrants married out, but often at great emotional cost. When Rosie Bloom married out in 1917 "it was a terrible blow to the community," and though her parents were "really broad minded," the marriage "really sort of broke up the family in a way."[51] Boxer Freddy Weinsummer's marriage to a beautiful young Gentile from Harold's Cross in the 1930s made him the envy of many young Gentile men, but "that was the end of him" as far as his own community was concerned. Even the feisty and unconventional Estella Solomons (1882–1968) held off marrying her longtime partner, Seamus O'Sullivan, until after both her parents were dead.[52] June Levine's father married out in the 1920s but was determined that she did not: "he would have thrown one of his famous tantrums and probably had a stroke."[53] Indeed, some of the first-generation immigrants sat shiva for offspring who married out and "treated them as if they had died."[54] A tailor from Portobello, Harry Isaacson, was one of the first to marry outside the community—certainly before 1920. Convinced that his action would cause the death of their devout father, a religious teacher, his brothers caught and beat him almost unconscious on the bank of the Grand Canal before being restrained by Gentile onlookers. However, shortly after the marriage, peace was restored when Isaacson's wife converted to Judaism, and the couple moved back to the Jewish neighborhood. Harry continued to attend shul and had a Jewish burial, but all seven of his children married out.[55] Of course, Gentile parents were just as unenthusiastic about their children marrying out. The taboo against mixed marriages set a boundary on Jewish-Gentile contacts.

As elsewhere, Freemasonry offered some of the more successful men in the Jewish community companionship with non-Jewish professionals and businessmen. Leaders of the Dublin Hebrew Congregation such as lawyers Ernest Harris and John D. Rosenthal, optician Maurice E. Solomons, and merchant Henry de Groot had already become members before 1895; stockbroker Edwin M. Solomons joined the Trinity College lodge in 1903, and Asher and Julius Leventon joined different Dublin lodges in 1907. Abraham W. Briscoe, whose son Robert would become lord mayor of Dublin, became a brother in 1906 and was one of the first of the Litvak community to join; other prominent Litvaks who joined later included Jacob Zlotover (1922), Isaac and David Eppel (1922 and 1923), and Gerald J. Goldberg. Goldberg, a prominent solicitor and future lord mayor of Cork, joined that city's Harmony lodge in 1938. Although Abraham Briscoe was a member of Dublin's Israel lodge, and Israel Kaitcer and Louis Solomon members of Belfast's Sholom lodge, Jewish masons were well spread across lodges. Intriguingly, the admission registers also include Hyman Kaitcer, who joined the Athy lodge in 1904, Joseph R. Khan (Carlow, 1914), and Isaac Khan (Baltinglass, 1915).[56]

At the outset, politics distanced the Litvaks from most of the native population. The Jewish community's loyalties were very firmly unionist to begin with. This followed from the rabbinical principle that diaspora Jews be loyal to the country in which they lived.[57] The Jews had come from anti-Semitic, despotic Russia and were presumably relieved and grateful to be in a more tolerant place. They genuinely regarded the British

monarch as guarantor of their liberties; moreover, they were suspicious
of Home Rule and Roman Catholicism. In eastern European Jewish eyes,
nationalism was almost invariably linked with unbridled xenophobia
and anti-Semitism; perhaps Irish nationalism also frightened them on
this score.

In the early years Jewish Ireland expressed its loyalty both in private
and in public. Queen Victoria's diamond jubilee in 1897 prompted com-
memorative services in Belfast and in Cork, and on Adelaide Road "a vast
concourse of Jews and Christians" heard Rev. L. Mendelsohn preach on
the theme that "Loyalty is the sentiment which beautifies our private life."
The elderly monarch's visit in 1900 prompted illuminated addresses and
further protests of loyalty and affection from the Dublin and Belfast congregations.[58] The visit occurred during the Boer War, when week after
week the *Jewish Chronicle* featured pictures of Jewish recruits to H.M.
forces. Reverend Mendelsohn preached again, taking as his theme "Many
daughters have done virtuously but thou excellest them all." According
to the *Jewish Chronicle*,

> He pointed out that in the Queen we have a thousand claims to rever-
> ence as mother, wife and queen. The stream is only sweet and re-
> freshing when the fountain-head is pure. By her example and in the
> choice of her Ministers, she has furthered every liberal movement.
> Slowly and surely, after we had also given our children as a ransom
> on battlefields, have prejudice been rooted out of the individuals that
> compose a nation, and our people has won the confidence of the
> nation by acts of loyalty.[59]

Mendelsohn's praise for Victoria's liberalism is noteworthy. Jessie
Bloom's parents were very loyal[60]; Joseph and Rebecca Reuben of Walworth Road had two portraits of Queen Victoria hanging on an upstairs
wall; and the Jewish Lads' Brigade ended its very first inspection and
display with "a sketch representing an attack by natives on a British
force and introducing an ambulance display."[61] A little over a decade after
Victoria's final visit, the Adelaide Road congregation marked King Edward VII's visit to Dublin with an address of welcome, and Rabbi Yossel-
sohn eulogized the king in front of the Litvak faithful at Lennox Street
shul, where the *beit midrash* (a place of study for male adults) was full to
overflowing.[62]

The choice of schooling created a further gap between the immigrants
and the majority of their neighbors. Most Jewish children steered clear of
Catholic national and secondary schools; only those who could afford
nothing else resorted to the Irish Christian Brothers. Before the establishment of Zion Schools on Bloomfield Avenue in 1934, the most popular
primary schools for Jewish children were St. Catherine's on Donore Ave-

nue and the Unitarian Damer School on Stephen's Green; for secondary schooling, Alexandra and Diocesan were the schools of choice for girls; Wesley College, St. Andrew's College, and the High School for boys.[63] Chaim Herzog attended Wesley College, "both fashionable and not Catholic, which was probably why my parents sent me there."[64] Third-level students opted for "Protestant" Trinity College and the Royal College of Surgeons rather than "Catholic" University College Dublin.

In due course, however, the community would integrate into the nationalist mainstream. The short-lived Judaeo-Irish Home Rule Association (JHRA), founded in 1908 by Joseph Edelstein and Jacob Elyan—two of "exactly half a dozen irresponsible individuals," according to one hostile source—against the wishes of some community leaders, marked a start in this respect. The opening meeting of the JHRA in the Mansion House's supper room on 10 September 1908 attracted about sixty Jews and three United Irish League M.P.s. Jacob Elyan explained on behalf of his fellow Jews that it was "in order to dispel the delusion and darkness which had surrounded them [that] they had formed this association." Edelstein's contribution referred to the overtaxation of Ireland, a burning issue at the time, while Arthur Newman lamented that the Jews were "used to seeing the discredited action of one being ascribed to the whole." "Mr. Wigoder"—almost certainly medical student Philip Wigoder—sought to move an amendment but was not allowed to do so by the chair. The meeting ended in mock-Irish style "with several interruptions and a free fight."[65]

The JHRA did not last long, but Jacob Elyan became a member of the Dublin executive of the United Irish League, and other second-generation Litvaks such as Michael Noyk and Robert Briscoe would play an important part in the Republican movement after the Easter Rising of 1916, as would Estella Solomons from the "English" community. From 1927 on, when he first contested the Dublin South constituency (which included the Little Jerusalem area) for the newly formed Fianna Fáil party, Robert Briscoe would have the support of most of the Dublin Jewish community.[66] A gregarious and amiable businessman with a finger in many pies, Briscoe served in the Dáil for nearly forty years (1927–65). In the 1960s an elderly Briscoe would represent the president of Ireland at the central Jewish service to mark the fiftieth anniversary of the Easter Rising of 1916, while his newly elected son, Ben Briscoe T.D., represented the prime minister. On that occasion, a specially composed prayer celebrated "a small heroic band of Irish citizens [sic] [who] struck an unforgettable blow for freedom," and "this friendly land in which the children of our own people, pursued and tormented among many nations, have found . . . rest and security, happiness and peace."[67]

Remembering Limerick

The main focus in this study is on economic and demographic aspects of Irish Jewry. Inevitably, given the tragic world history of Jewry, much of the historical and sociological discourse about Ireland's Litvaks and their descendants has focused instead on issues of racism and discrimination.[68] Even the tiny size of Ireland's Jewish population before the Litvak "invasion" has been attributed to Irish anti-Semitism, even though until very recently Ireland was an unpromising destination for immigrants from *any* quarter. Equally implausible is the link drawn between "Irish anti-Semitism" and what one observer has dubbed "the gradual decimation of the Dublin Jewish community" in recent years.[69] In reality, there was more anti-Semitism in the first half of the last century, when Jewish numbers were rising, than in the second half, when they plummeted.

Irish anti-Semitism existed, and traces doubtless still persist, but it was of a relatively mild variety. It reached its climax in Limerick in early 1904, when the rantings of a young Redemptorist preacher, Father John Creagh, led to the boycott that prompted the departure of several households in that city's small Jewish community. At the time, Limerick was a city of about forty thousand people. There was poverty aplenty: in the 1890s and 1900s one Limerick family in ten still lived in one-room tenements.

Limerick's Jews, like those of other Irish cities, were mainly middlemen traders. Apart from two "dental mechanics" and two clergymen, all male household heads and boarders listed in the 1901 census were described as peddlers, drapers, or shopkeepers. Most of the community lived in small houses on Colooney (now Wolfe Tone) Street, half a mile or so west of the city center; three families (those of Marcus Blond, Louis Goldberg, and Jacob Barron) lived in relative affluence on nearby Henry Street. One household in two could afford a live-in domestic servant in 1901, a sign that Litvak Jewry by then had achieved a modicum of comfort and respectability.

The community had been subject to much internal bickering since the 1880s. In early 1901 Louis Goldberg's family and several other families broke away because—so they claimed—they did "not want to associate [themselves] with moneylenders."[70] Their opponents responded that Goldberg and the others left "because they were not appointed by our Community as their leaders." In the following year the majority under Rabbi Elias Levin formed a burial society and purchased a graveyard; until then the remains of deceased congregants had to be transported by train for burial in Cork. Levin hoped that the community might thereby escape "the derision . . . of the gentiles in whose midst we live, who say: It is not enough that the Hebrews be wandering through their lifetimes, but also after their death." He promised that Goldberg and his associates—named and shamed as David Weinrank, Leib Goldberg, Saul Ginzburg, and Azriel Shabbtai Aranwitz—would never be allowed an appointment in the new burial society because they had "defiled the name of the congregation of Israel before the gentiles."[71] For a time Colooney Street housed two rabbis and two synagogues, but when the Goldbergs left Limerick for Cork in the wake of the boycott, the lease on their breakaway synagogue at 72 Colooney Street was snapped up by their rivals.[72] The split in the community can hardly have helped in 1904.

The Limerick events are often regarded, and rightly so, as the most serious outbreak of anti-Semitism in recent Irish history. Creagh's sermons mingled classic anti-Semitic rhetoric with accusations of exploitation by the weekly men: "Nowadays they [i.e., the Jews] dare not kidnap and slay children, but they will not hesitate to expose them to a longer and even more cruel martyrdom by taking the clothes off their backs and the bit out of their mouths." Creagh omitted to mention that Limerick's most prominent moneylenders were Gentiles, and that the credit extended by non-Jewish traders (including department stores such as Todds and Cannocks) dwarfed that supplied by Jewish drapers and house furnishers. In the wake of Creagh's sermons some Jews were physically assaulted and their property threatened; the late Gerald Goldberg recalled how his father and his cousin were waylaid and badly beaten and his father's house "attacked, its windows broken, its front door battered and the family driven into refuge in an upper room." Another house would have been ransacked but for the intervention of one John Daly, an elderly ex-Fenian.[73]

Creagh's sermons led to a boycott against the city's Jewish traders. This not only ruled out new business; it also led to opportunistic defaulting on outstanding debts. In the following months several households in a community of 170 souls left the city (though, significantly, not Ireland). In most cases, it seems, the breadwinners had lost their jobs as travelers or collectors for "the wealthier Jews . . . in consequence of the agitation." The decline from 170 in 1901 to 119 a decade later was not entirely due to the boycott, however: the Goldbergs left in part because of the split described above, and three other households left to join relatives in South Africa. The boycott exacerbated other sectarian tensions—those between Catholic and Protestant—in Limerick, and it is also possible that divisions within the Jewish community influenced the distribution of relief funds from outside, and forced some of the poorer families to leave.[74] The boycott was still in force in 1905, although dental mechanic Marcus Jaffe and furniture dealer Philip Toohey were exempt. Those who remained seem to have made good their losses, for more than half of them could afford domestic servants in 1911, and two had graduated from credit draper in 1901 to financier in 1911. The average household head "aged" only four years over the decade because some of those who left were replaced by younger immigrants.[75]

The story of the Limerick "pogrom"—which really does not deserve to be called a pogrom—has been told more than once, but much about those involved, both perpetrators and victims, and their motivations remains hidden.[76] Though Father Creagh's role has been highlighted, the events of 1904 were the culmination of sporadic attacks on Jewish traders since the mid-1880s.[77] Why Limerick, and not Cork or Dublin? Why 1904? Why *only* 1904? Was 1904 an aberration, or was there "no better year for summing up attitudes toward Irish Jewry in modern times?"[78] Surely, part of the answer is suggested by Father Creagh's residence in France at the height of the Dreyfus Affair, though it also bears noting that Limerick Jews had been subject to a series of smaller incidents in earlier years.[79]

A comparative perspective is offered by events occurring in south Wales seven years later. In the mining town of Tredegar in July 1882 Irish immigrant laborers had been the targets of local mobs, and two Irishmen had been murdered.[80] In 1911 it was the turn of Jewish immigrant traders. The anti-Jewish riots in south Wales in August of that year involved no fatalities, but in geographical range and intensity they dwarfed anything ever happening in Ireland. They began with "about 200 young fellows" wrecking and looting eighteen Jewish shops in Tredegar, but the trouble spread to several neighboring hillside towns (Ebbw Vale, Rhymney, Cwm, Victoria, Brynmawr, Bargoed, and Beaufort) in the following days, and required the presence of the Worcester Regiment to quell. In the wake of the outbreaks, the *Jewish Chronicle* put the damage and losses sustained by the Jewish population at "between £50,000 and £100,000"—or €7 million to €14 million in today's money.[81] Both the Welsh and Limerick outbreaks (despite Creagh's theological fulminations) were heavily "economic" in content: neither, it seems, involved the destruction of Jewish religious or communal property.

The Catholic bishop of Limerick, Dr. Edward O'Dwyer, was criticized both at the time and later for not condemning Creagh and the boycott publicly. In private, O'Dwyer tried to intervene, but he had little ecclesiastical authority over Creagh. Moreover, he had little sympathy for the local Jewish community, holding that the prejudice against them was mainly economic in origin, and instancing a report from one his priests that several Jews had left the town some years earlier, leaving behind unpaid debts of over £800. Rabbi Levin, spiritual leader of the majority faction, was alleged to have been one of the culprits. According to O'Dwyer Levin had absconded to America, only to return after a safe interval. Limerick tradesmen continued to deny him credit.[82] Nor was the reputation of Marcus Blond, a former clergyman and president of the Limerick congregation, an unblemished one: in 1900 he had been convicted of assaulting his father-in-law and given two months' hard labor in prison.[83]

The prejudice of "English" Jews toward their Litvak coreligionists may also have influenced their initial reaction to the events of 1904 in Limerick. The response of the Dublin Hebrew Congregation was to have its president accompany two delegates from the London Jewish Board of Deputies to Limerick, where they "spent some days in fully investigating the circumstances of each member of the community, their system of trading, and the character of each applicant for relief, and also the character of those who were once resident there and now live in other towns in Ireland." The group solicited information from "municipal officers, lending merchants, professional gentlemen, and Roman Catholic clergymen."[84] The mere existence of such an inquiry suggests that the "English" communities in Adelaide Road and London feared the worst of their "Russian" brethren. Indeed, the London Board had long been unsure about the Limerick community, and its attitude in 1904 is probably reflected in Samuel Montagu's remark in a letter to M. E. Solomons of the Dublin Hebrew Congregation in April of that year that "many of the Limerick Jews indulge in money lending under cover of peddling and this probably gave a hand to the attack."[85] Montagu's remark anticipates Lord Rothschild's regarding Tredegar's Jews in 1911: "They are a bad lot and probably deserve what they are getting."[86] The date of the Limerick boycott was probably a factor here: it took place at a time when legislation to control "alien" immigration was in the works, and when the Jewish establishment feared that the deceitful practices of the few would place the whole community at risk. In the event, however, the report cleared the Limerick traders of all wrongdoing. It found that with the exception of some five or six families the Limerick community was reduced to penury by the boycott, and inferred "strong evidence of fair trading" from how rare it was for Jewish traders to take proceedings to recover debts.[87]

Autobiographical Memory

They were lovely people . . . very, very friendly
people . . .
—*A woman who grew up on Raymond Street*[88]

Memoirs offer another source of insight into communal interaction. The impressions gleaned from Jewish memoirs are ambiguous on this score. Some give the impression of a rather closed community in the early days. For example, A. J. Leventhal (1896–1979), a native of Oakfield Place off Clanbrassil Street, reminisced in the 1940s about his childhood.

Between the cul-de-sac known as Oakfield Place [and] the lower end of Lombard Street West where non-Jews lived . . . might well have been a ghetto wall, so well drawn into their own loyalties were the young denizens of each locality.[89]

Indeed, in the late 1890s boys reenacted their own version of the Boer War on the side streets of Little Jerusalem, with Catholic lads playing the Boers and Jewish lads the British side. The young Max Nurock suffered for his parents' loyalties.

My unwise parents dressed me at the age of six in a little khaki suit with a hat like one of the volunteers—the CIV[90]—and I walked proudly down Emorville Avenue where I lived at the time, with a little wooden sword, and a small boy, he was certainly my size even more, of another persuasion, just walked and hit me one hit one biff in midriff which put me right out. I never wore that suit again. But we used to join up with a group and in the alleys around Lombard Street, you remember Louis? And have battles of sticks and stones with the Catholic boys, we representing the British and they the Boers.

Other Jewish memoirs imply a greater degree of personal contact and mutual empathy than as described by A. J. Leventhal. Jessie Bloom, who moved with her family to Windsor Terrace by the Grand Canal a few years after she was born, reminisced about "gradually beginning to be part of the neighborhood" in the 1890s, and recalled her closest friend, Molly Murphy, and her brother's friend Ned Smith, another Catholic who was friendly with many of the ultra-orthodox *shvartz frum*. She also related how she and her Jewish friends would frequently shift allegiances from Catholic to Protestant children in street battles.[91] And she noted,

The Sabbath observance among the children in Dublin naturally had great overtones of the *shtetl* influence and yet our Gentile playmates joined us on that day whenever possible, and enjoyed some of the good things of that Day. . . . There were . . . homes where we went calling, sometimes we would just come to sit down and visit, answer questions about our school work, etc. but always we felt we were welcome. It was a sort of get acquainted . . . to show our welcome to the new comers, and to further our good will with the people who were already in the town. It is strange that this feeling of solidarity should have become so important to us all, and perhaps in the Lithuanian *shtetl* the friendly feeling was only shown among our own, but in Dublin there was the acceptance of our Irish playmates, no wonder many of them could speak Yiddish as good as we did, and knew as much of the important religious observances as we did. . . . Since we were not allowed to eat *traifa* we rarely ate in the homes of our Gentile playmates, but gradually as we became more friendly they would ask us why we did not eat with them.[92]

Nick Harris, born in 1915, writes engagingly about friendships made and neighborly favors granted and received on Greenville Terrace in the 1920s.[93] Though his parents never managed to strike up close friendships with non-Jews of their own age, his earliest "clear memories" are being with "my friend John Kelly" watching British soldiers parading in Wellington Barracks when he was five years old. Later, at secondary school in Westland Row, he became close friends with one John Geraghty, whom he used to meet after school. "All my pals were non-Jewish," he remembers with feeling, "religion didn't come into it." "In all the years living in Greenville Terrace," he could not remember "any unpleasantness between our non-Jewish neighbors and ourselves."[94] On Saint Kevin's Road in Portobello, home of the Levitas family, the boys also all played together. Maurice Levitas's father, a tailor's presser, learned how to read and write English from a young next-door neighbor who was studying for the priesthood.[95] Harold Mushatt, who ran a tiny chemist's shop at 3 Francis Street with his brother between 1922 and 1967, remembered the inhabitants of the tenements around Francis Street and Engine Alley as "great people" with whom there was "a bond of trust." In a private family memoir, Simon Waterman described how in Downpatrick in 1941 and 1943 hundreds of local people accompanied the hearses carrying the remains of his parents as far as the railway station.[96] In Jerusalem in 1972 Max Nurock and Louis Wigoder, two elderly and distinguished ex-Dubliners, recalled the 1890s and the 1900s for an oral history project at the Hebrew University.

> LOUIS WIGODER. Westland Row Catholic School where I also had the wonderful experience of great friendship from all the Catholic priests, they were all priests teaching us there, and candidly, throughout my whole life in Ireland, I never experienced any anti-Semitism. There were the usual games, throwing stones at each other as boys were returning from Cheder and the Catholics were there, that was just among ourselves—but purely family quarrels.
> MAX NUROCK. [I]n our childhood, in our adolescence in Dublin, we met nothing but rare, superficial, unimportant, rather juvenile playfulness, as you would call it, we met nothing but friendship. We didn't feel any difference. And I don't know how the Jewish community in Dublin is integrated today, but we weren't held at arms length.[97]

Here we are eavesdropping, as it were, on conversations between elderly Dublin Jews. David Birkahn, a Cork-born Jew who had emigrated to Palestine in the late 1930s when he was in his twenties, corroborates. In July 1987 Birkahn confided to a Jewish American researcher in Jerusalem that "the Irish have been very tolerant, very lovable . . . and have been very accommodating to the Jews," and her response was, "Oh everything I have found in [my] research testifies to that totally."[98] In Belfast, too, a Jewish sociologist who interviewed elderly Jews in the 1990s found "little, if any, substantive evidence of anti-Semitism"; one interviewee reported that "we had good relations with our neighbors," another that "Northern Ireland was a good place to live."[99] For all the other evidence cited earlier, it is difficult to dismiss the claims of many who might have been at the receiving end of anti-Semitism that they never encountered more than mild prejudice in Ireland.

Recollections taken from members of the host community, if less reliable, broadly corroborate. Such recollections refer to the 1920s and later, by which time a pattern of neighborly relations had been set. In spring 2003 I contacted the residents of half a dozen streets in what used to be Little Jerusalem by mail, seeking memories of interaction with neighbors. In a follow-up exercise I interviewed several of those likely to be most knowledgeable. The following paragraphs give a flavor of the responses.[100]

BF of Greenville Terrace listed the three Jewish families still living on the street when he was younger; he and his wife "had good relations with all of them." He mentioned visiting two Jewish ex-neighbors in the Jewish Nursing Home in Rathmines and also attending their funerals. A neighbor in her eighties, a lifelong resident of the street and a treasure of vivid and colorful anecdotes, noted, "We never asked questions about their religion. We accepted them as neighbors. . . . Indeed I think we seemed to have more in common with them than with our few Protestant families who were more aloof." Sheila Cunningham remembers a neighbor, Mrs. Racusin of Brainboro, joking to her mother, "Mrs. Cunningham, you are such a good neighbor, I'd loan you my pot to cook a pig's cheek in!" News of Mrs. Cunningham's death in 1972 brought tears to the eyes of Isaac Eppel, an antique dealer who lived on the South Circular Road. But Sheila also noted, "Looking back now we realize that although the Jewish children came to our house we were never invited to theirs. In the surrounding streets people called us in to put a match to their fire or gas. Our neighbors never did this." Another resident of the street since the 1970s remembered its last Jewish residents as "very friendly"; "there was no hostility at all." AR, also a former resident, referred to two Jewish sisters in no. 22 who were somewhat private people, but "gave our family some of their Passover bread on a couple of occasions."

On Saint Kevin's Road, CM obtained most of her information on the street's history from the late Max Kravitz and his wife, "really public-spirited neighbors." On Saint Kevin's Parade, a neighbor remembered playing "in and out of each other's houses" as children with Linda Rick in the 1940s, one of the very few Jewish children on the street at that time. The Parade's last Jewish resident is elderly; "her non-Jewish neighbors are very attentive to her needs and visit her daily . . . to make sure she doesn't want for anything." Over twenty years ago eighty-four-year-old Mrs. O'Kelly, who lived on the Parade, remarked to a folklore collector that Jewish neighbors were liked and were "very kind if you were sick or that." SB, formerly of Dufferin Avenue, wrote that "Jewish neighbors . . . would more readily come to one's assistance in times of need than Irish neighbors," though his older sister "always seems to have had a dislike of Jews for no particular [reason]." Another resident described Jews as "very decent, quiet living people, who minded their own businesses, very easy to get on with and friendly." PB, who lived on the avenue as a boy in the 1960s, had "slight memories of the men, all somber-looking types making their way to the synagogue. Some were friendly but most ignored us kids. There were some Jewish kids in the neighborhood but they kept to themselves."

A man who has lived on the street since 1941 has "fond memories of many of [his] Jewish neighbors," but added,

> Getting to know your Jewish neighbors was easier for younger people . . . than it was for your parents. Adult Jews were not great mixers with their Christian neighbors other than those living near you. . . . [T]hey were a close-knit society and their main interest was in each other and each other's welfare. They were employers rather than employees and outside their ownership of the theatre and clothing businesses they were picture frame and scrap metal dealers, furniture restorers and money lenders and most important of all they, generally, they paid very low wages. . . . So overall, from the commercial point of view, there was no great love lost between the two factions. . . . Although I lived amongst them for most of my life and had a lot of contact with them I can't say I truly knew them. Of course I knew that they were different to us both in custom and habits but there was always that aloofness about them. But leaving that aside my memories of them are happy ones.[101]

On Longwood Avenue TH remembered "when [her] mother came home after an operation, a Jewess came and gave her the daintiest food items I've ever seen." She also wrote of "one Jewess [who] used to bring us water from the river Jordan when she visited it." Eighty-three-year-old Olive Sealy's sense that everybody on Martin Street got along "like a house on fire" was confirmed by seventy-seven-year-old George Kavanagh, a neighbor. He claimed that "we got on well with all our Jewish neighbors" and had a vivid recollection of Jewish friends waving at him through the window of his classroom in Grantham Street national school as they made their way home from Damer School. Another neighbor remembered the Malkinsons coming out on the street with glasses of wine to wish a bride-to-be well as she headed off to the church. A fifty-six-year-old Catholic who grew up on the street said his mother nursed Harry Isaacson, a neighbor, "till he died," and "thought the world of Mrs. Malkinson." The kindness to Harry Isaacson was reciprocated at the Lower Clanbrassil Street end of Lombard Street West, where a recently bereaved widow went to live with a Jewish family, who took care of her in old age. EK, who lived on nearby Lennox Street remembered her Jewish neighbors as "hard-working, good neighbors [who] never interfered." As far as she was concerned, there was complete integration. MB, who lived on Raymond Street, spoke of her former Jewish neighbors as "very, very friendly people."

Good relations, it is true, rarely implied socializing in Jewish homes. An elderly woman who spent all her life on Greenville Terrace, and who liked her Jewish neighbors, noted, "we were never in their homes—we only realized that afterward—but they'd share their food."[102] An eighty-two-year-old who grew up in poverty on Lower Clanbrassil Street declared that Jewish children would not be allowed play with him or his friends—but neither, probably, would the children of better-off Christian households.

Others remarked on how their Jewish neighbors dressed up for shul and for weddings, and some attributed their "flamboyant" attire to their connections in the clothing trade.[103] Social gradations within the Jewish community were implied, too. While Mrs. Racusin of Brainboro off Greenville Terrace had no compunction about hanging out her washing in front of her upstairs flat for all to see, on middle-class Dufferin Avenue servant girls seemed to spend a lot of time scrubbing in front of their Jewish employers' houses.

Catholic domestic servants probably learned more about the domestic life of the Jewish community than anyone else. Although they washed and scrubbed and brushed rather than cooked, they must have learned something also about kashrut and the hygienic practices associated with it. Nannie "Mack," who worked part-time for the Spiros from their arrival in Dublin in the late 1880s until her death in 1916, built a close relationship with all the household, and "would tell mother all the news of [Montague] Court and [Protestant] Row, how this neighbor lost his job, that one was expecting a baby, that one had a drunken husband."[104] The immigrants' understanding of and empathy with the host population grew with such contacts.

Memory lane, of course, is a thoroughfare marked by potholes and misleading signals. The pitfalls of interpreting snippets of autobiographical memory as relayed to a stranger, orally or by correspondence, need not be labored. Nonetheless, the overall impression left by written memoirs and oral evidence is of communal harmony at the local level.[105] The sense of harmony registered by the autobiographical evidence is supported by the fact that non-Jews never, it seems, acted in concert to keep Jews out of a street or neighborhood. Nor were there pressures on landlords or estate agents to discriminate against prospective Jewish tenants.

In 1893, when the Irish Litvak community was still in its infancy, Thomas Finlay S.J. described how "in some of the streets that open off the South Circular Road one may walk along the pavement from end to end and hardly hear a word of English spoken by the children who are at play on the footpath. We are in as completely a Jewish quarter as if we were wandering through some city of Poland or Southern Russia."[106] Finlay exaggerated, since as noted in chapter 5, even the most Jewish streets in Little Jerusalem nearly always contained non-Jewish families. But his account of the inward-looking character of the community rings true for that period. Even three decades later there was consternation among Dublin Litvaks "when a (Jewish) trader from Hungary arrived with his big red beard and a lot of children. It took him a long time to be accepted."[107]

Ironically, for all the red-bearded Hungarian's problems, there is a sense in which the Litvaks themselves wanted to be accepted from early on. This was reflected in their eagerness to learn English, in their participation in Irish cultural and political life, and in their determination to move away from their traditional "low-esteem" avocations toward ones that were more respectable and "acceptable." The streets and the neighborhoods became catalysts where initial hostility and mutual suspicion gave way to something between peaceful coexistence and mutual empathy. The acculturation of the Litvak immigrants and their descendants and their economic integration into Irish society turned them into Irishmen and Irishwomen. There were boundaries to neighborliness, however. Usually, it stopped short of intimacy and assimilation. In both Jewish and non-Jewish communities the strongest friendships were within the community.

SOCIAL LEARNING ACROSS COMMUNITIES?

What of the impact of intercommunal contacts on demographic patterns? In an area like family planning, where religious belief was a fundamental constraint, the impact is unlikely to have been significant. That Orthodox Jewish teaching on contraception was more liberal and flexible than was the Catholic position was really beside the point. However, there were other areas where who one's neighbor was could have made a difference. For instance, it is unlikely that Jewish children would have been completely immune from infectious diseases affecting their non-Jewish near neighbors. Greater attention to cleanliness and tidiness in one community is likely to have benefited the other, if only marginally. Given the close proximity of one group to the other over half a century or so, it is not implausible to expect such two-way cultural influences to have been at work.

But evidence on deliberate borrowing and learning is elusive. This is hardly surprising, since it is not even clear that non-Jews realized at the time that their Jewish neighbors were better at ensuring the survival of their infants and children. Present-day non-Jewish residents of Little Jerusalem never highlight this aspect, though they are quick to point to other perceived differences such as greater social mobility and business acumen. Given that even today we still do not fully understand why Jewish parents were so good at caring for their young offspring, it is surely expecting too much to expect their neighbors to have worked it out for themselves. The gap in infant and child survival chances was widely remarked on in scientific circles, but that is another matter.

Even if some intercommunal learning took place in realms such as personal hygiene, breastfeeding, or family planning, it would be very difficult to document. One area that is easier to document is food and diet. The influence of inadequate diets on infant and child mortality was probably more due to the primitive state of nutritional science and medical knowledge than to the lack of purchasing power.[108] There is no evidence of cross-cultural influences in this sphere: even after a Jewish presence of three-quarters of a century, no item in the Jewish diet had become part of occasional—never mind regular—non-Jewish fare. For as long as Little Jerusalem lasted, local non-Jews opted for beef and pork rather than the fish and poultry favored by their presumably healthier Jewish neighbors. The Jewish butchers and groceries on Lower Clanbrassil Street always catered to an overwhelmingly Jewish clientele. Perhaps one reason for the lack of crossover was that Jews and non-Jews rarely ate together.[109] Observant Jews avoided non-Jewish tables for religious reasons and tended not to invite their non-Jewish neighbors to dinner. Nor could non-Jews have acquired a taste for Jewish food through Jewish catering establishments; the few there were catered to an exclusively Jewish clientele, and indeed most Jewish weddings were catered in community halls adjoining their synagogues.

In summary, at the outset, a degree of mutual suspicion between native and newcomer was inevitable. In the course of their trading the Jewish immigrants found some of their stereotypes of the goyim confirmed, while the natives transferred some of their xenophobia and their contempt for moneylenders to the Jews. Doubtless, there was also an element of anti-

Semitism. Two factors helped minimize tensions between native and new-comer, however. First, the immigrants were always relatively few in number and keen to adapt to their new environment. They were unostentatious and law-abiding. In what was a new experience for those used to shtetl life, from the beginning they lived cheek by jowl with non-Jews. Second, they and their non-Jewish neighbors formed for the most part "noncompeting groups" insofar as employment was concerned. Native workers, by and large, did not feel threatened by the newcomers: their skills were broadly complementary. For that reason, neither Dublin nor Belfast ever witnessed anything to match the conflicts between Gentile and Jewish workers and householders in, say, early twentieth-century New York, in Latin America, or in London's East End in the 1930s.[110]

Another crucial point: attitudes almost certainly shifted over time. The sons and daughters of the immigrants grew up with Gentile neighbors and felt differently about them than their parents had. Children proved the catalysts for Jewish and Gentile householders getting to know and respect one other. The younger generation's contacts with Gentiles extended far beyond what Karl Marx dubbed the "callous cash payment." But even in the cases of the weekly business and moneylending, the tie between seller and buyer sometimes developed beyond the pure cash transaction. Some customers looked forward to the peddler's call, and even continued buying when they no longer needed to do so.[111]

In the end, however, although Jew and non-Jew learned to live peacefully together, the cultural independence of both sides argues against the kind of cross-communal networking and social learning that would have led to better health practices and a faster fertility transition.

A Note on Litigation between Jews

On the morning of Sunday, 25 March 1894, the bodies of a Jewish couple, Joseph and Rebecca Reuben, were found hanging in their house at 7 Walworth Road, in the heart of Dublin's Jewish quarter. What the *Dublin Evening Mail* dubbed "The Jewish Suicides" attracted a lot of interest. A crowd of curious onlookers followed the vehicle carrying the Reubens' remains to the city morgue, and the courtroom was full for the inquest. It seems that Reuben, who was a wholesale draper or *wholesalenik*, had heard that two of his clients, also Jewish, were about to abscond without paying for the £34 worth of dry goods he had advanced to them. He accordingly had informed the constabulary and had them arrested. The two, whose names were variously rendered as Milson/Wilson and Biljon/Bilgon in the Irish press, had appeared in court on the previous day, a Saturday. They were released on bail.

Why suicide? It came like a bolt from the blue, and a near relative could offer no explanation for their tragic decision. The couple were comfortably off; the policeman who discovered them found over £70 in cash and a considerable stock of goods on the premises. A report in the *Freeman's Journal* suspected that the Reubens were driven to suicide out of remorse for having brought two coreligionists to the police court on the Sabbath, a hypothesis echoed by the *Jewish Chronicle* in its next issue.[112]

The conjecture is plausible.[113] Indeed, in the event of a dispute between observant Jews, the ideal was to avoid the civil courts altogether and to leave the resolution of their disputes to a *din torah*, or rabbinical arbitration.[114] It was not in the interest of Jewish traders to be on bad terms with each other or to squabble among themselves; in the event of disputes, it made sense to settle in this semi-private fashion. Not all members of the community lived up to this ideal, however.[115] An inspection of civil court cases on the eve of World War I reveals many instances of Jews bringing coreligionists to court for unpaid bills. Examples in the 1909–12 period include moneylender Simon Watchman pursuing Bernard Wine and David Marks for £2 10s and L. S. Clien for £20 10s 6d; Hyman Barron, a successful Camden Street furniture merchant, seeking £2 11s in unpaid rent from Israel Lewis; *wholesaleniks* Cornick, Weinstock, Elyan & Co. of Lombard Street West looking for £23 10s from M. Isaacson, presumably a peddler, for goods sold; Solomon Sevitt pursuing Aaron Barron for £3 1s; Max Fine, a dealer of Upper Kevin Street, seeking £3 from Henry Posner, the value of "a bag of hair detained"; Max Coleman pursuing J. Rubin of the Camden Furnishing Company for £15, the principal and interest due on a bill of exchange; and Fanny Freeman, a litigious widow living on Lombard Street West, seeking £19 10s for "cash lent and board" from Mendel Garfinkle, who traded as "Goff Artist."[116] In June 1913, Joseph Zlotover, William Nurock, and L. Clein, trustees of the Dublin Hebrew Philanthropic Loan Fund and three of the most prominent men in the Litvak community, sued Abraham Cohen for £4 10s and Max Cohen for £3, "money lent" by the fund. Presumably some cases were indeed settled through arbitration; that brought by Hyman Barron against one Isaac Green for an unpaid loan of £9 0s 1d represents an intermediate case, since the parties agreed before a civil judge to let a rabbi decide between them.[117]

Chapter 10

ICH GEH FUN "IRE"LAND

Tell me something about Irishmen—something
intimate, something not generally known. You know,
your brother has been asking me so many questions
about Jews that I want to get even with him.
—*Italo Svevo to Stanislaus Joyce*[1]

"One-horse-town" they called him, disremembering
their peddling forebears. Disremembering, the sidelong
grin on the face of a lawyer whose father, dim as the
legend of Sweet Molly Malone, hawked his way to
opulence with rotten apples in the rain where
stopped the newest horse-trams.
—*Leslie Daiken, Dublin Jewish writer*[2]

THE ACCOUNT of Irish Jewry in economic and demographic context in the preceding pages began with James Joyce's fictional creation, Leopold Bloom. Bloom, the son of a Hungarian Jewish father and an Irish Protestant mother, married a Roman Catholic and befriended Litvak immigrants. In effect the multicultural Bloom had a foot in four camps, which makes him a historically implausible character. For Joyce, Bloom was the "modern" outsider to Dublin's parochial Gentiles; but had Bloom stepped from the written page into the real-life Little Jerusalem of Joyce's day, his mixed parentage, his non–east European background, and his atheism would have ensured him a rather cold welcome from that quarter.[3] So although Joyce's ear for accents and conversational nuances and his sense of place make *Ulysses* a very useful source for the historian of Dublin in the 1890s and 1900s,[4] the same cannot be said for its portrait of Dublin Jewry. The exhaustive searches by Joyce scholars for Leopold Bloom's Dublin cousins among the city's many Blooms turned out to be wild goose chases, and it turns out that Joyce himself did know anyone in the Litvak community personally. Almost certainly, Leopold Bloom owed more to information garnered by Joyce during his sojourn in Trieste between 1904 and 1915 than to any contacts with Irish Jewry before leaving Dublin at the age of twenty-two. Bloom's agnosticism would have been more acceptable in a city such as Trieste, where one Jew in five had renounced his or her faith, and where a significant proportion of marriages involving Jews were mixed. Triestine Jewry—more middle class,

more central European, more integrated, more worldly, more liberal—
would have appealed much more to both Joyce and Bloom than to their
Dublin coreligionists.[5]

RELIGION

By strictly confessional criteria, of course, Leopold Bloom was not a Jew.
His mother was a Gentile; his father was an apostate; their son was neither
circumcised nor bar mitzvah'd; he married out, going through the mo-
tions of conversion to Catholicism in the process; he flouted the Jewish
dietary laws; and he proclaimed himself an atheist. Unlike Bloom, Irish
Jews a century ago took their religion seriously, as their frequent disputes
about ritual and belief testify. The Dublin Hebrew Congregation (DHC),
which represented the community already settled in the city before the
arrival of the Litvaks, had worshiped in a converted chapel on Mary's
Abbey off Capel Street since the 1820s.[6] In 1892 the DHC shifted its
services south of the Liffey to the fine new shul at the bottom of Adelaide
Road. The move was prompted both by the decline and southward drift
of the "English" community and the location of the "new" Lithuanian
community within walking distance, a mile or so to the west. Yet although
old and new Jews shared a common creed, the social and cultural gap
between them was still very wide in the 1890s and 1900s. Most of the
newcomers would continue to support their own *hebroth* and educational
institutions, which proved remarkably resilient. In 1915 a fundraising
plea by the United Hebrew Congregation (UHC) in support of the
planned new shul on the South Circular Road noted the opening of a
temporary *minion*, "for the purpose of closing up a few of the [existing]
small congregations in order thereby (it is hoped) bringing about greater
unity in the community."[7] Those "small congregations" would prove remarkably resilient. Only Camden Street closed at the behest of the UHC;
Lombard Street West *hevra* was in use until 1960, Saint Kevin's Parade
until 1968, Lennox Street until 1974, and Walworth Road until 1981.
Indeed, Saint Kevin's Parade (most *frum*, i.e., most Orthodox of the *hevroth*) still survives as the Machzikei Hadass congregation, which meets
in Terenure Road North. At the same time, the new shul known as Greenville Hall—which finally opened in 1925—would increasingly provide a
focus for the east European newcomers, who preferred its Yiddish ethos
to that of the more staid and anglicized Adelaide Road. Some of the more
successful newcomers, it is true, graduated to Adelaide Road, although it
was not until 1910 that a "Russian" sat in the warden's box of the DHC.[8]

Adelaide Road boasted a congregation of over one hundred and fifty
members in the mid-1900s, but many lived some distance from the synagogue. Indeed its minyan room was so poorly attended in the early years

that its council voted a small sum to pay immigrant "minyan men" to attend so that services could be held regularly by those wishing to do so.[9] Only when the minyan room was relocated to Stamer Street within Little Jerusalem could the services of the minyan men be dispensed with.[10]

In Belfast it was a similar story: the awkward location of the "English" synagogue built on Great Victoria Street, about two miles from the "Russian" heartland north of the Carlisle Circus, induced many of the immigrant community to worship in the Jewish school on Regent Street instead. When in August 1901 the authorities at Great Victoria Street, who also controlled the school, had it padlocked, "our foreign brethren" made a forcible entry.[11]

There was also a class divide between the old and the new. It is noteworthy that while most of those leading the Adelaide Road congregation lived in the affluent townships on the south side of the Grand Canal, only one of the fourteen men on Greenville Hall's building committee in 1922 did so. Jews living south of the canal were wealthier; according to Sylvia Crivon, who grew up in Rathmines, "the most successful men had married English wives and they all lived on this side of the system . . . and didn't have much to do with the foreigners on the other side." It was not until she grew up and began to attend the Jewish Debating Society and the dances in Greenville Hall that Sylvia got to know the other side.[12] However, any lingering distinctions between English and Russian Jews had disappeared by mid-century.

Religious conviction and observance today are no match for those of a century or even a few decades ago. Shul services are shorter; fewer of the male congregants can lead the prayers or read from the Torah[13]; fewer households stick to a strict kosher regime; religious convictions and observance are attenuated; and the inevitability of some community members marrying out is accepted, albeit reluctantly. Despite the efforts in recent years of resident American Chabad rabbis, no more than one Jew in ten attends shul on a weekly basis in either Dublin or Belfast. And yet despite the falling off in numbers, the main Terenure synagogue still manages to organize twice-daily minyans, like its Little Jerusalem predecessors.[14]

From Little Jerusalem to Rathgar and Beyond

I felt *fer klempt* [very sad] as I walked out of the shop.
—*Nick Harris on the closure of Erlich's in 2001*

Leopold Bloom was born in 1866 on Upper Clanbrassil Street, the street that later would link Little Jerusalem proper with Harold's Cross on the other side of the Grand Canal. Though the wealthy Peisa Harmel lived on the same street for a while in the 1880s and 1890s, few other Jews ever lived or conducted business there. On *Lower* Clanbrassil Street it was a different story. An eighty-two-year-old Dubliner who grew up on Lower Clanbrassil Street recalled in April 2003 that during his childhood Sunday morning on the street "was like Grafton Street" (one of Dublin's main shopping thoroughfares). That was when "all the Jews came out." As non-Jewish Dublin rested or attended religious services, the kosher bakers, butchers, and grocers of Lower Clanbrassil Street did a roaring trade. My informant's future wife remembered as a teenager trying to wheel the big pram containing her niece through the crowds. Animated and voluble Jews in clusters kept getting in her way, oblivious to her ef-forts. Another longtime Gentile resident referred to Lower Clanbrassil Street in its heyday as "a terrific street—the best!" For Philip Rubinstein, a butcher on the street for three decades, "there was nothing like . . . Clanbrassil Street on a *shabbas* night. . . . All the women with their bar-rows of fish . . . and we'd open the butcher's from 11 P.M. to one or two in the morning. Then we'd have to be up at 6.30 on Sunday to get ready the orders!"[15] In 1926 the ever-enigmatic Joseph Edelstein declared in a letter to a friend from his temporary "Utopia" of Grangegorman mental hospital that he would gladly exchange it for "the perils of Clanbrassil Boulevard on Friday mornings (fish-days)."[16]

Lower Clanbrassil Street was the epicenter of Jewish Dublin for well over half a century. Even after many had left the original area of settle-ment, they came back to shop. In its heyday the three short blocks located between Leonard's Corner and Saint Kevin's Parade contained over twenty retail units catering almost exclusively to the Jewish community. As Oliver Samuel's photographs in the Dublin Zionist magazine *Nachlath Dublin* testify, even half a century ago Lower Clanbrassil Street on a Sun-day morning was still a lively and special place.[17] Its gradual decline there-after is reflected in the numbers of Jewish-run establishments: on the short stretch between Saint Kevin's Parade and Vincent Street, *Thom's Direc-tory* recorded sixteen in 1939, ten in 1960, and none in 2005. When the last of them—what used to be the late Beila Erlich's kosher shop—was sold, it stood between two stores serving Dublin's growing Muslim com-munity. Beila Erlich died in August 1998, and Jewish Clanbrassil Street died with her.[18]

Long before the opening of the new synagogue in Terenure in 1952, the center of gravity of the community had shifted, and the Jewish pres-ence along the South Circular Road was declining. Greenville Hall shul finally ceased to function in 1984, and Adelaide Road was deconsecrated in 1999. Now only the façade of Adelaide Road synagogue survives, al-most engulfed by the surrounding office blocks. By the early 2000s only a few elderly Jews still lived in the area that used to be known as Little

Jerusalem. One elderly Jewish woman remained on Oakfield Place; it was a similar story on Saint Kevin's Parade. There were no Jews left on Martin Street, Dufferin Avenue, or Greenville Terrace. Almost inevitably, the last families to remain were the less comfortably off who could not afford the move to middle-class Rathgar or Terenure. On Martin Street in Portobello, for example, the last Jewish male household heads included two journeymen tailors and a scrap dealer. The Jews who moved tended to sever links with their Gentile neighbors in Little Jerusalem, and the Jews who remained sometimes felt looked down on for their lack of financial and social success.[19]

Dublin's Little Jerusalem remained a vibrant and distinctive neighborhood for well over half a century. Then rising affluence drew its more affluent Jewish households into a leafier suburbia two or three miles further south, first across the Grand Canal to the Rathmines-Rathgar area and later as far as Terenure. In Belfast the shift to the suburbs is reflected in the location of successive synagogues. The stone for the first—thanks to the munificence of Daniel Jaffe—was laid at Great Victoria Street to the south of the city center in 1871; next, in 1904, came Annesley Street by Carlisle Circus, near where the late nineteenth-century immigrants settled; and, finally, in 1964, Somerton Road in the northern suburbs. Dublin and Belfast Jewries' shifts to the suburbs mirrored that of communities across the water. The "dynamic pattern" described by Shimon Stern, whereby "Jews move together with their institutions once in every 30 or 40 years along an axis leading outwards . . . on a leapfrog model" captures the shift in Dublin and Belfast. As in Stern's pattern, "the distance between the old and new centres [was] considerable, and the old neighborhoods [were] not adjacent to the new ones." As the old *hevroth* and communal facilities fell into disuse, new ones opened up "along the residential migration axis."[20]

The future was already being signaled in the mid-1920s. At the first meeting of the Adelaide Road "synagogue extension committee" one member noted that "he had been approached by certain parties who were interested in the building of a synagogue in the Rathmines district." His report was simply read into the minutes, but it is significant that only two on the extension committee were living in the Little Jerusalem area at the time. Both lived on Victoria Street, at its southern edge; most of the fourteen others lived in the Rathmines-Rathgar area. In 1935/36 a few Rathmines Jews decided to establish a minyan because their children were objecting to the long journey on foot "across the bridge" on the Sabbath. There was opposition, but the new group met first in private homes, then in the parochial hall on Leinster Road West, and finally in purchased premises on Grosvenor Road. It was the Grosvenor Road shul that acquired the site in Terenure.[21]

Judging by the number of schoolchildren with addresses in the area, Little Jerusalem was at its most vibrant in the 1900s and 1910s. Over a thousand children from the area attended school in the 1910s; thereafter, the numbers declined to about two hundred in the 1940s and about thirty in the 1960s. The Jewish presence did not decline as fast: instead, the community aged, while most of those who left came back to shop and, sometimes, to pray. For a district still very much alive half a century ago, Little Jerusalem has left few traces of its Jewishness. Today, the outward physical signs are scarce. Greenville Hall shul is now an office building. Gone, too, are all signs of the little shuls on Saint Kevin's Parade, Lennox Street, Lombard Street West, Camden Street, and elsewhere. Walworth Road synagogue now houses the Irish Jewish Museum, the Lennox Street shul is a business office, and Clein's bakery on Lennox Street, the last kosher bakery in the area, passed out of Jewish hands in 1960.[22] The physical appearance of the housing on streets such as Oakfield Place, Lombard Street West, Longwood Avenue, and Saint Kevin's Parade has changed little over the last century, but it bears no traces of its former Jewish residents. A few houses once occupied by Jewish families still contain a painted-over mezuzah.

Decline

"Ich geh fun 'ire' land und ich kum in unser land."
—Rabbi Isaac Halevi Herzog on leaving
Dublin for Palestine[23]

Ireland absorbed only about 0.15 percent of the pre-1914 Jewish exodus from eastern Europe. Its sluggish economic growth and relative poverty are the reasons for this. Moreover, the Jewish population of the two Irelands (north and south) was always miniscule in absolute terms; it peaked at somewhat over five thousand in the mid- to late 1940s.[24] Since then its decline has been uninterrupted until very recently. Jewish numbers in the republic have plummeted from 3,907 in 1946 to 2,127 in 1981 and 1,581 in 1991. The latest (2002) Republic of Ireland census put the number at 1,790, thus registering the first increase in the Jewish population since 1946. The increase is mainly due to the immigration of white-collar workers from Israel and the United States.[25] The indigenous Jewish community, alas, continues its decline and is now confined to Dublin (about 1,300) and Belfast (about 300). The congregations of Waterford, Derry, Lurgan, and Limerick are long gone, and the tiny presence in Cork now confines its communal activities to the High Holy Days (and with some help from outside).

The numerical vulnerability of Irish Jewry is sometimes interpreted as a barometer of anti-Semitism. One of the more unpleasant characters in *Ulysses*, schoolmaster Garret Deasy, had a ready explanation for the lack of anti-Semitism in Ireland a century ago: it was because "she never let them in." But Deasy's failure to account for either the Litvak immigration or well-known incidents of anti-Semitism in his own day made him doubly wrong in 1904. Applied to the late 1930s and early 1940s, when several Jewish refugees from Nazi Germany were denied political asylum in Ireland, Deasy's explanation is more convincing. The excuses made then bespeak a lingering anti-Semitism in the public service sector and in government.[26] In the private sector, elite anti-Semitism still constrained social contacts and professional advancement; rightly or wrongly, Jews who were passed over in their careers or never "invited to join the club" saw their Jewishness as only the stumbling block. Yet when compared to anti-Semitism elsewhere, or to the racist abuse and violence meted out in recent years to non-EU immigrants—more so in Belfast than in Dublin—the mistreatment suffered by Ireland's Litvak immigrants and their children and grandchildren was relatively mild. To dub Irish Jews "the archetypal 'others' of Ireland's national Catholicism," as Ronit Lentin has done, simply marginalizes the sufferings of these other groups—and of Jews elsewhere.[27] When the immigrants from Lithuania began to arrive in noticeable numbers in the 1870s and 1880s, nobody sought to prevent them from settling where they did; and when they began to move from where they initially settled, nobody put pressure on them to move out. Like New York's Lower East Side and Harlem and like London's East End, Dublin's Little Jerusalem and Cork's Jewtown ended up being victims not of persecution but of the upward social mobility of their Jewish populations. Few of those who left harbored any bitterness or resentment toward their non-Jewish neighbors or, when they emigrated, toward Ireland in general.

In economic terms Ireland's Jewish community made considerable progress between the 1870s and the 1940s. Several factors contributed to its success. First, at the outset its men were prepared to work hard at jobs that most people in the host community found distasteful, particularly peddling and petty moneylending, or dealing in scrap and rags and in secondhand furniture. Such jobs have always been the province of middleman minorities. In Ireland, discrimination did not shunt the immigrants into those jobs. On the contrary, the trading skills they had acquired in the shtetls were transferable to Ireland, and in due course their Irish children and grandchildren would be well represented in professions often denied Jews in tsarist Russia. Peddling required little start-up capital and only a rudimentary knowledge of English, though it also offered a good way of picking up colloquial English. In the short run at least, Ireland's relative economic backwardness arguably offered a better match for the peddling skills of its small number of immigrants than did a "modern" city like London.

Second, the immigrants saved and invested in property, education, and business. They worked harder, they probably saved more, and they were certainly economically more successful than their non-Jewish neighbors. In large part, those differences reflected different cultural priorities. The immigrants acquired a reputation for being tough but reliable business-men. They placed greater emphasis on schooling their children than their neighbors did. And, like other close-knit middleman minorities, the Jews helped one another. Their community was rich in networks and institu-tions offering mutual support. And there can be no doubt that non-Jewish Ireland benefited economically from its Litvaks.

Third, the demography of Irish Jewry was distinctive in a number of respects. While the pre-1939 increase took place at a time when the Irish population was falling, the subsequent decline occurred when aggregate numbers had begun to rise once more. Jewish demography was character-ized by adaptability and flexibility. While the first generation stood out for its low infant and child mortality, the second led the transition toward ever smaller families, trading child "quantity" for child "quality" to a much greater extent than did the majority population. The shift entailed a rise in living standards; moreover, to the extent that the return on human capital was an increasing function of the stock of human capital, that conferred an added boon. The career expectations of the second genera-tion stretched beyond those of the first, and many of the younger genera-tion received second- and even third-level education. For the third and fourth generations, absorption through intermarriage was never an im-portant factor; in a sense, the sturdy refusal to compromise constrained the size and viability of the community.

Despite the impact of the Great Depression and the increasingly confes-sional character of the Irish Free State (renamed Éire in the 1937 constitu-tion), the Jewish community maintained its numbers in the interwar pe-riod, when the population of the country as a whole continued to decline. There are several possible reasons for this. The most obvious is that the Jewish community was almost exclusively urban, and urban Ireland (north and south) held its own in demographic terms in these decades.[28] Moreover, there was little net emigration of Jews: entry into the United States was much more difficult than before, and the attractions of setting up a business in an ever more protectionist Irish Free State were increas-ing.[29] The post-1932 tariff regime even prompted the immigration from across the Irish Sea of some "tariff Jews," as they were known in the Jewish community.

The uninterrupted increase in Ireland's Jewish community between the 1870s and the 1940s was a measure of its prosperity and integration. In those decades the community showed every sign of being viable and long lasting. The suburban descendants of the pre-1914 generation were no longer the "sojourners" of the middleman minority model, always ready to pack their bags and move on.[30] To be sure, the second and third generations clung to their religious faith and their Zionist convictions. They also remained largely self-employed and their occupational profile was distinctive. Yet they were no longer primarily the proto-capitalist middlemen of old, and they dominated or monopolized none of the professions or industries that they joined. Some became heavily involved in the city's mainstream political and cultural life. In 1956 much was made of the election of Robert Briscoe as Dublin's lord mayor; a far more convincing measure of integration was the presence of three Jewish deputies—one for each of the main parties—in the Irish parliament in the 1980s and 1990s. Some invested heavily in manufacturing; others acquired skills requiring considerable acculturation, and not so readily transferable abroad. Lawyers, auctioneers, dentists, and doctors mixed freely with their Gentile counterparts. Several well-off Jews became active members of the nondenominational Masonic Order.[31] A degree in medicine or dentistry from Trinity College or the Royal College of Surgeons was archetypal human capital for a "sojourning" middleman. Acquired legal, political, and auctioneering skills were much less so, however, because they were not so readily transferable abroad. The Dublin community's sizable investments in its own golf club (1944), its own secondary school (1952), and its own sports grounds (1954) hardly hinted at its imminent decline.

Then, from the end of World War II emigration began to exact a heavy toll. A survey of 130 households in the Dublin Jewish community by Dublin-born Stanley Waterman in the early 1980s produced information on 221 emigrants, a very high number given the low fertility of the community in this era. More than half had emigrated to Britain, a fifth to North America, and, as noted above, another fifth to Israel.[32]

There are several likely reasons for the emigration. First, the underperformance and snail's-pace growth of the Irish economy in the postwar era undoubtedly played a part. The 1950s have been described more than once as "Ireland's lost decade." By its end the annual net emigration rate reached almost 2 percent of the population.[33] Jews left like everybody else. Thereafter, stark proof that the strategy of industrialization through import substitution was leading nowhere led to a sharp change in economic policy. The ensuing trade liberalization worked in time, but it proved the undoing of many indigenous, tariff-protected manufacturers. For the domestic clothing and textile industry (in which Jewish businessmen were very prominent) the going was particularly tough in the 1960s and 1970s. The numbers employed in the sector fell from about thirty-five thousand in 1958 to twelve thousand in 1986. For the sons of many factory-owning Jews, there was no business to inherit. And as one Dublin-born Jew put it, "Jews move to where the business is. If there is no business there are no Jews. That is what happened [in Dublin]."[34]

Young Jewish medical practitioners and dentists had always been emigration prone, but in the immediate postwar period the incentives to leave were stronger than ever before. Between 1946 and 1966 the number of physicians and surgeons in the republic rose very little—from 2,674 to 3,011—and that of dentists from 536 to 607. Moreover, the opportunities for specialist practice in Ireland were limited. Anti-Semitism in the medical profession almost certainly deterred some from aspiring to positions as consultants in Irish hospitals. Several Jewish medical professionals, it is true, reached the top in their specialist fields; they included cardiologist Leonard Abrahamson (1896–1961), who became president of the Royal College of Physicians of Ireland,[35] and his son-in-law, Ellard Eppel, who served as president of the Irish College of General Practitioners. Yet until recent decades Catholic hospitals restricted appointments to Catholics, while very few Catholics occupied consultancies in Protestant-run hospitals such as the Rotunda (where Bethel Solomons was elected Master in 1926), Mercer's (where surgeon Joseph Lewis, also Jewish, had a distinguished career), the Richmond, or the Meath.[36]

Second, Irish Jewry—probably to a greater extent than elsewhere—avoided assimilation through intermarriage. It did so through the emigration of a higher proportion of its young people. By the time the community reached its peak size, it seemed as if everybody was related to nearly everybody else. After World War II one could travel freely to Manchester, Canada, or Israel to seek a spouse. The proximity of England and the transferability of professional skills acquired in Ireland increased the mobility of young Irish Jews. The emigration of young single adults, rather than assimilation and marrying out, has been mainly responsible for Irish Jewry's decline in recent years. In other frontier Jewish communities—as in Australia, Denmark, or Finland—being a member of a small minority meant a higher risk of marrying out than in Ireland.[37]

Third, a sense of *galut* or *golus*—exile—has been part of the Jewish psyche since biblical times. This is epitomized by the motto of the Dublin Jewish Dramatic Society, founded in the 1920s by Larry Elyan and some others: "With a wanderer's staff in hand, without a home, without a land."[38] One chronicler of Irish Jewry has dubbed the land where her family settled as a "Gaelic Golus"; another referred to his route home from Dublin's Thomas Street to Little Jerusalem as his *"langer Goluth."*[39] Zionism, the creation of a Jewish state, and the Nazi Holocaust almost certainly increased the sense of insecurity and exile among diaspora

Jewry: according to Arnold Eisen, the Museum of the Diaspora in Jerusalem reminds non-Israeli Jews that "If you come from the Diaspora of the present, know that sooner than you think, your community too will be part of our past, a room in our museum."[40] From the outset, Irish Jewry supported the Zionist project. A small number of Irish Jews emigrated to Palestine in the 1920s and the 1930s, and more followed after 1948. In 1956 the Irish Department of Foreign Affairs guessed that the number of Irish citizens and their families in Israel "should not exceed about fifty," but the migration gathered pace thereafter; Stanley Waterman's 1981 study of Jewish emigration since mid-century found that roughly one in five of those who left had settled in Israel. Ireland's Jews (like Irish people generally) have always been migration prone, and this can only have increased their sense of being temporary or accidental sojourners in Ireland.[41]

Fourth, the fate of Irish Jewry needs to be placed in comparative context. It bears noting that today Israel seems to be one of the very few countries in the world with a growing Jewish population.[42] Jewish populations have been shrinking in most places due to a combination of low fertility and intermarriage, but the added pressure of migration to larger centers has placed even greater pressure on smaller communities. Once a community's size falls below a certain threshold, the decline risks becoming a free fall. Ireland's situation closely replicates that of many other small Jewish communities around the world in the past half-century or so. Across the Irish Sea, the Jewish communities of greater London and Manchester have held their own, while smaller provincial communities have dwindled or vanished. So, for example, Liverpool's Jewish population has dropped from an estimated 11,000 on the eve of World War I to about 3,000 today; Glasgow's from 10,000 in 1914 to fewer than 5,000; that of Edinburgh from 2,000 a century ago to less than half that. The same holds true for other smaller centers such as Newcastle, Hull, Southport, and Cardiff. The communities of Merthyr Tydfil and other towns in the Welsh valleys are no more. Similar trends are observable in Australia, Canada, and elsewhere.[43] The vulnerability of such small communities was (and is) exacerbated by the added difficulty and expense of acquiring kosher food.[44] By such yardsticks Irish—or at least Dublin—Jewry has not fared too badly.

Finally, a minority found the Irish Jewish community or Irish society as a whole claustrophobic and left to get away from it all. For some the determining factor was escape from what one expatriate dubbed the pressure of the "finding a Jewish [partner] and settling down syndrome."[45] Another informant whose family "lacked nothing, even during the war," and who saw in Ireland a "safe haven from bigotry [and] racism . . . [where the Jewish people] were allowed to follow any occupation they desired" was driven out in 1950 by the closed and repressive nature of mid-century Irish culture and by the bad weather.[46]

As noted in chapter 6, Irish Jewry a century ago was rich in institutions and social capital. As it ceased to be a largely middleman minority, the social capital associated with middleman minorities attenuated. The vibrancy of the middle-class suburban community never quite matched that of its predecessor. The plethora of social and cultural organizations survived the transfer for a time, and indeed new ones were formed. However, from the 1960s on they were already in decline, and by the 1980s "many [had] barely more than the committee to show as members."[47] In order to survive, communal institutions serving Dublin's Jewish suburbia such as Stratford College in Rathgar (founded in 1952) and Edmundstown Golf Club (founded in 1944 in response to the blackballing of Jewish golfers by established clubs) relied increasingly on Gentile involvement. Dublin Maccabi Association folded in 1997 and sold its grounds in 1999. Until the 1970s most Stratford students were Jewish but by the mid-1980s only three-fifths were, and the "Jewish atmosphere" was already waning.[48] In 2004 the Jewish Home in Rathmines (founded in 1950) admitted elderly Gentile residents for the first time. In Belfast the buildings housing a school and the Belfast Jewish Institute at Somerton Road have been sold and converted to commercial use, leaving only the synagogue lobby and sanctuary as spaces for communal functions.

Meanwhile, residents' memories of Little Jerusalem and its satellites are fading fast. The present occupant of 7 Saint Kevin's Parade, location of the first of the Litvak *hevroth* in the Little Jerusalem area, reported in early 2003 that "our house was apparently a synagogue around the turn of the last century," adding that he "had a visit from the chief rabbi of Ireland a while back asking about this," and that according to "a previous tenant who knew more about the subject . . . above our door there are two wooden blocks, now cut back flush with the brickwork, that apparently held the sign for the synagogue."[49] Residents' recollections corroborate the sense gained elsewhere that there was little sectarian or racial ill feeling between the residents of Little Jerusalem. Even allowing for the nostalgia and biases stemming from autobiographical memory, the impression gained from dozens of interviews and correspondence with elderly residents of the neighborhood is that they and their parents got along well with their Jewish neighbors. Elderly Jewish ex-neighbors or their families still drop by on occasion to chat and reminisce about the old days.

Appendix 1

LETTERS TO ONE OF THE LAST "WEEKLY MEN"

CHAPTER 3 described the importance of the itinerant trader—peddler, weekly payments man, or credit draper—in the immigrant community. The following is a selection of letters from customers to one of the last of Ireland's weekly men.[1] Mr. X supplied a variety of items on credit to clients living mainly in the poorer parts of Dublin city and its hinterland into the 1960s. He inherited the business, run from an office in central Dublin, from a connection through marriage c. 1950. He employed an agent to deliver the goods by car and to collect repayments. The geographical concentration of his rural custom suggests that it was built up by word of mouth, though Mr. X also engaged in advertising in a mass circulation evening newspaper to attract customers. Clearly, aspects of the business—the use of a car, the newspaper advertising, perhaps the letters like those reproduced below—would have been missing in earlier decades.

The letters—a representative selection of twelve out of over a hundred in the collection—date from between the late 1940s and the early 1960s. Almost all were from married women. They give a flavor of the straitened circumstances of the purchasers and, in many cases, the difficulties of conducting this kind of business. Several of the letters refer to illnesses in the family, to the breadwinner's loss of employment, or to some other misfortune. Several plead for more time for repayments. The goods purchased—essential items of clothing, bedding, footwear, overalls, curtains, "a leather jacket for a motorbike," a "dark sport coat with long arms"—hardly reflected frivolous consumption. The sums of money mentioned are modest. Some of the letters imply the right of the purchaser to have unsuitable or unsatisfactory goods returned or repaired free of extra charges.

Plainly this was not an avocation for the impatient or the short-tempered. For the most part the tone of the letters is both familiar and respectful, betokening repeat custom and mutual trust. In the interests of confidentiality names and addresses have been omitted. Otherwise, the letters are reproduced as they were written, with only occasional added punctuation.

Dear Mr. X

Could you please bring me a pair of boots. It is for the little lad that has the astma and his feet are wet. If you could please let me have them I would be much obliged. But before you do don't ask me to pay more money. I can't. Don't say I did not warn you. A fine boot size 2. Any colour. I would send my love only the wife might see it.

A.B.

Dear Sir

I wrote to you before to say that Miss Christina Murphy is not at this address, she went to England about a year ago. I don't know what she got off you, but I signed nothing so you cant take any action against me.

Yours faithfully
Mr. B.C.
Feather [i.e., father]

Mr X I am sorry for not sending you the 16/- as I am after being out of work for a week as I got a heavy cold on me . . . but it is all right now. I am going into work on Monday as I am sending up my little grand aughter with 10/- this week full next week.

Mrs. E.

To Mr. X

Please don't call on Friday as He has lost his job (with drink) and I've no money even to support the children but as soon as some arrangements are made I'll pay up the £1 18s that's due to you. Hoping you understand how things are at present.

Mrs. F.

[1960]
Dear Mr. X

The shirt you brought to me on yesterday Wednesday did not suit. It opens all the way from the front. If you can get me one of the ordinary shirts with the three buttons that is the kind of shirt my man wants.

Yours truly
Mrs. G

Dear Mr. X

I am sorry about this as my husban is in hosple and I am only on inshurons so I only be able to give 2–6 a week till I go back on my money. Terribly sorry about this.

Mrs H.

[January 1948]
Dear Mr. Y (Mr. X's father-in-law)

I received your letter on Saturday which I am not sending you on 5 shillings. You have not said what you wear going to do about the Spring of the Bed hoping you will see to it.

Yours faithfully
Mrs. I.

[May 1954]
Dear Sir

I Mary Giles wish to inform you that you have no call to threatening me with those solicitors of you[re]. I am widow with no means or property except old age pension which I have to support myself. The account I owe is not in debt to you but your father in law long since dead and was one decent person. I am willing to pay 2/6 every two weeks. So you may leave those legal advisors out of your head.

Yours sincerely
(Mrs.) J.K.

Dear Mr. X

Sorry my husband wont allow me to take any more on hands. He said he made only £8 a week and he has 28/- rent and milk 14/-. Pay for coal and food, so he said it was in posibale to manage. He came across this payment and discovered that the jumpers was £7 9s. He said he was going to see you during this week. Sorry again I am in terrible trouble over this. Hoping you won't mind but you will understand I have to live with him.

Yours faithfully
L. O'M.

Dear Mr. X

I'm very sorry for disapointing you so much in not giving you the couple of bob I owe you. So I hope you will excuse me for righting this letter to you. Well Mr. X I had to try and buy seed potatoes for the garden. So I had no money to send. So please don't call till the childrens allowance again and I will clear with you. As I don't want disapointing you when you call and I am going myself and the children down to my mother's place for a chong of ear [i.e., change of air] as my health is very bad.

Yours
Mrs. N

May 1961

Dear Sir: I just received your letter about Mrs. X's payment and I am her daughter writing to you. I just came home from England as she was very ill in hospital for the past three weeks and was unable to pay the account. She only came out of hospital last Sunday and will try to pull the account down as soon as she is able.

Yours faithfully
N.O.

Mr. X.

Just a line to let you know that I changed my mind about the Boots for Tony. He got a pair in Navan on Sat. But if you will please bring him two working shirts instead and bring good dark ones and not too dear he wants a good big size. . . . I will say no more till I see what you will bring me and if you don't bring me good value I will put you out.

Mrs. P.

Appendix 2

MR. PARNELL REMEMBERS

THE CONVERSATION reproduced below[1] between Séamus Mac Philib, then a young folklore collector, and Mr. George Parnell, an elderly resident of Dublin's south city, took place in 1980. It casts interesting light on moneylenders, Jewish and non-Jewish, and attitudes toward them in the first half of the last century. The conversation was recorded as part of the Irish Folklore Commission's Dublin Folklore Project. The text has been lightly edited for readability but its sense has not been altered. The unpleasant-sounding expression "Jewman," employed several times below, was common in Dublin a century ago. At the outset it did not have a negative connotation, any more than did "Corkman," "Kerryman," "Frenchman," or "Chinaman." Nevertheless, note that here the word is used only in the context of moneylending: otherwise the usage is "Jews."[2]

MR. P. There was a big lot of Jews then. They had their own kosher shops, I think there's two kosher shops up there—that's the meat they eat, you know, kosher meat. And they start—ah, I used to see the older men come round about, the Jews, they used to come around and they used to put in panes of glass. They'd have the sack with glass on their back. And some of the hard chaws would throw a brick at them. Break the glass, you know: but they [the Jews] used to do that and then they come along and they got into clothes.

But first of all they'd come with a picture, a picture of Jesus, they brought it to you, do you see, and a shilling a week of whatever it'd be, so you'd take it off them—most people took the picture. It might be . . . a Catholic saint actually was in the picture. . . . Well, then, there'd be a shilling every week for that. But then eventually he might come along and introduce maybe a suit. You know, he went in—once he got going, a suit, a topcoat, a pair of boots. And this is the way it went then, you see. But then they used to lend money.

I remember them coming around, always had pony and traps. And they always had a bouncer, a tough fellow driving the pony and trap. Mostly Monday morning that would be . . . and I remember well . . . there's a door at the back of the trap, and he'd be only just standing there, you know, getting shifted from house to house, and he'd get out of the cab and—or the trap—and go up to the house and get paid, and back again. But that was a regular thing.

S. MAC P. And what would they do if the people couldn't make the payments?

MR. P. Well they wouldn't do a thing; they were very, very fair. And I heard people say they'd rather deal with a Jewman than a Christian. I heard them say that. No . . . there's an old yarn about this Jewish man went up to the house, and the woman was coming down, she'd a bucket of slop, of course everything had to go down to the yard, no one had toilets or water upstairs at all, you see, and they all had to come down to the yard. So she was coming down. And the old Jewman was coming up. "There you are, Mrs. Murphy," he said, "you missed me last week." "Yes," says she, "but I won't miss you this week." Gave him the content of the bucket! (Laughs.) That's an old yarn told.

    . . . [A]nother Jewish man told me he was attacked by a dog once. He got a bite in the leg, and he wouldn't go up there anymore. That woman owed him money, he told me that, he wouldn't bother. He was afraid of his life of the dog, you know, our dogs, and he never went up again.

S. MAC P. They weren't liked to a certain extent, I don't think?

MR. P. Well, a certain crowd didn't like them and they began, I suppose to hurt the poor, you know that way, they got in on them, and I say they started with the picture, and then they come along with a suit or a pair of shoes. And then they got in for radios and big things like that. And delph—they went in for all that stuff.

    But there was an opposition then. There was a fellow around here, Alderman Kelly,[3] he was belonging to the Corporation, he opened a place down here on William Street, I heard the older men say. And he done the Jewman down there, he gave out stuff by the week. I think it's the old Civic Museum now, that's where it is now . . . and of course he was not on his own, he got a party to do it, and I believe they knocked him right, left and center, they wouldn't pay him at all, the people that got all the stuff off him. But he tried to beat the Jewman, but he didn't. So the Jewman is still going strong now, and he's not. But they're not as strong now as they used to.

    No . . . to lend money now you must have a premises, and so far as I know the law is that you must go to the premises to get your money. That's the way. Years ago the Jewman used to come up to all the houses, and gave them money, you see.

s. MAC P. People never tried to drive them out or anything like that?

MR. P. No, I never heard of—no, they didn't. No, they got a great welcome here in Ireland. They were never—they did hurt people alright, but then people got to live with them, and accept them, and found that they were very handy. And there was other people'd lend money, the Christians, well they'd charge maybe five shillings in the pound. . . .

And other people used to go to this woman too, the one of many, lots of dealers had that game. And they'd sell fish. You'd want a loan of five shillings, a lot of money then, and you got a loan of five shillings, you had to take five shillings' worth of fish. And then you had to pay one and three pence for the loan of five shillings. You had to pay six [shillings] and three [pence], plus the five shillings' worth of fish, which you threw out—that was eleven and three it cost you actually. For the loan of five shillings it cost you eleven and three. And the fish was thrown out—the cats were never as well fed! There were cats in every back street and lane and fish everywhere.

So that really they had to go to the Jewman because the Jewman . . . only charged what he was entitled to charge. I think it was three and nine or something at that time. And that's all the Jewman would charge. And he wasn't going up every week, if you gave him a pound off of it, well, that was a pound off your bill, but with the other people you only paid interest and you still owed the same amount of money. But the Jewman, as you gave money, it was getting knocked off your account.

LOUIS HYMAN, JESSIE BLOOM, AND

THE JEWS OF IRELAND

Louis Hyman labored at his *History of the Jews of Ireland* for nearly four decades before its publication in 1972. There were several reasons for its long gestation period: Hyman's residence in Palestine and Israel, his work as a schoolteacher and scoutmaster, and difficulties with financing its publication. Hyman's trips back to Dublin were few, and he relied on correspondents there and elsewhere for help.

Between the mid-1930s and the early 1970s he maintained a correspondence with fellow Dublin Litvak Jessie Bloom (née Spiro).[1] Jessie had been born in Cork in 1887, but the family moved to Dublin a few years later and she spent the rest of her childhood there. In 1912 she emigrated with her husband, Bob Bloom, to Fairbanks, Alaska, where they immersed themselves in frontier life. They returned to Dublin in 1928 in order to provide their four daughters with an upbringing in a Jewish environment. Hyman peppered Mrs. Bloom (who was about twenty years his senior) with detailed questions about Irish Jewry. She had originally intended to write her own history of Irish Jewry; in the first of Hyman's surviving letters to her (dated 20 March 1935), he asked about its progress and mentioned that another history, planned since 1925 and to be coauthored by Barney Shillman and Dr. Harris, might "trespass" on her work.[2] Since Bloom was mainly interested in the Litvaks, and Hyman's initial focus was on the pre-1880 period, they did not regard each other as rivals.

In the summer of 1935, Hyman moved to Haifa, where he would spend the rest of his life, and where he would be known as Uriel Hyman. There he kept up his determination to write "the history of the Jews in Ireland"; indeed, for a time he seems to have hoped to earn a doctorate from the Hebrew University for a dissertation on the subject.[3] His correspondence with Mrs. Bloom continued but, with one exception, only the letters from Hyman survive. Although containing interesting sidelights on life in Palestine and Israel, as well as some communal news, the letters consist mainly of questions and commentaries about Irish Jewry. At first Hyman urged Bloom to continue her own research into Irish Jewish history, but her writing plans were shelved when she and her family moved back to Fairbanks in 1937. Hyman could not rely on her anymore to check details, but he continued to ask her about connections for another three decades.

On 18 September 1945, Hyman informed Bloom that "Barney Shillman is first in the field this month with a 'History of the Jews in Ireland' (150 pages)," adding that "he got going quick when he heard of my work."[4] In March 1946 Hyman was "putting in whatever time I can to complete my history but it is rather difficult." He was relieved to find that Shillman's work was "by no means a scientific history," unkindly confiding to Bloom that a friend had written that "the Council of the Jewish Historical Society regard [Shillman's book] as an absurdity," and that Shillman had included too much material about himself and his family. By this time Hyman planned to extend his coverage beyond 1880; later he developed a keen interest in the Joycean connection and accordingly brought his end date forward to 1910. On 27 August 1948 Hyman was hinting wistfully that "one of the old crowd" could supply "living" data, "but I suppose I will never get that now"; in due course, however, he would build up an impressive network of contacts through correspondence in Dublin and elsewhere. A few months later he wrote asking Bloom for her view on the remarks about fin-de-siècle Dublin Jewry in Myer Joel Wigoder's memoir cited in chapter 1.[5] He also asked for information about "McDonagh's 'Irish Jew' produced at the Empire in 1921" and a long-lost skit on "the squabbling in the Hebrahs" by Mrs. Ida Briscoe.[6]

In May 1950 Louis Hyman had some hopeful news to report about his book. Fellow Dublin Litvak Max Nurock, also residing in Israel, had read the manuscript and returned it with a note to say that he was willing to edit it for publication, while community activist Philip Sayers had offered to defray "the expenses of publication." Eighteen months later, Hyman reported that Nurock had made many useful suggestions and had declared Hyman's work "superior in content, in learning, and in style . . . to Barney's [i.e., Bernard Shillman's] book."[7]

On 11 November 1952, Hyman wrote to congratulate Bloom on her evocative memoir of fin-de-siècle Jewish Dublin in the July 1952 issue of *Commentary Magazine*. However, he detected Larry Elyan's grandfather in the account of "Reb Meyer," the Cork rabbi who was the subject of a little ridicule by Bloom, adding that "I think Larry Elyan will also recognise him and be cut up by your characterising him as 'big bit of a fraud.' "[8] Hyman also questioned the wisdom of including remarks critical of the weekly payments system. In his next letter (dated 30 November 1952) he mentioned that he had added a reference to Bloom's article to his work-in-progress and an acknowledgment of her help. On 7 June 1953 he announced that he was dedicating the book to the memory of William and Rachel Nurock on the understanding that their son, Max Nurock, would help in getting it published. Then there was a long break in the correspondence, apart from one undated letter from Hyman.

The next item in the file is a copy of a letter from Jessie Bloom. It makes for rather uncomfortable reading, but deserves to be reproduced for the light it throws on communal tensions and the range of attitudes toward moneylending within the Litvak community. The distaste for moneylending displayed in her *Commentary* article is now directed at Max Nurock's father.

5901 Beach Drive, Seattle SW16
January 28, 1962
Dear Louis,

Yours of 22nd received. I hope you have now fully recovered from your operation. I was upset when I read of the offer of Max Nurock to help finance the publication of your manuscript on condition that you dedicate it to his parents. I don't know if you know that his father was a moneylender and did not bear a very reputable reputation in Dublin community. As I expect you would want your manuscript to be read by both the Jewish and Gentile community I think that dedicating it to Mr. Nurock would not enhance the reputation of the Jewish community in Ireland.

It is difficult to explain exactly what the position is but you would have to imagine the Dublin Community of the "early eighties" when our folks first arrived and when Mr. Nurock also arrived, at that time there was not very much for the Jews to do, and though the majority of them were men of learning as far as the Talmud was concerned, their knowledge of business was limited, nevertheless they struggled along, some selling pictures, at that time the development of reproductions was in its infancy, and pictures of Parnell, Queen Victoria, and reproductions of the Holy Pictures were popular, they also sold other things, and gradually worked their way, but the ones who became rich were the ones who lent money at an exorbitant rate of interest, and Mr. Nurock was among those. As the majority of the emigrants had a knowledge of Jewish History and realized what a scourge the practice of usury was to our people they had a contempt for moneylenders. We had to accept them in the community and many a time we blushed when we would hear of the way they treated their victims.

One year, I do not remember exactly when, Mr. Nurock was given the honor of Chosen Torah, and not satisfied to keep the honor in the community it was reported in the local press and it was explained that this particular honor was only given to one who was highly respected in the community, and I still blush when I remember what a time I had to explain to my gentile friends that we really did not honor moneylenders in our community. I've been thinking of your manuscript, it would probably be a work or reference and available to many scholars, and some might at a distant date try looking into the history of the man who was being honored by having the History dedicated to him, and I dread to think what a bad taste that would leave as to the integrity of the Jewish Community in Dublin.

Though the opportunities were limited yet there was always a chance for any bright boy or girl to work their way through school through scholarships, and many were the sacrifices our folks made to accomplish that, as you yourself know. I feel so keenly about this that if you should decide to have the manuscript dedicated to Mr. Nurock, I would want to disassociate myself entirely from the whole thing.

As a greener, Nurock père had started off by peddling small quantities of tea on credit in Athlone in the 1880s. Soon he took over a moneylending business in Dublin and in time prospered at it. In Dublin he first lived in a small terraced bungalow on Oakfield Place, but he would end his days in what was then 79 South Circular Road, an address with a respectable, middle-class resonance.[9] His son Max, who had offered to fund Hyman's work, was both a brilliant student in Dublin's High School and at TCD and a talented public servant, first in Palestine and Uganda, and later in Israel. In Dublin, he once hoped to fill the chair in classics in Trinity College; instead, he would end his career as Israeli ambassador to Australia.[10]

Hyman's next letter was dated 25 October 1967: there were no further mentions of the undertaking to the Nurock family, but this letter referred to the promise of help from the Dublin B'nei B'rith.[11] On 26 May 1968, Hyman wrote that he had given Bloom "honourable mention" because he had "found her notes most helpful." The next letter a few weeks later contains questions relating to James Joyce and Dublin Jewry. On 6 August he wrote to Alaska again "trying to clear up some points." Later that month he was writing again. "Max Nurock is on the board of the Israel University Press and he will have to have the final word about Larry Elyan's story of Bella Bloom." On 9 October 1970 Hyman wrote for old photographs and asking more questions about various Dublin Blooms. In his last surviving letter to Jessie Bloom, dated 4 May 1971, Louis Hyman was still looking for information and worrying about funding for publication. His last request was for "a list of first Jewish students in the [High School] in the last 2 decades of the last century." His book was published in 1972 by the Irish University Press, its dedication to the Nurocks intact,[12] and remains an indispensable source for all students of Irish Jewry.

NOTES

INTRODUCTION

1. See. e.g.. Magalaner 1953; Leventhal 1961; E. Steinberg 1981/82; G. Gold-berg 1986; Mac Aonghusa 1992; Nadel 1996; Davison 1998; Reizbaum 1999; Ó Gráda 2004.

2. In this period Ireland attracted far fewer East European Jews than either Belgium or Holland, but more than Denmark, where door-to-door peddling (a favored occupation of the immigrants) was illegal. It also attracted far more than either Norway or Finland, and about as many as Sweden.

3. Dublin-born Hyman conducted his research while based in faraway Haifa (where he emigrated in the early 1930s), but his invaluable book is based on exten-sive archival work and on correspondence and interviews with many Dublin Jews in the 1960s. Unfortunately none of his notes survives, although a little of his correspondence does.

4. The museum, which opened in 1985, was the brainchild of Asher Benson. In addition to its rich collection of memorabilia and artifacts, it contains a valuable documentary archive.

5. Slezkine 2004, ch. 1. Compare, e.g., Bonacich and Modell 1980.

6. On "frontier" Jewry, see, e.g., Elazar and Medding 1983; Gilman and Shain 1999.

7. *Jewish Chronicle* (henceforth *JC*), 9 August 1889 (as cited in Duffy 1985, p. 93).

8. Indeed, the alleged reluctance of some Jewish-Irish businessmen to employ fellow Jews may stem from a fear of competition from such employees, once trained (Nick Harris, interview by the author, 21 October 2004).

9. Henceforth "Litvak" is used as shorthand for the post-1870 immigrants, of whom a minority hailed from Russian Poland and Latvia, and a small number from elsewhere in eastern Europe.

10. E.g., Brockerhoff and Hewett 2000.

11. See Schmelz 1971; Collins 2001, pp. 79–80; Woodbury 1926; Preston and Haines 1991, pp. 28–29; Goldstein, Watkins, and Spector 1994; Garrett et al. 2001; Derosas 2003; Van Poppel, Schellekens, and Liefbroer 2002.

12. This term is still commonly used to describe the events of early 1904. See, e.g., Fanning, 2002, p. 42; Craig 2003; Flynn 2004. See also chap. 9.

CHAPTER 1. ARRIVAL AND CONTEXT

1. Cited in Lentin 2001.

2. Endelman 2002, p. 128.

3. Harrington 1992, p. 6.

4. Notable contributions include Miller et al. 2003; G. Fitzpatrick 1994; Doyle 1990, 1999.

5. Crane Lane then linked Dame Street and the River Liffey, and the synagogue was probably located in a house belonging to a Sephardic merchant. Indeed the graveyard deeds of the old Jewish cemetery at Ballybough on Dublin's north side are still kept in Bevis Marks synagogue in London. I am grateful to Asher Benson for this information.

6. Hyman 1972, p. 53.

7. For more on the pre-1870 history of Irish Jewry, see Shillman 1945; Hyman 1972 (whence the details here).

8. Ó Gráda 1994, p. 329; Moore 1984, p. 18, citing G. O'Brien 1918, pp. 20–21.

9. Godley 2001, pp. 80–81.

10. Derived from the 1926 census, vol. III(2), table 13B; 1936 census, vol. III(2), table 13B.

11. Berman and Zlotover 1966, p. 25; Moore 1981, p. 191; David Birkhan, interview by Carol Weinstock, July 1987, Acc. 5734, National Library of Ireland (NLI), Dublin. When Louis Brennan arrived in Ireland from Akmyan with his parents at the age of three, they joined the Isaacsons living at 24 Martin Street because "his mother was a Glasser who was related to the Hannah Glasser who married Elias Isaacson" (Michael Brennan, private communication with the author).

12. Dublin Metropolitan Police 1905; Hyman 1972, p. 328 n. 3. Few of those displaced by the Boer War could have remained in Ireland a decade later, since none of the Jewish children in our 1911 database described later was born in South Africa. Robert Baigel left Dublin for South Africa in 1902 because he found the community in Dublin too *"frum"* (pious) (Shalom Ireland Digest No. 239, December 2003).

13. E.g., Hatton and Williamson 1998; Wegge 1998.

14. Wischnitzer 1948, chs. 2–3; Vital 1999; Keogh 1998, pp. 8–11; Lentin 2001; Rivlin 2003, p. 140; for a more nuanced view, see Klier and Lambroza 1992.

15. Anon. 1965, p. 6.

16. Marcus 2001, pp. 5, 221, 266.

17. Levine 1988, pp. 105, 110; Levine 1982, p. 18.

18. Cesarani 1996, p. 248.

19. Cited in ibid.

20. Wischnitzer 1948; Joseph 1914.

21. Joseph 1914, p. 155; Diner 2000, pp. 19–25; Irving Howe, cited in Diner 2000, p. 23; Vital 1999, pp. 297–310, 365; *The Economist*, 23 December 2003, p. 87; see also Szreter 1996, p. 538.

22. Zborowski and Herzog 1995, pp. 260–61; Klier 1996; Cesarani 1996; Endelman 2002, pp. 128–29; R. Perlman 2001, p. 6.

23. Oshry 1995, p. v. Gordon Read's address to the International Academic Conference, held to mark the centenary of the Jewish Historical Society of England in 1993, began by describing the emigrants as "virtually fugitives," instancing the "barbarous Conscription Statute of 1827" and other discriminatory legis-

lation, and "mob violence" after 1881 (Read 1996). However, the contributions of John Klier and David Cesarani to the same conference forced him back to the metaphysical position that it was "not the actual suffering but the unlimited potential for it" that spurred the ouflow.

24. Seminal texts on collective and social memory include Halbwachs 1980; Fentress and Wickham 1992. Fentress and Wickham's analysis concerns a multi-layered "social memory"; they object to Halbwachsian collective memory as "curiously disconnected from the actual thought processes of any particular person" (ix–x).

25. Ó Gráda 2001, pp. 140–41.

26. Cesarani 1996; compare Donnelly 2001; Ó Gráda 2001.

27. I am grateful to Guy Beiner for this suggestion.

28. Compare Morawska 1996, pp. 29–30.

29. G. Wigoder 1985, p. 3; compare Myer Wigoder 1935, pp. 15, 23, 33. Keogh's study (1998, pp. 8, 65, 243, 244) conveys the impression that relations between Jews and non-Jews in Lithuania were no different than in the rest of the tsarist empire. It also conflates the horrors of the Holocaust in Lithuania with the treatment of Jews there before 1914. For maps of locations of the most important pogroms, see Klier and Lambroza 1992, pp. 43, 194, 290. A memoir of the town of Keidan notes that neither the town nor "all of Lithuania" was touched by the pogroms, and that relations between its Jews and non-Jews in the pre-1914 era were good (Kagan 1991, Keidan entry). Compare Hoffman (1999) on Russian Poland.

30. Keogh 1998, p. 65; Myer Wigoder 1935, pp. 22–23; JC, 20 July 1894; see also Gross 2003, pp. 33–34; http://www.shtetlinks.jewishgen.org/plunge/plunge.html; Zwi 1997, p. 21; Aleichem 1987, pp. 199–207, 247–55.

31. Berman 195-a, p. 11.

32. Kleanthous 2000.

33. Irish Times, 10 January 2003. Louis Goldberg gave his age as thirty-one in the 1901 census.

34. Hannah Berman (Berman and Zlotover 1966, p. 23) notes that only one of the Zlotover clan, Israel, was left behind in Lithuania, where he "experienced great poverty." He is the fifty-five-year-old Sroel Zlotov described in the 1897 tsarist census as a "deliverer of small wares," and living with his son Lemakh (12) and daughter Mushe (14) on Svinskaia Street in Akmyan.

35. Berman 195-a, p. 7; Berman and Zlotover 1966, pp. 21–22; Briscoe 1958, p. 10. One "Jewish history of Lithuania" (http://www.heritagefilms.com/LITHUANIA.html, accessed January 2003) notes, "Lithuania was a poor country, and the mass of its inhabitants, consisting of Lithuanian and Belorussian peasants, formed a low social stratum whose national culture was undeveloped. The Jews who had contacts with them as contractors, merchants, shopkeepers, innkeepers, craftsmen, etc., regarded themselves as their superior in every respect." For more on the Lithuanian background and context, see Schoenberg and Schoenberg 1991; Levin 2000; Oshry 1995.

36. Vital 1999, pp. 84–85; Rubinow 1907, pp. 492–95.

37. Rubinow 1907, p. 506; Levin 2000, p. 85.

38. Levin 2000, p. 77.

39. Burrows and Wallace 1999, p. 1113. See also Joseph 1969, p. 81; Kuznets 1975; Rubinow 1907, p. 559; Kahan 1986; Levin 2000, pp. 83–92.

40. Gregory 1982, pp. 80–102, 162.

41. Burds 1998, especially ch. 1.

42. Kuznets 1975, pp. 43–45; Joseph 1969, pp. 99–101.

43. U.S. Department of Commerce 1960, pp. 56–57; see also figure 1b. In all three cases the two biggest outflows occurred in 1907 and 1914. From Austro-Hungary 338,452 emigrated in 1907 and 278,152 in 1914; from Russia 258,943 in 1907 and 291,040 in 1914; from Italy 285,731 in 1907 and 283,738 in 1914.

44. Godley 2001, pp. 68, 87. Godley follows Hatton and Williamson 1998; see also Erickson 1996; Platt 2003.

45. Vital 1999, p. 308. The *Jewish Chronicle* was quick to point to the impact of economic downturns in the United States on the immigration rate. See *JC*, 27 March 1908, 8 May 1908.

46. Klier 1996; Joseph 1969, p. 9.

47. Vital 1999, pp. 300–301; Godley 2001, p. 66; also Kuznets 1975, pp. 117–18; Wischnitzer 1948, p. 69.

48. Perlmann 1996, 2000, p. 109.

49. Feldman 1994, p. 148.

50. There were reports of famine or near famine in 1867–68 and 1871. See http://www.sociumas.lt/Eng/Nr6/migracija.asp and http://www.jewishgen.org/databases/magid72.htm (accessed 15 December 2004).

51. Rubinow 1907, pp. 492, 502.

52. Vital 1999, p. 304; Rubinow 1907, pp. 528–29, 548; Keeling 1999.

53. Benson 1977, p. 7.

54. Morawska 1996, p. 26.

55. Myer Wigoder 1935, p. 47; Berman 195-b, pp. 9, 11; on Glasgow, compare Lindsay 1913, p. 23.

56. J. Edelstein 1908, p. 5; Myer Wigoder 1935, p. 6; J. Bloom 1952, pp. 21, 30; Keogh 1998, pp. 8, 243–44; Harris 2002, p. 1; Hyman 1972, p. 218; Marcus 2001, p. 77; Berman and Zlotover 1966, pp. 13, 23, 28. For pen pictures of all these shtetls see Schoenberg and Schoenberg 1991. In Dublin the Yiddish term *machudna* was used to describe people from the same village as well as relations by marriage, although strictly speaking it refers to in-laws only. I am grateful to Nick Harris for this information.

57. Schoenberg and Schoenberg 1991.

58. The data are taken from Schoenberg and Schoenberg 1991, pp. 327, 51, 390, 273, 232, 131, 218, 396, 309, 166. See also http://www.shtetlinks.jewishgen.org/telz/Telz1.html; http://www.shtetlinks.jewishgen.org/shavli/shavli3.html. According to Leah Yudeiken, Zhager "was more a shtot than a shtetl" (Zwi 1997, p. 72).

59. Arkin 1975, p. 216; Jacobson 1998, pp. 60–61.

60. Bernstein 1971, p. 11; G. Goldberg 1982; Lentin 2001; Harris 2002, p. 1; Marcus 2001, p. 266; Marcus 2004, p. 112; Price 2002, p. 30; Birkhan interview. The story about the delayed ship may have its origin in the saga of the *Hispania*, which was forced to spend some weeks in Cork for repairs in 1895. The male Russian Jewish passengers onboard were billeted in the houses of Cork coreligion-

ists, while the women and children remaining onboard were visited and cared for daily. Mr. A. H. Goldfoot, one of the leaders of the community, footed the grocery bills. A service was held onboard the *Hispania* before its departure to America (*JC*, 7 June 1895).

61. Cesarani 1996, pp. 251–52. Similarly, the claim (in Elazar and Medding 1983, p. 89) that Argentina was "a country of second choice" for the tens of thousands of Jews who went there in the 1900s overlooks the rapid growth of the Argentinian economy in that period and, indeed, its relatively high standard of living. According to Maddison (2001, pp. 185, 195) Argentine GDP per head was higher than that of western Europe on the eve of World War I (though considerably behind that of the United States).

62. Joseph 1969, pp. 140–45; Vital 1999, pp. 302–3; Kuznets 1975, pp. 100–112.

63. Rubinow (1907) notes the high proportion of traders who specialized in goods and services linked to agriculture.

64. Kuznets 1975, pp. 80–81; Rubinow 1907, p. 577.

65. Http://lethones.narod.ru/mem2.html (accessed 10 November 2003).

66. E.g., Sánchez-Alonzo 2000.

67. Morawska 1996, pp. 31–32.

68. Arkin 1975, pp. 216–17.

69. See, e.g., Vital 1999, pp. 158–63; Marcus 2001; J. Edelstein 1908, pp. 1–6; Eliach 1998, pp. 45–49. Maurice Abrahamson recalls that his parents and grandparents never talked about Lithuania "except on one occasion when my maternal grandmother was angry with me for going to see a display at the RDS [Royal Dublin Society] of Cossack riding feats" (Abrahamson to author, December 2004).

70. Stanislawski 1983, pp. 25–27; Petrovskii-Shtern 2001, pp. 378–79; Litvak 2005. According to Palmer (1901, p. 146), "as it by the richer classes that the rabbis and talmudists are chiefly supported, the *kahal* is practically in their hands."

71. On this point and on Jewish Russian recruits generally, see Litvak 2005.

72. Vital 1999, pp. 158–63; Berman 195-a, p. 5 (whence the anecdote).

73. I am grateful to Stephen Wheatcroft for these numbers, which come from *Obshchii Svod po Imperii. Rezultat razrabotki dannykh pervoi vseobshchii perepis' naseleniya 28/1/1897*, vol. 2 (St. Petersburg, 1905), pp. 296, 335. The number of Jews is also given in Rubinow 1907, pp. 490, 498.

74. Cesarani 1996, p. 250. See also Litvak 2006.

75. J. Bloom 1953.

76. Myer Wigoder 1935, pp. 66–67; Thelma Frye to the author, 1 November 2004. Philip Wigoder wrote as follows to Louis Hyman about his father Myer Joel's reaction: "My father's reactions on page 66 are quite understandable. It is the reaction against money counting more than education in communal life, one of the curses of the Galuth, and it is very depressing at times to witness the worship of Mammon and יובגעו גריבער [young "greeners"] often at the head of institutions. It is not unusual but often regrettable and the feelings of our old scholars and Baalabatim can be appreciated." Which, as Louis Hyman commented to Jessie Bloom, "brings us back where we started" (Hyman to Bloom, 15 December 1948,

Ms. Collection #93, box 4, folder 5, Jessie Bloom Papers (hereafter Bloom Papers), American Jewish Archives, Cincinnati.

77. Numbers derived from Godley 2001, p. 69; but see also Sarna 1981. Note, however, the significant numbers repatriated from Great Britain by the Jewish Board of Guardians in this period (Feldman 1994, pp. 302–3).

78. D. Fitzpatrick 1994, pp. 620–21; Harris 2002, p. 27; Heanue 2000.

79. Http://www.Jewishgen.org/databases/Lithuania/LithCensus1897.htm.

CHAPTER 2. "ENGLAND-IRELAND" AND DEAR DIRTY DUBLIN

1. Myer Wigoder 1935, p. 43.

2. Maddison's estimates of GDP per head in 1913 (in 1990 international dollars) are: United States $5,301, United Kingdom $4,921, Australia $5,715, Canada $4,447, Argentina $3,797 (Maddison 2001, tables A1-C, A2-C). Irish GDP per head was about $3,000 at this time.

3. Bairoch 1976, p. 320; Vaughan and Fitzpatrick 1978, pp. 29, 37, 42, 47. The statement holds, at least unless the outer suburbs of Kingstown and Blackrock are included as parts of Dublin.

4. Wright 1914, p. 15.

5. Bielenberg 1991, pp. 116–17; Rynne 1999, pp. 16–18. Ford citation in Rynne 1999, p. 18.

6. Hyman 1972, p. 160. Yet when E. Margoliouth attended Mary's Abbey in mid-August 1868 he found "a goodly number" there (Margoliouth 1868, entry for 15 August).

7. Hyman 1972, pp. 157–58, 160, 243–57. Compare Kokosalakis 1982, pp. 129–39; Henriques 1993. Duffy 1985, ch. 4, is a good source on intracommunal tensions in Dublin in the 1880s and 1890s.

8. One measure of the city's impoverished state in the 1900s was the one thousand or more school-age children who supplemented family incomes through street trading. Another was the high proportion—nearly one half—of all Dublin deaths occurring in charitable institutions. See Prunty 1998, pp. 153–57; J. O'Brien 1982, p. 175; Cameron 1908, p. 48.

9. J. O'Brien 1982, p. 98; Brady and Simms 2001, p. 164; *The Times*, 22 October 1913, cited in Fraser 1996, p. 67.

10. Cameron's efforts seem to have slackened toward the end of his tenure, however. See Daly 1984, pp. 287–89.

11. Cameron 1894, p. 41.

12. Grimshaw 1890; J. O'Brien 1982, p. 103; on Irish Americans, compare Morawska 1994, pp. 326–27.

13. Maguire 1993, pp. 74–75.

14. Craig, n.d., pp. 46–47; *Belfast Health Journal*, 1901, p. 8.

15. Cameron, in *Annual Reports*, passim.

16. Thus excluding the presumably small number of burials in parish graveyards.

17. Daly 1984, p. 242; Pim 1890, p. 7.

18. Using 2, 12, 29, 49, 69, and 85 years as age-group midpoints, the data generating figure 2.1 yield the following admittedly crude estimates (mainly because they make no allowance for migration) of the expectation of life (in years) in the mid-1880s and in the 1900s.

Class	Mid-1880s	1900s	Increase
I	53.4	60.3	6.9
II	37.0	42.1	5.1
III	27.9	33.75	5.85
IV	31.8	32.25	0.45
Average	32.6	35.2	2.6

19. The data are the focus of the especially detailed tables prepared for the 54th annual report of the British registrar general for 1891, as discussed in Woods 2000, pp. 258–59 (table 7.1); Woods and Shelton 1997, pp. 53–57. The high mortality towns were Blackburn, Leicester, and Preston; the low mortality counties were Dorset, Wiltshire, and Hertfordshire.

20. Preston and Haines 1991, p. 6; Rendle-Short 1955a, 1955b.

21. The number of deaths from measles was 567 in 1882 and 27 in 1883; 656 in 1899 and 7 in 1901. The number succumbing to diarrhea/dysentery was more than three times as high in 1899 (a particularly bad year for infectious diseases) as in 1903.

22. Compare Rendle-Short 1955a, 1955b.

23. They also confirm Belfast's advantage over Dublin in terms of infant mortality and the mortality of children aged 1–5 years. The data are taken from Vaughan and Fitzpatrick, 1978, pp. 28–29; *Thom's Almanac*, various years; *Returns of Births and Deaths in Dublin*, various years.

24. Meyer 1921, table VI.

25. Woods 2000. That mortality in the late 1890s was above trend does not alter this.

26. Woods 2000, p. 279 (citing Vallin 1991).

27. The Dublin wages series is an average of "low" and "high" five-year averages of wages earned by general building laborers. Compare D'Arcy 1989; Bowley (as reported in Feinstein 1990); compare also Knowles and Robertson 1951, app. table 1. On shifts in the cost of living in Ireland in this period, see Kennedy 2003.

28. Compare Ó Gráda 1994, p. 238.

29. Including "civic" areas of the county (i.e., municipal boroughs, townships, and towns of two thousand people or more) changes the percentages to 40.6 percent in 1861, 33.8 percent in 1881, and 26.2 percent in 1911. In 1841 the percentage of families living in fourth-class accommodation was 46.9 (*1841 Census*, p. 21). Most fourth-class housing in urban Ireland consisted of one-room tenement apartments.

30. Daly 1995, p. 226; Prunty 1999, pp. 173–77.

31. The townships, middle-class, low-tax enclaves, were distinct in ethos and proud of their independence. Though Catholics were in the majority in both townships, the property franchise qualification meant that political power in the town halls always eluded the majority population. Many of the townships' workforces,

particularly those in the professions and senior administrative positions, worked in the city proper.

32. Such tenement units constituted the bulk of Dublin's fourth-class housing in these decades and their number declined only slowly. It was 23,360 in 1881, 19,342 in 1891, and 20,564 in 1911. See Aalen 1992; J. Brady 2001; Daly 1982, 1984; J. O'Brien 1982; Ó Gráda 1998.

33. Cameron, in Dublin Corporation, *Annual Reports on Public Health, 1913*, pp. 127–28; Cameron 1914, pp. 82–83; Cameron, in Dublin Corporation 1906; Aalen 1992, pp. 293–94.

34. O'Brien 1982; Daly 1984; Prunty 1998.

35. *Housing Inquiry* 1944, p. 18; 1926 census, IV, table 2a; 1936 census IV, table 2a; Ó Gráda 1998.

36. Saorstát Éireann, *Annual Report of the Registrar General*, 1925–43. These are still very high rates compared to the average of about 7 per 1,000 today.

37. Alter 1997, p. 102. In a study of early twentieth-century Munich, John Brown (1998) found that infant mortality was concentrated in a small minority of households, and that those households were much less likely to own a water closet.

38. Daly 1981, pp. 237–38; J. O'Brien 1982, p. 19.

39. Pim 1892, p. 13.

40. J. O'Brien 1982; Daly 1981, pp. 238–41; Prunty 1998.

41. BPP 1880, p. v; BPP 1900.

CHAPTER 3. "THEY KNEW NO TRADE BUT PEDDLING"

1. Myer Wigoder 1935, p. 155; cited in Hyman 1972, p. 284.

2. Irish Folklore Commission Archive (IFCA), Ms. 1,964, pp. 40–42, Department of Irish Folklore, University College Dublin.

3. Arkin 1975, p. 44; Baron et al. 1975, pp. 110–11; Endelman 2002, p. 43; Elkin 1980, p. 104.

For more case studies, see Shain 1989; Friedman 1954; Kuznets 1960; Morawska 1996; Perlman 2001; Glanz 1945, 1961.

4. Kuznets 1960; Baron et al. 1975; Shatzmiller 1990; Botticini and Eckstein 2004a, 2004b; Slezkine 2004.

5. Aleichem 1987; Eliach 1998, p. 7.

6. Berman 1926, p. 324; Rubinow 1907, pp. 556–62.

7. *JC*, no. 1,953, 7 September 1906.

8. Baron et al. 1975, p. 260. Mendelsohn (1970, pp. 6–7) states that a majority of craftsmen in Belorussia-Lithuania were self-employed, and those who did not work alone or with the help of their families seldom hired more than a few assistants.

9. Perlmann 2000, p. 121.

10. Williams [2003]; Kokosalakis 1982, pp. 125–27; Collins 1990, pp. 47, 62, 153, 223; Henriques 1993, pp. 15–22, 51–55.

11. Hyman 1972, p. 161.

12. The Akmyan data are available at http://www.jewishgen.org/databases/ Lithuania/Lithcensus1897.htm#search. Several elderly household heads and wives with husbands absent were dependent on remittances from England, America, and Africa.

13. Berman 195-a, pp. 6, 9; Berman and Zlotover 1966, p. 26. Hannah Berman's novel *Ant Hills* (1926, pp. 249, 324) includes vivid accounts of the Lithuanian peddlers' lot.

14. Price 2002, p. 31.

15. J. Bloom 1952, p. 30; the story is repeated in a recorded interview with Jessie Bloom on 20 February 1976, Accession No. 2623, VF982, University of Washington Archives.

16. For similar reactions in London, New York, Glasgow, Edinburgh, and Cardiff, compare Gartner 1960; Burrows and Wallace 1999, pp. 1113–20; Collins 1990; Daiches 1956, pp. 97–8, 120–29; Henriques 1993, pp. 26–33.

17. Hyman 1972, p. 165.

18. The term "English" was used by the immigrants to refer to the English-speaking Ashkenazim, mainly of German origin. David I. Cohen, William Allaun, Joseph Levin, and Julius Goodman, all registered moneylenders, were among the free members in 1905. Cohen's daughter, Rosalind, was invited to perform a dance for guests at a vice-regal garden party in 1911 (*JC*, 21 July 1911). Ironically, in 1913 Joseph Edelstein defrauded Cohen of £2 2s. when Edelstein undertook to help him become a justice of the peace (Chief Secretary's Office Registered Papers [CSORP] 1913/7,854, National Archives of Ireland [NAI], Dublin).

19. Hyman 1972, p. 165, citing *JC*, 27 November 1885; also G. Wigoder 1985, p. 5. For more on Saint Kevin's Parade shul, see chap. 5 below. Compare Collins 1990, pp. 48.

20. J. Edelstein 1908, pp. 67, 109–10.

21. *JC*, 29 May 1992.

22. Compare Saorstát Éireann 1931, p. 147, where the total number of moneylenders in Dublin is given as 147 and the number of illegal moneylenders estimated at 50.

23. Dublin Metropolitan Police 1905; Moore 1984, p. 43.

24. Undated handbill, "Irish Manufacturers' Furniture Made by Sweaters," NLI, L.O. P 114, item 61. See too O'Riordan 1984. The petition involves a request to establish a branch of Chevovei Zion in Cork, 1 October 1893. The petition is in box 5, Irish Jewish Museum, Dublin.

25. Census household enumeration forms for Cork and Lurgan, 1901 and 1911, NAI.

26. I am grateful to Stewart Rosenblatt for his database of naturalized Jews, from which the numbers given here are derived.

27. In Latin America, where Jewish immigrants also resorted to peddling and kindred occupations, they were known as *klappers* (or door-knockers), *cuentaniks* (from *cuenta*, account), *semanalchiks* (from *semanal*, weekly), or *clientelchicks*. See Elkin 1980, p. 101. In Cork the peddlers were known as tallymen by their customers. The Scotch drapers so common in nineteenth-century England were also often called tallymen. See "Memoir by Esther Hesselberg," Acc. 5734, undated, NLI.

28. Not all: in Cork, "the casual poor who came . . . were also provided for during the [Passover] festival" in 1894 (*JC*, 4 May 1894). Mickey Brennan suggested to me in correspondence that "as the immigrant community . . . acclimatized they more readily settled into the 'classes' of their surrounding cultural environment." This might include working on Saturday mornings "when required to by their frequently Jewish employers in contravention of the religious laws."

29. Asher Benson, interview by the author, 30 May 2003.

30. Larry Elyan, interview by Carol Weinstock, July 1987, Acc. 5734, NLI.

31. J. Edelstein 1908, p. 14.

32. Benson, interview.

33. Berman 195-b, p. 10.

34. Children helped out after school. For example, Myer Joel Wigoder's son Harry traveled from door to door with his father's pictures from an early age, while his brother Philip sold sponges or helped with the making of pictures at home in Saint Kevin's Parade. Later their younger brother Louis contributed by selling sponges in pubs or helping Harry sell pictures for weekly payments ("Louis Wigoder Memoir," pp. 10, 12, 16. I am grateful to Thelma Frye for a copy of this valuable memoir).

35. *JC*, 9 February 1912. The society was chaired by Dr. G. S. Wigoder and its fund run for many years by Elias Weinstock, who left for London in 1913 (*JC*, 28 March 1913).

36. Godley 1996; J. Bloom 1953; Williams [2003].

37. Minutes of the Holy Burial Association, 13 February 1902, Irish Jewish Museum.

38. Transcript of interview with Louis Davis, December 1990, p. 9, Irish Jewish Museum; Harris interview, 21 August 2004.

39. Berman and Zlotover 1966, p. 30; see also Harris 2002, p. 36.

40. Jordan (1993, pp. 24–25) emphasizes the need for rich Jews to help (as opposed to exploit) the poor in order to maintain community solidarity, a precious defense in a hostile environment. Compare Greif 1989.

41. The word recurs as *laptseh* in Schlimeel 1954. For more on this somewhat derogatory term, see chap. 7 below.

42. E.g., J. Edelstein 1908, pp. 13–15; BPP 1897, pp. 148–49; Select Committee on Moneylenders Bill 1932, pp. 2, 4; Duffy 1985, p. 189.

43. Berman 195-b, p. 10; Berman and Zlotover 1966, p. 31.

44. In the 1902 *Thom's Directory*, for instance, Newman and Glasberg (no. 40), Cohen and Rubinstein (no. 60), and Sayers and Golding (nos. 28 and 29), are described as wholesale drapers.

45. Compare Elkin 1980, p. 103.

46. J. Edelstein 1908, p. 13.

47. Joyce [1922] 1969, pp. 290–91.

48. J. Bloom 1952, pp. 21–23. Louis Hyman related the following amusing story to Jessie Bloom (11 November 1952, Bloom Papers collection #93, box 4, folder 5):

My father tells me the story of a Dublin Jew who, proud of his business card which contained his home address, occupation as a bootmaker with the various notes and charges for soles and heels on it, sent it to his relations in Lithuania. Imagine his surprise when he received a reply with his name and address on the envelope as well as his charges for repairs.

49. Berman and Zlotover 1966, pp. 30–31.

50. Edelstein 1908, pp. 21, 31–34.

51. O'Brien 1982, p. 202.

52. Dublin Metropolitan Police 1905, report dated 13 February 1903, County Dublin; compare Ó Ciosáin 1997, pp. 68–71.

53. Asher Benson heard this from Yanks Marcus, himself a producer of holy pictures (Benson interview). See also Ruby and Frye 1997, pp. 21–22.

54. "Some 'tickmen' and their ways," 14 June 1894.

55. Duffy 1985, p. 35. The same goes for Italian and German immigrants. In 1911, 64 of the 411 Italians were ice-cream vendors, 33 confectioners or pastry cooks, and 20 musicians or music teachers. One hundred of the 963 Germans were teachers of one kind or another, 65 were indoor servants, and 45 were watch- or clockmakers (1911 census, *General Report*, p. 145).

56. Dahl 1959; Fontaine 1996; Pfister 2000; Glanz 1945, 1961, ch. 15; Friedman 1954.

57. Only 993 hawkers paid for a license in 1800, and only 841 paid in 1820 (BPP 1844, vol. 32 [123.], "Return relating to hawkers' licences").

58. Ó Ciosáin 1997, pp. 64–67. There are many accounts of peddlers in the archives of the Irish Folklore Commission (IFC) and in the pages of *Ireland's Own* (e.g., 28 January 1925, 21 June 1947, 7 May 1955). See also Ní Luain 1969; Molloy 1975.

59. Including general shopkeeper, dealer; grocer; butcher; meat salesman; draper; mercer; provisions curer; dealer; merchant; and corn, flour, seed merchant, dealer.

60. Compare Ó Gráda 1994, pp. 265–70.

61. IFC vols. 255/62, 256/4–5, 1,259/160 (Corca Dhuibhne, Kerry); vol. 1,839/178–82 (Craughwell, Galway); vol. 1,834/174–79 (Kiltoom, Roscommon); vol. 47/8–15 (Cill na Martra, Cork); vol. 692/322; vol. 434/8–11 (Kiltartan, Galway); vols. 733/359, 692/322 (south Kerry); vols. 1,113/459, 1483/122–61 (Armagh). For evocative accounts of Jewish peddlers and moneylenders from elderly Dubliners, see Irish Folklore Commission Archive, Ms. 1,964, pp. 40–44 (Mr. Parnell); Ms. 2003, pp. 125–28 (Mary Ann McLoughlin).

62. Harris, Naylor, and Selden 1961.

63. Rubin 1984, 1986; Finn 2001, p. 106; Finn 2003, pp. 283–84, 310–12. Several drapers testified to the Select Committee on Imprisonment for Debt (BPP 1873).

64. Baron et al. 1975, p. 263.

65. Coulter 1862, pp. 23–24; Ó Gráda 1994, pp. 268–70.

66. Cited in Hyman 1972, p. 213; see also "Letter to Editor," *Belfast Evening Telegraph*, 16 June 1894.

67. NAI, 1C-36–135 to 137 (Limerick City Circuit Court Bills Books, 1897 to 1905).

68. Philip Bash, writing as "Fair Play," *Belfast Evening Telegraph*, 26 June 1894. Bash was replying to the attack on Jewish credit drapers in "Some 'tickmen' and their ways."

69. E.g., Myer Wigoder 1935, p. 48; IFC/UFP 0651; Berman and Zlotover 1966, p. 5; J. Edelstein 1908, p. 16; O'Casey 1981.

70. Myer Wigoder 1935, p. 48.

71. Compare Endelman 2002, pp. 131–32. Compare Miriam Jordan, "Crédito Hispano: Trust in Poor Built Consumer Empire for Israeli Brothers," *Wall Street Journal*, 20 August 2004, p. 1, which describes a weekly business in the barrios of Los Angeles today very reminiscent of that prevalent in Dublin in earlier times. I am grateful to Arthur Sugerman for this reference.

72. Kennedy 1977; Hyman 1972, p. 212; Hyman to Bloom, 11 November 1952, American Jewish Archives. Compare the statement of Louis Stix (in J. R. Marcus, *Memoirs of American Jews*, 1:314):

> The first goods which we found profitable in our business throughout the country were made of German silver, manufactured by Hall & Elton. I sold them on credit and warranted that they would retain their bright color. Before long, however, they tarnished and looked like copper, and if left in acid, were nearly ruined. When I called upon my customers after six months or a year to collect the money due me, they showed me the goods, and although greatly disappointed that they had turned out so unsatisfactorily, yet, having sold them in good faith, believing them to be excellent metal as I represented, I left it with my patrons to decide the value, and pay me whatever they considered a fair price. This, of course, had the effect of increasing their confidence in me, which I never abused.

73. Hyman 1972, pp. 173–74; Asher Benson, oral communication with the author, August 2003.

74. J. Edelstein 1908, p. 29.

75. *JC*, 9 October 1896.

76. Duffy 1985, p. 85. Robert Bradlaw, "prince" of the immigrant community and one of the founders of Saint Kevin's Parade synagogue and the Dolphin's Barn cemetery, made his living as a moneylender (Duffy 1985, p. 88, citing *JC*, 27 November 1885; Hyman 1972, p. 166). He was related to Myer Joel Wigoder by marriage.

77. The list of moneylenders is given in a file in the National Archives (CSORP/ 23,538). This and other information relating to the commercial activities of the Jewish community were collected by the police in response to a memorandum from Sir Antony MacDonnell, undersecretary in Dublin Castle. See Keogh and McCarthy 2005, pp. 22–24.

78. Johnston 1985, p. 114; Blain 2000, pp. 103–4.

79. The Dublin Metropolitan Police file implies that those who resorted to Jewish moneylenders were poor risks rejected by other moneylenders. One such was a strong farmer with "a shocking reputation for not keeping his word or paying his debts, he couldn't get any credit in this neighbourhood and I hear that no neighbour would back a bill for him and that the Bank here are very shy of him" (NAI).

80. J. Edelstein 1908, pp. 28–29; de Barra 1997, p. 152; "Memorandum from S. Horwich . . . on behalf of those engaged in the business of small lenders of money ranging from one pound to £5," Attorney General's Office, 2000/14/498, 22 November 1932, NAI.

81. Kearns 1994, pp. 72, 196, 215; Nicholas Carolan (personal information); Johnston 1985, p. 114.

82. NAI 1C-40–24, City of Dublin and Kilmainham Division Civil Bill Book, April–June 1910. Duffy (1985, p. 72, citing CSORP, 16366) cites a Belfast police report referring to immigrants "recently arrived from Russia and Poland [who] prey upon the poorest class of the population in the most audacious fashion and every week the court is full of these." Contemporaries exaggerated the presence of Jewish traders in the courts (see Abbott 1907, p. 470, citing correspondence in the *Irish Times* in April 1904).

83. Rubin 1984.

84. Compare Rubin 1984, p. 332.

85. Kearns 1994, p. 152; Johnston 1985, p. 114. Several decades later the *Irish Jewish Yearbook* (1970–71, p. 20) noted that none of the 141 witnesses appearing before a tribunal relating to a television program on illegal moneylending suggested "any . . . Jewish association with the problem."

86. *JC*, 17 March 1893–14 April 1893.

87. BPP 1898, Q45, Q47. Similar sentiments prompted another communal leader in England to urge synagogues to bar those engaged in moneylending from membership. See Endelman 2002, p. 171; *JC*, 9 July 1897.

88. Copies are now very scarce and the work itself is largely forgotten.

89. J. Edelstein 1908, pp. 58–65; see also BPP 1898, p. 8, evidence of George Henry Lewis. Edelstein dedicated his curious and now largely forgotten work to "Reason" and to "Israel's friends," and "confidently" commended it "to the impartial judgement of the public, his object being rather to expose the causes of usury for eradication than the effects of vituperation." The book does not seem to have affected his standing in the Jewish community, because Edelstein continued to play an active part in it in the wake of its publication. He was behind the Judaeo-Irish Home Rule Association, founded in Dublin in September 1908 (see chap. 7), and in the following month claimed to have been appointed editor of the *Labour Gazette*, "the first Jew to hold this position in Ireland." A few years later, however, he declared his support for "the Palestine scheme formulated by Dr. Herzl" (*JC*, 18 September 1908, 16 October 1908, 6 December 1912).

Edelstein also played a leading role in the Jewish Literary and Social Society, which met at 57 Lombard Street West. In February 1909 the Rev. Abraham Gudansky proposed and Wigoder seconded a vote of thanks to him, following his lecture to that society on Heinrich Heine (*JC*, 26 February 1909). Edelstein was also a vocal opponent of Protestant missionaries seeking to convert Jews and a leading proponent of the Jewish dispensary established in 1913 (*JC*, 10 January 1913).

However, there was a darker side to Joseph Edelstein. In May 1911 he was found guilty of an indecent assault on a young girl, but the sentence was deferred and in the meantime he was committed to the Richmond mental hospital, where he was detained until February 1912. A few months later he was fined for "discharging firearms in a place of entertainment." When his parents and brother emigrated to Canada in early 1913 Edelstein remained in Dublin, mainly living with an aunt in Portobello. In 1912–13 he came under police suspicion for "the furtherance of appointments to the Commission of the Peace" under false pretenses. By then he was subject to bouts of mania. His police file contains a handbill announcing a forthcoming lecture in Belfast ("Time and place will be duly announced"), where he is described as "M.J.I, B.Litt., Ph.D.," "President of the Revolutionary Party in Russia, and Chief of the Nihilist Central Committee in Berlin." The title of his lecture was to be "The Children of Israel," with tickets to cost 3s, 2s, and 1s. Meanwhile Superintendent J. Low of the Dublin Metropolitan Police deemed him "not absolutely insane," but noted that he "has represented himself as a Secret Service Agent employed by the Home Office to watch foreign spies." During the Easter Rising of 1916 Edelstein became involved in a spying controversy that would dog him for years. His presence in Portobello barracks during the arrest and murder of Francis Sheehy-Skeffington led to accusations that he had "spotted" Sheehy-Skeffingon. Edelstein, who always claimed that he was an innocent bystander, was exonerated by a military tribunal, but the accusations persisted (see J. Edelstein 1933). Issue 56 of *The Fenian*, a clandestine Republic newssheet, ran the headline "Edelstein, the notorious Jew spy, now in the pay of the Free State government" (15 September 1922). It accused Edelstein of working for the "G" detective department in Great Brunswick Street, "where he wields considerable authority." It also referred to his "outrage on an Irish girl," and to his failing to gain entry to Canada where the Jewish community had sent him. From the 1910s on Edelstein suffered from intermittent bouts of mental illness and spent time in the Richmond and Grangegorman mental asylums. A friend, the artist Harry Kernoff, remembered Edelstein's "sanguine deep-set brown eyes" and his fondness for "red biddy" (a concoction of cheap red wine and methylated spirits). A few elderly present-day residents of the South Circular Road area remember Edelstein, who died in 1939 after being hit by a bus, as a courteous, well-spoken eccentric.

The Moneylender was reissued by Cahill in 1931; copies of either version are extremely scarce. Perhaps the reissue was prompted by the debate about Robert Briscoe's private member's bill to control moneylending. Re-publication, it seems, led to Edelstein's ostracism by some members of the Jewish community, although he had his loyal friends, too (including lawyer Herman Good). Edelstein's work bears comparison with Abraham Cahan's *Rise of David Levinsky* (New York, 1917), an equally scurrilous insider's appraisal of a Jewish *macher*. Like Moses Levenstein, Levinsky was born in Lithuania and began life abroad working as a peddler. See also Marowitz 1996, ch. 6.

For more on the maverick Joseph Edelstein, see CSORP 1913/7,854, NAI; Hyman 1972, pp. 185, 201, 336; Harris 2002, p. 82; Murray 2004; Kernoff 1974; Louis Wigoder and Larry Elyan, interviewed in Jerusalem in 1972, Oral History Department, Hebrew University, Jerusalem, call number (0111)0001, pp. 19–20. There are photographs of him in the handbill described above (enclosed in CSORP 7,584) and in *Nachlath Dublin Magazine*, no. 22 (1948): 5.

90. IFC/UFP 0259; IFC/UFP 0651; J. Edelstein 1908, pp. 64–65. Myer Joel Wigoder was no businessman, unlike his son Harry, who was largely responsible

for his brothers' education and for turning the family fortunes around. "Wigoder" would later become a familiar name in Dublin for wallpaper and other household furnishings. One Mrs. Monaghan, who once lived in Weavers" Square in the Liberties, claimed that her father offered Myer Wigoder a place in his stable to store his first rolls of wallpaper (IFC/UFP 607). One elderly Jewish informant recalled to the author that in the Dublin of his youth "many working class Jews were contemptuous of moneylenders and tended to empathize more with the clients than their coreligionists."

91. J. Bloom 1952, p. 23; Louis Hyman (Haifa) to Jessie Bloom (Fairbanks, Alaska), 11 November 1952, Ms. Collection 93, box 4(5), Bloom Papers.

92. *Jewish Standard*, 24 August 1888.

93. *JC*, 9 December 1892; cited in G. Moore 1981, p. 197, and in Price 2002, p. 33; Duffy 1985, p. 105 (citing *JC*, 20 May 1898).

94. Louis Goldberg, cited in Ryan 2002, p. 50.

95. *JC*, 15 February 1895.

96. G. Wigoder 1985, p. 13.

97. Cited in Yodaiken 1987, p. 42.

98. *Irish Independent*, 8 and 30–31 July 1926; *Irish Times*, 8 July 1926; *An Phoblacht*, 16 July–13 August 1926, 3–10 September 1926, 22–29 October 1926. I am grateful to Brian Hanley for guiding me to these references.

99. *An Phoblacht*, 22 October 1926, 11 February 1927.

100. Hanley 2002, pp. 76–77; *An Phoblacht*, 3 September 1926.

101. Briscoe 1958, p. 16; see also Keogh 1998, p. 89. Briscoe, who believed that some Jewish moneylenders were giving the community as a whole a bad name, was in a good position to broker the agreement between the IRA and the moneylenders. He was a successful businessman and the son of a Lithuanian immigrant who had started off in Dublin as a brush maker. Briscoe Senior, an ardent nationalist, named his sons Robert (Emmet) and Wolf Tone after Irish revolutionary heroes. Robert was a founding member of the Fianna Fáil party and the first member of the Jewish community to be elected to the Dáil (Irish parliament).

102. Wrightson 2000, pp. 205–9; Spufford 2002, pp. 45–49.

103. O'Callaghan 1825, p. 136.

104. The miseries wrought by Dublin's publicans and tenement owners on vulnerable households did not prevent them from being elected as aldermen and city councilors (J. O'Brien 1982, p. 98).

105. J. Edelstein 1908, p. 29.

106. Rubin 1984, p. 343; Black 1992, pp. 205–54; BPP 1873, 1897, 1898; Saorstát Éireann 1931.

107. Rowlingson 1994, pp. 28–31; Fitzpatrick 2001. The 1912 *Thom's Directory* lists thirty-nine pawn offices in greater Dublin. These include Mrs. Langan's at 53 Lower Clanbrassil Street, in the heart of the Jewish quarter. The average size of a transaction was small, and the interest charged was accordingly high.

108. *JC*, 30 May 1913. See also Marcus Blond, cited in Price 2002, p. 61; Lerner 1949.

109. Rubin 1986; Tebbutt 1983, pp. 182–83. Compare Kearns 1994, pp. 31–32, 100; Harris 2002, pp. 36–37.

110. O'Callaghan 1825, pp. 59, 136–37; Cleary 1914, pp. 170–71; Nelson 1969, pp. 124–32; "Burlington," *Catholic Encyclopedia.*

111. Anon. 1880.

112. Ó Gráda 1974; Kennedy 1977.

113. O'Callaghan (1825) conceded that "many pastors, shrinking from a contest, prefer to leave their flocks in their easy conscience, to the preaching of doctrine which they never would obey" (v).

114. The hostility toward moneylending was also reflected in Anglo-Irish literature. In William Carleton's *Black Prophet* (1847) and Liam O'Flaherty's aforementioned *House of Gold* (1929), the villains were gombeenmen.

CHAPTER 4. SELF-EMPLOYMENT, SOCIAL MOBILITY

1. Mitovsky 1959–60.

2. Baron et al. 1975, pp. 144–45, 147–57, 191–98.

3. Maitles 1995, p. 60.

4. Undated handbill, "Irish Manufacturers' Furniture Made by Sweaters," item 61, L.O. P 114, NLI. See also O'Riordan 1984.

5. Compare Collins 1990, p. 59.

6. O'Riordan 1988.

7. Baron et al. 1975, p. 264.

8. Harris 2002, pp. 1–3. In conversation, Nick Harris jokes about the risk entailed in employing Jewish workers, who were very likely to set up in competition as soon as they had learned the tricks of the trade (Harris interview, 21 October 2004).

9. On Sevitt, see the address by Manus O'Riordan on the occasion of the unveiling of a plaque at 52 Lower Camden Street, which once housed the Jewish Tailors and Pressers Union, 18 June 2002, at http://www.siptu.ie/news/easyprint.php?id=689. See also O'Riordan 1984.

10. Mitovsky 1959–60. In Germany the expression was "*balabos for sich*" (be one's own boss); see Wertheimer 1987, p. 92 (citing Kessner 1977, pp. 171–72).

11. Harris 2002, p. 148.

12. I am very grateful to Stuart Rosenblatt, indefatigable and knowledgeable genealogist of Irish Jewry, for a copy of the database underlying the analysis. For consistency, the occupations used are those reported at the date of the eldest child's admission to school.

13. Birkahn interview.

14. Thus Wolve Nurock is described as a traveler in the high school records and as a draper in those of the Diocesan School for Girls.

15. Cited in Aris 1970, pp. 232–33.

16. Hunt 1981, pp. 182, 184, cited in Lunn 1985, p. 34.

17. Burnett 1888, p. 571; Susser 1993, p. 120; Aris 1970, p. 232.

18. Feldman 1994, p. 155–65; Godley 2001.

19. Godley 2001, ch. 4.

20. Rubin 1984, p. 322; Godley 2001, p. 146 n. 19. The term "fringe" capitalist is Rubin's.

21. Godley 2001, pp. 120–21, 130.

22. Susser 1993, p. 113.

23. Endelman 2002, p. 130; J. White 1980, p. 245.

24. Goldman is cited in Green 1997, p. 28; see also Wechsler 1979, p. 288.

25. Cahan 1960, p. 167.

26. Wechsler 1979, p. 119; Model 1985, p. 75.

27. Wertheimer 1987, pp. 91–92.

28. As reported in Wechsler 1979, p. 111.

29. Wechsler 1979, pp. 117, 120–21; Green 2003, p. 43.

30. Wechsler 1979, p. 117; Lipman 1959, pp. 282–83; J. White 1980, pp. 255–57.

31. Wechsler 1979, ch. 7.

32. Wechsler 1979, p. 142. The variation in occupational distributions across counties and over time suggests that England's immigrants adapted to conditions as they found them. The increasing labor force shares of tailors and cabinet-makers in England and Wales (44.1 percent in 1891, 48.9 percent in 1911) at the expense of shoemakers, painters and glaziers, and commercial travelers (17.8 percent in 1891, 11.4 percent in 1911) probably reflected a shift toward better-paying occupations.

The statements about wages come from D. F. Schloss, "The Sweating System," *Fortnightly Review* 42 (December 1887): 848 (as cited in Wechsler 1979, p. 139) and Herbert Evans, Assistant Inspector of Factories (BPP 1903, q11726, p. 395). See also ibid., q22034, p. 807.

33. Godley 2001, p. 39.

34. Available through the Integrated Public Use Microdata Series (IPUMS). For more on IPUMS, see http://www.ipums.umn.edu/.

35. Wechsler 1979, p. 294; Rubinstein 1996, p. 108.

36. Personal communication, May 2003.

37. According to Nick Harris, the credit drapery business was already becoming dominant in the 1920s (conversation with the author, August 2003). Compare Gerlis and Gerlis 1986, pp. 100–105.

38. Curiously, perhaps, the immigrants never took to pawnbroking as in neighboring Wales. Compare Henriques 1993, pp. 19–22, 52–55.

39. Eppel 1992. The Eppels also invested in housing property.

40. On Arthur Newman, see Harris 2002, pp. 195–97; Hyman 1972, p. 341; Rivlin 2003, p. 105.

41. Hyman 1972, p. 342; Harris 2002, pp. 133, 195–96; Herzog 1997, p. 18. In Russia many Jews were prevented from entering the professions by a quota system.

42. On 25 September 1908 the *Jewish Chronicle* cites a report by Joseph Edelstein noting "the extraordinary fact that not a year has passed for quite a decade without a Jewish exhibitioner or prize-winner appearing." In a conversation recorded by A. Schlimeel (1954), the suggestion that "Mrs. So-an-so's son" would be better off giving up his medical studies, for which he was showing little aptitude, for his father's weekly led to a falling out between two Jewish women. In these years the *Chronicle* carried an occasional column on "university intelli-

gence," detailing the achievements of Jewish students (for more on schooling, see chap. 6).

43. Eppel 1992, p. 294; Berman and Zlotover 1966; Price 2002; Collins 1990, pp. 175–76; Kokosalakis 1982, p. 126–27; Henriques 1993, pp. 214–16.

CHAPTER 5. SETTLING IN

1. Berman and Zlotover 1966, p. 25.
2. For a brief but useful account of the Lurgan community, see McCorry 1993, p. 168. The *Jewish Chronicle* (18 October 1895) reports services being held at Abbey Street Hall in Armagh, conducted by Bernard White, A. Glicksman, and S. J. Parkes, with Parkes acting as president. During the High Festivals, families from Newry, Banbridge, and other surrounding towns came to Lurgan. According to Stanley Shapiro (Lurgan Jewry, *Belfast Jewish Record* 8[2] [April 1961]: 2), Lurgan's Board of Guardians "was so well known for its benevolence that the community was continually besieged by Schnorrers."
3. Danker 1960. Individual immigrants also set up businesses in towns such as Carlow (the Robinsons), Downpatrick (the Watermans), Tullow (the Khans), Gorey (the Cherricks), Newry (the Abrahamsons), Wexford (Simon Mann), and Drogheda (the Silvermans).
4. Hyman 1972, pp. 108–11.
5. Berman 195-a, p. 8. However, another account relates how Samuel Lewis Dutch, one-time president of Mary's Abbey congregation, broke his windows to give work to a Jewish glazier (Louis Hyman to Jessie Bloom, 29 September 1948, Bloom Papers).
6. Records of the Dublin Hebrew Congregation, p7517, NLI
7. O'Casey 1981, pp. 122–23. Compare Waterman and Schmool 1995.
8. Berman 195-a, p. 8; IFC/UFP 0471. There are photographs of nos. 28 (where Jacob Davis lived on arrival; see below), 29, 30, and 31 in the Irish Architectural Archive (63/100X1 and 54/85X1). These are copies of original glass negatives in the Royal Society of Antiquaries of Ireland collection. See also Ó Gráda 2005. Even in mid-century the street consisted, apart from the police station at no. 31, entirely of either tenements or workshops (Shaw 1850). See also Pearson 2000, pp. 135–37; Kearns 1994, plate 4.
9. Cameron 1883; Prunty 1998, pp. 136–37.
10. Hyman 1972, p. 146. Louis Wine, also from Lithuania, was another early arrival (Kleanthous 2000).
11. Margoliouth 1868, entry for 26 August.
12. Berman 195-a, p. 8; Berman and Zlotover 1966, pp. 25–26; Hyman 1972, pp. 136, 146, 155, 256–57.
13. A Dublin tourism plaque today marks the fictional birthplace of Leopold Bloom at 52 Upper Clanbrassil Street.
14. Fraser 1996, p. 72; Aalen 1985.
15. Duffy 1985, pp. 28, 32; J. Bloom 1952; Berman and Zlotover 1966, pp. 32, 39. Compare Marks (1994, pp. 60–61), who suggests that Jewish households tended to be concentrated in the best streets in the East End of London.

16. One of the moneylenders in Joseph Edelstein's *The Moneylender* is Oscar Whitingstone; see J. Edelstein 1908, p. 110.

17. Sheila and Carmel Cunningham, interview by the author, 21 March 2003.

18. Berman and Zlotover 1966, p. 30; Berman 195-b, pp. 4–5. George Mitovsky (1959–60) refers to *The Eye-Opener* "as a scurrilous sheet in which the cream and leaders of the community—whom my mother always dismissed airily as 'the rubbish'—were mentioned in blatantly libelous and deliciously scandalous terms" (16–17).

19. Shillman 1945, p. 96. In Glasgow the tension between the "old" community, focused on Garnethill shul, which was consecrated in 1879, and the "new" based in the Gorbals was analogous. There were no organized daily prayers at Garnethill; it was left to groups who wanted to pray to provide their own minyan, whereas in the new *hebroth* daily services were standard. See Collins 1990, pp. 48–56, 134.

20. J. Bloom 1953.

21. Berman 195-a, pp. 12–13; J. Bloom 1953, p. 27; see also Duffy 1985, p. 47–48. Perhaps there was something cultural in this penchant for domestic servants: a local history of Wilmington, Delaware, describes most Russian Jewish households as having black maids: "anyone could afford one—they only cost three or four dollars a week," and in a large sample of Jewish households constructed by the U.S. Census Bureau in 1890 over three-fifths of households had one or more servants. See David Goldberg, "An Historical Community Study of Wilmington Jewry, 1738–1925" (in Lucy Davidowitz Papers, box 2/1, American Jewish Historical Society (AJHS), New York); U.S. Census Bulletin No. 19 (30 December 1890), "Vital Statistics of the Jews in the U.S."

22. The elite of the Jewish community lived south of the canal in Rathmines or Rathgar. In the 1900s few of the socially exclusive council of the Adelaide Road shul lived in Little Jerusalem proper.

23. Minutes of the United Hebrew Congregation, 1914, Irish Jewish Museum.

24. *JC*, 5 April 1895.

25. Shillman 1964/5.

26. Marks 1994, pp. 16–18; Englander 1989; Fishman 1988.

27. Cited in Marks 1994, p. 22.

28. Endelman 2002, pp. 130–32; see also table 3.1 in chap. 3 above. The occupational profile of Dublin's Jews closely mirrored that of Liverpool. According to Bill Williams (undated), "A majority of [Liverpool's] newcomers took to some form of peddling, which underwent a marked revival in the city, to Scotch Drapery (that is, the sale of domestic textiles from house to house on a weekly-payment basis), or to itinerant glaziery, carrying panes of glass in frames strapped to their backs in search of broken windows."

29. Cited in Keogh 1998, p. 21; see also Kearns 1998, p. 170.

30. Borjas 1995; Wegge 1998; Cutler and Glaeser 1997; Cutler, Glaeser, and Vigdor 1999; Bertrand, Luttmer, and Mullainathan 2000; Chiswick and Miller 2003.

31. See Hyman 1972, pp. 189, 329.

32. *JC*, 27 November 1885 (cited in Duffy 1985, pp. 87–88).

33. Berman 195-b, p. 8.

34. Cited in Shillman 1945, p. 97.
35. Berman and Zlotover 1966.
36. Harris 2002, p. 23.
37. Meir Wigoder 2001.
38. The expected proportion is $[J-1]/[H-1]$, where J and H represent Jewish and total households.
39. Ó Gráda 2006.
40. Harris 2002, p. 23.
41. Sheila and Carmel Cunningham interview.
42. The proportions here are drawn from Stuart Rosenblatt's database of over seven thousand schoolchildren from all over Ireland.
43. See also Waterman 1981.
44. J. Bloom 1976. Clein (1989, p. 9) records: "According to family tales the Cleins devised an ingenious method of stealing horses. They walked backwards as they removed the horse from the barn, prepared to declare if they were caught, that they were returning the horse." For more on Cork Jewry, see Ó Grada 2006; Hyman 1972, pp. 218–24.
45. The proportion of households living in Hibernian Buildings probably declined over time. Seven of the thirty-nine couples in the 1911 database described were living in Hibernian Buildings.
46. Elyan interview.
47. Louis Marcus (personal communication, February 2004) often heard talk of *der alte Levi* in his youth.
48. Elyan interview. The *sefer torah* is a sacred parchment scroll on which portions of the Old Testament have been written by hand. It is kept in the ark in the synagogue. See also Hyman 1972, p. 219.
49. Esther Hesselberg, interview by Carol Weinstock, c. 1986, Acc. 5734 (unsorted), NLI.
50. Ibid.
51. On his visit in August 1888 the chief rabbi sought unsuccessfully to unite the two factions (*Jewish Standard*, 24 August 1888). See also *JC*, 30 December 1910.
52. Birkahn interview.
53. Marcus 1986, p. 111.
54. CSORP 1888/15,507, NAI; Hyman 1972, p. 219.
55. *JC*, 4 January 1896, 14 August 1896.
56. And described in greater detail in chap. 5.
57. For more on the early history of Cork Jewry, see Ó Gráda 2006.
58. I am grateful to Barry Chiswick for impressing the general point on me.
59. Hyman 1972, p. 203.
60. *HaYehudi*, 29 August 1901, 28 November 1912 (as cited in Schwartzman-Sharon 1971). I am grateful to Guy Beiner for these references.
61. See *JC*, 24 November 1911 (letter from Samuel Freeman); 1 December 1911 (letter from J. Myers); Hyman 1972, pp. 203–9; Warm 1998.
62. The streets included in our 1911 database are: Adela Street, Alloa Street, Annalee Street, Annesley Street, Antrim Road, Atlantic Avenue, Avoca Street, Bandon Street, Bristol Street, Brookhill Avenue, Carlisle Street, Cranburn Street,

Crumlin Road, Dargle Street, Duncairn Avenue, Fleetwood Street, Groomsport Street, Hillview Terrace, Kinnaird Terrace, Lincoln Avenue, Londsdale Street, Louis Street, Old Lodge Road, Pacific Avenue, Ponsonby Avenue, Roe Street, Somerton Road, and Vicinage Park.

63. *Belfast and Province of Ulster Directory,* 1910.

64. Stuart Rosenblatt's schools database (October 2004 version); Ordnance Survey of Northern Ireland, *Greater Belfast Street Map* (Belfast, 1980).

CHAPTER 6. SCHOOLING AND LITERACY

1. Olneck and Lazerson 1974, p. 473.

2. Kasovich 1929, pp. 127, 254. Compare Aleichem 1987, pp. 217–29.

3. Olneck and Lazerson 1974.

4. Bayor 1978, pp. 14–16; Diner and Lieff Benderly 2002, p. 280.

5. Dividing Jewish fathers and mothers into those under and over 40 gives the following result:

	< 40		40+	
Level (%)	M	F	M	F
Can't read	.208	.277	.275	.622
Read only	.048	.053	.056	.025
R & W	.744	.670	.669	.353

6. Harris 2002, p. 28.

7. On the importance of language acquisition in a somewhat different context, see Chiswick and Miller 2002, 2003.

8. Perlmann 1997.

9. Palmer 1901, p. 128; Joseph 1969, pp. 146–48; Vital 1999, p. 306; Harris 2002, p. 28; Stern 1997, p. 185; Kuznets 1975, pp. 80–81. Jessie Bloom's grandfather was a lawyer, but he supplemented his income by working as a *ronde-schreiber,* or someone who wrote petitions and letters for a fee. When he died her mother continued the business, and in Dublin she helped pay some of the bills by preparing naturalization forms and the like for immigrant Litvaks, all of which bespeaks less than universal literacy (J. Bloom 1976).

10. According to Price (2002, p. 132), many English public schools, particularly in London, imposed such quotas.

11. Rivlin 2003, pp. 109–10. Stratford was located at first on Terenure Road East and later on Zion Road in Rathgar.

12. G. Fitzpatrick 1994, pp. 86–88, 112.

13. Ibid., pp. 86–88.

14. Rivlin 2003, pp. 100–101. The surviving records in Synge Street contain no Jewish names, but they date only from 1923. I am grateful to Pádraig Ó Néill for this information. Perhaps Jewish students were deterred by a school schedule that included Saturday mornings (as some were in the case of St. Andrew's around this time).

15. L. Wigoder 1978, p. 23–24.

16. Harris 2002, p. 71; Rivlin 2003, pp. 104, 157. On an attempt to seek communal support for the education of the less well-off, see *JC*, 5 July 1912.

17. Diocesan School Admission Rolls 1902–36, Representative Church Body Library, Dublin.

18. Bloom 1953. On Max Nurock, see Wallace 2004, p. 162.

19. *JC*, 6 December 1895, 23 July 1897.

20. *JC*, 3 February 1899.

21. *JC*, 5 January 1894. The *Chronicle* often featured the Goldfoots. On 22 May 1891 it reported that Mr. and Mrs. Goldfoot made a presentation to the synagogue and ran a party for the entire community in the school room to mark their son's bar mitzvah. It also reported the achievement of Goldfoot's daughter "at the examination of Art and Science, recently held in Cork": "Miss Jenny Goldfoot passed in the following subjects: Freehand Drawing, Advanced Stage; Drawing in Life and Shade, Elementary Stage; Model Drawing, Elementary Stage" (*JC*, 24 September 1897). In the early 1890s the *Chronicle* also contained frequent glowing references to Miss Sarah de Groot, the actress daughter of a leading member of the Dublin "English" community (e.g., 5 February 1892).

22. L. Wigoder 1978, p. 30.

23. *JC*, 13 November 1908.

24. *JC*, 28 May, 1 July, 11 November 1898, 28 April, 14 July, 21 July, 4 August, 20 October 1899, 2 February, 30 March, 29 June 1900; 3 August, 11 August, 8 November 1901; 3 April, 22 May, 27 June 1908.

CHAPTER 7. THE DEMOGRAPHY OF IRISH JEWRY

1. Cited in Ellman 1982, p. 373.

2. Compare Entwistle et al. 1997; Watkins and Danzi 1995; Kohler, Behrman, and Watkins 2001; Kohler 2001.

3. Van Poppel, Schellekens, and Liefbroer 2002.

4. These are deposited and available for inspection in NAI.

5. E.g., Ó Gráda 1985; Guinnane, Moehling, and Ó Gráda 2001.

6. Soloway 1990, p. 10.

7. Haines 1985, p. 888; Watterson 1988, p. 292; Preston and Haines 1991; Garrett et al. 2001. Note that children born out of wedlock are thus left out of the reckoning in my analysis.

8. Duffy 1985, p. 47.

9. Another well-known pitfall of the 1911 census is the misreporting of ages prompted by the Old Age Pensions Act of 1908. Ireland lacked any civil registration before the 1860s and coverage was still far from complete in the 1900s, giving many of the not-so-elderly poor an incentive to exaggerate their ages. By matching couples in the 1901 and 1911 censuses, we can obtain a good sense of the extent of age misreporting. Fortunately, the outcome (not reported here) suggested that age misreporting was not serious in Dublin and that there was little difference between the three confessional groups in this respect. Age misreporting was slightly more common among women than men—unless women who had de-

clared too low an age in 1901 revealed their true ages in 1911. There was little variation in the gap by socioeconomic group. Admittedly the number of observations in some cases is small. See Ó Gráda 2002; Budd and Guinnane 1992. For the *Jewish Chronicle's* perspective on the old age pension, see *JC*, 15 May 1908.

10. A similar analysis of the Jewish quarter of Cork city in 1911 indicates that Jewish households (with 5.5 rooms per household) had the edge over their non-Jewish neighbors (4.5 rooms per household) in this respect.

11. However, some of those living on Martin Street and other streets with smaller houses employed the services of a daily rather than a live-in shikse (Michael Brennan, personal communication with the author). On the importance of status in eastern Europe, see Hundert 2004, pp. 90–92.

12. Reher 1999; Coale and Watkins 1986; Galloway, Hammel, and Lee 1994; Brown and Guinnane 2002; compare Iyer 2002.

13. The few exceptions include Irish Quaker women in the second half of the eighteenth century and the women of Quebec a century earlier. See Vann and Eversley 1992, pp. 133–43. Note that even where couples practiced no birth control, malnutrition might constrain family size (as perhaps in ancien régime France).

14. Ó Gráda 1993, pp. 206–7; Ó Gráda and Duffy 1995; David and Sanderson 1988; Guinnane Moehling, and Ó Gráda 2001. The Hutterite weights range from 0.550 for women aged 20–24 years to 0.061 for women aged 45–49 years. These weights represent the average number of children born per year to Hutterite women in those age groups in the 1920s. For more on I_g, see, e.g., Coale and Watkins 1986; Vann and Eversley 1992, p. 45.

15. Coale and Treadway 1986, p. 120; Ó Gráda and Walsh 1995; Ó Gráda 1997, pp. 193–95.

16. Livi-Bacci 1986; Knodel 1974, pp. 136–38; Goldscheider 1967; Kosmin 1982.

17. Harris 2002, p. 4.

18. Heer 1968; Gatrell 1986, pp. 54–55; Freeze 2002, p. 291; Kosmin 1982, pp. 253–56.

19. Freeze 2002, p. 53.

20. Ibid., pp. 53, 60, 61.

21. Coale, Anderson, and Härm 1979, pp. 78–80. See also Bushee 1903, p. 46. At first sight the Coale-Anderson-Härm finding would seem to conflict with that in Morgan, Watkins, and Ewbank 1994, who find that the fertility of U.S. Yiddish speakers c. 1910 was very different from that of other "new" immigrant groups, such as Poles and Italians. Morgan, Watkins, and Ewbank argue that Jewish immigrants had brought their knowledge of contraceptive techniques with them from Europe. The apparent contradiction is easily resolved. First, Coale, Anderson, and Härm were referring to Russian Jews, while the data used by Morgan, Watkins, and Ewbank refer to Yiddish-speaking mothers, some of whom would have been born in the United States. Second, Morgan, Watkins, and Ewbank assume that the precocious fertility transition documented by Livi-Bacci for west European Jewry applied equally to east European Jewry.

22. Livi-Bacci 1986, pp. 189–95. The birth registers reproduced in Hyman (1972, app. V) indicate an average interval of just less than two years (720 days)

between births. This is low but, unfortunately, reveals little about overall fertility, since the age of the mother is not given. The high proportion of fathers recording one, two, or three children could indicate a degree of "stopping"; but it could equally reflect a highly mobile population that yielded further births elsewhere.

23. On Orthodox Jewry in Israel today, see Dov Friedlander, "Fertility in Israel: Is the Transition to Replacement Level in Sight?" available at http://www.un.org/esa/population/publications/completingfertility/RevisedFriedlanderpaper.PDF (accessed May 2004).

24. Marks 1994, p. 69. Lev. 12:1–8 stipulates that women abstain from sex for forty days after the birth of a boy and for seventy-three days after the birth of a girl.

25. This is suggested by comparing the changes in the mean number of children from one duration category to the next for Jews and Catholics. In table 7.4 the increases for Jews are significantly greater between durations of 0–4 and 5–9 years and between 5–9 and 10–14 years, but not so thereafter. In Cork the Jewish advantage held at higher durations.

Mean Number of Children (Number of Households in Parentheses)

Duration	Jews	Others
0–4	0.75 (4)	1.18 (33)
5–9	3.86 (7)	2.00 (23)
10–14	4.83 (6)	3.27 (15)
15–19	6.00 (4)	4.21 (24)
20–29	6.73 (10)	5.94 (31)

26. For marriages where the female age at marriage was 20–24 years, the percentages of childless women were as follows:

	Jews		Catholics	
Marriage duration	Percentage childless	Number of obs.	Percentage childless	Number of obs.
0–4	20.7	29	21.6	37
5–9	5.6	36	6.7	45
10–14	2.6	39	12.8	39
15–19	14.3	21	15.2	33
20–29	7.2	28	11.6	43

On the relation between age at marriage and childlessness, see Wrigley 2004, pp. 410–11.

27. Ó Gráda 1991; Ó Gráda and Duffy 1995; Guinnane, Moehling, and Ó Gráda 2001.

28. On "stopping," see David and Sanderson 1988.

29. On the reluctance to control births in the Catholic community in this era, see Ó Gráda 1993, pp. 200, 219n. 41.

30. It is the number of children aged 0–2 divided by the weighted sum of married women aged 15–49. The weights used are the Hutterite weights described in

note 14 above, also used in constructing I_g. This means not allowing for illegitimate births, but their proportion was small in this period.

31. The underlying data are in Saorstát Éireann, *Census of Population 1946*, vol. 3, p. 32.

32. Compare Marks 1994, pp. 85–86, and the sources cited there.

33. As cited in Hyman 1972, p. 190.

34. For recent research, see Breschi and Pozzi 2004.

35. Peters 1908, pp. 213–15.

36. Guilfoy 1917, p. 10. Guilfoy's data are cited in Meyer 1921, table 10.

37. Woodbury 1926; Preston, Ewbank, and Hereward 1994.

38. See *Jewish Encyclopedia* (New York, 1901–6), article titled "Consumption (Tuberculosis)," available at http://www.jewishencyclopedia.com, and the sources cited there.

39. Preston, Ewbank, and Hereward 1994; Bushee 1903, p. 54.

40. Elkin 1980, p. 202.

41. Goldstein, Watkins, and Spector 1994; Marks 1994; Garrett et al. 2001, pp. 152–53.

42. Nick Harris (interview, August 2003) believed that Jews had built up immunity to infectious diseases over the generations.

43. I am grateful to Graham Mooney of Johns Hopkins University for sharing his data set of London births and infant deaths by registration subdistrict.

44. Mooney 1994; compare Huck 1997.

45. Schmelz 1971, pp. 22–33; Preston and Haines 1991, table 3.4.

46. Hyman 1972, pp. 244–66.

47. Schmelz 1971, pp. 21–23; Collins 2000, pp. 79–80. It would be nice to know whether Jewish infants were born with an advantage in terms of birth weight, which stood to them in infancy and childhood. As noted earlier, however, comparable birth-weight data are lacking. Peter Ward's sample of births in Dublin's Rotunda Hospital between 1870 and 1930 contains only eight Jewish infants. Their average birth weight—3,258 grams—was almost identical to those of Catholics (3,257 grams) and Protestants (3,249 grams). Peter Ward, personal communication with the author, 21 April 2003.

48. Very few of those born between these dates would have been buried in Ballybough cemetery (which served the community before Dolphin's Barn) or still be alive.

49. These statements are based on calculations from the evidence in Stuart Rosenblatt's recent invaluable compilation, whence also the citation from the Book of Genesis (Rosenblatt 2004b, p. 15). I am very grateful to Rosenblatt for enlightenment on this and other sources.

50. See chap. 2, note 24.

51. Guinnane 1997, pp. 112–13; Preston and Haines 1991, table 2.3.

52. Kosmin 1982, pp. 258–59.

53. On the negative binomial, see Long and Freese 2001, pp. 243–45. For a more extensive analysis using similar estimation techniques, compare Guinnane, Moehling, and Ó Gráda 2001.

54. The resulting negative binomial regression produced:

	Coefficient	z
aamw	−.0367	−2.84
aamh	−.0244	−2.43
hrupol	−.4561	−3.66
doms	−.3402	2.68
cmr	.0258	11.63
constant	−2.564	−5.61
Pseudo R^2		.083
N		1,079

55. Preston and Haines 1991, pp. 88–90; Haines and Preston 1997. Garrett et al. (2001) also apply the index in their study of mortality in England.

56. On mortality, see Ó Gráda 2002. I also experimented with dividing the area in two, with the South Circular Road as dividing line, but this produced no worthwhile results.

57. Arguably, neither of these variables is entirely exogenous, but our restricted choice of socioeconomic variables makes us treat them as such here.

CHAPTER 8. CULTURE, FAMILY, HEALTH

1. H. Edelstein (1950, p. v). Born in Dublin in the early 1890s, Hyman Edelstein (Joseph Edelstein's brother) emigrated to Canada in the early 1910s with his parents. He had been a brilliant student both at the high school and Trinity College, though a nervous disposition prevented him from completing his degree in Trinity. For much more on Hyman Edelstein, see http://www.uwo.ca/english/canadianpoetry/cpjrn/vol06/fisher.htm (accessed 21 January 2006). The other epigraphs are taken from Levine 1988, p. 105, and *Journey to the Dawn*, as cited in Olneck and Lazerson 1974, p. 474.

2. The classic source is McCloskey 1970. See also Fogel and Engerman 1977; Lewis and McInnis 1980.

3. Temin 1997; Blanchard 1978; Cipolla 1965, 1967; Mokyr 1991; Clark 1987.

4. Bonacich 1973, p. 585.

5. Botticini and Eckstein 2004a.

6. Petty 1899, p. 264. For the literature on middleman minorities, see Bonacich and Modell 1980; Botticini and Eckstein 2004a, 2004b.

7. Bowles and Gintis 2003.

8. S. Steinberg 1981 (citation at p. 132); see also S. Steinberg 2000; Perlmann 1988, pp. 215–16.

9. I am grateful to Barry Chiswick for this suggestion.

10. Olneck and Lazerson 1974; Rubinstein 1999.

11. "Jews and the Old Age Pension Scheme," *JC*, 15 May 1908.

12. Compare Collins 1990, p. 44.

13. *Jewish Standard*, 25 January 1889. The disputes that divided both the Limerick and Cork communities were settled in 1895. However, a new dispute broke

out in Limerick, marked by the opening of a second synagogue in 1901. The break-away group, swayed by Chief Rabbi Adler's advice, disassociated themselves from the "money-lenders" (*JC*, 26 April 1895, 13 September 1895; letters in *Limerick Leader*, 9 and 10 January 1901 from M. J. Blond and Louis Goldberg, cited in Ryan 1997; Morrissey 2003, p. 326).

14. Jessie Bloom, 26 April 1965, Ms. Collection 13/1, Bloom Papers.

15. DHC committee minutes, February 1914, p. 8880, NLI.

16. Levine 1988, pp. 109–10. However, Asher Benson (interview, 29 May 2003) notes that perhaps not too much should be made of this: "That's all part of the service . . . you don't go to the service necessarily to pray . . . [you go] to talk."

17. Daiken 1946, p. 33.

18. Michael Brennan, e-mail correspondence with the author, March 2004.

19. I am grateful to Arthur Sugerman for this information.

20. Ms. 93/12/8, AJA.

21. Compare J. White 1980, p. 44, on London.

22. "The Sanitation of the Mosaic Law," *JC*, 29 September 1899; *Irish Jewish Year Book* (1964–65), p. 64. Beila Erlich ran the water virtually all day long in her shop in Clanbrassil Street. From time to time an upstairs tenant (and employee) would go down and ask her to "turn off that water" (interview at St. Kevin's Community Centre, March 2003).

23. *JC*, 4 September 1908.

24. Eliach 1998, pp. 203–9; J. O'Brien 1982, p. 102; citing Dublin Corporation Reports and Documents, 1901-III, no. 212.

25. Esther Hesselberg, interview by Carol Weinstock, 1987 (typescript in Acc. 5374, NLI); also Harris 2002, p. 60.

26. Fogel 2004; Mokyr 2002, ch. 5.

27. Jones 2001, pp. 101–26; Mokyr 2002; Ó Gráda 1995, pp. 248–49. Awareness of the link has recently prompted the creation of a much-hyped public-private partnership between the World Bank and a group of soap companies, following a suggestion from Valerie Curtis of the London School of Hygiene and Tropical Medicine ("Hand-washing: How to Save 1 Million Children a Year," *The Economist*, 6 July 2002, p. 83).

28. "Hand-washing."

29. J. Bloom 1952, pp. 25, 26; Harris 2002, pp. 18–19, 67; see also Fishman 1988, p. 148; Berman 195-b; J. White 1980, pp. 48–49.

30. According to Michael Brennan (e-mail communication, 8 February 2004), "when my oldest brother was born in 1920 one of his older twin sisters (born a year earlier) developed whooping cough and was ill enough to be admitted to the Cork St. Fever Hospital, so my mother, my oldest brother and the other twin also had to be admitted because my mother was breast-feeding all three."

31. Presumably there was some overlap in the categories used.

32. Cameron 1912, pp. 130–37; Preston and Haines 1991, p. 28. See also Chiswick 1986.

33. BPP 1903, Q3963, Qs. 21412–15.

34. BPP 1903, Qs. 16298, 17513, 17515; Marks 1994, pp. 74–75; Collins 2001, p. 78.

35. *JC*, 20 January 1911, cited in Collins 1990, pp. 164–65; Collins 2001, p. 79.

36. Preston, Ewbank, and Hereward 1994, pp. 68–69; Woodbury 1926.

37. Harris 2002, pp. 27–29, 221.

38. Bruce Misstear (grandson of H. S. Misstear), interview by the author, 25 March 2003. In the interwar period this extensive business employed as many as twelve people.

39. Goldstein, Watkins, and Spector 1994.

40. A database of nearly ten thousand Rotunda Hospital mothers created by Peter Ward for his study of birth weights c. 1870–1930 (Ward 1993) contains at most eight Jews.

41. May Smith, another Jewish midwife, lived on Warren Street and delivered numerous Jewish babies for a few decades up to the 1930s. I am grateful to Michael Brennan for this information.

42. The business book is kept in the Irish Jewish Museum. In the 1896–1901 period Ada Shillman delivered nearly four hundred infants. She charged Mrs. Briscoe and about twenty-five other mothers £1 5s. (or £1.25 in terms of decimal currency) or more per delivery, while she charged another twenty or so 10s. (£0.50) or less per delivery.

43. Shillman 1945, pp. 117–18.

44. Compare Chiswick 1986.

45. IFC/UFP 0682; compare Marks 1994.

46. Daly 1984, p. 112.

47. Mr. and Mrs. Louis Davis, interview by Irish Jewish Museum, December 1990.

48. Diner 2002, pp. 112, 178; D. Fitzpatrick 1994, p. 265. For an interesting perspective on evolving Jewish cuisine in Edinburgh, see Storrier 1992–93.

49. Daly 1984, pp. 268–69; J. O'Brien 1982, pp. 164–68; Marks 1994, p. 72–73; BPP 1904, Q10,975; J. Bloom 1953.

50. Daiken n.d., 33,491.

51. Esther Hesselberg, interview by Carol Weinstock, 1987 (typescript in Acc. 5734, NLI).

52. KC, private communication with the author, May 2003.

53. Crowley 1988, p. 44.

54. Ibid.; Levine 1982, p. 76; Levine 1988, p. 108; Schlimeel 1954.

55. "Erev Passach," box 12, folder 8, Bloom Papers.

56. Information from Maria Byrne. Another informant (Iris Misstear) remembered a Jewish neighbor's maid coming looking for caster sugar. She was duly given some, but returned it because she couldn't use it out of "a Christian container."

57. J. O'Brien 1982, pp. 164–66; Daly 1984, pp. 110–12.

58. Lindsay 1913, p. 23; Collins 1990, pp. 163–64.

59. Admittedly, like all such studies, this is subject to some likely biases. Some households are likely to have been on their best behavior while under Lindsay's scrutiny.

60. Lindsay 1913, p. 11.

61. BPP 1904, Q11,086; Lindsay 1913, pp. 31–34.

62. Marks 1994, pp. 72–74.

63. Ibid., pp. 66–67; Lindsay 1913, pp. 23–24.

64. In an address to the Second International Congress on Eugenics, cited in Bales 1980, p. 24. Philip Cowan's papers (box 4/7, AJHS) contain the records of eighteen Jewish inmates in the New York County Almshouse in the early 1890s; all were described as "temperate."

65. Guilfoy 1917, app. table 1. Deaths included are those from "alcoholism" and "cirrhosis of the liver." For deaths in the 45–64 age group the Irish disadvantage was less marked.

	Males	*Females*
Ireland	4.2	1.7
Russia	1.1	0.6
Austro-Hungary	2.8	0.9

Also of interest in this respect are the data in Bales's classic study of Irish American and Jewish American attitudes to alcohol; see Bales 1980.

66. Hyman 1972, p. 186; Harris 2002, pp. 3–4, 83; Crowley 1988, p. 44; interviews with Olive Sealy, Sheila and Carmel Cunningham, and Dominick Casey. Curiously, perhaps, Jews played no part in the Dublin drinks trade, though they dominated both the production and supply of alcohol in tsarist Lithuania.

67. Jessie Bloom to Sherry Abel (*Commentary Magazine*), 26 June 1961, box 93/3/8, Bloom Papers.

68. BPP 1900, Q4360, 4383–84; Grimshaw 1890. Regressing the death rate (DR) and the infant mortality rate (IMR) on the number of cases of drunkenness per thousand ($DRUNK$) with Grimshaw's data on major British and Irish cities produced the following outcome. In the second case IMR data for Salford and Nottingham are lacking. The statistical correlation between the DR and $DRUNK$ is indeed striking, although the correlation disappears when the overall death rate is replaced by the *infant* mortality rate. T-statistics are given in parentheses.

Dependent Variable	*DR*	*IMR*
DRUNK	0.221	−0.126
	(6.08)	(−0.24)
Constant	19.17	164.1
	(32.99)	(18.42)
N	14	12
Prob > F	0.00	0.81
Adjusted R^2	0.73	−0.01

69. J. O'Brien 1982, p. 188; Daly 1984, pp. 81–83. Calculated from the police reports described in BPP 1902, appendix. The evidence from C Division, where nearly all the parents' children were routinely reported as "poor," "respectable," and "industrious," is omitted.

Grimshaw's remarks recall those of his English counterpart, Dr. William Ogle, who in his fifty-fourth annual report for 1891 (p. xvi) noted how two or three times as many infants died of suffocation on Saturday nights as on any other night of the week.

CHAPTER 9. NEWCOMER TO NEIGHBOR

1. Montgomery 1984, p. 9.

2. *Irish Times*, 29 January 2004.

3. Cited in Price 2002, p. 34.

4. D. Power 1992, p. 11.

5. The incident is cited in the entry on Ireland by Joseph Jacobs and L. Hühner in the 1906 *Jewish Enyclopedia* (http://www.jewishencyclopedia.com/view.jsp?artid=169&letter=I).

6. Kleanthous 2000; Berman 195-a, p. 10; Price 2002, p. 53; Yodaiken 1987, p. 48.

7. Marcus 1986, p. 111; G. Goldberg 1945, pp. 140–41. In a short story by the Dublin Jewish writer Leslie Daiken, a recent arrival from Lithuania exclaims, "See, see how they stare at us! We're a barabarick (i.e. barbaric) primitive people. I suppose we're a sight for sore eyes" (Daiken collection, Ms. 33,491, NLI).

8. Berman 195-b; Rivlin 2003, p. 73.

9. In this they were no different than the "street urchins" who pelted would-be peddler Israel Kasovich with stones and lumps of coal in New York in the early 1880s, or the "loafers" who assailed his father, "ran after him, pulled his beard, kicked him, and showered him with refuge from garbage cans," or the "city toughs and hooligans" who prompted their victims in Detroit to form the Jewish Peddlers Protective Association. In Latin America, too, peddlers were "subjected to constant personal harassment," though hardly because they were Jewish. See O'Casey 1981; Rockaway 1974, p. 103; Kasovich 1929, p. 178; Elkin 1980, pp. 102–3.

10. *Jewish Standard*, 16 March 16 1888 (juxtaposing the anti-Semitism of the Cork Trade Council and the sympathy of the Irish parliamentary party).

11. Bulfin 1907, pp. 307–9; *The Leprecaun* 1907 (reproduced in Farmar 1991, p. 51). On Griffith, see Rivlin 2003, pp. 33–34, 192.

12. The term "Jewman" or "Jewmen" was used on at least half a dozen occasions in the Irish Dáil between 1922 and 1958, most recently in 1950 by the Labour Party's William Davin (*Parliamentary Debates Dáil Éireann*, vol. 106, 18 June 1947, and vol. 119, 23 March 1950) and Fianna Fáil's J. Griffin (*Parliamentary Debates Dáil Éireann*, vol. 168, 12 June 1958). See also Golding 1982, pp. 129–35.

13. Compare Endelman 2002, pp. 199–201.

14. Liebman and Cohen 1990, pp. 37–38.

15. Zborowksi and Herzog 1995, pp. 152, 156.

16. Slezkine 2004, pp. 108–9.

17. Morawska 1996, p. 16; Hundert 2004, pp. 50–51; see also Bushee 1903, pp. 156–57.

18. Odile Suganas, in Minczeles and Plasseraud 1996, p. 80.

19. Hundert (1992, p. 38), referring to eighteenth-century Poland, states that "personal relations between Poles and Jews were mediated, decisively, by their religious difference. The *halakha* and the traditions of Jews, no less than the canon law and the traditions of Christians, sought to limit contacts with outsiders of the other religion." Anti-Gentile passages in the Talmud and the halakha are highlighted in Shahak 1994; http://www.kokhavivpublications.com/2002/forum/israel_fund_demo/shahak_letters.html; and http://www.biu.ac.il/Spokesman/Stories/jul_14_2002.htm (exchange between Yaron Yadan and Jeffrey Woolf). Moses Maimonides' interpretation of the passage on usury in Deut. 32:19–20 is an extreme case in point: "We have been condemned to burden the Gentile with interest, and thus to lend to him, not to help him, but rather to harm him, even in the case of a loan at interest of a sort we have been cautioned against making to Israelites" (cited in Penslar 2001, p. 53). Such passages are played down in Anon. (2003); see also Nelson (1969, pp. xx–xxi, n. 3).

20. Compare Minczeles and Plasseraud 1996, p. 115.

21. *JC*, 3 April 1891.

22. Halberstam 1997, pp. 207–8; Liebman and Cohen 1990, pp. 50–55.

23. Shimoni 1999, pp. 142, 152nn. 29, 30.

24. Daiken 1963, p. 19; Berman 195-b.

25. Michael Brennan, personal communication with the author, 28 January 2004. For more on *Yoshke Pandre*, see *Mendele: Yiddish literature and language*, vol. 8.129 (10 February 1999), http://shakti.trincoll.edu/~mendele/vol08/vol08.129.

26. Schlimeel 1954; J. Edelstein 1908; Michael Brennan, e-mail communication with the author, February 2004.

27. According to Shahak 1994, p. 26, *shikse* is the feminine version of *sheqetz*, which means (according to the *Megiddo Modern Hebrew-English Dictionary*) "unclean animal; loathsome creature, abomination (colloquial—pronounced shaygets) wretch, unruly youngster; gentile youngster." In this context note the comment of a Jewish dentist in Pennsylvania: "Believe me, I hear the word *goy* a lot more than I hear the word *kyke*" (Halberstam 1997, p. 216). On the currency of such derogatory terms, also see Slezkine 2004, pp. 107–9.

28. J. Bloom 1952. Compare Schlimeel 1954.

29. Information from Israel Schachter on ShalomIreland; Daiken 1939, p. 30.

30. Brennan, personal communication with the author, 28 January 2004; Louis Wigoder memoir, p. 9. Wigoder and his classmates were always outnumbered, but the fighting later served him well as a champion university boxer. Max Nurock recalled such fights, too, at the turn of the century; he was no hero himself, but "the Wigoder boys and the Buchhalter boys and the Hool boys, they were a very stout lot" (Max Nurock, interviewed in Jerusalem in 1972, Oral History Department, Hebrew University, Jerusalem, call number 0111/0001, p. 13.

31. Compare Brady 1975, p. 172, and Meek 1985 (on Dublin); Daiches 1956, p. 135 (on Edinburgh). Jessie Bloom, who grew up in Little Jerusalem in the 1890s and 1900s, cites a few jingles "about the Catholic and Protestant problem" but none referring to Jews.

32. Leventhal 1945, p. 208; Daiken 1963, pp. 18–19; parts cited in Hyman 1972; Price 2002; Rivlin 2003, p. 74; compare Johnston 1985, pp. 24–25. It is

not inconceivable that either Daiken or Leventhal composed the Jewish ripostes. Dermot Power (1992, pp. 10–11) recorded a local version of the same song, which was sung to the tune of "The Old Orange Flute," in Waterford, noting that it was very popular "among the workers of Denny's Bacon Factory over sixty years ago." In Limerick the following lines, which I owe to my neighbor Luke Leonard, were still current in the 1930s:

Give me my shillie,
Or give me my shawl,
Or I'll take the pictures off the wall,
Or the blanket off the bed.

33. Compare the following depiction of Russian Jews in Wilmington, Delaware, a century ago: "Although relations were friendly, there was little socializing with neighbors. Daily religious observance, language problems, a daily two-hour religious school (after regular classes) for the boys, and common problems with obtaining kosher meat, are only partial explanations. The feeling that some felt with this group was of 'one big family'. They would go to the beach together, celebrate holidays together, visit constantly" (David Goldberg, "A Historical Community Study of Wilmington Jewry, 1738–1925," p. 38, Lucy Davidowitz Papers, AJHS).

34. Herzog 1997, pp. 13–14.

35. Daiken 1939, p. 29. June Levine's early memories of Clanbrassil Street were less nostalgic; "that cloying, incestuous quality that threatens destruction" bothered her (1982, p. 75). Compare Marks 1994, p. 38.

36. J. Bloom 1952, pp. 23–24, 29–30; Duffy 1985, pp. 114–41.

37. The *Jewish Chronicle* (6 March 1908) reproduces a list of categories of Jewish charitable societies operating in Russia. In the 1890s welfare organizations proliferated in Kovno province; in 1898 they helped out nearly one Jewish family in four. See Levin 2000, p. 92.

38. *JC*, 3 January 1890, 18 May 1892.

39. In later years a member of the Board of Guardians would do the rounds of Jewish businessmen and solicit a contribution of £5 or £10 toward an unspecified purpose. The money would be paid back in due course. Harris, interview, 21 October 2004.

40. Mentioned in the *Weekly Irish Times*, 21 January 1905. I am grateful to Tim Harding for this reference.

41. The "slow progress" of this society, inaugurated at a meeting presided over by Maurice Solomons (*JC*, 15 November 1985), was noted in the *Jewish Chronicle*, 12 June 1896.

42. *JC*, 13 January 1899.

43. Hyman 1972, pp. 135–36; Black 1992; Dublin Hebrew Congregation (DHC), Annual Report 1905–6, p8880, NLI. In January 1910 the DHC held a memorial service in Lewis's honor (*JC*, 7 January 1910).

44. CSORP, 1905/23,538, NAI.

45. Herzog 1997, p. 9.

46. CSORP, 1888/15,507, NAI.

47. Hesselberg 1974.

48. Dublin Jewish Amateur Boxing Club, Programme for Annual Tournament, Saturday, 28 January 1939 (copy in NLI).

49. Harris 2002, pp. 88–98; Rivlin 2003, pp. 211–29.

50. This does not include those who converted to facilitate marriage.

51. J. Bloom 1976.

52. Solomons 1956, p. 204.

53. Levine 1988, p. 107.

54. See Price 2002, pp. 195–96; Herzog 1997, p. 18; Elyan 1948 (a fictional account of a mixed marriage in a small Jewish community like that in Cork); transcript of interview with Mr. and Mrs. Aubrey Yodaiken, 10 January 1991, Irish Jewish Museum. "Sitting shiva" refers to the period of mourning that follows a Jewish burial, when family members focus on remembering the deceased. At the outset most marriages within the Jewish community were arranged (transcript of interview with Esther Hesselberg, 11 December 1990, Irish Jewish Museum). On attitudes toward marrying out in France, see Schnapper 1983, pp. 16–18, 37–38, 123–25.

55. KC, interview by the author, April 2003; Nick Harris, interview by the author, August 2003. According to Michael Brennan, the tailor's wife became "a proper, strictly kosher, Jewish wife, who was resented by some of the Jewish women for her extensive knowledge and skill in Jewish practice" (e-mail communication with the author, February 2004).

56. Membership admission registers, 1875–1942, Grand Lodge of Ireland, Freemasons' Hall, Dublin; Berman and Zlotover 1966, p. 90.

57. J. Bloom 1952; Myer Wigoder 1935, pp. 73, 81–82; H. Edelstein 1921, 1950, p. 53; G. Wigoder 1985, pp. 12, 14; Rivlin 2003, p. 191.

58. JC, 27 April 1900.

59. JC, 13 April 1900.

60. This although the IRA's clandestine newspaper, An t-Óglach, was printed in Abraham Spiro's printing works on Charlotte Street, where Oscar Traynor, officer-in-command of the IRA's Dublin Brigade, worked as a compositor (http:// www.siptu.ie/news/easyprint.php?id=689, accessed 15 February 2003).

Cork seems to have differed from Dublin and Belfast. Larry Elyan, who grew up in the southern capital, remembered being "brought up with very Irish pro-nationalist sentiments in the Jewish school. My recollection is that my first seeds of nationalism were sown there, in the songs we sang" (Elyan interview).

61. J. Bloom 1952; Freeman's Journal (hereafter FJ), 26 March 1894; JC, 3 April 1908.

62. JC, 21 July 1911; HaYehudi, 26 May 1911 (as reported in Schwartzman-Sharon 1971). I am grateful to Guy Beiner for the last reference. Invitations to the Viceregal Lodge for Mr. and Mrs. I. L. Bradlaw and Mr. and Mrs. Bernard Jackson were noted in the Jewish Chronicle on 25 August and 1 September 1911.

63. Nick Harris still does not know why his mother chose to send him to the Christian Brothers at Westland Row (Harris 2002, pp. 71–73; Harris interview, August 2003).

64. J. Bloom 1952, p. 30; Harris 2002, p. 49; I. Power 1997, pp. 39–40, 49–50; Herzog 1997, p. 13. My database implies that members of the Church of Ireland were marginally more likely to live on more heavily Jewish streets. For

Catholic households the average value of *jethos* (the proportion of a population on a street which was Jewish) was 0.166 while for Church of Ireland households it was 0.210.

65. *FJ*, 11 September 1908; report of meeting by Dublin correspondent and letter from Philip Wigoder, *JC*, 25 September 1908. The M.P.s present were Stephen Gwynn, William Field, and Timothy C. Harrington.

66. As Asher Benson reminds me, Briscoe was not Ireland's first Jewish parliamentary representative. That distinction fell to economist David Ricardo, M.P. for the borough of Portarlington between 1819 and his death in 1823. Admittedly Portarlington was a "rotten" borough, i.e., its votes were controlled by a member of the landed elite.

67. *Irish-Jewish Year Book*, no. 16 (1966–67): 5, 70–71.

68. E.g., Moore 1984; O'Riordan 1984–85; G. Goldberg 1986; Keogh 1998; Lentin 2001.

69. Reizbaum 1999, pp. 36–38; Craig 2003; Lentin 2001; also Ronit Lentin, "Racialising the Other, Racialising the 'Us': Emerging Irish Identities as Processes of Racialisation," Trinity College Dublin seminar titled "Emerging Irish Identities," 27 November 1999.

70. In the 1901 census enumeration forms most of the male household heads are described as drapers or peddlers. Louis Goldberg was a "wholesale draper," Marcus Blond a "draper and grocer." None is described as a "moneylender" or "financier," though there are two "financiers" by 1911.

71. "Record of the Holy Burial Society of the Limerick Hebrew Congregation," Ms. 22, 436, NLI.

72. Mark Duffy's account of the boycott (1985, pp. 168–94) also highlights the divisions within the Jewish community.

73. As cited in Rivlin 2003, p. 32. It is said that Creagh's sermon was prompted by press reports of the wedding of Fanny Tooch (or Toohey) and Maurice Maissel on 7 January 1904.

74. Duffy 1985, pp. 186–87.

75. Ibid., p. 186; Ryan 2002, p. 50; Keogh 1998, p. 256 (citing CSORP, 1905/ 23,538, NAI). My reading of Ryan's interesting article is that it was the combination of boycott and communal split that drove Louis Goldberg and family out of Limerick. The 1901–11 comparisons are derived from the manuscript census. The 1901–11 comparison hardly supports the claim that the boycott "destroyed the viability of Limerick city's small Jewish community" (Fanning 2002, p. 42).

76. See, e.g., the accounts in Abbott 1907, pp. 470–72; Magalaner 1953; Hyman 1972, pp. 212–17; Moore 1984, pp. 57–61, 167–94; Keogh 1998, pp. 26–53; Fanning 2002, pp. 42–48; Rivlin 2003, pp. 32–33; Ryan 1997, 2002; O'Flynn 2004, pp. 156–224. On St. Patrick's Day 2004, RTÉ 1 (the main channel of the public television service) carried a useful account of the events of a century ago.

77. There had been some trouble in Limerick earlier. The first attacks on Jews occurred in April 1884 and lasted two months. They seem to have been prompted by a combination of factors. One Jacob Barron let off a firework on Good Friday, innocent of the ill-feeling that might cause; then, on Easter Sunday, a maidservant spied Lieb Siev engaged in the ritual slaughter of a chicken in his backyard. An

attack on Siev's house followed (Ryan 1984). However, in 1888 Cork's lord mayor suggested that "some of the prejudice existing in the Limerick neighborhood a few years ago . . . was due to . . . the attempted sale of indecent cards and pictures by foreign hawkers among a peasantry who, whatever charges have been levelled against them, are pure-minded and pure-living. There being until lately no foreigners in Ireland, all those passed as Jews" (*The Times*, 15 March 1888). The *Jewish Chronicle* reported several more attacks on Jews in Limerick in the following years. On 24 November 1896, for example, the house of Moses Leone was attacked. The police quickly intervened on that occasion and one of the assailants was sentenced to two months in prison with hard labor (*JC*, 4 December 1896; Moore 1984, p. 169; Hyman 1972, p. 211).

78. Magalaner 1953, p. 1219.

79. On the French connection, see Duffy 1985, pp. 177–78.

80. Parry 1983; O'Leary 1991.

81. Alderman 1972–73; 1979, 2000–2001; Holmes 1983; Glaser 1993; Rubinstein 1997; *JC*, 25 August to 8 September 1911. Anti-Jewish riots in June 1917 in the Leylands, Leeds' run-down Jewish neighborhood, involved a mob of three thousand people, also dwarfing the events in Limerick.

82. As Ryan (2002, p. 49) notes, the 1901 census lists one of Levin's children as born in America in 1894.

83. See Moore 1984, pp. 58–59, 180; Morrissey 2003, pp. 319–26. Perhaps here, too, Tredegar provides a parallel. The author of a study of events there, while pronouncing them still "something of an enigma wrapped in a mystery," concludes that the "bad reputation" of a few Jewish landlords may have led to the emergence of "an anti-Semitic element to smear the whole community." (Glaser 1993, pp. 173). The *Jewish Chronicle* (1 September 1911) supported the call of one Jewish editorialist "to deal drastically ourselves with those in our midst who constitute a distinct danger to Jewry at large."

84. Dublin Hebrew Congregation Annual Report 1903–4.

85. Cited in Duffy 1985, pp. 179–80. The London Board also suspected the leadership of Limerick's Jewish community.

86. Glaser 1993, p. 169.

87. Circuit court records suggest that Jewish moneylenders and traders accounted for only a small fraction of the cases taken against debtors in Limerick City circuit court in the years before the boycott. Creagh's claim that Jews issued 337 summonses in 1902 and 226 in 1903 entirely ignores the comparative aspect. I don't know the source of Creagh's data; perhaps he was adding together cases taken before the circuit court and before the lord mayor's court of conscience (which had jurisdiction over only very small claims). See Moore 1984, app. B; Morrissey 2003, p. 320; but also Ryan 2002.

The boycott did not sour Jewish-Gentile relations in the long run. The late Joe Morrison, star of Valerie Lapin's 2003 film documentary *Shalom Ireland*, attended the Christian Brothers' Sexton Street school in the 1930s "without encountering any prejudice or discrimination" (http://www.jewishjournal.com/old/Ireland.5.5.0.htm).

88. Maria Byrne, 54 Dufferin Avenue, interview by the author, 19 March 2003. However, a woman from the Liberties told a student folklore collector in 1980 that "we didn't mix with them. We lived beside Jews" (IFC/UFP 0480).

89. Leventhal 1945, p. 207; see also Myer Wigoder 1935; Berman and Zlotover 1966; Marcus 2001, pp. xiii, 16.

90. This is a reference to the City of London Imperial Volunteers.

91. J. Bloom 1952, pp. 27, 32.

92. Box 13/1, Bloom Papers.

93. Compare Marks (1994, p. 12n. 4), who refers to "the interaction many of the Jews had with their non-Jewish neighbors in the streets and with their fellow-workers in the workplace."

94. Harris 2002, pp. 13, 55, 73.

95. O'Riordan 2001; Davis and Davis interview; Harris interview, 21 October 2004.

96. Harold Mushatt, interview by the Irish Jewish Museum, 1993–94. Waterman 1998.

97. Excerpts from a conversation among five elderly Dublin Jews recorded in Jerusalem in 1972, Oral History Archive, Hebrew University Jerusalem. Also Wilson 2004, p. 62.

98. Birkahn interview.

99. Warm 1998, p. 236. Louis Davis's father lived in Belfast in the early decades of the last century. There his best friend was a Gentile police inspector, and neighbors of all religious persuasions looked after each other (Davis and Davis interview).

100. In 1980 Johnnie McDonnell and Ambie Collins of Iveagh Buildings remembered "knocking around" with Jewish kids as children and being very close to some Jewish neighbors. See IFC/UFP 0287, UFP 0471.

101. DC, interview by the author, April 2003.

102. Sheila Cunningham, interview by the author, March 2003.

103. This "flamboyance" seems to have been the catalyst for the Limerick boycott of 1904, when envious locals took exception to the elegant clothes worn by some of those attending a Jewish wedding on 7 January. On fears that displays of sartorial extravagance would provoke hostility from the majority community in eighteenth-century Poland, see Hundert 2004, pp. 88–89.

104. J. Bloom 1953.

105. Blain (2000, pp. 113–20) recalls the good and the bad: friendship between a working-class Catholic and a well-off Jewish girl threatened by Catholic bigotry, and ended by the class divide when the Jewish girl went to a "swanky private school somewhere in the city" and her friend returned to St. Mary's on Haddington Road. See also Maxton 1997, pp. 76–77.

106. Cited in Keogh 1998, p. 21.

107. Price 2002, p. 35; JC, 29 May 1992.

108. Preston and Haines 1991, pp. 44–47.

109. Compare Schnapper 1983, pp. 39–42, 125–26.

110. Bayor 1978, pp. 24–30; Elkin 1980, p. 103.

111. Private information, 29 September 2004.

112. *FJ*, 26 March 1894; *JC*, 30 March 1894. Rivlin (2003, p. 117) documents another Jewish suicide, that of an unsuccessful nineteen-year-old hawker, found hanging in his lodgings in Warren Street in early November 1905.

113. An alternative hypothesis (which I owe to Michael Brennan) is that the charge against the two peddlers was spurious, part of a psychotic breakdown leading to the double suicide.

114. For an instance involving two ministers at Greenville Hall in 1953, see Rivlin 2003, pp. 64–65.

115. Pace Herzog 1997, p. 14.

116. See also the account in the *Dublin Evening Mail* of 16 June 1904 (as recounted in Mac Aonghusa 1992) of an emigration swindle perpetrated by one "James Wought, 27 Warren Street and 49A Lr. Clanbrassil Street" against members of the Litvak community.

117. Herzog 1997, p. 14; civil bill book, 1C-40–24; 1C-40–25/40, NAI.

CHAPTER 10. *ICH GEH FUN "IRE" LAND*

1. Cited in Hartshorn 1997, p. 63.

2. Daiken 1946, p. 33.

3. Leopold Bloom was thus doubly "modern": vis-à-vis Irish Catholics and also—although Joyce failed to recognize this—Dublin Litvaks. For more on Joyce and Dublin Jewry, see Ó Gráda 2004 ("Lost").

4. Note, however, the reservations noted in Cullen 1995.

5. Ellmann 1982, p. 375; Hyman 1972, pp. 173–74. Trieste's Jews included very few *Ostjuden* in Joyce's time, and the Jews he met were all urbane, well-integrated Triestine Jews. Though some east European Jews had reached Trieste in the 1880s and 1890s, in Joyce's day the bulk of its Jews spoke Italian, German, or Greek as a first language. Many Jews spoke the Triestine dialect; German was the lingua franca of the Hapsburg Empire of which Trieste was then a part. On Joyce's years in Trieste, see McCourt 2000.

6. According to Ned Lambert, a character in *Ulysses*, "the original jews' temple" had occupied "the most historic spot in all Dublin . . . where silken Thomas proclaimed himself a rebel in 1534."

7. Notice regarding the building of Greenville Hall, 1915, box 47, Irish Jewish Museum.

8. In November 1905 the Litvak members included a Yodaiken, an Elyan, a Noyk, a Wigoder, a Mushatt, two Briscoes, and three Ellimans. The "Russian" was Hosias Weiner of 33–34 Talbot Street and Riga House, Howth. In 1907 Weiner had been co-opted to a seat on the DHC Council (DHC Council minutes, 3 November 1907, p8880, NLI).

9. Admittedly the DHC was not alone in this. In London, where minyan men were common in the 1900s, they "did not err on the side of extreme piety or Hebrew scholarship" (*JC*, 24 January 1908), and in Belfast there was talk of employing minyan men at two shillings a week for the Great Victoria Street shul in the 1890s ("History of the Belfast Hebrew Congregation, Part V," *Belfast Jewish Record* 18[3] November 1971).

10. Dublin Hebrew Congregation Annual Reports 1906–7, 1907–8, p8880, NLI. Zion Schools, established at the corner of Bloomfield Avenue and the South Circular Road in 1934 by Little Jerusalemers or former Little Jerusalemers, would also prove more successful than the "English" school established next to the Adelaide Road shul in the 1890s.

11. *JC*, 23 August 1901.

12. Sylvia Crivon, interview by Carol Weinstock, 14 October 1987, Acc. 5734, NLI.

13. Beginning in the mid-1930s, several Jewish ministers berated the community for failing to support its Talmud Torah. See Rivlin 2003, p. 112.

14. Harris 2002, pp. 121–22; Funke 2003, p. 55. While the ethos of the community remains very Orthodox, since 1946 Dublin has also had its smaller Progressive synagogue. Progressive or liberal Judaism's origins lie in early nineteenth-century Germany. It views itself as "blending ancient traditions with the changing world of today" (see http://wupj.org/about/index.html). Aside from some important doctrinal differences, it distinguishes itself from Orthodox Judaism by allowing mixed seating and mixed choirs, the use of the vernacular in services, and single-day observance of festivals.

15. Philip Rubinstein (as cited by Katrina Goldstone in *Irish Times*, 27 June 1984), interview at Saint Kevin's Community Centre, March 2003.

16. Joseph Edelstein to Herman Good, 4 April 1926, box 36, Irish Jewish Museum. Elaine Crowley (Crowley 1988) remembered the "exoticness" of Clanbrassil Street.

17. The photographs, published in *Nachlath Dublin* (1950), were taken by Oliver Samuels of London at the request of Asher Benson, who supplied the captions.

18. Harris 2002, pp. 200–204; Rivlin 2003, pp. 20–21. The Jewish Representative Council tried to keep the shop going, but closed it on 1 May 2001 as losses accumulated.

19. Brennan, e-mail correspondence with the author, February 2004.

20. Waterman 1981; Stern 1997, p. 188.

21. Dr. S. Eppel, "Memoir of the Rathmines Hebrew Congregation," Acc. 5,734 (unsorted), NLI.

22. However, its bread conformed to kashrut requirements until the early 1990s (Harris 2002, pp. 39–40). For an architectural perspective on the area in the 1970s, see de Blacam and Kealy 1975.

23. This was in 1936. In translation, Rabbi Herzog's quip means "I go from your country and I come to our country," but note the pun on "ire" (Yiddish for "your"). I am grateful to Israel Schachter for this information.

24. Perhaps the decline was delayed by World War II, although emigration from Ireland to Great Britain was considerable during the war.

25. A distinction between community and population is apposite here. In the Celtic Tiger era of the 1990s hundreds of Jews were drawn to Ireland, leading to an increase in the Jewish population, but most did not identify with the aging Irish Jewish community.

26. Fanning 2002; Goldstone 2000; Lentin 2001.

27. Lentin 2001; also *New York Times*, 13 June 2004. Equally unconvincing is the link drawn between the murder (allegedly by the IRA) of Leonard Kaitcer, a Belfast antique dealer who was kidnaped from his home in February 1980, and the subsequent decline of Northern Ireland's Jewish community. In fact, Northern Ireland's Jewish population declined by far less in 1981–91 than in 1971–81; moreover, the decline during the 1980s was much greater in the South than in the North. On recent racist attacks in Belfast, compare "Racist War of the Loyalist Street Gangs," *The Guardian*, 10 January 2004 (where Belfast is dubbed "the race-hate capital of Europe"), and "Race Hate on Rise in Northern Ireland," http://news.bbc.co.uk/2/hi/uk_news/northern_ireland/3390249.stm.

28. The population of the five biggest cities on the island rose from 852,384 in 1901 to 1,093,217 in 1936/37, and their share of the total rose from 19.1 percent to 25.7 percent.

29. Only Cork does not fit this pattern. There the recorded Jewish population reached a peak in 1911. Between 1911 and 1936 all religious denominations other than Catholic suffered losses in both Cork city and county—considerably more than in the Irish Free State as a whole. Most of the decline predated 1926: no doubt, the War of Independence of 1919–21 and the ensuing radical shift in Cork's political and cultural complexion were partly responsible for this. However, Cork's Jewish population declined more in 1926–36—a decade when the Jewish population of the state as a whole rose marginally—than in 1911–26.

30. Compare Bonacich 1973; Bonacich and Modell 1980; Slezkine 2004, ch. 1.

31. Hyman 1972, pp. 197, 202; Berman and Zlotover 1966, p. 90. Leopold Bloom was also a mason: see Ito 2001.

32. Waterman 1985. On the motives for Jewish migration to Palestine, see Metzer 1998, ch. 3.

33. Compare the titles of Garvin 2004; Keogh, O'Shea, and Quinlan 2004.

34. Cecil Lee, interview by Carol Weinstock, July 1987, Acc. 5734, NLI; for more on the economic background, see Ó Gráda 1997, ch. 4. The employment data, taken from the Census of Industrial Production, refer to clothing and leather.

35. Leonard Abrahamson was also appointed to the first board of the House of Industry hospitals by Seán McEntee, Minister for Local Government and Public Health, in 1941.

36. For more on Jewish medical men in Ireland, see Rivlin 2003, pp. 139–46; Solomons 1956. On sectarian tensions about appointments in Dublin hospitals, see Findlater 2001, pp. 464–46.

37. Elazar and Medding 1983, p. 329. The high incidence of intermarriage in Denmark may be inferred from the significant numbers of part-Jews (1,301) and Christians (686) accompanying the 5,191 Jews evacuated to neutral Sweden in 1943 (European Jewish Congress). Finnish Jewry, too, is characterized by very high rates of secularization and intermarriage.

38. Morris 1976.

39. Berman and Zlotover 1996, dustjacket; "Louis Wigoder memoir," p. 22.

40. Arnold Eisen, as cited in Sander Gilman's introduction to Gilman and Shain 1999, p. 1.

41. Keogh 2004, p. 269; Waterman 1985. Those listed in 1956 exclude some prominent Irish-born Jews such as Max Nurock and the Herzogs, perhaps because they had traveled on British passports.

42. http://www.mfa.gov.il/MFA/Archive/Israel%20Line/2002/Israel%20 Line%20-%203-Dec-2002.

43. Compare Henriques 1993; Newman 1985; Endelman 2002, pp. 230–31.

44. For the Robinsons, one of two Jewish families in the town of Carlow, keeping kosher in the era before freezers entailed either driving up to the butchers in Dublin, over fifty miles away, or arranging to have meat sent by rail. Later a "large deep freezer" reduced commuting costs. On the High Holy Days, the Robinsons went to Dublin and stayed with relatives. Shopping for Pesach involved a special expedition (Philippa Blatt, née Robinson, private communication with the author). On Jews in Carlow, see also "Letter to the editor," *Irish Jewish News* 7(2) (October–December 1981): 17.

45. AP to author, private communication. See also Levine 1982, p. 19.

46. Theo Garb to author, December 2004.

47. Waterman 1987, p. 30; Rivlin 2003, pp. 126–27.

48. Taub 1986, pp. 43, 49, 161–66.

49. Alan Eustace to author, March 2003. Compare Hyman 1972, plate XV.

Appendix 1. Letters to One of the Last "Weekly Men"

1. The letters are contained in an unsorted collection in the National Library. I am grateful to Gerard Lyne for pointing me to this source.

Appendix 2. Mr. Parnell Remembers

1. IFC/UFP, no. 00081. I am grateful to Professor Séamus Ó Catháin and the Irish Folklore Commission for permission to reproduce this material.

2. Compare the use of the pejorative *judío* for "small peddler and market merchant" in interwar Mexico. Jewish white-collar workers and professionals were not called *judíos*, however. See Elkin 1980, p. 116.

3. Alderman Thomas Kelly (1868–1942), Sinn Féin's first alderman on Dublin city council and later Fianna Fáil T.D. for Dublin South, cofounder of the Municipal Gallery and the *Dublin Historical Record*. Vol. 4 of the *DHR* contains an obituary of Alderman Kelly.

Appendix 3. Louis Hyman, Jessie Bloom, and The Jews of Ireland

1. The letters form part of the Bloom Papers (collection #93, box 4, folder 5).

2. Bernard Shillman was a Dublin solicitor, well-known for his acerbic wit. "Dr. Harris" is presumably prominent community activist Ernest Wormser Harris (1859–1946).

3. Hyman to Bloom, 1 May 1936.

4. The reference is to Shillman 1945.

5. See p. 29 above.

6. So far I have been unable to trace either of these items.

7. Hyman to Bloom, 6 June 1951, box 4, folder 5, Bloom Papers.

8. Hyman to Bloom, 11 November 1952, box 4, folder 5, Bloom Papers. Indeed, Elyan, then a resident of Israel, would write to *Commentary* protesting Bloom's memoir. See Elyan 1952.

9. For more on "79," see Berman and Zlotover 1966. On Wolve Nurock's prominence in the community, see *JC*, 25 April, 7 June, 13 December 1912.

10. The Oral History Archive at the Hebrew University of Jerusalem contains an interview of Max Nurock by historian Bernard Wasserstein on 15 September 1969 (OHD 82/1). Wasserstein describes Nurock the septuagenarian as "silver-haired, quirky, affable, prejudiced, candid and aphoristic . . . [who] says of himself: 'Max Nurock has a certain charisma, you know.' Staunch Zionist: highly contemptuous of the Arabs and of black Africans . . . a would-be Max of the Middle East." In the interview Nurock claimed that he had been instrumental in persuading the chief rabbi of Ireland, Isaac Herzog, to move to Palestine.

11. See Rivlin 2003, p. 127. The well-known Irish American politician Paul O'Dwyer also contributed to the publication of Hyman's work through the Irish Institute Inc. I am grateful to Maurice Abrahamson for this information.

12. The dedication reads:

In grateful memory of
WILLIAM and RACHEL NUROCK
of Dublin
themselves in their lifetime a noble part of the later history
of Irish Jewry
and of
Professor LEONARD ABRAHAMSON
illustrious teacher and compassionate physician
and selfless servant of Dublin Jewry.

Leonard Abrahamson (1896–1961), eminent surgeon and "from the 1920s to the 1960s . . . natural leader of the Jewish community" (Rivlin 2003, p. 144), was married to Max Nurock's sister. Melisande Zlotover had dedicated *Zlotover Story* to Joseph Zlotover (her grandfather) and to William Nurock (to whom she was related through marriage).

BIBLIOGRAPHY

Jewish Ireland

Abrahamson, Maurice. 1978. "My uncle Max." *Dublin Jewish News* 5(2) (September–October): 10.

Anon. 1965. *The Noyek Story 1890–1965: A Record of Achievements over 75 Years,* Dublin: Noyek.

Anon. 2005. "Hats, ribbons and refugees." In *Holocaust Memorial Day 2005: Learning from the Past: Lessons for Today.* Dublin: Holocaust Memorial Committee, pp. 6–7.

Bales, Robert Freed. 1980 [1944]. *The "Fixation Factor" in Alcohol Addiction: An Hypothesis Derived from a Comparative Study of Irish and Jewish Social Norms.* New York: Arno Press.

Bayor, Ronald H. 1978. *Neighbors in Conflict: The Irish, Germans, Jews, and Italians of New York City, 1929–41.* Baltimore: Johns Hopkins University Press.

Benson, Asher. 1993. "Jewish Genealogy in Ireland." In *Aspects of Irish Genealogy: Proceedings of the First Irish Genealogical Congress.* Dublin: Irish Genealogical Congress Committee, pp. 17–27.

Benson, Sylvia. 1977. *Down Memory Lane.* Tel Aviv: Published by the author.

Berman, Hannah. 195–a. "Zlotover story." Unpublished typescript. Robert and Jessie Bloom Papers, Jacob Rader Marcus Center of the American Jewish Archives, Cincinnati.

———. 195–b. "Berman story." Unpublished typescript. Robert and Jessie Bloom Papers, Jacob Rader Marcus Center of the American Jewish Archives, Cincinnati.

Berman, Hannah, and Melisande Zlotover. 1966. *Zlotover Story: A Dublin Story with a Difference.* Dublin: privately printed.

Bernstein, Mashy. 1971. *A Portrait of the Jews in Ireland.* Dublin: Jewish Representative Council of Ireland.

Bloom, Cecil. 1996. "Jewish Dispersion within Britain." In Newman and Massil, eds., pp. 31–47.

Bloom, Jessie. 1952. "The Old Days in Dublin: Some Girlhood Recollections of the 1890s." *Commentary* (July): 21–32.

———. 1976. "Jessie Bloom Interviewed by Erica Gottfried, Seattle, Washington, February 20, 1976." University of Washington Library, Manuscripts, Special Collections, Acc. 2623, folder VF 982.

Bresnan, Pauline. 2001. "Little Jerusalem: A Study of the Clanbrassil Street/South Circular Road Jewish Community 1900–1950." Project completed for NUI (Maynooth) Certificate in Local History.

Briscoe, Robert (with Alden Hatch). 1958. *For the Life of Me.* Boston: Little, Brown.

Clein, Michael A. 1989. *The Clein Family.* Coral Gables: Judaic Studies Program, University of Miami.

Daiken, Leslie. 1939. "Juvenilia." *Dublin Magazine* (January–March): 29–43.

———. 1946. "As the Light Terrible and Holy." *Dublin Magazine* (January–March): 32–37.

———. n.d. Unpublished papers and correspondence. Mss. 33,487–33,507. National Library of Ireland, Dublin.

Danker, Trevor. 1960. "Derry's Jewish Community." *Belfast Jewish Record* 7(2): 3.

"*DJN* Talks to Louis Hyman." 1976. *Dublin Jewish News* 3(5) (October–November): 4–5.

Duffy, Mark J. 1985. "A Socio-economic Analysis of Dublin's Jewish Community 1880–1911." M.A. diss., National University of Ireland.

Edelstein, Hyman. 1921. *Canadian Lyrics and Other Poems.* Montreal: Belles Lettres.

———.1950. *The Spirit of Israel and Other Poems.* Toronto: Ryerson Press.

Edelstein, Joseph. 1908. *The Moneylender.* Dublin: Dollard.

———. 1933. *Echo of Dublin Rebellion, 1916. Verbatim Report of the Proceedings before the Royal Commission. Vindication of Mr. Joseph Edelstein.* Dublin: Drought.

Elyan, Laurence. 1948. "A Strange Atonement." *Nachlath Dublin Magazine* no. 22:18–20.

———. 1952. "The Jews of Cork," *Commentary* (November): 614.

Eppel, Cissie 1992. *A Journey into Our Ancestry: Chronicles of the Rosenheim, Levy, Eppel Families.* Jersey: Bennie Linder.

[Finlay, Thomas A.] 1893. "The Jew in Ireland," *Lycaeum* 6 (no. 70), 215–18; 7 (no. 71), 235–38; 8 (no. 72), 251–55.

Flynn, Kevin Haddick. 2004. "The Limerick Pogrom, 1904." *History Ireland* 12(2):31–33.

Funke, Phyllis Ellen. 2003. "The Jewish Traveller: Belfast," *Hadassah Magazine* (November): 53–59.

Goldberg, Dan. 1998. "The Last Jews of Belfast: A Diaspora Community Caught in the Crossfire." *Eretz* 58:34–39.

Goldberg, Gerald Y. 1945. "Note on the Jewish Community in Cork." In Shillman, *Short History,* pp. 138–42.

———. 1986. "Ireland Is the Only Country . . . Joyce and the Jewish Dimension." In M. P. Hederman and Richard Kearney, eds., *The Crane Bag Book of Irish Studies, vol. 2 (1982–1985).* London: Colin Smythe, pp. 5–12.

Golding, G. M. 1982. *George Gavan Duffy 1992–1951: A Legal Biography.* Dublin: Irish Academic Press.

Goldstone Katrine. 2000. " 'Benevolent Helpfulness'? Ireland and the International Reaction to Jewish Refugees, 1933–9." In M. Kennedy and J. M. Skelly, eds., *Irish Foreign Policy, 1919–66: From Independence to Internationalism.* Dublin: Four Courts Press, pp. 116–36.

Harfield, Eugene. 1893. *A Commercial Directory of the Jews of the United Kingdom.* London.

Harris, Nick. 2002. *Dublin's Little Jerusalem.* Dublin: A. & A. Farmer.

Heanue, Michelle. 2000. *The Decline of the Use in the Yiddish Language in Ireland*. Dublin: Irish Jewish Museum.

Herzog, Chaim. 1997. *Living History: A Memoir*. London: Weidenfeld & Nicholson.

Hesselberg, Ackie. 1974. "I Remember." *Dublin Jewish News* 1(2): 6.

Huhner, Leon. 1902–5. "The Jews of Ireland: An Historical Sketch." *Transactions of the Jewish Historical Society of England* 5, 226–42.

Hyman, Louis. 1972. *The Jews of Ireland to the Year 1910*. Dublin: Irish Academic Press.

Irish-Jewish Year Book. 1964–. Dublin: Office of the Chief Rabbi.

Ito, Eishiro. 2001. "Is Leopold Bloom a Jewish Freemason?" *Journal of Policy Studies* (Policy Studies Association, Iwate Prefectural University), 3(2). Downloadable at p-www.iwate-pu.ac.jp/~acro-ito/Joycean_Essays/U_Jewish Freemason.html.

Keogh, Dermot. 1998. *Jews in Twentieth-century Ireland: Refugees, Anti-Semitism, and the Holocaust*. Cork: Cork University Press.

———. 2004. " 'Making Aliya': Irish Jews, the Irish State and Israel." In Dermot Keogh, Finbarr O'Shea, and Carmel Quinlan, eds. *The Lost Decade: Ireland in the 1950s*. Cork: Mercier Press, pp. 252–72.

Keogh, Dermot, and Andrew McCarthy, eds. 2005. *Limerick Boycott 1904: Anti-Semitism in Ireland*. Cork: Mercier Press.

Kernoff, Harry. 1974. "Harry Kernoff reminisces." *Dublin Jewish News* 1(5): 5.

Kleanthous, Loretta. 2000. "Memoir of Louis and Hanchen Wine." Unpublished.

Lentin, Ronit. 2001. "Ireland's Other Diaspora: Jewish-Irish within, Irish-Jewish without." *Golem: European Jewish Magazine* 3(6).

Leventhal, A. J. 1945. "What It Means to Be a Jew." *The Bell* 10(3): 207–16.

———. 1961. "The Jew Errant." *The Dubliner* 2(1): 11–24.

Levine, June. 1982. *Sisters: The Personal Story of an Irish Feminist*. Dublin: Ward River Press.

———. 1988. "June Levine." In Johnston 1988, pp. 104–11.

Mac Aonghusa, Proinsias. 1992. "Why Joyce Used "Bloom." *Irish Press*, 13 June, pp. 18–19.

McCann, John. 1927. "Jews in Dublin." *Ireland's Own* 49 (282) (April 27).

Magalaner, Marvin. 1953. "The Anti-Semitic Limerick Incidents and Joyce's 'Bloomsday.' " *Proceedings of the Modern Language Association* 68(5): 1219–23.

Marcus, David. 1986. *A Land Not Theirs*. New York: Bantam Press.

———. 2001. *Oughtobiography: Leaves from the Diary of a Hyphenated Jew*. Dublin: Gill & Macmillan.

———. 2004. *Buried Memories*. Cork: Mercier Press.

Margoliouth, E. 1868. "Missionary Work in Ireland" (Journal of a visit to Dublin in July–August). Ms. Coll. 318, 6/1, Representative Church Body Library, Dublin.

Maxton, Hugh. 1997. *Waking: An Irish Protestant Upbringing*. Belfast: Lagan Press.

Mitovsky, George. 1959–60. "When Zionism Was Slightly Traife." *Nachlath Dublin*, pp. 16–17.

Montgomery, Niall. 1984. "Abraham Jacob Leventhal: A eulogy." In Eoin O'Brien, ed., *Abram Jacob Leventhal: Dublin Scholar, Wit and Man of Letters*. Dublin: Con Leventhal Scholarship Committee, pp. 9–13.

Moore, G. 1981. "Some Socio-economic Aspects of Anti-Semitism in Ireland 1880–1905." *Economic and Social Review* 12(3): 187–201.

———. 1984. "Anti-Semitism in Ireland 1880–1905." Ph.D. diss., Ulster Polytechnic.

Morris, Ralph. 1976. "From Mother's Scrapbook." *Dublin Jewish News* 3(2): 14.

Murphy, Daniel J. 1978. "Yiddish at the Abbey Theatre, Dublin." *Bulletin of Research in the Humanities* 81(4): 431–35.

Murray, Peter. 2004. "Joseph Edelstein." Paper presented at the conference on Jewish Ireland, Linenhall Library, Belfast, 2–3 September.

O'Casey, Seán. 1981. "Vandering Vindy Vendhor." In *Autobiographies*, vol. 1. London: Macmillan, pp. 122–27.

O'Flynn, Criostoir. 2004. *Beautiful Limerick*. Dublin: Obelisk Books.

Ó Gráda, Cormac. 2004. "Lost in Little Jerusalem: Was Leopold Bloom Really an Irish Jew?" *Journal of Modern Literature* 27(4): 17–26.

———. 2005. "Dublin's Jewish Immigrants a Century Ago: Settling In." *Field Day Review* 1: 87–99.

———. 2006. "Notes on the History of Cork Jewry." In Dermot Keogh, ed., *In Memoriam Gerald Goldberg*. Cork: Mercier Press.

———. 2006. "Dublin Jewish Demography a Century Ago." *Economic and Social Review*, forthcoming.

Ó Meachair, Micheál. 2004. *An Giúdachas: Buneolas ar Chreideamh agus ar Chleachtais na nGiúdach*. Dublin: Foillseacháin Ábhair Spioradálta.

O'Riordan, Manus. 1984. "Jewish Trade Unionism in Dublin." In Labour History Workshop, *The Rise and Fall of Irish Anti-Semitism*. Dublin: Labour History Workshop, pp. 25–36.

———. 1984–85. "Anti-Semitism in Irish Politics." *Irish-Jewish Yearbook* 34: 15–17.

———. 1988. "Connolly Socialism and the Jewish Worker." *Saothar* 13: 120–30.

———. 2001. "Maurice Levitas: An obituary." *Saothar* 26: 7–9.

Price, Stanley. 2002. *Somewhere to Hang My Hat: An Irish-Jewish Journey*. Dublin: New Island Books.

Rivlin, Ray. 2003. *Shalom Ireland: A Social History of the Jews in Modern Ireland*. Dublin: Gill & Macmillan.

Rosenblatt, Stuart. 2004a. *Irish Jewish Memorial Inscriptions, vol. 1: Aughavannagh Road, Dolphins Barn, Dublin 8. 1898–2003*. Dublin: Jewish Genealogical Society of Ireland. Copies in National Library of Ireland and in the National Archives, Dublin.

———. 2004b. *Irish Jewish Memorial Inscriptions, vol. 2: Ballybough, Dublin (1748–1908) and Early Synagogues*. Dublin: Jewish Genealogical Society of Ireland.

———. 2004c. *Irish Jewish Museum Listings to 1992*. Dublin: Jewish Genealogical Society of Ireland.

————. 2004d. *Belfast Irish Jewish Memorials 1873–2003*. Dublin: Jewish Gene-alogical Society of Ireland.

————. 2005a. *Alien Registration 1914–1922. Dublin Non-national Jewish Ex-tracts*. Dublin: Jewish Genealogical Society of Ireland.

————. 2005b. *Ada Shillman's (Midwife) Birth Records 1896–1908*. Dublin: Jew-ish Genealogical Society of Ireland.

————. 2005c. *Limerick Hebrews 1904*. Dublin: Jewish Genealogical Society of Ireland.

Ryan, Des. 1984. "The Limerick Jews." *Old Limerick Journal* 17:27–30.

————. 1997. "Jewish Immigrants in Limerick: A Divided Community." In David Lee, ed., *Remembering Limerick*. Limerick: Civic Trust, pp. 168–69.

————. 2002. "The Jews, Fr. Creagh, and the Mayor's Court of Conscience." *Old Limerick Journal* no. 38:49–52.

Salmon, John. 1915. "Jews in Ireland." *Belfast Telegraph*, 24, 25, 29 September.

Schachter, Jacob. 1967. *Ingathering: Collected Papers, Essays and Addresses*. Je-rusalem: Bazak Press.

Schlimeel, A. 1954. "A Trip Down Clanbrassil Street." *The Jewish Leader* (incor-porating *Halapid*) 2(3): 2.

Schwartzman-Sharon, Ephraim. 1971. *Milhemet HaErim L'Atzmautam* (The Irish struggle for independence). 3rd enlarged ed. Jerusalem: Rubin Mass.

Shillman, Bernard. 1945. *A Short History of the Jews in Ireland*. Dublin: Eason.

————. 1964/65. "The Dublin Board Shechita." *Irish-Jewish Yearbook* 1:18–21.

Solomons, Bethel. 1956. *One Doctor in His Time*. London: Johnson.

"Some Tickmen and Their Ways." 1894. *Belfast Evening Telegraph*, 14 June.

Taub, David. 1986. "A Critical Analysis of the Provision and Development of Educational Facilities for Members of the Jewish Community in Ireland and in Great Britain." Ph.D. diss., University College Dublin.

"Uncovering Down's Links with Russia." 2004. *Down Recorder*. 21 July.

Warm, David D. 1998. "The Jews of Northern Ireland." In Paul Hainsworth, ed., *Divided Society: Ethnic Minorities and Racism in Northern Ireland*. London: Pluto.

Waterman, Simon. 1998. "Memoir." Unpublished typescript.

Waterman, Stanley. 1981. "Changing residential patterns of the Dublin Jewish community." *Irish Geography* 14:41–50.

————. 1985. "A Note on the Migration of Jews from Dublin." *Jewish Journal of Sociology* 37(1): 23–27.

————. 1987. "On the South Side of the Liffey." *Jewish Quarterly* 34(1): 28–30.

Waterman, Stanley, and Marlena Schmool. 1995. "Literary Perspectives on Jews in Britain in the Early Twentieth Century." In Russell King, John Connell, and Paul White, eds., *Writing across Worlds: Literature and Migration*. London: Routledge, pp. 180–97.

White, J. D. 1992–93. "The Dublin Hebrew Congregation: A History of Adelaide Road Synagogue 1892–1992." *Irish-Jewish Year Book* 41:7–23.

Wigoder, Geoffrey. 1985. *In Dublin's Fair City*. Jerusalem: World Zionist Organization.

Wigoder, Louis. 1978. "Memoir." Ashkelon: Privately published.

Wigoder, Meir Joel. 2001. "A Family Album: Photography versus Memory in Sigfried Kracauer and Roland Barthes." *History and Memory* 13(1): 19–59.

Wigoder, Myer J. 1935. *My Story.* Leeds: J. Porton & Son.

Wilson, Jonathan. 2004. "The Fading World of Leopold Bloom." *New York Times Magazine,* 13 June, pp. 60–63.

Yodaiken, Len. 1987. *The Judeikens: A Jewish Family in Dispersion.* Privately printed (copy in National Library of Ireland).

OTHER JEWISH

Abbott, George F. 1907. *Israel in Europe.* London: Macmillan.

Alderman, Geoffrey. 1972–73. "The Anti-Jewish Riots of August 1911 in South Wales," *Welsh Historical Review* 6(2): 190–200.

———. 1979. "The Jew as scapegoat? The Settlement and Reception of Jews in South Wales before 1914." *Transactions of the Jewish Historical Society of England* 26:62–70.

———. 2000–2001. "The Anti-Jewish Riots of August 1911 in South Wales: A Response." *Welsh History Review* 20:565–71.

Aleichem, Sholem. 1987. *Tevye the Dairyman and the Railroad Stories.* New York: Schocken Books.

Anon. 1965. *The Noyek Story 1890–1965: A Record of Achievements over 75 Years.* Dublin: Noyek.

Anon. 2003. *The Talmud in Anti-Semitic Polemics.* Washington, DC: Anti-Defamation League.

Aris, Stephen. 1970. *Jews in Business.* London: Jonathan Cape.

Arkin, Marcus. 1975. *Aspects of Jewish Economic History.* Philadelphia: Jewish Publication Society of America.

Baron, Salo W., Arcadius Kahan, et al. 1975. *Economic History of the Jews,* ed. Nachum Gross. Jerusalem: Keter Publishing House.

Berman, Hannah. 1926. *Ant Hills.* London: Faber & Gwyer.

Black, Gerry. 1992. *Lender to the Lords, Giver to the Poor.* London: Valentine Mitchell.

Botticini, Maristella, and Zvi Eckstein. 2004a. "From Farmers to Merchants: A Human Capital Interpretation of Jewish Economic History." Typescript, Boston University.

———. 2004b. "Jewish Occupational Selection: Education, Restrictions, or Minorities?" Typescript, Boston University.

Cahan, Abraham. 1960. *The Rise of David Levinsky.* New York: Harper.

Cesarani, David. 1994. *The Jewish Chronicle.* Cambridge: Cambridge University Press.

———. 1996. "The Myth of Origins: Ethnic Memory and the Experience of Emigration." In Newman and Massil, eds., pp. 247–54.

Chirot, Daniel, and Anthony Reid, eds. 1997. *Essential Outsiders: Chinese and Jews in the Modern Transformation of Southeast Asia and Central Europe.* Seattle: University of Washington Press.

Chiswick, Barry R. 1986. "Labor Supply and Investment in Child Quality: A Study of Jewish and Non-Jewish Women." *Review of Economics and Statistics.* 68(4): 700–703.

Chiswick, Barry R., and Paul Miller. 2003. "Do Enclaves Matter in Immigrant Adjustment?" Mimeo, University of Illinois, Chicago.

Clare, George. 1981. *Last Waltz in Vienna: The Destruction of a Family 1842–1942.* London: Macmillan.

Collins, Kenneth E. 1990. *Second City Jewry: The Jews of Glasgow in the Age of Expansion.* Glasgow: Scottish Jewish Archives Committee.

———. 2001. *Be Well! Jewish Health and Welfare in Glasgow, 1860–1914.* East Linton: Tuckwell Press.

Daiches, David. 1956. *Two Worlds: A Jewish Childhood in Edinburgh.* London: Macmillan.

Davison, Neil R. 1998. *James Joyce, Ulysses, and Construction of Jewish Identity.* Cambridge: Cambridge University Press.

Della Pergola, Sergio, and Judith Even, eds. 1997. *Papers in Jewish Demography 1993 in Memory of U. O. Schmeltz.* Jerusalem: Avraham Harman Institute of Contemporary Jewry.

Derosas, Renzo. 2003. "Watch Out for the Children! Differential Infant Mortality of Jews and Catholics in Nineteenth-Century Venice." *Historical Methods* 36(3): 109–30.

Diner, Hasia R. 2000. *Lower East Side Memories.* Princeton: Princeton University Press.

———. 2002. *Hungering for America: Italian, Irish, and Jewish Foodways in the Age of Migration.* Cambridge, MA: Harvard University Press.

Elazar, Daniel J., with Peter Medding. 1983. *Jewish Communities in Frontier Societies: Argentina, Australia, and South Africa.* New York: Holmes and Meier.

Eliach, Yaffa. 1998. *There Once Was a World: A Nine-Hundred-Year Chronicle of the Shtetl of Eishyshok.* Boston: Little, Brown.

Elkin, Judith Laikin. 1980. *Jews of the Latin American Republics.* Chapel Hill: University of North Carolina Press.

Endelman, Todd M. 2002. *The Jews of Britain, 1656 to 2000.* Berkeley: University of California Press.

Englander, D. 1989. "Booth's Jews: The Presentation of Jews and Judaism in *Life and Labour of the People of London.*" *Victorian Studies* 32(4): 551–73.

Erickson, Charlotte. 1996. "Jewish People in the Atlantic Migration, 1850–1914," in Newman and Massil, eds., pp. 1–20.

Feldman, David. 1994. *Englishmen and Jews: Social Relations and Political Culture 1840–1914.* New Haven: Yale University Press.

Fishman, William J. 1988. *East End 1888: A Year in a London Borough among the Labouring Poor.* London: Duckworth.

Freeze, ChaeRan. 2002. *Jewish Marriage and Divorce in Tsarist Russia.* Waltham, MA: Brandeis University Press.

Friedman, Lee M. 1954. "The Problems of the Nineteenth Century American Jewish Peddlers." *Proceedings of the American Jewish Historical Society* 44:1–7.

Gartner, L. P. 1960. *The Jewish Immigration in England 1870–1914.* London: Allen and Unwin.

Gerlis, Daphne, and Leon Gerlis. 1986. *The Story of the Grimsby Jewish Community*. North Humberside: Humberside Leisure Services.

Gilman, Sander, and Milton Shain, eds. 1999. *Jewries at the Frontier: Accommodation, Identity, Conflict*. Champaign: University of Illinois Press.

Glanz, Rudolf. 1945. "Notes on Early Jewish Peddling in America." *Jewish Social Studies* 7(1): 119–36.

———. 1961. *The Jew in Old American Folklore*. New York: Waldon Press.

Glaser, Anthony. 1993. "The Tredegar Riots of 1911." In Henriques, pp. 151–76.

Godley, A. 1996. "Jewish Soft Loan Societies in New York and London and Emigrant Entrepreneurship, 1880–1914." *Business History* 38(3): 101–16.

———. 2001. *Jewish Immigrant Entrepreneurship in New York and London, 1880–1914*. London: Palgrave.

Goldscheider, Calvin. 1967. "Fertility of the Jews." *Demography* 4(1): 196–209.

Goldstein, Alice, S. C. Watkins, and Ann Rosen Spector. 1994. "Childhood Health-Care Practices among Italians and Jews in the United States, 1910–1940." *Health Transition Review* 4(1): 45–61.

Green, Nancy L., ed. 1998. *Jewish Workers in the Modern Diaspora*. Berkeley: University of California Press.

Gross, Jan T. 2003. *Neighbours: The Destruction of the Jewish Community in Jedwabne, Poland, 1941*. London: Arrow Books.

Halberstam, Joshua. 1997. *Schmoozing: The Private Conversations of American Jews*. New York: Penguin.

Harfield, Eugene. 1893. *A Commercial Directory of the Jews of the United Kingdom*. London.

Henriques, Ursula R. Q. 1993. *The Jews of South Wales: Historical Studies*. Cardiff: University of Wales Press.

Hoffman, Eva. 1999. *Shtetl: The History of a Small Town and an Extinguished World*. London: Vintage.

Holmes, C. 1983. "The Tredegar Riots of 1911: Anti-Jewish Disturbances in South Wales." *Welsh History Review* 11:214–23.

Huhner, Leon. 1902–5. "The Jews of Ireland: An Historical Sketch." *Transactions of the Jewish Historical Society of England* 5:226–42.

Hundert, Gershon David. 1992. *The Jews in a Polish Town: The Case of Opatów in the Eighteenth Century*. Baltimore: Johns Hopkins University Press.

———. 2004. *Jews in Poland-Lithuania in the Eighteenth Century*. Berkeley: University of California Press.

Jacobson, Dan. 1998. *Heshel's Kingdom: A Family, a People, a Divided Fate*. London: Hamish Hamilton.

Joseph, Samuel. 1914. *Jewish Immigration to the U.S. from 1880 to 1910*. New York: Arno Press.

Kagan, Berl. 1991. *Jewish Cities, Towns, and Rural Settlements in Lithuania: Historic-Biographic Sketches*. New York: B. Kohen.

Kahan, Arcadius. 1986. "The Impact of Industrialization in Tsarist Russia on the Socioeconomic Conditions of the Jewish population." In *Essays in Jewish Social and Economic History*. Chicago: University of Chicago Press, pp. 1–69.

Kasovich, Israel. 1929. *The Days of Our Years: Personal and General Reminiscences (1859–1929)*. New York: Jordan Publishing.

Kessner, Thomas 1977. *The Golden Door: Italian and Jewish Immigrant Mobility in New York City, 1880–1915*. New York: Oxford University Press.

Klier, John D. 1996. "Emigration Mania in Late-Imperial Russia: Legend and Reality." In Newman and Massil, eds. pp. 21–30.

———. 2000. "What Exactly Was a Shtetl?" In Gennady Estraikh and Mikhail Krutikov, eds., *The Shtetl: Image and Reality*. Oxford: Legenda, pp. 23–35.

Klier, John D., and Shlomo Lambroza. 1992. *Pogroms: Anti-Jewish Violence and Modern Russian History*. Cambridge: Cambridge University Press.

Kokosalakis, N. 1982. *Ethnic Identity and Religion: Tradition and Change in Liverpool Jewry*. Washington, DC: University Press of America.

Kosmin, Barry A. 1982. "Nuptiality and Fertility Patterns of British Jews 1850–1980: An Immigrant Transition?" In D. A. Coleman, ed., *The Demography of Immigrants and Minority Groups in the UK (Proceedings of the 18th Annual Symposium of the Eugenics Society 1981*. London: Academic Press, pp. 245–61.

Kuznets, Simon. 1960. "Economic Structure and Life of the Jews." In Louis Finkelstein, ed., *The Jews: Their History, Culture, and Religion*. Philadelphia: Jewish Publication Society of America.

———. 1975. "Immigration of Russian Jews to the United States: Background and Structure." *Perspectives in American History* 9:35–124.

Lerner, Abba. 1949. "The Myth of the Parasitic Middleman." *Commentary* 8(1). Available at http://www.commentarymagazine.com.

Levin, Dov. 2000. *The Litvaks*. Jerusalem: Yad Vashem.

Liebman, Charles S., and Steven M. Cohen. 1990. *Two Worlds of Judaism: The Israeli and American Experiences*. New Haven: Yale University Press.

Liedke, Rainer. 1998. *Jewish Welfare in Hamburg and Manchester c. 1850–1914*. Oxford: Clarendon Press.

Lipman, Vivian David. 1959. *A Century of Social Science, 1859–1959: The Jewish Board of Guardians*. London: Routledge and Kegan Paul.

Litvak, Olga. 2006. *Russia's First Jewish Soldiers and the Making of Russian-Jewish Memory*. Bloomington: Indiana University Press.

Maitles, Henry. 1995. "Attitudes to Jewish Immigration in the West of Scotland to 1905." *Scottish Economic and Social History* 15:44–65.

Marks, Lara V. 1994. *Model Mothers: Jewish Mothers and Maternity Provision in East London, 1870–1939*. Oxford: Oxford University Press.

Marowitz, Sanford E. 1996. *Abraham Cahan*. New York: Twayne.

Mendelsohn, Ezra. 1970. *Class Struggle in the Pale: The Formative Years of the Jewish Workers' Movement in Tsarist Russia*. Cambridge: Cambridge University Press.

Metzer, Jacob. 1998. *The Divided Economy of Mandatory Palestine*. Cambridge: Cambridge University Press.

Minczeles, Henri, and Yves Plasseraud, eds. 1996. *Lituanie juive 1918–1940. Message d'un monde englouti*. Paris: Éditions Autrement.

Mitovsky, George. 1959–60. "When Zionism Was Slightly Traife." *Nachlath Dublin*, pp. 16–17.

Model, Suzanne. 1985. "A Comparative Perspective on the Ethnic Enclave: Blacks, Italians, and Jews in New York City." *International Migration Review* 19(1): 64–81.

Morawska, Ewa. 1996. *Insecure Prosperity: Small-town Jewry in Industrial America, 1890–1940*. Princeton: Princeton University Press.

Nadel, Ira B. 1996. *Joyce and the Jews: Culture and Texts*. Gainesville: University Press of Florida.

Newman, Aubrey, and Stephen W. Massil, eds. 1996. *Patterns of Migration, 1850–1914*. London: Jewish Historical Society of England.

Newman, D. 1985. "Integration and Ethnic Spatial Concentration: The Changing Distribution of the Anglo-Jewish Community." *Transactions of the Institute of British Geographers* 10(3): 360–76.

Oshry, Rabbi Ephraim. 1995. *The Annihilation of Lithuanian Jewry*. Brooklyn: Judaica Press.

Penslar, Derek J. 2001. *Shylock's Children: Economics and Jewish Identity in Modern Europe*. Berkeley: University of California Press.

Perlman, Robert. 2001. *From Shtetl to Milltown: Litvaks, Hungarians, and Galizianers in Western Pennsylvania, 1875–1925*. Pittsburgh: Historical Society of Western Pennsylvania.

Perlmann, Joel. 1988. *Ethnic Differences: Schooling and Social Structure among the Irish Italians, Jews, and Blacks in an American City, 1880–1935*. Cambridge: Cambridge University Press.

———. 1996. "Geographic Origins of Russian Jews." Paper presented at the European Social Science History Meetings, Noordwijkerhout, the Netherlands, May.

———. 1997. "Russian Jewish Literacy in 1897: A Reanalysis of Census Data." In Della Pergola and Even, eds., pp. 123–36.

———. 2000. "What the Jews Brought. East-European Immigration to the United States, c. 1900." In Vermeulen and Perlman, eds., pp. 103–23.

Peters, Madison C. 1908. *Justice to the Jew: The Story of What He Has Done for the World*. New York: McClure.

Petrovskii-Shtern, Yohanan. 2001. "Jews in the Russian Army: Through the Military to Modernity." Ph.D. diss., Brandeis University.

———. 2004. *Drafted into Modernity: Jews in the Russian Army, 1827–1914*.

Platt, Leah. 2003. " 'America Was in Everybody's Mouth': An Economic Evaluation of Jewish Emigration from the Russian Empire, 1881–1914." Unpublished paper, Harvard University.

Read, Gordon. 1996. "Indirect Passage: Jewish Emigrant Experiences on the East Coast-Liverpool Route." In Newman and Massil, eds., pp. 267–82.

Reizbaum, Marilyn. 1999. *James Joyce's Judaic Other*. Stanford: Stanford University Press.

Rockaway, Robert A. 1974. "The Eastern European Jewish Community of Detroit, 1881–1914." *YIVO Annual of Jewish Social Science* 15:82–105.

Rubinow, I. M. 1907. *The Economic Condition of the Jews in Russia*. Repr., New York: Arno Press, 1975.

Rubinstein, W. D. 1997. "The Anti-Jewish Riots of 1911 in South Wales: A Reexamination." *Welsh History Review* 18(4): 667–99.

———. 1996. *A History of the Jews in the English-Speaking World: Great Britain.* London: Macmillan.

———. 1999. "The Weber Thesis and the Jews." In Elise S. Brezis and Peter Temin, eds., *Elites, Minorities and Economic Growth.* Amsterdam: North Holland, pp. 137–48.

Sarna, J. 1981. "The Myth of No Return: Jewish Return Migration to Eastern Europe, 1881 to 1914." *American Jewish History* 71: 256–68.

Schmelz, Usiel Oskar. 1971. *Infant and Early Childhood Mortality among the Jews of the Diaspora.* Jerusalem: Institute of Contemporary Jewry, Hebrew University of Jerusalem.

Schnapper, Dominique. 1983. *Jewish Attitudes in France: An Analysis of Contemporary French Jewry* (originally published in French in 1980). Chicago: University of Chicago Press.

Schoenberg, Nancy, and Stuart Schoenberg 1991. *Lithuanian Jewish Communities.* New York: Garland.

Shahak, Israel. 1994. *Jewish History, Jewish Religion.* London: Pluto Press.

Shain, Milton.1989. " 'Vant to puy a Vaatch?' The Smous and Pioneer Trader in South African Jewish historiography." *Jewish Affairs* 44(5).

Shatzmiller, Joseph. 1990. *Shylock Reconsidered: Jews, Moneylending, and Medieval Society.* Berkeley: University of California Press.

Shimoni, Gideon. 1999. "From One Frontier to Another: Jewish Identity and Political Organization in Lithuania and South Africa, 1890–1939." In Sander L. Gilman and Milton Shain, eds., *Jewries at the Frontier: Accommodation, Identity, Conflict.* Urbana: University of Illinois Press, pp. 129–54.

Slezkine, Yuri. 2004. *The Jewish Century.* Princeton: Princeton University Press.

Stanislawski, Michael. 1983. "The Transformation of Traditional Authority in Russian Jewry: The First Stage." In David Berger, ed., *The Legacy of Jewish Migration: 1881 and Its Impact.* New York: Brooklyn College Press, pp. 23–30.

Steinberg, Erwin. 1981/82. "James Joyce and the Critics Notwithstanding, Leopold Bloom Is Not Jewish." *Journal of Modern Literature* 9(1): 27–49.

Steinberg, Stephen. 1981. *The Ethnic Myth: Race, Ethnicity, and Class in America.* Boston: Beacon Press.

———. 2000. "The Cultural Fallacy in Studies of Racial and Ethnic Mobility." In Vermeulen and Perlmann, pp. 61–71.

Stern, Shimon. 1997. "Patterns of Spatial Behaviour among Jews in West European and North American Cities." In Della Pergola and Even, eds., pp. 177–90.

Storrier, Susan. 1992–93. "Jewish Cuisine in Edinburgh." *Scottish Studies* 31:14–39.

Susser, Bernard. 1993. *The Jews of South-West England: The Rise and Decline of Their Medieval and Modern Communities.* Exeter: University of Exeter Press.

Trachtenberg, Henry. 1996. "Peddling, Politics, and Winnipeg's Jews, 1891–1895: The Political Acculturation of an Urban Immigrant Community." *Histoire Sociale* 29:159–86.

Tye, Larry. 2001. *Home Lands: Portraits of the Jewish Diaspora.* New York: Holt.

Vital, David. 1999. *A People Apart: The Jews in Europe, 1789–1939*. Oxford: Oxford University Press.

Wechsler, Robert Steven. 1979. "The Jewish Garment Trade in East London, 1875–1914." Ph.D. diss., Columbia University, New York.

Wertheimer, Jack. 1987. *Unwelcome Strangers: East European Jews in Imperial Germany*. New York: Oxford University Press.

White, Jerry. 1980. *Rothschild Buildings: Life in an East End Tenement Block, 1887–1920*. London: Routledge and Kegan Paul.

Williams, Bill. [2003]. "History of Liverpool's Jewish Community," http://www.ljgs.org/Documents/Bill-Williams1.html. Accessed 24 January 2003.

Wischnitzer, Mark. 1948. *To Dwell in Safety: The Story of Jewish Migration since 1800*. Philadelphia: Jewish Publication Society of America.

Zborowski, Mark, and Elizabeth Herzog. 1995. *Life Is with People: The Culture of the Shtetl*. New York: Schocken.

Zwi, Rose. 1997. *Last Walk in Narishkin Park*. North Melbourne: Spinifex.

OTHER IRISH

Aalen, F. H. A. 1985. "The Working-Class Housing Movement in Dublin, 1850–1920." In Michael Bannon, ed., *A Hundred Years of Irish Planning: The Genesis of Modern Irish Planning*. Dublin: Turoe Press, pp. 131–88.

———. 1992. "Health and Housing in Dublin c. 1850–1921." In F. H. A. Aalen and K. Whelan, eds. *Dublin, City and County: From Prehistory to Present*. Dublin: Geography Publications, pp. 279–304.

Anon. 1880. "An Irish Fishing Village." *Harper's New Monthly Magazine* 60:682–89.

Bielenberg, Andy. 1991. *Cork's Industrial Revolution, 1780–1880: Development or Decline?* Cork: Cork University Press.

Blain, Angeline Kearns. 2000. *Stealing Sunlight: Growing Up in Irishtown*. Dublin: A. & A. Farmar.

BPP (British Parliamentary Papers). 1880. *Report of the Royal Commissioners Appointed to Inquire into the Sewerage and Drainage of the City of Dublin*. Vol. 27 [.2605].

———. 1900. *Report of the Committee Appointed by the Local Government Board for Ireland to Inquire into the Public Health of the City of Dublin*. Vol. 39 [.243].

———. 1902. *Report of the Select Committee on Street Trading Children*. Vol. 49 [.1122].

———. 1908. *Belfast Health Commission: Report to the Local Government Board of Ireland*. Vol. 31 [.4128].

———. 1913. *Vice-regal Commission on the Irish Milk Supply*. Vol. 29.

———. 1914. *Report of the Departmental Committee Appointed by the Local Government Board for Ireland to Inquire into the Housing Conditions of the Working Classes in the City of Dublin*. Vol. 19 [.7273].

Brady, Eilis. 1975. *All In, All In*. Dublin: Coimisiún Béaloideasa Éireann.

Brady, Joseph. 2001. "Dublin at the Turn of the Century." In Brady and Simms, eds., pp. 221–81.

Brady, Joseph, and Anngret Simms, eds. 2001. *Dublin through Space and Time.* Dublin: Four Courts Press.

Budd, John, and T. W. Guinnane. 1992. "Intentional Age-Misreporting, Age Heaping, and the 1908 Old Age Pensions Act in Ireland." *Population Studies* 45(3): 497–518.

Bulfin, William. 1907. *Rambles in Eirinn.* Dublin: Gill & Son.

Cameron, Sir Charles. 1883–. *Report Upon the State of Public Health and the Sanitary Work Performed in Dublin during the Year 1882–.* 1908 issue. Dublin: Dollard.

———. 1913. *Reminiscences.* Dublin: Hodges, Figgis.

———. 1914. *A History of Municipal Health Administration in Dublin.* Dublin: Hodges, Figgis.

Cameron, Sir Charles, and E. D. Mapother. 1879. "Report on the Means for the Prevention of Disease in Dublin." *Reports and Printed Documents of the Corporation of Dublin.* 1:343–52.

Coulter, Henry. 1862. *The West of Ireland: Its Existing Condition and Prospects.* Dublin: Hodges & Smith.

Craig, Patricia. 2003. "Elementary Schooling." *Times Literary Supplement,* 28 November, p. 28.

Crowley, Elaine. 1988. "Elaine Crowley." In Johnston, pp. 41–48.

Cullen, L. M. 1992. "The Growth of Dublin, 1600–1900: Character and Heritage." In F. H. A. Aalen and K. Whelan, eds., *Dublin, City and County: From Prehistory to Present,* Dublin: Georgraphy Publications, pp. 252–77.

———. 1995. "The Joyce Country: Joyce's Dublin." *Joycean Japan* (6):19–40.

Daiken, Leslie. 1963. *Out Goes She: Dublin Street Rhymes with a Commentary.* Dublin: Dolmen Press.

Daly, Mary E. 1981. "Late Nineteenth and Early Twentieth Century Dublin." In David Harkness and Mary O'Dowd, eds., *The Town in Ireland: Historical Studies XIII.* Belfast: Appletree Press, pp. 221–52.

———. 1982. "Social Structure of the Dublin Working Class, 1871–1911." *Irish Historical Studies* 22 (90): 121–33.

———. 1984. *The Deposed Capital: A Social and Economic History of Dublin, 1860–1914.* Cork: Cork University Press.

———. 1995. "Working Class Housing in Scottish and Irish Cities on the Eve of World War I." In S. J. Connolly, R. Houston, and R. J. Morris, eds., *Conflict, Identity, and Economic Development, 1600–1939.* Preston: Carnegie Publishing, pp. 217–27.

D'Arcy, Fergus. 1989. "Wages of Labour in the Dublin Building Industry, 1667–1918." *Saothar* 14:17–32.

de Barra, Eibhlís. 1997. *Bless 'em All: The Lanes of Cork.* Cork: Mercier Press.

de Blacam, Shane, and Loughlin Kealy. 1975. "City Housing Improvement." In Patrick M. Delany, ed., *Dublin: A City in Crisis.* Dublin: RIAI, pp. 61–68.

Donnelly, James S. 2001. *The Irish Potato Famine.* London: Sutton.

Doyle, David N. 1990. "The Irish as Urban Pioneers in the United States, 1850–1870." *Journal of American Ethnic History* 10:36–59.

Doyle, David N. 1999. "Cohesion and Diversity in the Irish Diaspora." *Irish Historical Studies* 31(123): 411–34.

Doyle, Pat, and Louis P. F. Smith. 1989. *Milk to Market: A History of Dublin Milk Supply in Celebration of the 50th Anniversary of the Founding of the Leinster Milk Producers' Association*. Dublin: Leinster Milk Producers' Association.

Dublin Corporation. 1906. *Official Report on the Sanitary Circumstances and Administration of the City of Dublin with Special Reference to the Causes of the High Death Rate*. Dublin: Thom.

Dublin Metropolitan Police. 1905. "Report on Jews." CSORP 23538, National Archives of Ireland.

Ellman, Richard. 1982. *James Joyce*. 2nd ed. Oxford: Oxford University Press.

Fanning, Bryan. 2002. *Racism and Social Change in the Republic of Ireland*. Manchester: Manchester University Press.

Farmar, Tony. 1991. *Ordinary Lives: Three Generations of Irish Middle Class Experience, 1907, 1932, 1963*. Dublin: Gill & Macmillan.

Findlater, Alex. 2001. *Findlaters: The Story of a Dublin Merchant Family*. Dublin: A. & A. Farmar.

Fitzpatrick, David. 1994. *Oceans of Consolation: Personal Accounts of Irish Migration to Australia*. Ithaca: Cornell University Press.

Fitzpatrick, Georgina. 1994. *St. Andrew's College, 1894–1994: Ardens sed Virens*. Dublin: St. Andrew's College.

Fitzpatrick, Jim. 2001. *Three Brass Balls: The Story of the Irish Pawnshop*. Dublin: Collins Press.

Flinn, Col. D. Edgar. 1906. *Official Report of the Sanitary Circumstances and Administration of the City of Dublin with Special Reference to the Causes of the High Death Rate*. Dublin: Thom for HMSO.

Flynn, Kevin Haddick. 2004. "The Limerick Pogrom, 1904." *History Ireland* 12(2):31–33.

Fraser, Murray. 1996. *John Bull's Other Homes: State Housing and British Policy in Ireland, 1883–1922*. Liverpool: Liverpool University Press.

Garvin, Tom. 2004. *Preventing the Future: Why Was Ireland So Poor for So Long?* Dublin: Gill & Macmillan.

Grimshaw, T. W. 1890. "Child Mortality in Dublin." *Journal of the Statistical and Social Inquiry Society of Ireland* 9, appendix, 1–19.

Guinnane, Timothy W. 1997. *The Vanishing Irish: Households, Migration and the Rural Economy in Ireland, 1850–1914*. Princeton: Princeton University Press.

Guinnane, Timothy, Carolyn Moehling, and C. Ó Gráda. 2001. "Fertility in South Dublin a Century Ago: A First Look." Yale University Economic Growth Center Discussion Paper No. 838.

Hanley, Brian. 2002. *The IRA, 1926–1936*. Dublin: Four Courts Press.

Housing Inquiry. 1944. *Report of Inquiry into the Housing of the Working Classes of the City of Dublin, 1939–43*. Dublin: Stationary Office.

IFC/UFP. 1980. Irish Folklore Commission Urban Folklore Project. University College Dublin.

Johnston, Máirín. 1985. *Around the Banks of Pimlico*. Dublin: Attic Press.

———. 1988. *Dublin Belles: Conversations with Dublin Women*. Dublin: Attic Press.

Jones, Greta. 2001. *"Captain of All These Men of Death": The History of Tuberculosis in Nineteenth and Twentieth Century Ireland*. Amsterdam: Editions Rodopi.

Joyce, James. [1922] 1969. *Ulysses*. Harmondsworth: Penguin Books.

Kearns, Kevin C. 1994. *Dublin Tenement Life: An Oral History*. Dublin: Gill & Macmillan.

———. 1998. *Dublin Voices: An Oral Folk History*. Dublin: Gill & Macmillan.

Kennedy, Liam. 1977. "A Sceptical Note on the Reincarnation of the Irish 'gombeenman.' " *Economic and Social Review* 8(3): 213–22.

———. 1978. "Retail Markets in Rural Ireland at the End of the Nineteenth Century." *Irish Economic and Social History* 5:46–63.

———. 2003. "The Cost of Living in Ireland over Three Centuries c. 1660–1960." In D. Dickson and C. Ó Gráda, eds., *Refiguring Ireland*. Dublin: Lilliput Press, pp. 249–76.

Keogh, Dermot, Finbarr O'Shea, and Carmel Quinlan, eds. 2004. *The Lost Decade: Ireland in the 1950s*. Cork: Mercier Press.

Maguire, William A. 1993. *Belfast*. Keele: Keele University Press.

McCorry, Francis Xavier. 1993. *Lurgan: An Irish Provincial Town, 1610–1970*. Lurgan: Inglewood Press.

McCourt, John. 2000. *The Years of Bloom*. Dublin: Lilliput.

Meek, Bill. 1985. *Moon Penny: A Collection of Rhymes, Songs, and Play-verse for and by Children* Dublin: Ossian.

Miller, Kerby, Bruce Boling, David Doyle, and Arnold Schrier. 2003. *Irish Immigrants in the Land of Canaan: Letters and Memoirs from Colonial and Revolutionary America*. New York: Oxford University Press.

Molloy, M. J. 1975. "The Paddy Pedlar." In *Three Plays*. Newark, DE: Proscenium Press, pp. 97–122.

Morrissey, Thomas J. 2003. *Bishop Edward Thomas O'Dwyer of Limerick, 1842–1917*. Dublin: Four Courts Press.

Ní Luain, Siobhán. 1969. "The Packman." In *The Sally Patch & Other Poems*. Belfast: Irish News, pp. 8–9.

O'Brien, George A. P. 1918. *The Economic History of Ireland in the Eighteenth Century*. Dublin: Maunsel.

O'Brien, Joseph. 1982. *Dear, Dirty Dublin: A City in Distress, 1899–1916*. Berkeley: University of California Press.

O'Callaghan, Jeremiah. 1825. *Usury or Interest Proved to be Repugnant to the Divine and Ecclesiastical Laws, and Destructive to Civil Society*. London: Clemens.

Ó Ciosáin, Niall. 1997. *Print and Popular Culture in Ireland, 1750–1850*. London: Macmillan.

O'Flaherty, Liam. 1929. *The House of Gold*. Leipzig: B. Tauchnitz.

Ó Gráda, Cormac. 1974. "Soláthar Creidmheasa Don Íseal-Aicme San Naoú Céad Déag." *Central Bank of Ireland Quarterly Bulletin* 120–35.

———. 1985. "Did Ulster Catholics Always Have Larger Families?" *Irish Economic and Social History* 12:79–88.

———. 1991. "New Evidence on the Fertility Transition in Ireland." *Demography* 28(4): 535–48.

Ó Gráda, Cormac. 1993. *Ireland before and after the Famine: Explorations in Economic History, 1800–1925.* 2nd ed. Manchester: Manchester University Press.

———. 1994. *Ireland: A New Economic History, 1780–1939.* Oxford: Oxford University Press.

———. 1995. "The Rotunda Hospital and the People of Dublin, 1745–1995." In Alan Browne, ed., *Masters, Midwives, and Ladies-in-Waiting: The Rotunda Hospital 1745–1995.* Dublin: A. & A. Farmar, pp. 240–63.

———. 1997. *A Rocky Road: The Irish Economy since the 1920s.* Manchester: Manchester University Press.

———. 1998. "James Larkin: The Socio-economic Context." In Donal Nevin, ed., *James Larkin: The Lion of the Fold.* Dublin: Gill & Macmillan, pp. 8–16.

———. 2001. "Famine, Trauma, and Memory." *Béaloideas* 69:121–44.

———. 2002. "The Greatest Benefit of All: Old Age Pensions in Ireland." *Past & Present* 175: 124–61.

———. 2004. "Infant and Child Mortality in Dublin a Century Ago." In Breschi and Pozzi, eds., pp. 89–104.

Ó Gráda, Cormac, and Niall Duffy. 1995. "Fertility Control Early in Marriage in Ireland a Hundred Years Ago." *Journal of Population Economics* 8:423–31.

Ó Gráda, Cormac, and Brendan M. Walsh. 1995. "Fertility and Population in Ireland, North and South." *Population Studies* 49(2): 259–80.

O'Leary, Paul. 1991. "Anti-Irish Riots in Wales, 1826–1882." *Llafur* 5(4), pp. 27–36.

Parry, J. 1983. "The Tredegar Anti-Irish Riots of 1882." *Llafur* 3(4): 20–23.

Pearson, Peter. 2000. *In the Heart of the City.* Dublin: O'Brien Press.

Pim, Frederic W. 1890. *The Growth of Sanitation in Dublin: Being an Address Delivered at the Nineteenth Annual General Meeting of the Dublin Sanitary Association, 27th March, 1890.* Dublin: R. D. Webb.

Power, Dermot. 1992. *The Ballads and Songs of Waterford from 1487.* Waterford: Scoláire Bocht Publishing.

Power, Irene Wilson. 1997. *To the School in the City: St. Catherine's National School Donore Avenue, Dublin.* Dublin.

Prunty, Jacinta. 1999. *Dublin Slums, 1800–1925: A Study in Urban Geography.* Dublin: Irish Academic Press.

———. 2001. "Improving the Urban environment: Public health and Housing in Nineteenth-century Ireland." In Brady and Simms, eds., pp. 166–220.

Rynne, Colin. 1999. *The Industrial Archaeology of Cork City and Its Environs.* Dublin: Oifig an tSoláthair.

Saorstát Éireann. 1931. *Report of the Select Committee on the Moneylenders Bill* [T.74]. Dublin: Government Publications.

Shaw, Henry. 1850. *The Dublin Pictorial Guide and Directory.* Dublin: Shaw. Repr., with a new introduction by Kevin B. Nowlan. Dublin: Friar's Bush Press, 1988.

Tebbutt, Melanie. 1983. *Making Ends Meet: Pawnbroking and Working-Class Credit.* Leicester: Leicester University Press.

Vann, Richard T., and David Eversley. 1992. *Friends in Life and Death: The British and Irish Quakers in the Demographic Transition*. Cambridge: Cambridge University Press.

Vaughan, W. E., and A. J. Fitzpatrick. 1978. *Irish Historical Statistics: Population, 1821–1971*. Dublin: Royal Irish Academy.

Wallace, W.J.R. 2004. *Faithful to Our Trust: A History of the Erasmus Smith Trust and the High School, Dublin*. Dublin: Columba Press.

Webb, Ella G. A., and Lily Anita Baker. 1910. "First Annual Report of the Dublin Pasteurised Milk Depot." *Dublin Journal of Medical Science* (January–June): 59–65.

Wonfor, William J., and Sidney R. Pontifex. 1862. "On the Quality of the Milk Supplied to the Poor and Other Districts of Dublin." *Dublin Quarterly Journal of Science*. Dublin: McGlashan and Gill, pp. 337–46.

Wright, Arnold. 1914. *Disturbed Dublin*. London: Longman.

General

Alter, George. 1997. "Infant and Child Mortality in the US and Canada." In Bideau, Desjardins, and Brignoli, eds., pp. 91–108.

Atkins, P. J. 1992. "White Poison: The Health Consequences of Milk Consumption." *Social History of Medicine* 5(2): 207–27.

———. 2003. "Mother's Milk and Infant Death in Britain circa 1900–1940." *Anthropology of Food* 2. Available at http://www.aofood.org/JournalIssues/02/atkins.pdf.

Bairoch, Paul. 1976. "Population urbaine et tailles des villes en Europe de 1600 à 1970." *Revue d'Histoire Économique et Sociale* 54:304–35.

Becker, Gary S., and George Stigler. 1977. "*De gustibus non est disputandum*." *American Economic Review* 67(1): 76–90.

Bertrand, Marianne, Erzo F. P. Luttmer, and Sendhil Mullainathan. 2000. "Network Effects and Welfare Cultures." *Quarterly Journal of Economics* 115(3): 1019–55.

Bideau, Alain, Bertrand Desjardins, and Hector Perez Brignoli, eds. 1998. *Infant and Child Mortality in the Past*. Oxford: Oxford University Press.

Blanchard, Ian. 1978. "Labour Productivity and Work Psychology in the English Mining Industry." *Economic History Review* 31(1): 1–15.

Bonacich, Edna. 1973. "A Theory of Middleman Minorities." *American Sociological Review* 38:583–94.

Bonacich, Edith, and John Modell. 1980. *The Economic Basis of Ethnic Solidarity*. Berkeley: University of California Press.

Borjas, George. 1995. "Ethnicity, Neighbourhoods, and Human Capital Externalities." *American Economic Review* 85:365–90.

Bowles, Samuel, and Herbert Gintis. 2003. "Persistent Parochialism: Trust and Exclusion in Ethnic Networks." *Journal of Economic Behaviour and Organization* 55(1): 1–23.

BPP (British Parliamentary Papers). 1873. *Report from the Select Committee on Imprisonment for Debt*. Vol. 15 [348].

BPP (British Parliamentary Papers). 1893–94. *Report of Select Committee of the House of Lords on the Debtors Act* (HL 156). Vol. 9.
———. 1897, 1898. *Report of the Select Committee on Moneylending*, 1897. Vol. 11 (364.), 405; 1898, vol. 10 (260.), 101.
———. 1903. *Report of the Royal Commission on Alien Immigration: Minutes of Evidence* [.1742].
———. 1904. *Report of the Interdepartmental Committee on Physical Deterioration: Minutes of Evidence.* Vol. 32, [.2210].
Breschi, Marco, and Lucia Pozzi, eds. 2004. *The Determinants of Infant and Child Mortality in Past European Populations.* Udine: Forum.
Brockerhoff, M., and P. Hewett. 2000. "Inequality of Child Mortality among Ethnic Groups in Sub-Saharan Africa." *Bulletin of the World Health Organisation* 78(1): 30–41.
Brown, David. 2000. " 'Persons of Infamous Character': The Textile Pedlars and the Role of Peddling in Industrialization." *Textile History* 31(1): 1–26.
Brown, John C., and Timothy W. Guinnane. 2002. "Fertility Transition in a Rural, Catholic Population: Bavaria 1880–1910." *Population Studies* 56(1): 35–49.
Burds, Jeffrey. 1998. *Peasant Dreams & Market Politics: Labor Migration and the Russian Village, 1861–1905.* Pittsburgh: University of Pittsburgh Press.
Burnett, John. 1888. "Report to the Board of Trade on the Sweating System of the East End of London . . ." App. G to "Report from the Select Committee on the Sweating System," BPP 1888, vol. 21.
Burrows, Edwin G., and Mike Wallace. 1999. *Gotham: A History of New York City to 1890.* New York: Oxford University Press.
Bushee, Frederick A. 1903. "Ethnic Factors in the Population of Boston." *Publications of the American Economic Association*, 3rd ser., 4(2): 1–171.
Chiswick, Barry R., and Paul W. Miller. 2002. "Immigrant Earnings: Language Skills, Linguistic Concentrations and the Business Cycle." *Journal of Population Economics* 15(1): 31–57.
———. 2003. "The Complementarity of Language and Other Human Capital: Immigrant Earnings in Canada." *Economics of Education Review* 22:469–80.
Cipolla, Carlo. 1965. *Guns and Sails in the Early Phase of European Expansion, 1500–1700.* London: Collins.
———. 1967. *Clocks and Culture.* London: Collins.
Clark, Gregory. 1987. "Why Isn't the Whole World Developed? Lessons from the Cotton Mills." *Journal of Economic History* 47(1): 141–74.
Cleary, Patrick. 1914. *The Church and Usury: An Essay on Some Historical and Theological Aspects of Money-Lending.* Dublin: Gill and Son.
Coale, A. J., and D. Treadway. 1986. "A Summary of the Changing Distribution of Overall Fertility, Marital Fertility, and the Proportion Married in the Provinces of Europe." In Coale and Watkins, eds., pp. 31–181.
Coale, A. J., and S. C. Watkins, eds. 1986. *The Decline of Fertility in Europe.* Princeton: Princeton University Press.
Coale, Ansley J., Barbara Anderson, and Erna Härm. 1979. *Human Fertility in Russia since the Nineteenth Century.* Princeton: Princeton University Press.
Cutler, David M., and Edward L. Glaeser. 1997. "Are Ghettos Good or Bad?" *Quarterly Journal of Economics* 132(3): 827–72.

Cutler, David M., Edward L. Glaeser, and Jacob L. Vigdor. 1999. "The Rise and Decline of the American Ghetto." *Journal of Political Economy* 107(3): 455–506.

Dahl, Sven. 1959. "Travelling Pedlars in Nineteenth Century Sweden." *Scandinavian Economic History Review* 7(2):167–78.

Dansel, David L. 2001. *Village Mothers: Three Generations of Change in Russia and Tataria*. Bloomington: Indiana University Press.

David, Paul A., and Warren Sanderson. 1988. "Measuring Marital Fertility Control with CPA." *Population Index* 54 (Winter): 691–731.

Diner, Hasia R., and Beryl Lieff Benderly. 2002. *Her Works Praise Her: A History of Jewish Women in America from Colonial Times to the Present*. New York: Basic Books.

Entwistle, B., R. R. Rindfuss, S. J. Walsh, T. P. Evans, and S. R. Curran. 1997. "Geographical Information Systems, Spatial Network Analysis, and Contraceptive Choice." *Demography* 34(2): 171–86.

Farrow, Thomas. 1895. *The Money-lender Unmasked*. London: Roxburghe Press.

Feinstein, C. H. 1990. "New Estimates of Average Earnings in the United Kingdom, 1880–1913." *Economic History Review* 43(4): 595–632.

Fentress, James, and Chris Wickham. 1992. *Social Memory*. Oxford: Blackwell.

Finn, Margot. 1998. "Working-class Women and the Contest for Consumer Control in the Victorian County Courts," *Past & Present* 161:116–54.

———. 2001. "Scotch Drapers and the Politics of Modernity: Class and National Identity in the Victorian Tally Trade." In Matthew Hilton and Martin Daunton, eds., *The Politics of Consumption: Citizenship and Material Culture in Europe and America*. London: Palgrave Macmillan, pp. 89–108.

———. 2003. *The Character of Credit: Personal Debt in English Culture, 1740–1914*. Cambridge: Cambridge University Press.

Flinn, Col. D. Edgar. 1906. *Official Report of the Sanitary Circumstances and Administration of the City of Dublin with Special reference to the Causes of the High Death Rate*. Dublin: Thom for HMSO.

Fogel, R. W. 2004. *The Escape from Hunger and Premature Death, 1710–2100: Europe, America, and the Third World*. Cambridge: Cambridge University Press.

Fogel, R. W., and S. Engerman. 1977. "Explaining the Relative Efficiency of Slave Agriculture in the Antebellum South." *American Economics Review* 67(3): 275–96.

Fontaine, Laurence. 1996. *History of Pedlars in Europe*. Cambridge: Polity Press.

Galloway, Patrick R., Eugene A. Hammel, and Ronald D. Lee. 1994. "Fertility Decline in Prussia, 1875–1910: A Pooled Cross-section Time Series Analysis." *Population Studies* 48:135–58.

Garrett, Eilidh, Alice Reid, Kevin Schürer, and Simon Szreter. 2001. *Changing Family Size in England and Wales*. Cambridge: Cambridge University Press.

Gatrell, Peter. 1986. *The Tsarist Economy, 1850–1917*. London: Batsford.

Green, Nancy L. 1997. *Ready-to-Wear and Ready-to-Work: A Century of Industry and Immigrants in Paris and New York*. Durham: Duke University Press.

Green, Nancy L. 2003. "Fashion, Flexible Specialization, and the Sweatshop." In D. E. Bender and R. A. Greenwald, eds., *Sweatshop USA: The American Sweatshop in Historical and Global Perspective*. London: Routledge.

Gregory, Paul R. 1982. *Russian National Income, 1885–1913*. Cambridge: Cambridge University Press.

Greif, Avner. 1989. "Reputation and Coalitions in Medieval Trade: Evidence on the Maghribi Traders." *Journal of Economic History* 49(4): 857–82.

———. 1993. "Contract Enforceability and Economic Institutions in Early Trade: The Maghribi Traders' Coalition." *American Economic Review* 83(3):525–48.

Guilfoy, William H. 1917. *The Influence of Nationality upon the Mortality of a Community, with Special Reference to the City of New York*. New York: Department of Health of the City of New York.

Haines, Michael R. 1985. "Inequality and Childhood Mortality: A Comparison of England and Wales, 1911, and the United States, 1900." *Journal of Economic History* 45:885–912.

———. 1992. "Occupation and Social Class during Fertility Decline: Historical Perspectives." In J. R. Gillis, Louise A. Tilly, and D. Levine, eds., *The European Experience of Declining Fertility, 1850–1970*. Cambridge: Blackwell, pp. 193–226.

———. 1995. "Socio-economic Differentials in Infant and Child Mortality during Mortality Decline: England and Wales, 1890–1911," *Population Studies* 49:297–315.

Haines, Michael R., and Samuel Preston. 1997. "The Use of the Census to Estimate Childhood Mortality: Comparisons from the 1900 and 1910 United States Census Public Use Samples." *Historical Methods* 30(2): 77–97.

Halbwachs, Maurice. 1980. *The Collective Memory*. New York: Harper and Row.

Harrington, James. 1992. *The Commonwealth of Oceana; and, A System of Politics*. Ed. J. G. A. Pocock. Cambridge: Cambridge University Press.

Harris, Ralph, Margot Naylor, and Arthur Selden. 1961. *Hire Purchase in a Free Society*. 3rd ed. London: Institute of Economic Affairs.

Hartshorn, Peter. 1997. *James Joyce and Trieste*. Westport, CT: Greenwood Press.

Hatton, T., and J. G. Williamson. 1998. *The Age of Mass Migration: Causes and Economic Impact*. New York: Oxford University Press.

Heer, D. M. 1968. "The Demographic Transition in the Russian Empire and in the Soviet Union." *Journal of Social History* 1:193–240.

Huck, Paul. 1997. "Seasonal Shifts in the Seasonality of Infant Deaths in Nine English Towns during the Nineteenth Century: A Case for Reduced Breast Feeding?" *Explorations in Economic History* 34:363–86.

Hunt, E. H. 1981. *British Labour History, 1815–1914*. London: Weidenfeld & Nicholson.

Iyer, Sriya. 2002. *Demography and Religion in India*. Oxford: Oxford University Press.

Jordan, William C. 1993. *Women and Credit in Pre-Industrial and Developing Societies*. Philadelphia: University of Pennsylvania Press.

Keeling, Drew. 1999. "The Transportation Revolution and Transatlantic Migration, 1850–1914." *Research in Economic History* 19:39–74.

Knodel, John E. 1974. *The Decline of Fertility in Germany, 1871–1939*. Princeton: Princeton Univeristy Press.

Knowles, K.G.J.C., and D. J. Robertson. 1951. "Differences between the Wages of Skilled and Unskilled Workers, 1880–1950." *Bulletin of the Oxford University Institute of Statistics*. 13: 109–27.

Kohler, Hans-Peter. 2001. *Fertility and Social Interaction: An Economic Perspective*. Oxford: Oxford University Press.

Kohler, Hans-Peter, Jere R. Behrman, and Susan C. Watkins. 2001. "The Density of Social Networks and Fertility Decisions: Evidence from South Nyanza District, Kenya." *Demography* 38(1): 43–58.

Kunitz, Stephen L., and S. L. Engerman. 1992. "The Ranks of Death: Secular Trends in Income and Mortality." *Health Transition Review* 2 (supplementary issue): 29–46.

Lewis, Frank D., and R. Marvin McInnis. 1980. "The Efficiency of the French-Canadian Farmer in the Nineteenth Century." *Journal of Economic History* 40:497–514.

Lindsay, Dorothy E. 1913. *Report upon a Study of the Labouring Classes in the City of Glasgow (Carried Out during 1911–12 under the Auspices of the Corporation of the City)*. Glasgow.

Livi-Bacci, Massimo. 1986. "Social-Group Forerunners of Fertility Control in Europe." In Coale and Watkins, eds., pp. 182–200.

Long, J. Scott, and Jeremy Freese. 2001. *Regression Models for Categorical Dependent Variables Using Stata*. College Station, TX: Stata Press.

Lunn, Kenneth. 1985. "Immigrants and Strikes: Some British Case Studies, 1870–1914." In K. Lunn, ed., *Race and Labour in Twentieth-century Britain*. London: Frank Cass, pp. 30–42.

McCloskey, D. N., ed. 1970. *Essays on a Mature Economy*. Oxford: Oxford University Press.

Maddison, Angus. 2001. *The World Economy: A Millennial Perspective*. Paris: Organization for Economic Co-operation and Development.

Marcus, David. 1986. *A Land Not Theirs*. New York: Bantam Press.

———. 2001. *Oughtobiography: Leaves from the Diary of a Hyphenated Jew*. Dublin: Gill & Macmillan.

———. 2004. *Buried Memories*. Cork: Mercier Press.

Maxton, Hugh. 1997. *Waking: An Irish Protestant Upbringing*. Belfast: Lagan Press.

Meek, Bill. 1985. *Moon Penny: A Collection of Rhymes, Songs, and Play-verse for and by Children* Dublin: Ossian.

Mercier, Michael E., and Christopher G. Boone. 2002. "Infant Mortality in Ottawa, Canada, 1901: Assessing Cultural, Economic and Environmental Factors." *Journal of Historical Geography* 28(4): 486–507.

Meyer, Ernest Christopher. 1921. *Infant Mortality in New York City*. New York: Rockefeller Foundation International Health Board.

Miller, Kerby, Bruce Boling, David Doyle, and Arnold Schrier. 2003. *Irish Immigrants in the Land of Canaan: Letters and Memoirs from Colonial and Revolutionary America*. New York: Oxford University Press.

Millward, Robert, and Frances Bell. 2001. "Infant Mortality in Victorian Britain: The Mother as Medium." *Economic History Review* 54(4): 699–713.

Mokyr, Joel. 1991. *The Lever of Riches*. New York: Oxford University Press.
———. 2002. *The Gifts of Athena: Historical Origins of the Knowledge Economy*. Princeton: Princeton University Press.

Mooney, Graham. 1994. "Did London Pass the 'Sanitary Test'? Seasonal Infant Mortality in London, 1870–1914." *Journal of Historical Geography* 20(2): 158–74.

Morawska, Ewa. 1994. "Afterword: America's Immigrants in the 1910 Census Monograph: Where Can We Who Do It Differently Go from Here?" In Watkins, ed., 319–50.

Morgan, S. Philip, S. C. Watkins, and Douglas Ewbank. 1994. "Generating Americans: Ethnic Differences in Fertility." In Watkins, ed., pp. 83–124.

Morrissey, Thomas J. 2003. *Bishop Edward Thomas O'Dwyer of Limerick, 1842–1917*. Dublin: Four Courts Press.

Nelson, Benjamin. 1969. *The Idea of Usury: From Tribal Brotherhood to Universal Otherhood*. Chicago: University of Chicago Press.

O'Callaghan, Jeremiah. 1825. *Usury or Interest Proved to Be Repugnant to the Divine and Ecclesiastical Laws, and Destructive to Civil Society*. London: Clemens.

O'Flaherty, Liam. 1929. *The House of Gold*. London: Jonathan Cape.

Olneck, Michael R., and Marvin Lazerson. 1974. "The School Achievement of Immigrant Children: 1900–1930." *History of Education Quarterly* 14(4): 453–82.

Orchard, Dorothy, and Geoffrey May. 1933. *Moneylending in Great Britain*. New York: Russell Sage Foundation.

Palmer, Francis H. E. 1901. *Russian Life in Town and Country*. London: Geo. Newnes.

Petty, Sir William. 1899. *Economic Writings of Sir William Petty*. Ed. C. H. Hull. Cambridge: University Press.

Pfister, Ulrich. 2000. "Von Kiepenkerl zu Karstadt. Einzelhandel und Warenkultur im 19. und frühen 20. Jahrhundert." *Vierteljahrschrift für Sozial- und Wirtschaftsgeschichte* 87:38–66.

Phillips, J., and M. French. 1999. "State Regulation and the Hazards of Milk." *Social History of Medicine* 12(3): 371–88.

Pim, Frederic W. 1892. *Preventible Diseases: Why Are They Not Prevented?* Dublin: Webb.

Preston, Samuel H.. and Michael R. Haines. 1991. *Fatal Years: Childhood Mortality in the United States in the Late Nineteenth Century*. Princeton: Princeton University Press.

Preston, Samuel H., Douglas Ewbank, and Mark Hereward. 1994. "Child Mortality Differences by Ethnicity and Race in the United States: 1900–1910." In Watkins, ed., pp. 35–82.

Rajakumar, Kumaravel. 2001. "Infantile Scurvy: A Historical Perspective." *Pediatrics* 108(4): E76.

Reher, David. 1999. "Back to the Basics: Mortality and Fertility Interactions during the Demographic Transitions." *Continuity and Change* 14(1): 9–31.

Rendle-Short, J. 1955a. "The Causes of Infantile Convulsions Prior to 1900." *Journal of Pediatrics* 47:733–39.

———. 1955b. "The History of Teething in Infancy." *Proceedings of the Royal Society of Medicine* 48:132–35.

Rowlingson, Karen. 1994. *Moneylenders and Their Customers*. London: Policy Research Institute.

Rubin, Gerry R. 1984. "The Country Courts and the Tally Trade, 1846–1914." In G. R. Rubin and D. Sugarman, eds., *Law, Economy and Society, 1750–1914: Essays in the History of English Law*. Abingdon: Professional Books, pp. 321–48.

———. 1986. "From Packmen, Tallymen, and 'Perambulating Scotchmen' to Credit Drapers' Associations, c. 1840–1914." *Business History* 28(2): 206–25.

Ruby, Thelma, and Peter Frye. 1997. *Double or Nothing: Two Lives in the Theatre*. London: Janus.

Sánchez-Alonzo, Blanca. 2000. "Those Who Left and Those Who Stayed Behind: Explaining Emigration from the Regions of Spain, 1880–1914." *Journal of Economic History* 60(3): 730–55.

Scott, Peter. 2002. "The Twilight World of Interwar British Hire Purchase." *Past & Present* 177:195–225.

Soloway, Richard A. 1990. *Demography and Degeneration: Eugenics and the Declining Birthrate in Twentieth-century Britain*. Chapel Hill: University of North Carolina Press.

Spufford, Peter. 2002. *Power and Profit: The Merchant in Medieval Europe*. London: Thames and Hudson.

Strauss, Nathan. 1913. *Disease in Milk: The Remedy Pasteurization*. New York: Privately published.

Szreter, Simon. 1996. *Fertility, Class and Gender in Britain, 1860–1914*. Cambridge: Cambridge University Press.

Temin, Peter. 1997. "Is It Kosher to Talk about Culture?" *Journal of Economic History* 57(2): 267–87.

Thornton, Patricia A., and Sherry Olson. 1991. "Family Contexts of Fertility and Infant Survival in Nineteenth-Century Montreal." *Journal of Family History* 16(4): 401–17.

United Nations. 1985. *Socioeconomic Differentials in Child Mortality in Developing Countries*. New York: United Nations.

U.S. Department of Commerce. 1960. *Historical Statistics of the United States*. Washington, DC: U.S. Department of Commerce.

Vallin, Jacques. 1991. "Mortality in Europe from 1720 to 1914: Long-term Trends and Changes in Patterns by Age and Sex." In Roger Schofield, David Reher, and Alain Bideau, eds., *The Decline in Mortality in Europe*. Oxford: Clarendon Press, pp. 38–67.

Van Poppel, Frans, Jona Schellekens, and A. Liefbroer. 2002. "Religious Differentials in Infant and Child Mortality in the Netherlands, 1855–1912." *Population Studies* 56:277–89.

Vann, Richard T., and David Eversley. 1992. *Friends in Life and Death: The British and Irish Quakers in the Demographic Transition*. Cambridge: Cambridge University Press.

Vermeulen, Hans, and Joel Perlmann, eds. 2000. *Immigrants, Schooling and Social Mobility: Does Culture Make a Difference?* London: Macmillan.

Ward, W. Peter. 1993. *Birth Weight and Economic Growth: Women's Living Standards in the Industrializing West.* Chicago: University of Chicago Press.

Watkins, Susan C., ed. 1994. *After Ellis Island: Newcomers and Natives in the 1910 Census.* New York: Russell Sage Foundation.

Watkins, Susan C., and Angela D. Danzi. 1995. "Women's Gossip and Social Change: Childbirth and Fertility Control among Italian and Jewish Women in the United States, 1920–1940." *Gender & Society* 9(4): 469–90.

Watterson, P. A. 1988. "Infant Mortality by Father's Occupation from the 1911 Census of England and Wales." *Demography* 25:289–306.

Webb, Ella G. A., and Lily Anita Baker. 1910. "First Annual Report of the Dublin Pasteurised Milk Depot." *Dublin Journal of Medical Science* (January–June): 59–65.

Wegge, Simone. 1998. "Chain Migration and Information Networks: Evidence from Nineteenth-century Hesse-Cassel." *Journal of Economic History* 58(4): 957–86.

Whetham, Edith. 1976. "The London Milk Trade, 1900–1930." In Derek Oddy and D. S. Miller, eds., *The Making of the British Diet.* London: Croom Helm, pp. 65–76.

Wonfor, William J., and Sidney R. Pontifex. 1862. "On the Quality of the Milk Supplied to the Poor and Other Districts of Dublin." *Dublin Quarterly Journal of Science* 2:337–46.

Woodbury, R. M. 1926. *Infant Mortality and Its Causes.* Baltimore: Williams and Wilkins.

Woods, Robert I. 2000. *The Demography of Victorian England and Wales.* Cambridge: Cambridge University Press.

Woods, Robert I., and Nicola Shelton. 1997. *An Atlas of Victorian Mortality.* Liverpool: Liverpool University Press.

Wrightson, Keith. 2000. *Earthly Necessities: Economic Lives in Early Modern Britain.* New Haven: Yale University Press.

Wrigley, E. A. 2004. *Poverty, Progress, and Population.* Cambridge: Cambridge University Press.

INDEX

Abrahamson, Leonard, 78–79, 213, 267n35, 269n12
Abrahamson, Maurice, 233n69
accidental arrival: myth of, 25, 232–33n60
acculturation, 3, 87, 185, 200
Adelaide Road synagogue, 67, 91, 102, 124, 164, 189, 205, 207, 208, 266n10
Adler, Herman (chief rabbi), 67, 117, 124, 255n13
age at marriage, 126, 138–40
Akmyan (Akmene), 23, 24, 25, 29, 46, 47, 115, 230n11, 237n12
alcohol: the Irish and, 176–77, 185, 243n104, 257n65, 257n68; Jews and, 171, 176–77, 257n65, 257n66
Aleichem, Sholem, 16, 46, 182
Alexandra College, 124, 126
Annals of Inisfallen, 179
anti-Semitism, 16, 118, 179–81, 188, 210, 267n27; in Russia, 12–21, 188, 245n41. *See also* Limerick
Argentina, 30, 233n61
Aris, Stephen, 85
Athlone, 23, 168, 180
autobiographical memory, 4, 16–17, 194–200, 221–23

baitz, 184
Ballybough cemetery, 11, 253n48
Banbridge, 247n2
Belfast, 3, 5, 11, 30, 31, 32, 197, 206; decline of community in, 215; Jewish demography in, 148–49; settlement patterns in, 119–21
Benson, Asher, 230n5, 239n53, 255n16, 262n66
Berman, Hannah (writer), 23, 28, 46, 47, 48, 94, 95, 102, 168, 180
Berman, Lieb, 16, 51, 53, 54, 55, 180
Bialystok, 12
Blond, Marcus, 191, 193–94, 262n70
Bloom, Benny, 60–61
Bloom, Jessie, 28, 67, 102–3, 115, 168, 172, 195, 233n76, 238–39n48; and Louis Hyman, 224–27

Bloom, Leopold, 1, 2, 60, 106, 176, 204, 205, 206; Triestine Jewry as a context for, 204–5
Boer War, 189, 195
Botticini, Maristella, 46, 161
boxing, 187, 259n30
Bradlaw, Robert, 106, 127, 240n76
Brainboro (Dublin), 197, 199
breastfeeding, 168, 201
Brennan, Louis, 230n11
Brennan, Michael, 184, 255n30, 261n55
Bride Street, 96, 97, 124
Briscoe, Robert, 190; attitude of to money-lenders, 68, 243n101; as lord mayor of Dublin, 212
Bulfin, William, 180

cabinetmakers and carpenters, 50, 80, 118
Camden Street shul, 205, 209
Cameron, Sir Charles, 34, 143, 167, 168, 169, 175
capmakers, 74, 106, 126
Carlisle Circus (Belfast), 44, 120, 206, 208
Carlisle Cricket Club, 187
Carlow, 188, 246n3, 268n44
Carpenters. *See* cabinetmakers and carpenters
Catholicism: and anti-Semitism, 191, 264n105; and usury, 70–71
Cesarani, David, 15, 26, 28, 231n23
Chain migration, 12
Chancery Lane, 95, 96, 97, 98, 246n8
childlessness: low incidence of among immigrants, 141, 153, 252n26
civil courts, 64–66, 241n82, 263n87
Clanbrassil Street, Lower, 3, 105, 172, 199, 243n107, 260n35; on Sunday mornings, 207
Clara, 180
Coale, Ansley J., 134, 138, 157, 251n21
collective memory, 14–15, 27, 231n24
communal tensions, 117, 120, 206–7, 226, 248n51, 254–55n13
conscription. *See* Russian army
contraception, 130, 251n21; and social networks, 135

Cork, 5, 11, 30, 31, 32, 44, 48–49, 115–19, 187, 225; decline of Jewish community in, 209, 267n29; Jewish-Gentile relations in, 118; religiosity of Jewish community in, 117–18; state-funded Jewish school in, 186
Cossacks, 13, 233n69
Coulter, Henry, 59
Crane Lane synagogue, 10, 230n5
Creagh, Rev. James, 191–93, 263n87
credit drapers, 3, 50, 53, 64, 91, 193, 240n68, 245n37, 262n70; last of, 61
culture, 34, 152–53, 164–76

Daiken, Leslie, 68, 184, 185, 204, 258n7, 260n32
Damer School, 124
Davis, Jacob, 95, 96, 98, 102
dentists, 83–84, 86, 213
Derry: Jewish community in, 94, 209
diarrhea/dysentery, 145; in London, 147; seasonality of deaths from, 147
diaspora Jewry, 213–14
diet, 146, 171–76, 201; role of fish in, 172, 174, 175, 207, 223
Din torah (rabbinical arbitration), 203
Diner, Hasia, 171
Diocesan School, 124, 127, 244n
Dixon, Daniel, M.P., 35
Dolphin's Barn cemetery, 151–52, 253n48
domestic servants, 103, 107, 157, 165, 170, 192, 199, 247n21, 251n11, 256n56; and child mortality, 150
Downpatrick, 196, 246n3
Drogheda, 9, 63, 246n3
Dublin: high mortality in, 33–39; housing conditions in, 40–41; interwar, 41–42; Jewish population of, 32, 209; relative poverty of, 30–31
Dublin Artisans Dwelling Company (DADC), 99, 107
Dublin Corporation, 34, 40–41
Dublin Hebrew Congregation. See Adelaide Road synagogue
Dublin Maccabi Association, 187; sale of grounds of, 215
Dublin Metropolitan Police, 96, 98, 240, 242n89
Dufferin Avenue, 100, 102, 108, 134, 173, 176, 198
Duffy, Mark, 2, 131, 262n72

Easter Rising (1916), 190
Eckstein, Zvi, 46, 161
economic conditions in Ireland, 40–42, 212–13
Edelstein, Hyman, 125, 127, 128, 160, 254n1
Edelstein, Joseph, 29, 51, 54–55, 56, 66–67, 69, 125, 190, 237n18, 241–42n89
Edinburgh, 96, 174, 214
Edmundstown Golf Club, 215
education. See schooling
Elkin, Judith, 146
Elyan, Jacob, 51, 69, 190, 242n89
Elyan, Larry, 90, 117, 213, 225, 261n60, 269n8
emigration from Russia, Jewish, 16–22
Encyclopedia Judaica, 68, 182
Endelman, Todd, 9
Eppel, Ellard, 185
Erlich, Beila, 206, 207, 255n22

Feldman, David 85
fertility: decline in, 134–36; among immigrants, 138–43, 154–57, 200–201; in Israel, 252n13; in Russia, 136–38
fertility transition, 129–31, 134–36, 152–53; and Catholicism, 5, 135, 156; and "spacing," 135, 139; and "stopping," 141
Finlay, Thomas, S.J., 104, 200
Finn, Margot, 58
fish. See diet
Fitzpatrick, David, 29, 171
Fogel, Robert, 167
food. See diet
Freemasons, 188, 212
Freeze, ChaeRan, 137–38
friction between "English" and immigrant Jews, 33, 95, 164, 182, 206, 237n18, 247n19
Friedlander, Dov, 252n23
frontier Jewry, 4

Galut, 213–14, 233n76
Galway, 23, 94
Gentile butchers, 103
Glasgow, 47, 87, 169, 173–76, 214, 247n19
glaziers, 45, 50, 86, 95–96, 221, 246n5, 247n28

Godley, Andrew, 19, 22, 29, 85, 87, 89
Goldberg, Gerald, 17, 25, 188, 192
Goldberg, Louis, 17, 192, 262n70
Goldstein, Alice, 146
Gorey, 246n3
Grand Canal, 2, 3, 23, 99, 104, 107, 125, 166, 195, 206
greeners, 72, 105, 227, 233n76
Greenville Hall synagogue, 103, 164, 206, 207, 209, 265n114; opening of in 1925, 205
Greenville Terrace, 99, 100, 102, 172, 197, 199
Grimshaw, T. W., 34, 177, 257n69
Gudansky, Rev. Abraham, 107, 164
Guilfoy, William: on child mortality in New York, 144

Harfield's *Commercial Directory*, 51, 52, 119
Harmel, Peisa, 102, 106, 206
Harrington, James, 9
Harris, Nick, 29, 73, 100, 102, 110, 126, 136, 196, 206
Hebrew Philanthropic Loan Society, 53, 203
Herzog, Chaim, 91, 185, 187, 190
Herzog, Moses, 55, 64, 106, 176
Herzog, Rabbi Isaac, 209, 266n23, 269n10
Hesselberg, Esther, 118, 119
Hevra/hevroth, 48, 102, 164, 215, 225, 247n19
Hibernian buildings, Cork, 44, 49, 116
High School: Jewish students at, 125
holy pictures, 29, 45, 51, 54, 56, 117, 198, 221, 226
housing: in Dublin, 33, 35, 40–42, 102–3, 236n32; in Little Jerusalem, 43–44, 97–101, 103
Howe, Irving, 14
Huguenot immigrants, 10
Hunt, E. H., 84, 85
Hutterite weights, 135, 251n14
hygiene: as an influence on mortality, 34–35, 144, 167–68, 169
Hyman, Louis, 2, 47, 106, 224–27, 229n3, 233n7, 238–39n48

immigration: to Britain, 213; to Ireland, 4–5, 9–29; to Israel, 213–14; to United States, 19–21

intermarriage, 8, 185, 187, 188, 214, 261n54, 267n37
IRA moneylending raids, 68
Irish Christian Brothers, 126, 189, 196, 249n14, 261n63, 263n87
Irish Jewish Museum, 2, 261n54
Irish Jewry: decline of, 208–215

Jaffe, Daniel, 208
Jaffe, Sir Otto, 120
Jakobovitz, Rabbi I., 125
Jervise Street, 97
Jewish communities: in Bolivia, 45; in South Africa, 12, 183, 230n12; in South Wales, 47, 91
Jewish mothers, 168, 169, 170–71
Jewish weddings, 201, 262n73, 264n103
Joseph, Samuel, 13, 26
Joyce, James, 1, 2, 4, 60, 106, 129, 134, 143, 180, 204, 225, 265n5
Judaeo-Irish Home Rule Association, 190

Keogh, Dermot, 2, 14
Kernoff, Harry, 242n89
Kilkenny, 94, 180
Kishinev pogrom, 12
Klier, John, 231n23
Knodel, John, 136
kosher, 26, 103, 118, 173, 186, 199, 209, 221, 261n55; and health, 166; koshering for Passover, 166
Kosmin, Barry, 153
Kovno, 17, 18, 21, 22
Kuznets, Simon: on the economic factors behind migration, 19; on economic implications of minority status, 45–46; on Jewish propensity for urban locations, 161; on the skills of Jewish emigrants, 26

Lapin, Valerie, 2, 263n87
laptseh, 54, 238n41
Leeds, 12, 43
legal profession, 128, 212
Lennox Street, 164–65, 199, 209; shul on, 164–65
Lentin, Ronit, 25, 262n69; on decline of Jewish community, 210
Levenstein, Moses, 51, 55, 61, 66–67, 69
Leventhal, A. J. (Con), 185, 194, 195, 260n32

Levin, Rabbi Elias (Limerick), 191, 193, 263n82

Levine, June, 13, 160, 188

life expectancy in Jewish Dublin, 151–52

Limerick, 7, 209, 260; anti-semitism in, 179, 191–94, 262–63n77

Lindsay, Dorothy: survey by of Glasgow diets, 173–75

literacy and illiteracy, 46, 122–24, 249n5, 249n6

Lithuania, 12, 13, 22, 26, 47, 53, 182, 231n35

litigation, 63–66; between Jews, 202–3

Little Jerusalem, 5, 109–10, 200, 204, 206, 207–8, 209; decline of, 209; first settlers in, 97; social differentiation in, 104, 108

Litvaks, 5, 12, 43, 46, 60, 84, 104, 119, 200, 211, 229n9; *mentalité* of, 46, 181, 231n35

Liverpool, 87, 169, 169, 214, 247n28

loan banks, 61, 62, 65

Lombard Street West, 97, 99, 125, 195, 199, 209

London, 27, 85–90, 103–4, 147, 210

London Jewish Board of Guardians, 12, 25, 88, 146; and Limerick in 1904, 194

Longwood Avenue, 101, 107, 198, 209

Lord Rothschild, 103, 194

Lurgan: generosity of community in, 246n2; Jewish community in, 50, 94, 209

Machzikei Hadass, 205

Manchester, 51, 214

Marcus, David, 2, 13

Marks, Lara, 146, 175, 246n15

marrying out. *See* intermarriage

Martin Street (Dublin), 126, 134, 166, 172, 176, 184, 198, 208

Marx, Karl, 202

Mary's Abbey synagogue, 48, 96, 97, 106, 164, 205

May Laws, 12, 14, 17, 21

medicine, as a career, 78–79, 82, 86, 91, 128, 170, 213, 245n42, 267n36

Mendelsohn, Rev. L., 67–68, 189

middleman minorities, 3, 17, 161, 211, 212, 254n6

mikvah, 168; at Tara Street baths, 166

milk, adulteration of, 168, 169

minorities, economic role for, 161, 163

minyan, 94, 164, 205, 206, 208, 247n19; minyan men, 206, 265n9

Misstear's pharmacy, 170, 256n38

Mokyr, Joel, 167

Moneylender, The. See Edelstein, Joseph

Moneylender Unmasked, The (1895), 69

moneylending, 3, 61–71, 119, 161, 237n22; Leslie Daiken on, 68; Jewish attitudes to, 66–68, 226–27; Geoffrey Wigoder on, 68

Moore Street, 96, 97

Moore, Gerry E., 2

Morawska, Ewa, 27, 182

mortality: in Dublin, 34–42; in Dublin and Belfast compared, 38; infant and child, 39, 42, 148–52, 157–59; in Jewish Ireland, 147–52

Mushatt family, 108, 170, 196, 264n96

New York, 27, 85–90, 210, 257n64

Newman, Arthur, 91, 118

Newry, 246n2

Noyk family, 13, 16, 125, 190

Nurock, Max, 122, 125, 127, 132, 195, 196, 225–27, 259n30, 269n10, 269n12

Ó Ciosáin, Niall, 57

Oakfield Place (Dublin), 50, 61, 97, 101, 105–06, 126, 195, O'Callaghan, Rev. Jeremiah, 70, 244n113

O'Callaghan, Rev. Jeremiah, 70, 244n113

O'Casey, Seán, 95, 180

occupations, 72–91

O'Dwyer, Dr. Edward, 193

O'Flaherty, Liam, 70, 244n114

O'Grady, Standish Hayes, 59, 209

Pale of Settlement, 14, 15

Parnell, George, 221–23

Passover, 165, 166, 173

pawnbrokers, 71, 243n107

peddling and peddlers, 3, 5, 45–71, 73, 210, 237n27; earnings of, 55–56; harassment of, 45, 63, 258n9; in Ireland, 57–58; in Lithuania, 16, 24, 46, 58, 237n13; and the railway network, 18, 46, 53, 57, 62; Sholem Aleichem on, 46; stock-in-trade of, 56–57

percentnik, 69

Perlmann, Joel, 22, 46, 124

personal hygiene, 165–66
Pesach. See Passover
Peters, Madison: on low Jewish mortality, 144
Petty, Sir William, 161
pogroms, 12, 14, 17, 21, 231n24
politics: unionist sympathies of Jewish immigrants, 188–90; in Cork, 261n60
Portobello (Dublin), 53, 99, 164, 166, 190
poultry. *See* diet
Price, Stanley, 2, 48, 91
provincial Jews in England, 47, 214

Queen Victoria, 189

Railroad Stories. See Aleichem, Sholem
Rambles in Eirinn. See Bulfin, William
Rathgar, 3, 104, 125, 206, 208
Rathmines, 44, 102, 104, 208, 215
Raymond Street, 99, 194
religion and immigrant Jews, 47, 48, 117, 118, 164, 164–65, 173, 230n12
replacement effect, 141
residential clustering, 108–15, 148, 161
Reuben, Joseph and Rebecca: suicides of, 202–3
Rise of David Levinsky, The, 88, 242n89
River Liffey, 34, 43
Rivlin, Ray, 2
Rosenblatt, Stuart, 77
Rotunda maternity hospital, 167, 170
Royal College of Surgeons, 127–28, 190, 212
Rubin, Gerry, 58
Rubinow, Isaac, 22, 233n63
Rubinstein, W. D., 163
Russell, George (AE), 70–71
Russian army: conscription in, 25, 27–28, 230n23; Jews in, 13, 27–28

Saint Andrew's College: Jewish students at, 125, 190
Saint Kevin's Parade, 61, 97, 99, 106, 128, 132, 197–98, 205, 209; shul on, 48, 91, 106, 164, 215
Saint Kevin's Road, 107, 190, 197
Samuels, Oliver, 207
sanitation, 42–43, 44, 129, 167
Sayers, Philip, 91, 118, 225
Schmeltz, U. O., 7
schooling, 31, 122–28, 211
second generation, 122–28

self-employment, 17, 50, 53, 72–91, 107, 236n8
Sephardic Jews, 10, 230n5
serfdom, 18, 19
shabbas goyim, 164, 197
shikse, 183, 184, 251n11
Shillman, Ada (midwife), 170, 256n42
Shillman, Bernard, 2, 126, 224, 225, 268n2
shochet/shochtim, 91, 94, 103, 118, 163, 166
shtetls, 18, 29, 90, 122, 181, 195, 232n56
Slezkine, Yuri, 3, 181–82, 259n27
smoked salmon, 172
snobbery, among Litvaks, 102
social capital, 186–87
social mobility, 78–84, 128, 129, 210; *Jewish Chronicle* on, 163
Solomons, Bethel, 84, 170
Solomons, Mr. and Mrs., 110; tragic death of, 107
Sombart, Werner, 161
South Africa, 12, 27, 128, 230n12; and Jewish attitudes toward black population, 183
South Circular Road, 6, 56, 99, 102, 146, 148, 157, 184, 197, 200, 205, 207
sport, 185, 186, 187, 215
St. Catherine's School (Donore Avenue), 124
Stamer Street, 165
start-up capital, 53, 203; 260n39
Steinberg, Stephen, 162–163
stereotyping: Irish of Jewish, 84, 95–96, 181–85, 262n69; Jewish of Irish, 180–181
suburbanization, 3, 207–8; beginnings of, 115

tailoring, 3, 47, 49, 50, 73, 86, 196
tariff Jews, 211
Temin, Peter, 161
Terenure, 3, 205, 206, 208
the "never-never,", 3, 58
Thom's Directory, 102, 106, 108, 110
Trade Unions: in Cork, 118, 187; Jewish, 72, 73, 244n9
Tredegar: anti-Jewish riots in, 193, 194, 263n83
Trieste: Jewish community of, 204–5, 265n5

Trinity College, Dublin, 254n1
Tullow, 180
typhoid fever, 42

Ulysses. See Joyce, James
United Hebrew Congregation, 205

Vilna, 21, 26, 138, 165
Vincent Street, 166
Vital, David, 14, 21; on the skills of Jewish emigrants, 26

wages, 40, 42, 235n27; in London, 89
Walworth Road, 2, 97, 99, 103, 209; closure of shul on, 205
Ward, Peter, 253n47
Waterford, 94, 209, 260n32
Waterman, Simon, 196
Waterman, Stanley, 212, 214
Wechsler, Robert, 88
weekly men, 47–56, 117, 217–20
Wesley College: Jewish students at, 125, 126, 190
Wexford, 9, 246n3
White, Jerry, 88

wholesaleniks, 54, 202, 203
Wigoder, Harry, 91, 238n34, 242–43n90
Wigoder, Myer Joel, 23, 30, 68, 108, 225, 233n76, 238n34, 242–43n90; hopes of for family, 122; on peddling, 45, 60; as a poor businessman, 91; reason of for coming to Ireland, 16; regrets materialism of immigrants, 29
Wigoder, Philip, 122, 190
Williams, Bill, 247n28
Wine, Louis, 16–17, 180
women in labor force, 77, 133
Woodbury, R. M.: on infant mortality in U.S. cities, 144, 146
Woods, Robert, 39
Wright, Arnold, 31

Yiddish language and culture, 29, 57, 73, 90, 96, 118, 123, 195, 232n56

Zion Schools, 91, 124, 189
Zionism, 119, 212, 213–14
Zlotover family, 17, 91, 101, 107, 188, 231n34, 237n24, 269n12